ESSAY WRITING FOR CANADIAN STUDENTS

SECOND EDITION

ESSAY WRITING FOR CANADIAN STUDENTS

SECOND EDITION

KAY L. STEWART

MARIAN E. KOWLER
Grant MacEwan Community College
Edmonton, Alberta

CHRIS BULLOCK
University of Alberta
Edmonton, Alberta

PRENTICE-HALL CANADA INC., SCARBOROUGH, ONTARIO

Canadian Cataloguing in Publication Data

Stewart, Kay L. (Kay Lanette), 1942-
  Essay writing for Canadian students

Includes index.
ISBN 0-13-283706-4

1. Exposition (Rhetoric).   2. English language —
Rhetoric.   I. Kowler, Marian, 1945-
II. Bullock, Chris, 1945-   III. Title.

LB2369.S87 1985   808'.042   C84-099582-2

Prentice-Hall Inc., Englewood Cliffs, *New Jersey*
Prentice-Hall International, Inc., *London*
Prentice-Hall of Australia, Pty., Ltd., *Sydney*
Prentice-Hall of India Pvt., Ltd., *New Delhi*
Prentice-Hall of Japan Inc., *Tokyo*
Prentice-Hall of Southeast Asia (Pte.) Ltd., *Singapore*
Editora Prentice-Hall do Brasil Ltda., *Rio de Janeiro*
Prentice-Hall Hispanoamericana, S.A., *Mexico*
Whitehall Books Ltd., Wellington, *New Zealand*

ISBN 0-13-283706-4

Production editors: Maura Brown/Clare Rundall
Design: Helmut Weyerstrahs
Typesetting: Q Composition
Printed and bound in Canada by Imprimerie Gagné Ltée.

3   4   5   IG   89   88   87

Contents

PART 3 HANDBOOK FOR FINAL EDITING

Acknowledgments

In revising *Essay Writing for Canadian Students,* we have attempted to practice what we preach by systematically rethinking and reorganizing our material. We would like to take this opportunity to introduce our third co-author, Chris Bullock, Professor of English at the University of Alberta, whose creative contributions and meticulous attention to detail have helped to make this version of our text what it is.

Like our first edition, this text is not only *for* Canadian students but also *by* them. Once again we thank the students at the University of Alberta, the University of British Columbia, and Grant MacEwan Community College who participated in the testing of earlier versions and who allowed us to use their work. In particular we thank Marlyn Lyall, who worked so conscientiously to write the history essay on the Red River Settlement and Fort Victoria. We would also like to thank all the students and instructors who used the first edition and passed on to us their suggestions for its improvement.

More thanks go to colleagues who commented on portions of the manuscript: Professor Kelly Barratt (University of Ottawa); Dr. A. Harding (University of Saskatchewan); Professor P. Denham (University of Saskatchewan); and Ms. Sharon McKenzie (Northern Secondary School, Toronto). Dr. W. Beard (University of Alberta) shared his knowledge of film criticism; Professor James Reither (St. Thomas University) influenced our thinking about research; and Doris Burghardt made useful suggestions on several chapters. We would especially like to thank Karin Capri, who proofread most of the manuscript, and Sean Stewart, whose parenthetical comments as he typed the first draft onto a word processor provided comic relief and pointed out problem spots.

Our thanks go as well to the editors at Prentice-Hall for their unfailing encouragement and patience and for the occasional prod to hurry up and get finished.

To all the friends, colleagues, and students who provided us with the support and encouragement to go on, we extend our sincere thanks, and to Dan Kowler, for his special assistance, we express a special thank-you. For the final shape of this edition, the three of us, of course, accept sole responsibility.

Preface to the Revised Edition

To the Student

Like carpentry and chemistry, farming and finance, writing is a skill that you can learn, not a talent you either have or don't have. Great writers, it is true, may have a special talent; but most writers are made, not born. And these days, everyone is a writer.

As we have moved from the Industrial Revolution to the information revolution, communication has become more and more the focus of our business and personal lives. We read and write business letters, memos, technical reports, instruction manuals, legal documents. We read newspapers, magazines, books, advertisements; watch films, plays, television programmes; listen to songs, newscasts, lectures—all written by someone, somewhere.

Much of this writing is based on three simple steps that you can learn: defining your purpose, organizing your material to suit your purpose, and presenting what you have to say clearly and concisely. In this book we show you how to follow these steps for a particular kind of writing: the essays you write in many college and university courses. We illustrate this process with examples drawn from a wide range of sources—literary and non-literary, Canadian and non-Canadian—to provide models for your own thinking and writing.

Once you have learned how to define your purpose, to organize your material, and to present your ideas clearly and effectively when you write essays, you will find it easy to apply these skills to other types of writing.

To the Instructor

If you chose to use the first edition of *Essay Writing for Canadian Students*, you no doubt believe as firmly as we do in the value of revision. You will therefore understand our desire to revise this text so that it better meets your needs and those of your students. Our goal has been to maintain our emphasis on the process of revision and our use of a broad range of material, Canadian and non-Canadian, literary and non-literary, while making the text easier to use and, more importantly, giving students a better understanding of the preparatory thinking necessary for writing papers in college and university.

A change we had originally conceived of as simply a means of making the text easier to use turned out to have far-reaching consequences. To increase the number of chapters while making them shorter, we discovered, we would need to make each chapter more self-contained. That required a fundamental change in the organization of the text. In the first edition, chapters move from an overview of the revision process to a step-by-step examination of how to rethink and rewrite the parts of the college and university essay: thesis, middle paragraphs, overall structure, introduction and conclusion.

Our first major change is to differentiate college and university essays according to the basic skills they require: the skills of analysis, comparison, evaluation, and research. Within each of these areas, we give equal attention to topics that ask students to focus on content and to those that ask students to focus on the relation between form and content. We use the terms *content* and *textual* analysis, comparison, evaluation, and research to distinguish these two approaches. Because analysis is central to so much thinking and writing at the college and university level, we devote separate chapters to content analysis and textual analysis. The chapter on textual analysis should be especially valuable for students in literature courses.

Our second major change is to divide our treatment of these basic cognitive skills into two parts. The "Preparing to Write" chapters outline a step-by-step procedure for understanding essay assignments; for gathering material efficiently; for analyzing, comparing, or evaluating material, as required; and for finding a thesis. In addition, "Preparing to Write: Research" includes a search strategy for locating library materials and guidelines for using secondary sources. In each chapter, we have linked our discussion of general principles to typical writing assignments so that students will have concrete models of the kind of thinking and writing they are expected to do.

In the "Writing" chapters, we have maintained the emphasis on the process of revision that was the core of the first edition. In each "Writing" chapter, we briefly review the preparatory steps covered in the previous chapter, using a new essay topic, and then take students through the process of writing and revising a first draft. In "Writing Analysis Essays" we set out general strategies for organizing essays and developing paragraphs to support a thesis; in the "Writing" chapters on comparison, evaluation and research we focus on the special strategies appropriate to these forms. Each chapter concludes with a sample essay that provides a model for student writing.

We have maintained not only our emphasis on the process of revision but also our use of both literary and non-literary material. If you have used the first edition, you will see much that is familiar: analyses of poems by Alden Nowlan and Raymond Souster; the comparison of historical accounts by Ernest Wallace and Dee Brown; and the research material on the founding of the Red River Settlement and Fort Victoria, for example. You will also find new material, including analysis of a passage from *The Stone Angel* and analysis of a scene from *Hamlet*. This edition provides sample analyses of a wider range of literary forms: fiction, poetry, drama, film, and expository prose.

Although we have included both literary and non-literary material, you may want to emphasize one or the other. If you teach writing through the study of literature, you may want to concentrate on the discussions of textual analysis, comparison, and evaluation and the chapter on research on literary topics. If you teach courses in which students write on a broad range of topics, you may want to give equal attention to the analysis, comparison, and evaluation of content. The inclusion of non-literary examples benefits students in both kinds of writing classes, we feel, by showing them that the principles they are learning also apply to the work they do for other courses.

To make the text easier to use, we have introduced several changes in format. The most noticeable change is the use of a question-and-answer format for preparation and revision. This method of presentation should have several advantages over the more discursive method of the first edition. Maintaining the same format makes material easier to find within each chapter, reinforces the basic processes of preparation and revision, and allows students to see similarities and differences between various kinds of essays.

The other major change in format is in our placement of material on final editing. In the first edition, we put material on style, grammar, and format into the last chapter, to reflect our attitude that these are matters that should be attended to only after the larger issues of content and organization have been resolved. In teaching writing, however, it is not always possible, nor even desirable, to leave all consideration of these details until the end of the course, as the arrangement of the text might suggest.

We have therefore introduced Chapter 6, "Final Editing," at the end of Part One, "Preparing, Writing, Editing: The Basic Analysis Essay," in order to emphasize the importance of this stage of the revision process. The "Checklist for Final Editing" and sample revisions in this chapter should help alert students to some of the most common problems in style, grammar, and format. Detailed explanations are reserved for Part Three, the "Handbook for Final Editing." The exercises in each section of the handbook will allow students to test their understanding of the material. Answer keys for these exercises are provided in the accompanying Instructor's Manual.

By emphasizing the skills common to all academic disciplines, we aim to help students develop the ability to think more analytically and to communicate their ideas more effectively. We trust that the revised edition of *Essay Writing for Canadian Students* will be a practical guide to both thinking and writing for college and university students.

Kay Stewart / Marian Kowler / Chris Bullock

PART 1

Preparing, Writing, Editing: The Basic Analysis Essay

Chapter 1

Writing Essays

While you are at college or university, you are likely to do various kinds of writing as part of your course work. One common type is **report writing**. When you write reports, your aim is to present factual information in an orderly manner. You may write lab reports in science courses, observation reports in education courses, business reports in commerce courses, or technical reports in engineering courses.

Another type of writing you might do is **creative writing**. When you write poems, plays, or fiction, your aim is to communicate your vision of the world through imagined characters and situations. Even if you do not take a creative writing course, you might find yourself using imaginary characters and situations to explain a point in philosophy or to hold the attention of grade six students for a geography lesson.

The kind of writing you will likely do the most in college or university courses, however, is **essay writing**. If you take a first-year course in English or communications, you may write several short papers and perhaps a longer research paper. Many other courses, especially in the humanities, social sciences, education, and fine arts, will require you to write research papers, if not short essays.

This book is about essay writing. It focuses on essay writing for two reasons. The first reason is that the analytical thinking you practice in the process of writing essays is central to the work you do in college or university. The second is that the procedures you learn for writing and revising essays will help you with many others kinds of writing assignments.

ESSAY WRITING: PURPOSE

Exploration

How will writing essays help you to develop analytical thinking? One way is by giving you a systematic method for exploring your ideas.

This purpose is reflected in the French word from which the term **essay** comes: *essai*, meaning "attempt." The term was first used to refer to a particular kind of writing by the French author Montaigne, who published a book of short prose pieces entitled *Essais* in 1580. This title suggests the personal, exploratory nature of Montaigne's attempts to understand the world around him by writing on everyday subjects such as "Liars" and "The Art of Conversation." Many of the essays you study in literature courses are likely to be of this type.

Since Montaigne's day, however, the term essay has also come to include formal writing on a wide range of subjects, from the nature of love in Shakespeare's *King Lear* to theories about the origins of the universe. It is this more formal type of essay writing that you will most often be called upon to do in your university and college courses.

Whether the essays you write are informal or formal, they provide you with an opportunity to develop an opinion about a particular subject. In the process of writing on the nature of friendship, for example, you may discover which qualities you most value in your friends. Similarly, you may not know what you really think about issues such as Canada's role in NATO, the desirability of genetic engineering, or the preservation of endangered species until you write about them, because you have not had to define your opinion or to defend it.

Another benefit of writing essays is that you are able to transform passive learning into active learning. If you were taking a painting course, you would recognize that no matter how good the instructor's lessons might be, you would only learn how to paint by painting. The same holds true for learning to write. What may be less obvious is that you learn the theories, concepts, and procedures of disciplines such as history, sociology, psychology, and literary criticism in two ways: by reading about them and hearing them explained, and by actively employing them in writing papers. Using the tools of these disciplines in your writing helps you to understand them better. Writing essays, then, enables you to explore a particular subject and to develop your opinions about it.

Communication

Exploration is not the only purpose of writing essays. Another is communication. To communicate effectively, you must consider how best to present the results of your exploration.

Essays, as we have seen, develop an opinion about facts or experience. But if you want your opinion to be taken seriously, you have to do more than make pronouncements such as "Genetic research should be stopped" or "The government should spend more money on genetic research." To make your point convincing to a reader, you need to support your opinion by giving your reasons for holding it.

Consider an argument in which you claim that genetic research should be stopped and your friend claims it shouldn't. At this level each statement is "just an opinion" and your discussion isn't likely to go very far. But suppose that you extended your statement to say that genetic research should be stopped because of the possibility that lethal organisms could be released into the environment, thereby endangering millions of lives. Now that you have given a reason for your opinion, you can try to persuade your friend that such an occurrence is likely.

In an essay, this combination of an opinion and the reason(s) supporting it is called a **thesis**. A thesis is like a hypothesis in a scientific experiment; it is the thing to be proved. An opinion, of course, can't be proven experimentally. Proof in an essay consists of the logical, orderly **development** of the thesis through explaining your reasons and giving evidence (such as factual information, examples, and quotations from authorities) to support them.

Your thesis is the backbone of your essay. If in the body of your essay you explain your thesis carefully and support it adequately, you are likely to persuade your readers to take your opinion seriously, whether or not they agree with it. Writing essays is thus a means of sharing your understanding of a particular issue with others.

This account of the purposes of essay writing may help you to see why essays are assigned in many college and university courses. Writing essays gives you the opportunity to explore a variety of subjects in depth, to formulate carefully considered opinions about those subjects, and to communicate your opinions clearly and effectively.

ESSAY WRITING: PRODUCT

Although every essay presents the writer's point of view on a particular subject, how the writer chooses to present that point of view will depend upon the audience for whom the piece is written.

Audience

Most of the essays you are likely to study in literature courses were originally published in magazines or newspapers where they had to compete for readers' attention with photographs, advertising, and a host of other articles. In these circumstances, essay writers may attempt to catch the reader's eye by starting with a controversial claim they will eventually reverse, or by describing a dramatic event in their lives. Having caught the reader's attention, popular essayists may try to hold it by maintaining suspense as to their thesis, or by narrating a series of events with an unexpected outcome.

Formal essays on academic subjects, in contrast, are written for specialized audiences whose interest in the subject the writer can take for granted. Readers of these essays want to know from the beginning what the author's point of view is and to have the evidence supporting that view laid out in a logical, orderly fashion. Most of the essays you write in college and university courses will be of the second type. You will be writing for instructors and classmates who are familiar with the subject, but who need to be told, clearly and efficiently, what *you* make of it.

Structure

You can meet your reader's needs and demonstrate your understanding of your subject most effectively by writing essays that have these main structural elements:

INTRODUCTION
The introduction establishes the context for the discussion (i.e., defines necessary terms, gives historical background) and presents the thesis of the essay.

MIDDLE PARAGRAPHS
Each middle paragraph discusses a single subpoint of the thesis. The purpose of the paragraph is defined by a topic sentence that links the paragraph to the thesis. Middle paragraphs usually contain both explanations of the point made in the topic sentence and specific details illustrating that point. Transitional words and phrases signal the movement from point to point and establish the relationship between points and the details that support them.

CONCLUSION
The conclusion ties together the points developed in the middle paragraphs and mentions the wider implications of the discussion, if any.

Sample Essay: Analysis of a Film

So that you can see what this kind of essay might look like in practice, here is an example. The topic asked students to choose their favourite film and explain its appeal. The main structural elements of the essay have been labelled:

ROMANCE AND REALISM IN CASABLANCA

Introduction   Since its release in 1942, the movie Casablanca, directed by Michael Curtiz, has become a classic. Even people who have never seen the film recognize the theme song, "As Time Goes By," and the line "Play it

	again, Sam," even though this line never actually occurs in the film. Why has <u>Casablanca</u> remained so popular? The answer to this question undoubtedly lies partly in the appeal of its two stars, Humphrey Bogart and Ingrid Bergman, and talented supporting actors like Claude Rains, Sidney Greenstreet, and Peter Lorre.
Thesis	Its main appeal, however, is the mixture of romance and realism in its plot, setting, and characterization.
Topic sentence	The obvious romanticism of the plot tends to obscure its realistic elements. Consider the details. After a few shots of a spinning globe and Casablanca street scenes, we are introduced to Rick Blaine (Humphrey Bogart),
Middle paragraph 1	a mysterious American expatriate who owns the Café Américain, meeting place of Casablanca's smart set, and who appears to care for nothing and nobody. Into Rick's café walk Victor Laszlo (Paul Henreid), a famous Resistance leader, and Ilsa Lund (Ingrid Bergman), his wife, in search of stolen letters of transit that would guarantee them a safe exit from Casablanca to Lisbon and America. In a flashback we learn that just before the Nazis occupied Paris, Rick and Ilsa met there and fell in love. Because of their agreement not to speak of their pasts, however, Ilsa does not tell Rick of her marriage to Laszlo, whom she believes to have died in a concentration camp. On the day that the two are to leave Paris together, Ilsa discovers Victor is still alive and, without explanation, sends Rick a note saying she still loves him but can never see him again.
Transition Topic Sentence	Rick and Ilsa's past, then, is a romantic tale of love and self-sacrifice. When they meet and fall in love again in Casablanca, they must confront more realistic problems: Rick's cynicism, a product of his sense of
Middle paragraph 2	betrayal; Ilsa's love, respect, and admiration for Victor; Victor's own sense of honour; and the very real threat posed to them all by the Nazis' determination to prevent Victor's escape.
Topic sentence	The reality of this threat is emphasized by the director's use of the setting. On the one hand, Casablanca is a romantic city. In its sun-baked streets, merchants in fezzes haggle with prospective buyers; inside Rick's Café Américain, the scene of much of the action, the wealthy gamble. On the other hand, Casablanca, gov-
Middle paragraph 3	erned by French authorities who are subservient to German "advisers," is the major point of escape for refugees from Nazi-occupied Europe. Consequently, we see the marketplace turn into a place of terror when a member of the Free French underground is shot by

French police in front of the law courts bearing the motto "Liberty, Equality, Fraternity." Similarly, the glamour of Rick's café is offset by the plight of the refugees who frequent it and by the ease with which the Germans order the place closed. The setting thus emphasizes the film's mixture of romance and realism.

Transition

Topic sentence

Middle
paragraph 4

What gives the film its appeal is not just the romantic hope that the good guys will eventually defeat the Nazis, however; it is the film's recognition of the struggle that goes on within characters who, while basically good, may make wrong choices. This issue arises for several of the minor characters, but is most fully explored in the relationship between Rick and Ilsa. Although Rick's past (running guns to Ethiopia, fighting in the Spanish Civil War) suggests that he is capable of idealism, his refusal to shield the man who stole the letters of credit raises the possibility that he will refuse to help Laszlo and Ilsa. Similarly, Ilsa's shift from threatening to shoot Rick for the letters of transit one minute, to planning to go away with him the next, makes us wonder whether she will again be capable of sacrificing her love for Rick to her duty to her husband. To emphasize these inner struggles, scenes between Rick and Ilsa are often shot in half-light, creating the juxtaposition between light and shadow that is one of the film's trademarks. Since most of us are faced with difficult moral choices, we identify more fully with characters who face similar struggles than we do with those who never question their own motives or behaviour.

Conclusion

In the end, it is the romantic ethic of love and self-sacrifice that triumphs, as Rick puts Ilsa and Victor on the plane for Lisbon and, with Captain Renaud, strides off into the fog to join the resistance fighters. But in its use of plot, setting, and characterization, the film reminds us that such triumphs arise out of our struggles against opposition, both without and within. It is this realistic recognition of the difficulty of living up to our best selves that gives the film its continuing appeal.

Discussion of the Sample Essay

"Romance and Realism in *Casablanca*" illustrates the effective use of the structural elements common to college and university essays. In the first few sentences of the introduction, the writer establishes the context of the essay by providing basic information about the film and by introducing the issue of the film's popularity. The introduction concludes with the statement of the **thesis** signalled by the transitional phrase "Its main appeal, however, ..." By placing the thesis at the end of the paragraph, preceded by a transitional device that signals its importance, the writer focuses attention on the main point: the relation between the film's popularity and the combination of romance and realism in its plot, setting, and characterization.

The thesis also serves as a guide to the structure of the essay as a whole. It sets out the order in which the three aspects of the film will be discussed. This order is one of **ascending interest**. That is, the writer puts the paragraph on the plot first because the point about the mixture of romance and realism in the plot is the most obvious and most easily explained. Next, the writer discusses details of the setting that illuminate the contrast between romance and realism. Then the point about characterization comes last to emphasize its importance.

In the middle paragraphs of the essay, each of these points is clearly made in a **topic sentence**. Each topic sentence identifies the aspect of the film to be discussed (such as plot) and connects that aspect to the thesis by stating how it contributes to the film's popularity. The topic sentences also provide **transitions** between one paragraph and the next.

The framework you create by establishing this kind of relationship between the thesis, topic sentences, and transitional devices will give your reader valuable assistance in following your line of thinking.

Important as this framework is, the essay would not be convincing if the middle paragraphs did not contain **details** to support the points made in the topic sentences and **explanations** to clarify what the details mean. In the first middle paragraph, for example, the point that the plot seems "romantic" would not seem very convincing without details of the plot. Details alone are not enough to define "romantic," however. And so the writer provides the explanation that the plot is romantic because it is a "tale of love and self-sacrifice."

The conclusion sums up the relationship the writer has established between the film's popularity and the mixture of romance and realism in its plot, setting, and characterization. Notice that the conclusion does not merely repeat what the writer has said in the thesis and topic sentences.

"Romance and Realism in *Casablanca*" thus illustrates how you can use the structure common to most college and university essays to present your opinion on a subject in a clear, straightforward way. This structure is appropriate for a wide range of topics that ask you to analyze a single subject. You will find step-by-step procedures for writing this kind of essay in Chapters 3, 4, and 5. Later chapters will suggest modifications to this basic structure to use when you are writing essays that require comparison, evaluation, or research.

ESSAY WRITING: PROCESS

We began with the sample on *Casablanca* so that you would have a clear idea of the final form in which most college and university essays appear. Most people don't write an essay—or anything intended to be read by others, for that matter—by sitting down with paper and pen (or typewriter) and rising an hour later with a finished product. The finished product is simply the last stage of a highly complex process of thinking and writing, rethinking and rewriting. If you want to produce an interesting, thoughtful essay, like the one on *Casablanca*, you have to be prepared to give time and serious attention to your subject. Without that willingness, you will not "learn how to write," from this book or from any other.

But it is our belief that if you are willing, you can learn to write essays that have something to say and say it well. These are the five skills you need:

1. Making sure you understand your assignment.
2. Asking questions that will yield a good thesis about your subject.
3. Finding research material when necessary.
4. Organizing your ideas so the reader can follow your train of thought.
5. Presenting your ideas in a style appropriate to your audience and purpose.

In this book you will find step-by-step procedures for acquiring each of these skills.

Understanding Essay Assignments

Although instructors attempt to make their assignments clear, students sometimes have trouble with writing essays because they are unsure about what to do. If you make sure you understand your assignment before you begin, you will be able to use your preparation and writing time more efficiently. This book therefore includes several aids to understanding the requirements of common types of essay topics. In the next chapter, "Clarifying Essay Topics and Gathering Material," you will find explanations of terms frequently used in assignments, examples of common types of essay topics, and a chart of "Questions to Ask about Essay Topics" to remind you of what to look for in your own topics. In each of the "Preparing to Write" and "Writing" chapters we review these questions in order to point out the specific demands of various kinds of essays. The third place you will find help with understanding essay assignments is in the reference section. Charts showing the appropriate questions to ask about specific kinds of topics are reprinted there so that you can easily consult them for your own assignments.

Asking Questions

The second key to writing good essays is knowing what kind of questions to ask. Those questions will depend not only on what your subject is, but also on how you have been asked to think about it. We have organized much of this book around the following four ways of thinking and writing:

1. Analyzing a single subject (Chapters 3, 4, and 5).
2. Comparing two or more subjects (Chapters 7 and 8).
3. Evaluating one or more subjects (Chapters 9 and 10).
4. Using research materials (Chapters 11 and 12).

We have emphasized the skills of analyzing, comparing, evaluating, and doing research because they are ones you will use constantly, whenever you read or do an experiment or prepare for an exam, as well as when you write essays.

You will find suggestions on how to ask effective questions in three locations.

1. Chapter 2, "Clarifying Essay Topics and Gathering Material," outlines several procedures for generating ideas.

2. The "Preparing to Write" chapters (3, 4, 7, 9, 11) give you step-by-step procedures for asking questions when you are analyzing, comparing, evaluating, or doing research. These questions will help you to collect appropriate material on your subject, to arrive at an opinion about this material, and to find reasons to support your opinion so that you will have a good thesis for your essay. The wide range of topics used in the examples will help you to formulate appropriate questions when you are writing essays for other courses.

3. In the reference section at the end of the text you will find charts of questions you can usefully ask when you are analyzing poetry, fiction, drama, film, and non-fictional prose, as well as suggested questions for analyzing non-literary topics.

Finding Research Material

One problem that every beginning student faces is that of learning how to use a college or university library. If you wrote research papers in high school, you probably relied on the small collection available in your school library and perhaps some material from the public library. Or you may never have written a research paper. In either case, you may feel unsure about your ability to make efficient use of the wealth of books, journals, and other material in a college or university library.

By the end of this century, you may be able to do all your library research by typing a few key words into a computer, which will then print out a list of books and journal articles on your subject. In some places, you may already be able to request this service. Because of limitations in the kind of material that is easily located through computer searches, however, you will still need to know how to use card catalogues, periodical indexes, and other reference material.

In this book you will find two chapters on doing library research. Chapter 11 outlines a basic strategy for deciding what kind of material you need and how to find it, and then shows how you would use this strategy to do research for a paper in a discipline such as history. Chapter 12 shows you how to find material on a work of literature and how to integrate your research with your own interpretation. These chapters should give you a clear idea of how to do research for a wide range of topics.

Organizing Your Ideas

Understanding your assignment, asking questions, and finding material are steps you take in preparing to write an essay. Your next concern is how to organize your ideas and evidence so that you can present them effectively to a reader. The "Writing" chapters (5, 8, 10, 12) carry the process of essay writing from the preparation stage through the first stage of revision: revising a first draft for content and structure. Each of these chapters contains (1) a checklist for evaluating first drafts, with specific questions for the type of essay discussed in that chapter; (2) a sample first draft; (3) an evaluation of the strengths and weaknesses of that draft; and (4) a demonstration of how to make the revisions most commonly needed in the type of essay being discussed. Each "Writing" chapter concludes with a sample essay.

Using an Appropriate Style

The last requirement for a good essay is that you communicate your ideas clearly and persuasively. Potentially good ideas are wasted if your reader cannot understand how points are related or what a particular sentence means; if your reader is distracted by mistakes in grammar, punctuation, or spelling; or if your reader dismisses what you say because your tone is too belligerent or too apologetic.

If you follow the procedures we give for preparing, writing, and revising your first draft, you may find that much of your difficulty in "getting your ideas on paper" has disappeared. Nevertheless, all writers give their work a final editing to improve a sentence here or there and to check for lapses in format or accepted usage. To assist you with these changes, you will find a demonstration of final editing in Chapter 6, with a checklist that is keyed to Part 3 of the text, the "Handbook for Final Editing." In the handbook you will find explanations of the most common problems in grammar, punctuation, and spelling. You will also find guidelines for maintaining an appropriate tone, for using sentence structure effectively, and for setting out quotations, footnotes, bibliographies, and essays as a whole.

SUMMARY

This book is designed to give you the help you need at each stage of the writing process, from understanding the requirements of your topic to putting the finishing touches on your final draft. As you use this book, you will develop both thinking skills—analyzing, comparing, evaluating—and writing skills—organizing material, revising it, polishing it. These skills will be equally useful for the essays and term papers you write in English courses and for those you write in other fields. Furthermore, they will remain with you long after you have written your last essay for college or university.

Chapter 2

Clarifying Essay Topics and Gathering Material

As we noted in Chapter 1, the main purpose of writing assignments is to help you understand course material by exploring it in detail and communicating an opinion about it. Essay topics are designed to allow you to come to terms with the concepts you have studied, the novels you have read, or the data you have collected. But in order to write an essay that demonstrates your understanding of your subject, you first need to know what the topic means. Then you need to know how to find something to say.

CLARIFYING ESSAY TOPICS

When you first look at a list of topics for your courses, you may feel unsure about what to do. Consider these typical assignments for first-year college and university courses:

> What is the function of the graveyard scene in *Hamlet*?
> Discuss the concept of the state in Plato's *Republic*.
> Compare the use of the vampire myth in the films *Dracula* and *Nosferatu*.
> Explain the concept of narcissism as the term is used by Freud and his followers.
> Is Alice Munro's "The Red Dress" a good story? Why or why not?
> Compare Chomsky's and Skinner's theories of language acquisition.
> Discuss the development of Canadian abstract painting.
> Evaluate Canadian and U.S. policies on pollution in the Great Lakes.
> Write a 1000-word essay on some aspect of computers.

If you were faced with these topics, or similar ones, would you be able to answer "yes" to the following questions?

Questions About Essay Topics

Do I understand the terms used in the topic?
Do I understand the directions the topic gives me?
Do I know what kind of material to use in my essay?
Do I know how to limit the topic if necessary?
Do I know how to choose a topic that fits my interest, knowledge, time, and writing skills?

If your answer to any of these questions is "no," read on. You'll find the answers in this chapter.

Defining Unfamiliar Terms

The first step in writing an essay on a set topic is to make sure that you understand exactly what the assignment means. To write on the sample essay topics listed above, for example, you would have to know the meaning of the terms narcissism, abstract painting, myth, and language acquisition.

Learning about a subject includes learning the vocabulary that specialists use in talking about issues that interest them. If you are interested in computers, for example, you quickly learn the meaning of terms such as byte, printout, and software. In psychology courses, you may learn the meaning of such terms as conditioned response, narcissism, and depression. In literature courses you are likely to discuss the meaning of terms such as myth, point of view, and tragedy.

As these examples suggest, the specialized vocabulary of each discipline is likely to include both terms that are seldom used outside the field and terms that are used in a more restricted way than in everyday speech. When you say, "I feel depressed," for example, you may be disappointed about an exam mark, sad about a friend's moving, or temporarily in low spirits for any one of a number of reasons. But you are not using the word **depressed** in the way a psychologist or psychiatrist would. Similarly, the term **tragedy**, as used in literary criticism, is not simply a disastrous event, but a certain kind of play.

Making sure you know the meaning of such terms is the first step in understanding your essay topics. Since your instructor may not be available when you need to find out what such terms mean and your standard dictionary may not contain specialized definitions, you need to be aware of other ways of finding explanations. The two principal sources for such information are your text(s) for the course and specialized dictionaries.

Many texts, including this one, contain **glossaries** that briefly define concepts and other terms with which their readers may be unfamiliar. Check the table of contents to see whether the text contains a glossary; if there is one, see if it defines the word adequately for your purposes. If there is no glossary, or if you are still puzzled, check the index to see whether there is a discussion of the term elsewhere in the text.

If your text doesn't provide all the information you need, consult the specialized dictionaries in the reference area of the library. This list will give you an idea of the wide range of dictionaries available:

> **Examples of Specialized Dictionaries**
>
> Abrams, M.H. *A Glossary of Literary Terms*, 3rd ed. New York: Holt, Rinehart, and Winston, 1971.
>
> Ammer, Christine, and Dean S. Ammer. *Dictionary of Business and Economics*. New York: Free Press, 1977.
>
> Angeles, Peter Adam. *Dictionary of Philosophy*. 1st ed. New York: Barnes and Noble, 1981.
>
> Henderson, I.F., and W.D. Henderson. *A Dictionary of Biological Terms*. 8th ed. by J.H. Kenneth. Princeton, N.J.: D. Van Nostrand, 1963.
>
> Holman, C. Hugh. *A Handbook to Literature*. 3rd ed. New York: Odyssey Press, 1972.
>
> Mayer, Ralph. *A Dictionary of Art Terms and Techniques*. New York: Crowell, 1969, 1975.
>
> Preminger, Alex, et. al., eds. *Princeton Encyclopedia of Poetry and Poetics*. Princeton: Princeton University Press, 1974.

For help in finding similar dictionaries in other fields, consult your library holdings or a reference librarian.

If you have consulted your text and an appropriate dictionary and you are still unsure about the meaning of a particular term, ask your instructor. You can't write well on a topic if you are unclear about what the topic means.

Understanding Directions

The second step in coming to terms with an essay topic is to make sure you understand the directions you are given for how the essay is to be written.

If you take another look at the list of sample topics, you may wonder, "What directions?" If you were doing math, you would easily recognize the symbols that told you whether to add, subtract, multiply, or divide; if you were cooking, you would know what to do if the recipe said to mix, bake, or fry. But you may be less familiar with the terms that give you directions for writing essays.

One reason for your uncertainty about directions for writing essays is that essay topics are stated in a wide variety of ways. Most of the essays you write for college and university courses, however, employ only three basic procedures: **analysis, comparison,** and **evaluation**. Below you will find a description of the three basic procedures, with examples to show how to recognize which procedure or procedures a particular assignment calls for.

Analysis   The main purpose of analysis is to illuminate something, such as a concept, a text, an event, or a set of data, by examining its parts in detail. When you analyze something, you will answer questions like these:

> What parts can the thing I am analyzing be divided into?
> What is the nature of the thing I am analyzing?
> Why does it have this particular nature?

If you were analyzing the artifacts from an archaeological site, for example, you would divide them into parts according to types of artifacts (flints, trade goods, animal remains, and so forth) and according to the location where they were found. From your analysis of this material, you would decide what kind of site this is: for example, a winter camp used by Assiniboian Indians over a period of a hundred years. To complete the analysis, you would explain why these artifacts indicate this kind of camp. Combining your generalization about the nature of the thing you are analyzing with your explanation of why it has this particular nature would give you a thesis for your essay.

There are two basic ways of analyzing material: content analysis and textual analysis.

CONTENT ANALYSIS is the examination of behaviour, data, written works, and other sources of information without regard to the form in which the information is communicated. "Explain the concept of the state in Plato's *Republic*" and "Discuss the causes of the English Civil War" are examples of the kind of topic that requires content analysis. In Chapter 3, "Preparing to Write: Analyzing Content," you will find step-by-step procedures for doing this kind of analysis, with two sample topics.

TEXTUAL ANALYSIS is the examination of written works or performances (such as plays, television programmes, and films) with attention both to what is being said and to how the work or performance is presented. If you were writing on the significance of the title in Joseph Conrad's "Heart of Darkness," for example, you would discuss not only what the story says but also the techniques Conrad uses in presenting the story. You will find a detailed examination of textual analysis, with sample topics, in Chapter 4, "Preparing to Write: Analyzing Texts."

Few topics actually use the word **analyze**. Analysis, however, is the basis of almost all writing you are likely to do in college or university. Topics that require only analysis ask you to divide a single thing—Plato's concept of the state, the causes of the English Civil War, the significance of a story's title—into its parts. Other topics may ask you to compare or to evaluate. Before you can compare or evaluate, however, you must first analyze. Thus it is important to make sure you understand the basic procedures of analysis.

Comparison   The main purpose of comparison is to examine the similarities and differences of two or more things in such a way as to lead to a clearer understanding of the things themselves and of your basis of comparison. The **basis of comparison** tells you which features of the things you are comparing are relevant. You could compare apples and oranges, for example, as foods, as cash crops, or as objects to throw. Depending on which of these you chose as your basis of comparison, your comparison would illuminate not only the individual properties of apples and oranges, but also the general properties of foods, cash crops, or objects to throw.

Since comparison is based on analysis, your first step in comparing things is to divide them into parts and compare the parts. The questions you answer in making comparisons are therefore modifications of the questions for analysis:

> What is the basis of comparison?
> What matching parts can these things be divided into?
> What is the central likeness or difference between these things?
> Why are the things I'm comparing similar or different?

If you wanted to compare downhill and cross-country skiing, for example, you would first need to choose your basis of comparison. Would you compare them as competitive sports, as forms of exercise, or as recreational activities? Your basis of comparison would determine the parts you divide the two sports into, their central likeness or difference, and the reasons for that similarity or difference. At each step, you would analyze in terms of similarities and differences.

You might find comparison topics stated in these ways:

> Choose two poems and show how they either attack or celebrate aspects of contemporary life.
> How are the principles of solar heating systems similar to or different from the principles of geothermal systems?
> Compare Chomsky's and Skinner's theories of language acquisition.
> Discuss the symbolism of roses in three poems.
> Compare two films.

When you are asked to write on two or more things, you are being asked to compare them, whether or not the topic says so explicitly. Some of these topics state the basis for comparison (compare these poems as **attacks or celebrations of contemporary life**; compare solar and geothermal heating systems **in terms of their principles**; compare **the use of symbolism** in three poems). When the topic does not provide a basis of comparison (compare Chomsky's and Skinner's theories of language acquisition; compare two films), you will have to find one. Suggestions about how to do so appear later in this chapter and in Chapter 7, "Preparing to Write: Making Comparisons."

Evaluation The main purpose of evaluation is to determine the strengths and weaknesses of something—a plan, a performance, a work of art, or a theory, for example. Like comparison, evaluation starts with analysis. To evaluate a hockey forward, for example, you would first analyze the player's skills as a skater, shooter, stick-handler, and play-maker. Your knowledge of the game and of other hockey forwards would give you a sense of what constitutes excellence in each of these categories. To evaluate a particular player, you would therefore measure that person's strengths and weaknesses against your standard of excellence.

In order to evaluate one or more things, you will need to answer questions like these:

> What standard of evaluation is appropriate?
> What strengths and weaknesses can I divide my material into?
> What is the nature of my evaluation of this material?
> Why have I come to this evaluation?

The common standards of evaluation are practical, ethical, aesthetic, and logical. Since it is possible to evaluate things according to various standards, you have to define which one or ones you have chosen to use. If you chose to evaluate proposed federal policy on pollution in the Great Lakes on practical grounds, for example, you might consider the cost to participants, the technology used to control pollution, and the enforcement of government regulations. Your analysis of these areas might lead you to conclude that the federal policy is good because it would provide cost-efficient, technologically sound, and easily enforced methods for reducing pollution. If you had evaluated the proposal on ethical grounds, however, your conclusion might have been quite different; you might have decided, for example, that you found the proposal ethically unacceptable because it would infringe on native fishing rights.

Because of the wide variety of possible viewpoints, essay topics seldom give the standard of evaluation you should use. For each of these topics, you would have to decide on an appropriate standard of evaluation:

> Is J.D. Salinger's *Catcher in the Rye* a good novel?
> Was the Riel Rebellion justified?
> Are individual rights better protected under the Canadian Charter of Rights or under the U.S. Constitution?

You will find more information on how to evaluate in Chapter 9, "Preparing to Write: Making Evaluations."

Other Terms Although most essay topics require that you analyze, compare, or evaluate, these terms may not appear in the topics, as you will have noticed from the examples. You will therefore need to think about what the topic actually requires. For instance, the word **discuss**, used in a wide range of topics, may seem to mean "summarize the relevant information." **It doesn't**. It may appear in topics that require analysis, comparison, or evaluation. **Explain**, **examine**, and **assess** are other words whose meaning may be ambiguous. You may also discover that some topics ask you to **compare** things when you are actually expected to both **compare and evaluate** them. If you are in doubt about the meaning of the directions you are given, ask your instructor.

Choosing Material: Primary and Secondary Sources

So far we have discussed how to find out what each of your topics means and how to decide which procedure or combination of procedures (analysis, comparison, and evaluation) each topic requires. Next you would consider what sources to use. Is your essay to be based solely on **primary sources**, or are you expected to consult **secondary sources** as well?

Primary Sources Primary sources of information are first-hand experiences or first-hand accounts of experiences. Your own knowledge, experience, and observations would be considered primary sources of information. This would include the novels you read, the plays you see, and the questionnaires you collect for your sociology class. It would also include sources such as official documents (e.g., the British North America Act, the Canadian Charter of Rights and Freedoms), eyewitness accounts of events, letters, diaries, and contemporary newspaper accounts. Assignments based solely on primary sources are designed to give you practice in thinking analytically about what you have read, observed, or experienced. When you analyze, compare, or evaluate texts, your primary source of information and ideas is the texts themselves.

Secondary Sources   Secondary sources of information consist of second-hand (or third- or fourth-hand) accounts of experience, such as books and articles written by contemporary historians about past events. They are secondary sources because they select and present material to support a particular point of view. Only some facts are included and usually only one point of view is argued. Assignments based on secondary sources are designed to acquaint you with the important issues in your discipline and also with its methods of research and analysis. Although you may use your prior knowledge and experience as a source of information for some content topics, most will require you to use secondary sources. As a beginning student in the social sciences, for example, you would probably have to rely on books and articles about your subject because you would not have ready access to primary sources or the skills necessary to collect and analyze data.

You can also use secondary sources to supplement your analysis of primary sources. Let's say you have been asked to analyze the function of the graveyard scene in *Hamlet*. Do you rely solely on your own reading of the play, or do you also look up what literary critics have said about it?

It depends, in most cases, on the length of your essay. If this is the topic for a short paper (about 500-1000 words), your instructor probably wants you to demonstrate your ability to use your own skills of literary analysis to arrive at an interpretation. If you were to take your interpretation from secondary sources, you would defeat the purpose of the assignment. On the other hand, if this is the topic for a "term paper" (usually 1500 words or more), your instructor may want you to supplement your analysis of the scene by considering what other writers have said about it. If your assignment for a long essay does not indicate whether you are expected to do library research, be sure to ask. That way you won't discover the awful truth the day before your paper is due.

Essays that require you to use both primary and secondary sources are often difficult to write because of the additional demands of finding relevant secondary sources and integrating others' opinions with your own. You will find a detailed discussion of how to do this kind of paper in Chapter 12.

Limiting the Topic

Most essay topics set definite limits for your investigation: the concept of the state in Plato's *Republic*; the use of the vampire myth in *Dracula* and *Nosferatu*; Canadian and U.S. policies on pollution in the Great Lakes. Occasionally, however, you may be given an indefinite topic like the last one on the list at the beginning of this chapter: "Write a 1000-word essay on some aspect of computers." Or you may be invited to come up with your own topic: "Write a short essay on any work we've discussed in the course so far." In these cases, you will save yourself a great deal of time, and ensure a better essay, by limiting the topic before you begin preparing to write.

Why should you limit the topic? Your examination of your subject should be thorough enough that you can speak as an "expert" to less well-informed readers. If you try to write a five-page essay on broad subjects such as computers or every aspect of the novel *Great Expectations*, your treatment is likely to be fairly superficial. Narrowing your focus enables you to explore your subject in greater depth. It also helps you organize your thinking, your information-gathering, and your writing.

To limit a broad topic, begin by using one of the discovery techniques outlined later in this chapter to generate a list of narrow topics. Then you can choose your narrow topic by following the advice in the next section.

Choosing a Topic

How do you decide which topic to choose from a list you have made up or been given? You are likely to produce your best work when you choose a topic that offers the best "fit" to the combination of interest, knowledge, time, and writing skills you bring to it.

Interest   It is a truism that we all write better when the subject interests us than when it doesn't. You won't always find a topic you are passionately interested in, and you certainly shouldn't twist every topic to fit your preoccupations. But you should try to avoid writing on a topic that you find totally uninteresting, however easy the topic might seem. If you are bored with your subject, you are likely to communicate your boredom to your reader, and a bored reader is not likely to be favourably disposed to what you have to say.

Knowledge   Interest alone will not result in a successful piece of writing. You have to have something to say. How much do you already know about each topic? How much reading or other information-gathering would you need to do to answer the question adequately? Suppose, for example, that for your course in adolescent psychology you have been asked to write an essay on one of these questions:

1. How adequate are the special programmes that the province provides for problem adolescents?
2. Much has been said about the influence of peer pressure during adolescence. From your own experience, would you say this influence is more harmful than beneficial, or vice versa?

Which topic would you choose? The first would be a reasonable choice if you have worked with problem adolescents, or if you are familiar with the relevant agencies, or if you know how to get information about government programmes quickly and easily. If you lack that kind of specialized knowledge, the second topic would be easier because your own experience, and your knowledge of the experience of other adolescents, would provide all the material you need.

Time Both interest and knowledge need to be balanced against the time that you have to finish a particular assignment. The more time you have, the more reasonable it is to follow your own interests even if you have very little knowledge about the subject. Conversely, if your essay is due in two days, you are wise to choose a topic about which you are already fairly well informed.

How much time is it reasonable to spend on a given subject? In an ideal world, you would spend as much time as you needed to explore the subject fully, to let your ideas develop and mature, and to write draft after draft until you were satisfied that you could do no better. This is not an ideal world. You are always having to juggle the demands of one assignment against the demands of other assignments, other courses, your personal life. As you consider the requirements of your assignment, work out a schedule for completing your essay. Be sure to allow time for several drafts, with an interval between them. You are more likely to see what changes need to be made if you've left the essay for a day or two.

Writing Skills Sometimes you may feel that all of the possible topics are fairly equal in terms of your interest, knowledge, and time. In that case, you might consider whether there are differences in the writing skills involved. As we have seen, comparison and evaluation are based on analysis. Therefore topics that require only analysis may be easier than those that require a combination of procedures. On the other hand, if you have trouble finding enough to say about a single subject, you might choose a comparison topic instead. By taking such considerations into account, you can often increase your chances of writing a good essay.

Gathering Material

After you have decided what your topic requires, your next step is to gather appropriate material. This is another stage of preparing to write that you may be inclined to rush through because you feel you should be writing your paper. All too often, however, essays that are well organized and grammatically correct have disappointingly little to say because the writers have made only superficial points or have not used specific examples to support their points.

In the "Preparing to Write" chapters we will demonstrate how to **collect** material from textbooks, literary works and performances, and library references. In this section we will focus on how to gather material for assignments that start from what you already know. These assignments may leave you facing a blank sheet of paper for hours on end, or give you an uncomfortable feeling that you have left some areas of your topic unexplored. Fortunately there are several techniques you can use to stimulate your thinking and to lead you into areas of your topic you might otherwise have overlooked. We will consider four discovery techniques: (1) freewriting; (2) brainstorming; (3) tree diagramming; and (4) asking questions about specific categories of analysis.

Freewriting   Each time you come up with an idea, does another part of your brain say, "That's no good," or "You'll look silly if you say that"? The ability to distinguish strong ideas from weak ones is very useful when you are revising, but it can be a nuisance when you are trying to get started.

Freewriting is one way of circumventing this mental editor. Freewriting consists of writing continuously for ten minutes or longer, without stopping to organize, correct, or evaluate what you are doing. If you tend to agonize over a blank page, then you may find that freewriting on the subject of your essay will set your mind in motion.

If your freewriting material seems too limited, try variations on the basic freewriting process. You might, for example, look over your first freewriting for material most relevant to your assignment and then do a second freewriting using this material as a springboard. Or if you are writing an essay on a text, you might freewrite a fantasy dialogue with the author, asking questions and recording the "author's" replies. This dialogue may lead you to insights that you would not have reached by more conventional means.

Freewriting can be a valuable way of starting the process of gathering material. It will rarely provide you with all the material you need, however. You may therefore want to combine freewriting with other discovery techniques.

Brainstorming   Brainstorming is another way of circumventing your mental editor. Brainstorming consists of putting down, in point form, everything you can think of about your topic, however obvious or bizarre the ideas might seem. You begin by putting your subject in the middle of a page, and then you jot down ideas as they come to you. When you finish, you will have a mixture of generalizations and details radiating from your central subject. You can then draw lines to connect related points.

For example, if you were asked to write an essay on fitness, you might come up with the following brainstorming diagram:

The advantage of recording your ideas in the form of a diagram is that you can link points as you think of them, and thus make them easier to categorize. Much of the material in the above diagram, for example, relates to the effects of fitness. You might therefore decide to make the effects of fitness the focus of your essay.

Tree Diagramming   Tree diagramming is a more systematic form of brainstorming. When you use this technique, you gather material by thinking of the categories and subcategories of the topic in the form of an ever-expanding "tree." For example, if you were asked to write an essay evaluating one of the transportation systems in your province, you might begin by setting out the following tree diagram.

Tree diagramming is useful for narrowing a broad topic and for developing equivalent categories of information.

Asking Questions Within Analytical Categories   Each discipline of thought, such as sociology or history or English, has its own set of questions about the world and its own way of organizing the answers to those questions. In this text we call these questions **heuristic questions** and these ways of organizing the answers **special categories of analysis**. You can use these questions and categories to generate material for your essays.

Heuristic questions are questions that encourage the asker to explore particular areas of a subject. They range from the familiar five W's of news reporting—Who? What? When? Where? Why?—to complex questions of philosophical enquiry. If you ask each of the appropriate heuristic questions about your subject, you can ensure that your coverage will be thorough.

The only problem is that in lectures and textbooks you are usually presented with the answers to a particular set of questions rather than the questions themselves. Since these answers are organized according to the categories of analysis specific to that discipline, however, you can use these **special categories** as a starting point for asking questions.

For example, let's suppose you have been asked to write an essay on the subject of manhood in a short story. On a first reading, you may have little idea of what questions to ask in order to discover something about the story's treatment of manhood. If you know the categories for the analysis of fiction, however, you can ask how each of the categories (narrative structure, setting, characterization, and so forth) contributes to a particular theme about the nature of manhood. You will have plenty of material for your essay by the time you have asked yourself questions such as these: What is the setting of the story, and how does it make a point about manhood? Does characterization in the story make a point about manhood?

If you do not know the special categories applicable to your subject, you can use questions based on more **general categories of analysis**. In Chapter 3 we show how you can use the general categories of causes, effects, and features for analyzing content. You can also use heuristic questions based on these categories for limiting topics or for generating material. If you were asked to analyze Freud's concept of narcissism, for example, you might begin by asking yourself questions such as these: What are the features of this concept? What caused Freud to develop this concept? What effect did this concept have on Freud's other theories and on the development of psychoanalysis?

We have outlined four techniques to help you discover what to say about a particular subject. You may find one technique that you can use for every assignment, or you may shift from one to another to meet specific needs. In our examples of the preparation process, we emphasize heuristic questions based on categories of analysis. We find this the most useful discovery technique because it organizes material into appropriate categories at the same time.

SUMMARY

In this chapter we have discussed the first two steps in preparing to write an essay: clarifying essay topics and gathering material. Asking yourself the appropriate questions about essay topics will help you to plan your writing tasks efficiently, confident that you know what you are doing. Using the discovery techniques outlined in this chapter will help you to limit broad topics as well as to explore ideas for your essay.

At this stage of the preparation process, allow yourself to explore a wide range of possible responses to your topic. If you make judgments about the relevance of ideas and details too soon, you may leave yourself too little material to work with. You can't build a good building with shoddy materials, and you can't write a good essay without good ideas. The stage of gathering material is a vital element in the preparation process, worth all the attention you can give it.

EXERCISES

A. In the following essay topics, identify the terms you might need to define either because they belong to the specialized vocabulary of a discipline or because they are used in a more restricted sense than in everyday speech. Then give definitions for two of the terms you have identified, using a specialized dictionary if necessary. List where you found your definitions.

1. Write a 750-word essay on the use of biofeedback in the treatment of chronic pain.

2. How does Dee Brown use the concept of "manifest destiny" in *Bury My Heart at Wounded Knee* to explain Indian-white relations during the settlement of the American West?

3. Write a 750-word essay comparing the kinship systems of the Cree and Chipewyan Indians.

4. Analyze the film *Butley* in terms of the unities of action, time, and place.

5. Write a 750-word essay explaining why, according to economists, scarcity is a subjective concept and thus a permanent part of the human condition.

B. In a sentence or two each, explain whether the essay topics below require analysis, comparison, evaluation, or a combination of these procedures.

1. Explain how the weakening of the Ottoman Empire contributed to the conflicts that led to World War I.

2. Write a 750-word essay discussing Freud's and Jung's concepts of dreams.

3. Write a 750-word essay showing how Charlie Chaplin's rise to fame in the 1920s introduced a more complex kind of comedy into American films.

4. Your economics text implies that every nation goes through a "characteristic sequence of stages" as it passes from the 'young debtor' to the 'mature creditor' stage of economic development. Cy Gonick argues that this model does not hold for Canada because it does not consider factors peculiar to foreign investment in Canada. Which of these two positions more accurately accounts for Canada's economic development?

5. Comment on the significance of the title *In a Free State* in any two sections of this book.

C. In a few sentences each, explain what would constitute **primary sources** and what would constitute **secondary sources** of material for essays on each of the following topics. For each topic, also explain under what circumstances you would use only primary sources, only secondary sources, or a combination of both.

1. What are the disadvantages of the Utopian society William Morris describes in *News from Nowhere*?

2. Write a 1500-word essay explaining why the British were disorganized and inefficient during the early years of World War I.

3. Comment on the implications of John Dewey's statement that the teacher's primary task is to motivate students to learn, that "There is the same exact equation between teaching and learning that there is between buying and selling."

4. Show how television conveys, or does not convey, traditional masculine and feminine stereotypes.

D. The subjects below are too general to make good topics for a 1000-word essay. Choose two subjects. For each subject you choose, use one of the discovery techniques outlined in this chapter to arrive at a list of 5-10 narrow essay topics.

1. The struggle between the British and the French for control of North America

2. Alcoholism in Canada

3. The development of abstract art in Canada

4. The impact of television

5. The legal system in Canada

E. Choose one of the four discovery techniques to generate material you might use in a short essay on one of the following topics. Save your material for possible use in a later exercise.

1. Does our legal system serve the needs of everyone in our society? Explain why or why not.

2. Does television perpetuate traditional masculine and feminine stereotypes?

3. We blame many problems on "lack of communication." Discuss three causes or three effects of communication failure.

4. Embryo cloning is now an established technique for improving the characteristics of dairy cattle. The technology is available to extend embryo cloning into many other fields, including human reproduction. What are the implications of cloning human embryos?

Chapter 3

Preparing to Write: Analyzing Content

It's the second week of classes, and you are looking over the writing assignments you've been given so far:

SOCIAL ANTHROPOLOGY 101
We have discussed the "rites of passage" that mark the transition from adolescence to adulthood in traditional hunting and gathering societies. Does Canadian society possess such rites?

PHILOSOPHY 250
Discuss the concept of the state in Plato's *Republic*.

EDUCATION 200
Keep a journal over the term about your experiences as a student or the experiences of some member of your family in an educational setting: a day-care centre, kindergarten, public or private school. At the end of the term, you will use your entries to write a 1000-word essay on what you have learned about some aspect of the educational system.

HISTORY 280
Write an essay on the British war effort in the early years of World War I.

SOCIAL PSYCHOLOGY 213
Why do people who are fully aware of the health hazards continue to smoke?

Here you are, with five essays to think about, and the topics are so different. How will you ever be able to write satisfactory essays on such a wide range of topics?

Relax. Although the topics for these courses look quite different, they all require the same mode of thinking: content analysis. **Analysis,** as you may recall from Chapter 2, is the process of dividing something into parts in order to understand better both the parts and the whole. **Content analysis** is the examination of behaviour, data, written works, and other sources of information without regard to the manner in which the information is communicated. Content analysis is a basic mode of understanding material in many disciplines. Essays based on content analysis are commonly required in disciplines such as education, the social sciences, and the humanities. Once you have a good grasp of what content analysis is and how to do it, you will have a good foundation for much of the writing you will do in college and university.

In this chapter we will first examine the basic questions and procedures for topics that require content analysis. Then we will follow those procedures to show how you would prepare to write on two of the topics given at the beginning of this chapter. By the end of this chapter, you should have a clear understanding of the principles involved in doing content analysis. You should also be able to apply the procedures to topics you encounter in a wide range of courses.

BASIC QUESTIONS AND PROCEDURES FOR CONTENT ANALYSIS

When you analyze for content, your subject is usually an event, such as the Russian Revolution or the exploration of Canada; a concept, such as the Oedipus complex or the state; a theory, such as Keynesian economics or the "big bang" theory of the origin of the solar system; or a set of data, such as observations of infant behaviour or questionnaires about voting habits.

Your purpose in analyzing is to answer two questions. The first is a "what" question: What is the nature of the thing I am analyzing? The second is a "why" question: Why does the thing I am analyzing have this particular nature? Together the answers to these questions will give you a thesis for your essay. The steps outlined below will show you how to go about answering these questions.

Once you have completed these steps, you will be ready to write the first draft of your essay. You will have a thesis to work from; you will have categories of information to serve as the basis for your paragraph divisions; and you will have material to provide explanations and details to support your points. By giving yourself enough time to prepare in this systematic way, you will ensure that you begin with a thorough, thoughtful analysis of your subject. So when you are faced with a content analysis topic, ask yourself the following questions.

Step 1

CLARIFYING THE TOPIC

Do I understand the terms used in the topic?

For definitions of terms within a particular discipline, check the glossary in textbooks or a specialized dictionary of the kind discussed in Chapter 2.

Do I understand the directions the topic gives me?
A. Am I asked to analyze, to compare, or to evaluate?
B. Does this topic require content analysis or textual analysis?

A. Topics for analysis ask you to examine the causes, effects, or features of a single subject or to examine the relationship between a part and the whole to which it belongs.

B. Content analysis asks you to focus on an event, a concept, a theory, or a set of data. Textual analysis asks you to consider how a particular work, written or performed, is presented, as well as what it says.

Do I know what kind of material to use in my essay?

Content analysis may be based on primary sources (such as experiences you have had or data you have collected); on secondary sources (books and articles on your subject); or on both. These topics often require research (see Chapter 11).

Do I know how to limit the topic if necessary?

Topics for content analysis are often broad and therefore need to be limited. See the suggestions for limiting topics in Chapter 2.

Do I know how to choose a topic that fits my interest, knowledge, time, and writing skills?

For suggestions on choosing topics, see Chapter 2. Once you have chosen a topic, decide how much time to allow for completing the assignment, depending upon its length and the kind of material required. The more reading or other information-gathering you have to do, the longer you'll need for the preparation stage.

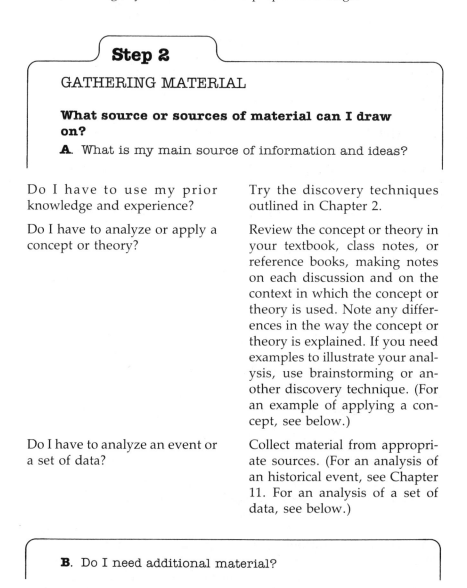

Step 2

GATHERING MATERIAL

What source or sources of material can I draw on?

A. What is my main source of information and ideas?

Do I have to use my prior knowledge and experience?	Try the discovery techniques outlined in Chapter 2.
Do I have to analyze or apply a concept or theory?	Review the concept or theory in your textbook, class notes, or reference books, making notes on each discussion and on the context in which the concept or theory is used. Note any differences in the way the concept or theory is explained. If you need examples to illustrate your analysis, use brainstorming or another discovery technique. (For an example of applying a concept, see below.)
Do I have to analyze an event or a set of data?	Collect material from appropriate sources. (For an analysis of an historical event, see Chapter 11. For an analysis of a set of data, see below.)

B. Do I need additional material?

Look up unfamiliar words in a standard dictionary, an unabridged one if possible. Check specialized dictionaries like those mentioned in Chapter 2 (p. 16) for definitions of terms within a specific discipline.

Consult an encyclopedia for a general overview of a subject. For help in finding books and articles on your subject, see Chapter 11.

Step 3

CATEGORIZING MATERIAL

What categories should I divide my material into?

Once you have defined the event, set of data, concept, or theory you are analyzing, you need to establish categories for your analysis. These categories are the parts you will divide your material into.

Special Categories   Each discipline has sets of categories used in analyzing specific kinds of material. These are the **special categories** of that discipline. Some topics will indicate the categories you are to use ("Discuss the social and psychological causes of alcoholism"). Others will assume that you know the appropriate categories ("Discuss the concept of the state in Plato's *Republic*"—you must know the "parts" that make up a state). Whenever these special categories are given or implied, use them to organize your material.

General Categories   You may also find topics for which there are no obvious categories for organizing your material. In the absence of appropriate special categories, begin your analysis by using one or more of these **general categories**:

> **Features**: What are the main parts of this event, set of data, concept, or theory?
>
> **Causes**: What has brought about, or might have brought about, the event, data, concept, or theory I am analyzing?
>
> **Effects**: What has happened, or might happen, as a result of this event, data, concept, or theory?

After you have put your information under these broad headings, you can organize it further by using appropriate subcategories. If you were writing an analytical essay on smoking, for example, you might come up with half a dozen causes of this behaviour. You might discover, however, that you could group these causes under subcategories such as psychological causes and social causes.

Step 4

FINDING A THESIS

What generalization can I make about the nature of the thing I am analyzing?

What is the nature of rites of passage in Canadian society?
What is the nature of the state in Plato's *Republic*?
What is the nature of the educational setting I have observed?
What was the nature of the British war effort at the beginning of World War I?
What is the nature of the smoking habit?

To answer this question, examine the information in each of your categories to see what pattern or patterns you can discover. Then ask yourself: what attribute or attributes are common to some or all of the categories?

When you have defined these attributes, combine them in a generalization about the subject you are analyzing. This generalization will constitute the opinion portion of your thesis statement. Your information on the British war effort at the beginning of World War I might lead you to a generalization such as this:

The British war effort at the beginning of World War I was disorganized and inefficient.

Why does the thing I am analyzing have this particular nature?

Why are the rites of passage among Canadian adolescents as they are?
Why did Plato have this particular conception of the state?
Why is this aspect of the educational system as it is?
Why was the British war effort disorganized and inefficient?
Why do people smoke when they know smoking is bad for them?

The answer to this "why" question will complete your thesis by providing one or more reasons to support your opinion. You can answer this question in two ways: (1) by re-examining the material in your categories with the "why" question in mind; or (2) by calling upon your broader knowledge of the subject. In either case, you will be defining the features, causes, or effects that will justify your generalization about your subject.

If you were analyzing the British war effort in World War I, for example, your final thesis might be something like this:

> The British war effort during the early years of World War I was disorganized and inefficient (generalization) because Asquith's indecisiveness and the confusion among government administrators created conflict between the politicians and the military (definition of causes).

Much of this preparation is essentially a thinking process, and therefore not as time-consuming as it may appear. With practice you will find that following these steps—clarifying your topic, dividing your subject into appropriate categories for content analysis, making reasonable generalizations about it, and explaining your reason(s)—will enable you to write better essays more efficiently.

SAMPLE TOPICS: ANALYZING CONTENT

To show how you would prepare to write essays requiring content analysis, we will follow the steps outlined above for two topics listed at the beginning of this chapter. One of the topics will demonstrate using special categories for content analysis, and the other will demonstrate using general categories.

Using Special Categories to Apply a Concept

Most of your essay topics in fields such as anthropology, history, psychology, and sociology will ask you to analyze content. In many cases, your topics will require you to apply the concepts and methods of the discipline to a particular body of material. You might be asked to demonstrate your understanding of the economic concept of supply and demand and of the method of case study analysis, for example, by analyzing the growth and decline of a particular industry.

The topic from social anthropology at the beginning of this chapter is an example of this kind of assignment:

> SOCIAL ANTHROPOLOGY 101
> We have discussed the "rites of passage" that mark the transition from adolescence to adulthood in traditional hunting and gathering societies. Does Canadian society possess such rites?

We will follow the steps for preparing to write on this topic by showing what your responses might be when you are using the special categories of a particular discipline to apply a concept.

Step 1

CLARIFYING THE TOPIC

A. Do I understand the terms used in the topic?
B. Do I understand the directions the topic gives me?
   1. Am I asked to analyze, to compare, or to evaluate?
   2. Does this topic require content analysis or textual analysis?
C. Do I know what material to use?
D. Do I need to limit the topic?
E. Have I chosen a topic that fits my interest, knowledge, time, and writing skills?

A. I'll need to check the definition of "rites of passage" in my textbook and possibly in an encyclopedia.

B. No mention of comparison or evaluation. To answer the question, I'll have to analyze the transition from adolescence to adulthood in Canada. Since I'm not analyzing a particular writer's essay on adolescence in Canada, this will be content analysis.

C. No mention of research. In addition to finding a good explanation of rites of passage, I'll need to think of examples of events in Canadian society that might fit the definition of rites of passage.

D. The topic is quite specific; I may need to limit my examples.

E. No choice of topic. The essay is only supposed to be 500 words, due in one week. There's little reading to do. I could review my notes and write the first draft tomorrow, and then revise my essay over the weekend.

Step 2

GATHERING MATERIAL

What source or sources of material can I draw on?

From class lectures, I know that in some societies males go through rites of passage at puberty to show their change in status from children to adults. Canadian society certainly doesn't put adolescents through tests of courage or mark their bodies as a sign of adult status.

My textbook and an encyclopedia give me a more complete definition of this concept. Most rites of passage, it seems, are characterized by three phases: (1) **separation** from both younger children and adults, often in a special place; (2) a **transition** period for learning the rules of the adult community and passing certain tests; and (3) **reincorporation** as an adult member of the community, marked by ceremonies or celebration.

I'll try one of the discovery techniques discussed in Chapter 2 to think of occasions in Canadian society that might fit these three phases.

Step 3

CATEGORIZING MATERIAL

What categories should I divide my material into?

Some of the examples I've thought of, like being able to drink or to vote, are rights that you receive automatically when you reach a certain age. Others, like getting your own apartment, seem more informal. I think I'll begin by dividing my examples into Legal Rights and Social Rights. Then I'll use the special categories of separation, transition, and reincorporation to see whether my examples fit the concept of rites of passage.

Legal Rights
1. Getting a driver's licence
   - separation: minimum age established by provincial law
   - transition: learning driving skills, passing a test
   - reincorporation: considered adult driver, but discriminatory insurance rates
2. Being able to drink in public
   - separation: minimum age established by provincial law
   - transition: ?
   - reincorporation: entry into places reserved for drinking adults, often marked by celebration
3. Being able to vote
   - separation: age established by law
   - transition: ?
   - reincorporation: voting at the next election
4. Having the right to quit school
   - separation: minimum age established by provincial law; school-leavers often isolated from classmates
   - transition: ?
   - incorporation: may join the adult working world

Social Rights
1. Getting a full-time job
   - separation: may involve leaving school and/or home
   - transition: may involve period of training or apprenticeship and certification, but may not
   - reincorporation: membership in the working world, with adult pay; sometimes celebrated by worker and friends or family
2. Establishing a Residence
   - separation: leaving the family home
   - transition: learning the skills to take care of self
   - reincorporation: membership in the community of self-supporting adults, sometimes celebrated with party
3. Getting Married
   - separation: giving up single life
   - transition: sometimes formal period of engagement
   - reincorporation: membership in the community of married adults, marked by wedding

Step 4

FINDING A THESIS

What is the nature of the thing I am analyzing?

First I should see if there are any patterns in my examples. Do all the examples show the phases of separation, transition, and reincorporation?

Separation stage   Among the social rights, getting a full-time job and getting married sometimes involve a change of residence and of household members, but establishing a residence is the only one that requires this kind of separation. For the legal rights, on the other hand, separation between adult and non-adult status is determined almost exclusively by age. Furthermore, the age at which these rights are obtained differs, both from one kind of right to another and from province to province.

Transition stage   In some of my examples there is a transition phase. Getting a driver's licence requires passing a test on a specific body of skills. Some jobs require periods of apprenticeship or training; some couples have a period of engagement. But these conditions do not apply to everyone. Some of these events show no transition stage. People become eligible to vote, or to drink in public, for example, simply by reaching a designated age.

Reincorporation stage   Reincorporation into the adult world is equally hit and miss. Weddings are the clearest example of celebrations marking the entry into a new community of adults. But obviously many people hold adult status long before they marry. Few other occasions are commonly marked by special recognition of the person's new status.

Although my examples show some elements of traditional rites of passage (they do involve the granting of adult rights and privileges), there is no set of steps that all Canadian adolescents go through at the same time to become recognized as adult members of the community.

On the basis of my data, then, I'd say that the transition from childhood to adulthood in Canadian society happens piecemeal, with individuals achieving signs of adult status at different ages and not necessarily participating in all these ritual occasions. (There are no significant differences between my examples of legal rights and my examples of social rights; if there were, my generalization would have to account for those differences.)

Why does the thing I am analyzing have this particular nature?

Why is the transition from childhood to adulthood in Canadian society a piecemeal one, instead of being similar to the rites of passage of more traditional societies? I will re-examine my material to see what might be a reasonable explanation of the cause or causes of this situation.

What I notice is that the social and legal rights I have examined admit adolescents into one segment of adult society, but do not grant them adult status in the society as a whole. There are distinct rites of passage for becoming a driver, drinker, voter, worker, self-supporting adult, or spouse. There is no single rite of passage that is recognized by the society as a whole. This lack of a single socially recognized ritual conferring adulthood accounts for the piecemeal nature of the transition from childhood to adulthood.

Now I can write my thesis:

> The transition from adolescence to adulthood in Canada is a piecemeal one rather than a true rite of passage because adult status is granted independently by various segments of the society rather than by the society as a whole.

You have now completed the steps in preparing to write on a topic that requires you to do content analysis using special categories. The special categories here are the "parts" of the concept "rites of passage"—the phases of separation, transition, and reincorporation. As you can see, the special categories give you a way of generating examples of possible rites of passage in Canadian society and analyzing them. You can use this procedure whenever you are asked to analyze content—a concept, a proposal, a set of data, or an event—within the framework of a particular field of study.

Using General Categories to Analyze Data

As we have seen, some topics will indicate the major categories you can use in analyzing your material. Other topics may ask you to provide the "content" from your own knowledge or experience and then to analyze it, without specifying a particular frame of reference. When your topic does not state or imply a set of categories, you can begin your analysis by using the general categories of Causes, Effects, and Features.

To see how you would use general categories for content analysis, we will take the topic from Education 200:

> EDUCATION 200
> Keep a journal over the term about your experiences as a student or the experiences of some member of your family in an educational setting: a day-care centre, kindergarten, public or private school. At the end of the term, you will use your entries to write a 1000-word essay on what you have learned about some aspect of the educational system.

Step 1

CLARIFYING THE TOPIC

A. Do I understand the terms used in the topic?
B. Do I understand the directions the topic gives me?
   1. Am I asked to analyze, to compare, or to evaluate?
   2. Does this topic require content analysis or textual analysis?
   3. Are general or special categories for content analysis appropriate for my topic?
C. Do I know what material to use?
D. Do I need to limit the topic?
E. Do I know which topic I can handle most successfully?

A. There are no unfamiliar terms.

B. (1) The topic doesn't say, specifically, but there is no mention of comparison or evaluation. It seems as though I'm being asked to analyze the data I collect about an educational setting. (2) In analyzing my journal I will be doing content analysis rather than textual analysis, because I will focus on what happened, not on how the journal is written. (3) I'm not asked to look for specific kinds of material or to analyze my entries in terms of any theories of education, so I'll start with the general categories of Features, Causes, and Effects.

C. Whose experiences shall I write about? Not my own—I'd forget to take notes. I want to know how my son Tommy gets on in the day-care centre while I'm taking courses, so I'll keep a journal about what happens there. During the term, I'll talk to Tommy and the staff and make notes about their experiences as well as notes on my observations. The topic does not mention library research.

D. The topic says to focus on "some aspect of the educational system." I'll have to define my focus. Not all of my journal entries will be useful.

E. No choice of topics. 1000-word essay, due at the end of term. I'll take notes to the end of November; that will give me two weeks to sort and analyze my journal entries and to write two or three drafts of my essay.

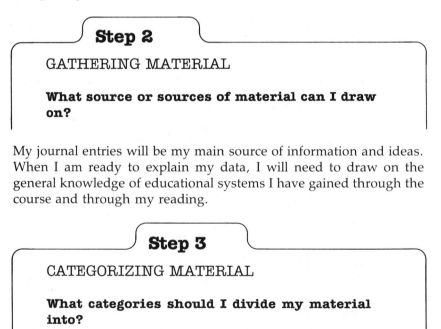

Step 2

GATHERING MATERIAL

What source or sources of material can I draw on?

My journal entries will be my main source of information and ideas. When I am ready to explain my data, I will need to draw on the general knowledge of educational systems I have gained through the course and through my reading.

Step 3

CATEGORIZING MATERIAL

What categories should I divide my material into?

I am using the general categories of Features, Causes, and Effects. I will need to begin with an accurate description of the situation at the day-care centre, so I will use Features as my first category. I'll subdivide my material into these smaller categories: (1) the kind of centre it is; (2) the facilities; (3) the staff; and (4) the programme.

DAY-CARE CENTRE: FEATURES

Kind
Privately run; fees: $250/month full-time, $150/month part-time; government subsidy applied for; enrollment: 29 children ages 2-6 in September; 12 in kindergarten, 17 in playschool; most full-time; 13 from single-parent families

Facilities
Church basement: 1 large and 2 small rooms (one for kindergarten); kitchen; washroom. No playground, but park within 1 block. Near the university and downtown.

Staff
a) Director: helped with 2-4 year olds until kindergarten teacher left; then took over kindergarten
b) Kindergarten teacher: offered full kindergarten programme in Sept.; left in October because of long hours and low pay
c) 1 full-time child-care worker: plans and carries out activities for playschool
d) 1 part-time child-care worker: assists with afternoon outings and special projects

Programmes
September: full kindergarten programme; varied indoor activities and daily trips to park for playschool; 2 field trips; lunches and snacks provided.
October: kindergarten programme reduced (5 children withdrawn); excursions to park reduced when staff reshuffled after kindergarten teacher left; field trips cancelled.
November: lunches and snacks no longer provided; parents asked to help with activities (many single and/or working parents cannot)

Step 4

FINDING A THESIS

What generalization can I make about the nature of the thing I am analyzing?

Many things that happened at the centre seem to be effects of the kindergarten teacher's leaving. In reading through my entries for each category, I notice that the number of staff and students has declined; that the programmes have been reduced; and that the facilities are less adequate, since the children now spend all their time at the centre instead of going to the park or taking field trips. Both the parents and children seem unhappy with the cutbacks in programmes and services. It's clear that the centre has deteriorated over the last three months. This generalization best defines the nature of the day-care centre.

Why does the thing I am analyzing have this particular nature?

To find a reason to support my generalization, I must re-examine my notes to look for possible causes of the day-care centre's deterioration.

All the centre's difficulties seem to have occurred as a result of the kindergarten teacher's leaving. Is this a reason? Not a very good one, because it would make the situation purely personal. I need a reason that will explain both this particular situation and similar ones.

Why did the kindergarten teacher leave? Because of long hours and low pay. Why wasn't she paid more? Why wasn't she replaced? Five children were withdrawn when she left; that meant less money in fees, and therefore less money to hire staff. The day-care centre's problems in all areas seem to be caused by inadequate funding. But why is the funding inadequate? Low fees are not the problem. This centre's fees are comparable to those charged by other day-care centres. If the centre raised its fees substantially, more parents might withdraw their children because they couldn't afford the increase.

In September the centre applied for a government grant, which it still has not received. If this centre had been subsidized as other centres are, its services would not have deteriorated. The lack of government funding, then, seems to be a principal reason for the deterioration of this day-care centre.

Would I have an adequate thesis if I said that conditions at the day-care centre had deteriorated over the last three months because of the lack of government funding? I'd better check my topic.

My topic asks me to use my experience to say what I have learned about "some aspect of the educational system." That seems to call for a more general thesis. How do the problems of the day-care centre relate to problems in the educational system as a whole? Without adequate government funding, any educational institution is likely to experience the same problems: too few teachers, inadequate programmes, and inadequate facilities. And as a result, its students are likely to suffer.

I can now write a thesis that will show how my experiences with the day-care centre relate to larger issues within the educational system:

> The deterioration I observed in a privately run day-care centre because of lack of government funds suggests that the quality of education we can offer students in any educational setting is dependent upon adequate public funding for teachers, programmes, and facilities.

Now that I have a thesis, I can write the first draft of my essay.

SUMMARY

The sample topics in this chapter should give you a good idea of how to use the special categories for content analysis within a particular discipline as well as the general categories for content analysis when your topic does not indicate appropriate special categories. Special and general categories provide a systematic means of categorizing and analyzing your material. By the time you have completed these steps, you should have an adequate thesis for your first draft. You will find specific suggestions for writing and revising essays of analysis in Chapters 5 and 6.

EXERCISES

Save your responses to the following exercises for possible use in the exercises for Chapter 5.

As you know, the purpose of content analysis is to determine the nature of the thing you are analyzing and to explain why it has this particular nature. So that you can practice the preparation process for essays requiring content analysis, let's suppose that you have been asked to write an essay on this topic: "Why do people who are fully aware of the health hazards continue to smoke?"

Follow these steps for arriving at a thesis about this subject:

1. From the information given below, select appropriate items for these three categories:
    - features of smoking
    - causes of smoking
    - effects of smoking

2. See if you can find a pattern in your material that will answer this question: "Why do people who are fully aware of the health hazards continue to smoke?"

3. Give one or more reasons to support your generalization. These reasons may be based either on a re-examination of the material in your categories or on your broader knowledge of human behaviour.

ITEMS OF INFORMATION

a. Cigarette smokers continue to smoke because their experience seems to indicate that cigarettes will provide pleasure or reduce tension or promote good fellowship.

b. If you smoke 20 cigarettes a day and inhale 10 times per cigarette, you will apply 400 coats of a deadly mixture of tars to the parts of your body that come into contact with cigarette smoke. These tars will cause abnormalities in all smokers; sometimes these abnormalities will develop into cancer (Olshavsky, p. 34).

c. Advertising does not seem either to promote or to inhibit cigarette smoking. Cigarette smoking is a major health problem in countries such as Russia and China that have banned cigarette advertising (Olshavsky, p. 98).

d. Most smokers smoke part of the time simply through habit. They automatically smoke when they are drinking coffee or liquor, or when they are playing cards, typing, reading, or driving (Mausner and Platt, p. 15).

e. Recent studies confirm the well-known observation that a great deal of smoking is stimulated by the smoking of others.

f. Mausner and Platt report that two researchers, Brock and Balloun (1967), performed an ingenious experiment in which they discovered that "smokers work harder to eliminate static from a tape recorded message opposing the smoking-cancer link than from a message supporting the relation. Non-smokers, in contrast, more frequently eliminated the static from the message supporting the smoking-cancer relation" (Mausner and Platt, p. 93).

g. Many smokers report that they think of smokers as daring and sophisticated, whereas they think of non-smokers as sensible and careful (Mausner and Platt, p. 7).

h. Both adolescents and adults say that they smoke partly because of a strong sense of fellowship with other smokers (Mausner and Platt, pp. 8-9, 13-14).

i. Cigarette smoking reduces the ability of the blood to carry oxygen, thickens the arteries, increases the rate and output of the heart, increases blood pressure, and increases the rate at which blood clots (Olshavsky, p. 35).

j. In his study of the smoking habits of British schoolboys, J. M. Bynner discovered that "fewer smokers than non-smokers thought that anti-smoking advertisements would be effective and more smokers (48%) than non-smokers (13%) thought that 'too much fuss was being made about smoking' " (p. 34).

k. Cigarette smoking first "slows the motion of and then completely destroys" the cilia, tiny hair-like projections that line the bronchial tubes. These cilia help the lungs clean themselves; so if they are destroyed, the lungs are more susceptible to disease (Olshavsky, p. 34).

l. Olshavsky remarks that people who think that it is healthier for them to smoke than to gain weight if they stopped smoking should know that "a man of average weight who smokes two packs a day would have to gain 75 pounds to offset the improvements in his life expectancy if he stopped smoking" (p. 26).

m. Most smokers will admit on an abstract level that smoking is dangerous but will minimize the dangers on a personal level. Often smokers will claim that their consumption of cigarettes is well below the danger level, or that they do not inhale, or that scientists will find a cure for cancer before they become victims.

n. Bynner discovered that "Boys who smoke thought of themselves as being fairly tough but not as tough as they would really have liked to be. They, more than any other group, saw non-smokers as completely lacking in toughness, and thus the act of giving up smoking involved identification with a group which had a very unattractive characteristic" (p. 93).

o. Current studies show that smokers and non-smokers have the same emotional needs. Smokers satisfy some of these needs by smoking, but their needs are the same as those of non-smokers.

p. Mausner and Platt conclude their study of smoking among college students with this observation: "Our research supports the widely held concept that smoking is initiated by forces in the social environment of adolescents. It also presents some evidence for the thesis that smoking throughout life is highly dependent on the social environment" (p. 171).

References

Bynner, J. M. *The Young Smoker*. London: Her Majesty's Stationery Office, 1969.

Mausner, Bernard, and Ellen S. Platt. *Smoking: A Behavioral Analysis*. New York: Pergamon Press, 1971.

Olshavsky, Richard. *No More Butts: A Psychologist's Approach to Quitting Cigarettes*. Bloomington: Indiana University Press, 1977.

Chapter 4

Preparing to Write: Analyzing Texts

If you are like most students entering college or university, you have studied two or three plays by Shakespeare, lots of short stories, a few novels, and perhaps a little poetry. You have also seen quite a few movies and television programmes, and possibly a few plays. In discussing these works in class or with your friends, however, you may have spent more time in talking about whether you liked the work or agreed with its point of view than you spent in examining how it was put together.

If your experience has been something like this, you have probably had little practice in doing textual analysis. You may therefore have only a vague idea of what to do when you are asked to write an essay analyzing a piece of writing or a performance.

Textual analysis, you will recall, is the examination of a written work or performance with attention both to what is being said and to how the work or performance is presented. Your purpose in analyzing a text is to determine the relation between the work's form (its manner of presentation) and its content. In this chapter you will find out how to use both general categories for analyzing texts and special categories for analyzing specific literary forms. By the end of the chapter you should have a good understanding of the principles of textual analysis and the ability to apply these principles to a wide variety of topics.

BASIC QUESTIONS AND PROCEDURES FOR TEXTUAL ANALYSIS

When you are learning how to do textual analysis, it is helpful to develop a sense of how all the parts of a poem, short story, or essay, for example, fit together to convey the work's theme or thesis. We will therefore explain the basic process of textual analysis according to the questions you would ask for topics like these:

Analyze the following passage from Hugh MacLennan's essay
" 'By Their Foods . . . .' " (no mention of relating the passage to
the essay as a whole)
Analyze Alden Nowlan's poem "Warren Pryor."
What point about North American society is being made in the
film *Network*?
Analyze a television documentary.
Discuss David Suzuki's essay "Genetics: Will This Science Save Us
or Kill Us?"

The first sample topic will demonstrate the preparation process for
this kind of textual analysis.

As you learn more about the techniques used in various forms of
expression, you will probably encounter essay topics that ask you to
show how a specific part of a work, such as point of view, or setting,
or symbolism, relates to the work as a whole, as in these topics:

Choose a short passage from Margaret Laurence's novel *The Stone
Angel* and show how the passage illuminates the novel as a whole.
Discuss the use of Christ symbolism in Alden Nowlan's poem
"The Bull Moose."
Discuss point of view in James Joyce's story "Araby."
What is the significance of the stage setting in Arthur Miller's play
Death of a Salesman?

The second sample topic will show you how to adjust the basic procedures of textual analysis to fit this purpose.

In both types of textual analysis you must show how the features
of the work or performance relate to its theme or thesis, whether or
not the topic says so explicitly. The basic questions to ask in order to
arrive at a thesis are the same: What is the nature of the thing I'm
analyzing? Why does it have this particular nature? Here are the steps
to follow when you are analyzing texts.

Step 1

CLARIFYING THE TOPIC

Do I understand the terms used in the topic?

Topics for textual analysis often contain specialized terms such as
point of view and **dramatic monologue**. If you are unsure of the
meaning of a term, look it up in the glossary of your textbook or in
a handbook of literary terms.

> ### Do I understand the directions the topic gives me?
> **A.** Am I asked to analyze, to compare, or to evaluate?
> **B.** Does this topic require textual analysis or content analysis?

A. Topics for textual analysis ask you to examine a single written work or performance, or one or more features of a single work or performance. Evaluation is not required unless the topic specifically asks for it.

B. Topics for textual analysis ask you to focus on the relationship between what is communicated in a written work or performance and how it is communicated. Most topics in literature and film studies courses require textual analysis; topics in other courses may. If you are not sure, ask your instructor.

> ### Do I know what kind of material to use in my essay?

The work or performance you are analyzing will be your primary source of material. You may need to consult reference works for explanations of literary and historical allusions. If you are doing a research paper, you will need to consult secondary sources as well. Some instructors expect library research for term papers; others do not. If you are in doubt, ask.

> ### Do I know how to limit the topic if necessary?

If you have been given a broad topic, such as, "Write a paper on any aspect of *Great Expectations* that interests you," see the suggestions for limiting topics in Chapter 2.

> ### Do I know how to choose a topic that fits my interest, knowledge, time, and writing skills?

If you are given a choice of topics, consider which work or performance you find most interesting; how much reading or viewing each topic involves; how well you understand the special focus of each topic; and which writing skills each will require. For every assignment, decide how much time to allow for preparing to write, writing, and revising.

Step 2

GATHERING MATERIAL

What source or sources of material can I draw on?

A. What is my main source of information and ideas?

For textual analysis, your main source of information and ideas is the work or performance you are analyzing. If you are analyzing a written work, you will need to read and perhaps reread it until you have a good general understanding of what it says. If you are analyzing a performance—a play, film, or television programme—you may have only one chance to watch it. In these circumstances, you can gather information more efficiently if you prepare beforehand by doing such things as reading reviews and making a list of names to which you may need to refer (actors, directors, costume designers, etc.). You may also be able to find a script to read either before or after the performance. If possible, see the performance more than once. You will be able to concentrate on details much more easily the second time, just as you can with written works.

B. Do I need additional material?

These sources will help you with difficulties you may find in analyzing texts: (1) a standard dictionary (preferably an unabridged one) will tell you the meaning of unfamiliar words; (2) specialized dictionaries and reference books will identify historical and literary allusions and clarify the symbolic associations of words; (3) reviews and scholarly books and articles will provide interpretations. For suggestions about how to find this library material, see Chapters 11 and 12. Be sure to give credit to these sources for any ideas or information you use from them.

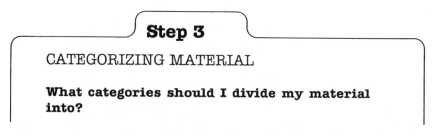

Step 3

CATEGORIZING MATERIAL

What categories should I divide my material into?

When you have a basic understanding of the work you are analyzing, make notes about its features under appropriate categories of analysis.

General categories of textual analysis give you a starting point for writing essays when you are not familiar with the special categories for analyzing a particular kind of text, or when you are writing under time limitations (in-class essays and exams). They also provide ways of organizing your thinking about the things you read and watch, whether or not you write about them. The following chart outlines the general categories of analysis commonly used in literary criticism to analyze written or performed texts.

GENERAL CATEGORIES OF TEXTUAL ANALYSIS

Subject: What is the work about?

Structure: How is the work put together?

Development: What are the particular details that give the work substance?

Style: How does the author or director use the 'language' of the medium?

Tone: What is the author's or director's attitude towards the subject, as conveyed by the work?

Theme or Thesis: What is the central idea of the work? (Though you may make tentative statements about theme or thesis at this stage, your final statement of theme or thesis will come later.)

Categorizing your material in this way serves two main functions. When you are preparing to write, these categories provide the data for your interpretation of the work's theme or thesis and for your own thesis; when you are ready to write your first draft, these categories determine your paragraph divisions and provide the specific details you need to support your points.

Step 4

FINDING A THESIS

A thesis, you will recall, is an opinion with one or more reasons to support it. When you are analyzing a text as a whole, your opinion is your interpretation of the theme or thesis of the work you are analyzing; your reasons are your attempts to explain why the theme or thesis is as it is.

To find a thesis for your essay, then, you must first determine the theme or thesis of the work you are analyzing.

What is the nature (theme or thesis) of the thing I am analyzing?

What is MacLennan's thesis in the passage from " 'By Their Foods . . .' "?
What is the theme of Alden Nowlan's poem "Warren Pryor"?
What is the theme of *Network*?
What is the thesis of the television documentary I'm analyzing?
What is the thesis of Suzuki's essay?

In essays and other non-fictional works, the thesis is often stated explicitly. In such cases, the thesis is usually given near the beginning or at the end of the work, and often in both places. Occasionally you will find the thesis elsewhere. When you are analyzing non-fictional works, then, check first to see whether the author has stated the central idea explicitly.

Don't assume, however, that what seems to be the thesis is the fullest statement of the work's central point. If you analyze the work carefully, you will sometimes find that the stated thesis does not completely account for the work as a whole—perhaps because the full thesis would seem too controversial or too obvious; perhaps because the author or director had not thought through his or her ideas sufficiently to state a definite thesis (even professional writers sometimes have this problem!).

In some non-fictional writing, and in all imaginative works, the thesis or theme is not stated explicitly; instead, it is implicit in the relation among the parts of the work. Your analysis of those parts will allow you to arrive at a statement of the work's theme or thesis. Examine the material in your categories to answer these questions:

A. What pattern of conflict does the work establish between sets of values?

Begin by asking yourself what values particular characters, actions, or modes of thought represent. Be as specific as possible. Let's suppose, for example, that you are attempting to determine the theme of Alden Nowlan's poem "Warren Pryor":[1]

---

[1] Alden Nowlan, "Warren Pryor," from *Under the Ice* (Toronto: Ryerson, 1961), pp. 18-19; reprinted in *Fifteen Canadian Poets Plus Five*, ed. Gary Geddes and Phyllis Bruce (Toronto: Oxford University Press, 1978), p. 188. By permission of the author.

WARREN PRYOR

When every pencil meant a sacrifice
his parents boarded him in town,
slaving to free him from the stony fields,
the meagre acreage that bore them down.

They blushed with pride when, at his graduation,
they watched him picking up the slender scroll,
his passport from the years of brutal toil
and lonely patience in a barren hole.

When he went in the Bank their cups ran over.
They marvelled how he wore a milk-white shirt
work days and jeans on Sundays. He was saved
from their thistle-strewn farm and its red dirt.

And he said nothing. Hard and serious
like a young bear inside his teller's cage,
his axe-hewn hands upon the paper bills
aching with empty strength and throttled rage.

In determining the theme of this poem, you might decide that the
conflict is between the parents' need for their son to escape from their
life of poverty and the son's need to escape from the "successful" life
they have forced him into. This is a much better statement of the
conflict than merely saying the conflict is between parents and children, or between dreams and reality, because it identifies the specific
nature of the conflict in this poem, instead of merely labelling it in a
way that would apply equally well to thousands of other literary
works.

   If you think of this conflict as a conflict between sets of values,
rather than as a conflict between characters, you will see that this
step will work for non-fictional works as well as for fictional ones.
You might say, for example, that the basic conflict in Suzuki's essay
is between the advantages and the disadvantages of doing genetic
research. To have an adequate statement about this conflict, however,
you would have to be specific about what, in Suzuki's view, these
advantages and disadvantages are.

B. How is this conflict resolved?

The question here is which set of values wins and which loses, and
why. Reconsider your notes in light of your statement about the
nature of the conflict in the work. In the conflict between the parents'
dreams of their son's material success and the child's own needs in
"Warren Pryor," for example, the parents win. Why? Because their

sacrifices have created a trap of duty from which the son cannot escape.

C. What is the work's theme or thesis?

Combine your answers to the previous questions about the nature of the conflict and its resolution into a statement of the work's theme or thesis. This will be a generalization about the central idea of the work, based on your analysis of the work as a whole. When you are analyzing an imaginative work, you put your statement of theme in a form that applies to people and situations generally, rather than to particular characters and situations within the work. You might decide, for example, to state the theme of "Warren Pryor" like this:

> This poem suggests that children who are forced to fulfill their parents' dreams end up with lives as imprisoning as those their parents dreamed of escaping from.

Notice that a work's theme or thesis is different from its subject, and is also different from a summary of what happens. If you were analyzing a television documentary, for example, you might say that its subject is war. In summarizing its content, you might say that it showed government posters from World War I and II, films of military training, and interviews both with former "enemies" and with soldiers in training. Your statement about the thesis of the television documentary, in contrast, might be something like this:

> This documentary makes the point that war is evil because it leads us to treat others as less than human.

Why does the thing I am analyzing have this particular nature?

> Why does the passage from MacLennan's essay have this thesis?
> Why does "Warren Pryor" have this particular theme?
> Why does *Network* portray North American society this way?
> Why does this documentary make this particular point about war?
> Why does Suzuki make this particular point about genetic research?

The primary meaning of this "why" question is "What features of the work led me to my interpretation?" This is the question you will need to answer whenever you are analyzing texts, and therefore the question we will focus on in our sample topics.

A secondary meaning of this question is "Why do you think the author or director takes this particular point of view?" As a beginning student you may not have the knowledge or the analytical skill necessary to answer this question. By being aware of this question, however, you can increase your sensitivity to the work's literary and historical context.

Here are suggestions for arriving at answers to these questions.

A. What features of the work led me to my interpretation?

To answer this question, you define the features of the text that support your interpretation. Let's suppose, for example, that you want to explain your reasons for defining the theme of "Warren Pryor" as you have. To support your interpretation, you would indicate the features of the poem that illustrate this theme: its images, its diction, and its structure. Putting together the answers to your "what" and "why" questions would give you a thesis like this for your essay:

> Together the images, diction, and structure of "Warren Pryor" suggest this theme: that children who are forced to fulfill their parents' dreams end up with lives as imprisoning as those their parents dreamed of escaping from.

B. Why does the author or director present this particular point of view?

This is a more speculative question than the previous one. To give a reasonable answer, you need to have a good grasp of some context relevant to the work. That context might be literary (other works by the same author or director, or other works of the same kind, for example); historical (the work as a response to issues, events, or ideas of its time); or psychological (the work's relation to the author's or director's life or to psychological theories).

If you were analyzing the television documentary on war, for example, you might ask, "Why would this director want to make this particular film at this time?" From your reading about the director's political views and your knowledge of current affairs, you might conclude that the director's purpose was to create a climate of public opinion that would influence government defence policy. Combining your interpretation of the documentary's thesis with your sense of its purpose, you would arrive at a thesis similar to this for your essay:

This documentary makes the point that war is evil because it leads us to treat others as less than human. It does so in order to create a climate of public opinion opposed to increased military spending.

Because the question "Why does the author or director present this particular point of view?" asks you to speculate about the work's possible causes or possible effects, you will often need to support your opinion with factual information or with the opinions of authorities in the field. Consequently, this type of interpretation is more appropriate for research papers than for shorter essays.

SAMPLE TOPICS: ANALYZING TEXTS

Now that you have a sense of the basic principles of textual analysis, you can see how to put these principles into practice in the two sample topics below. The first shows you how to use the general categories of textual analysis; the second shows you how to use special categories for analyzing poetry.

Using General Categories to Analyze Non-Fictional Prose

To show how you would use the general categories of textual analysis to analyze essays and other types of non-fictional prose, we will follow the steps in preparing to write on this topic:

ENGLISH 101
Write an essay of about 750 words in which you analyze the given passage from Hugh MacLennan's essay " 'By Their Foods . . . .' "

Step 1

CLARIFYING THE TOPIC

A. Do I understand the terms used in the topic?
B. Do I understand the directions the topic gives me?
   1. Am I asked to analyze, to compare, or to evaluate?
   2. Does this topic require content analysis or textual analysis?
C. Do I know what kind of material to use in my essay?
D. Do I know how to limit the topic if necessary?
E. Do I know how to choose a topic that fits my interest, knowledge, time, and writing skills?

A. There are no unfamiliar terms.

B. The topic says to analyze the passage; we've been studying the relation between form and content in essays by other writers, so I should consider both what MacLennan says and how he says it. Since we are not given the whole essay, the passage will be the whole that I will divide into parts to analyze. I'm not sure what special categories would be appropriate, so I'll use the general categories of textual analysis: Subject, Structure, Development, Style, Tone, and Thesis.

C. The passage is the only material I need.

D. No need to limit the topic.

E. No choice of topics. I will need to analyze the passage and write the first draft three or four days before the essay is due so that I will have time to revise it.

Step 2

GATHERING MATERIAL

What source or sources of material can I draw on?
A. What is my main source of information and ideas?

This passage from MacLennan's essay, reprinted in our class anthology:[2]

> Favourite dishes can be as revealing as recurrent dreams; even the neophyte traveller learns as much about a nation's character by observing what its people eat as by talking for hours to its cab drivers.
>
> Germans, for instance, have an obsession with caraway, and caraway lurks in every dish, a fatal undertone beneath the heavy, seemingly honest surface of German food, and you get into the habit of waiting for those black, curled little seeds to catch in your teeth, for the abrupt incongruousness of the caraway taste to shock your taste buds, just as you get into the habit of expecting a fatally recurrent behaviour-pattern to show up in German politics.
>
> Austrians love pastries and whipped cream, succulent torten and rich brioches, bread with little nutriment but baked with crunchy crusts delicious to tongue and teeth. Charming they indubitably are, these people who suffer the tragedy of living just

---

[2]Hugh MacLennan, " 'By Their Foods . . .,' " in *Scotchman's Return and Other Essays* (Toronto: Macmillan of Canada, 1960), pp. 13-14; reprinted in *Modern Canadian Essays*, ed. William H. New (Toronto: Macmillan of Canada, 1976), pp. 64-65.

below a nation of caraway-eaters, and wise (or infatuated) in their determination to disguise the bitterness of life wherever possible. The coffee drunk by the Austrians is a dark and heavy brew, but as your taste dwells with the whipped cream floating on top, its bitterness is revealed only in the final drops.

Perfect in its ardour is the food of Italy. Not only the pizzas, spaghettis, macaronis, and raviolis with their divine harmonies of parmesan, ground meats, onion, tomatoes, and herbs, but the chianti, so honestly rough on the tongue it forms a bridge from the pastas to the fresh figs, oranges, tangerines, and walnuts that cap a true Italian meal—such a diet breeds people of a fine but delicate vanity, opera singers, and beautifully understanding women, but few successful lusters after power.

Most complicated, and complicated without being subtle is the diet of that intricate people, the Swedes. Strong, contrasting textures, robust flavours implicitly critical of each other, an immense variety of carefully thought-out detail enclosed within a single central idea—that is smorgasbord. The smoked eels, fish, and meats of Sweden are beyond compare, the pickles blunt but seldom sour, the vegetables fresh. Neither delicate nor rich, masculine but not uneasily so, neither one thing or the other but everything simultaneously, all excellent, smorgasbord is the logical calculation of Swedish life.

B. Do I need additional material?

I need to look up **neophyte** and **incongruousness**. Maybe I'd better check **smorgasbord** to see if the original meaning is different from the way the word is used now.

I'm not sure what MacLennan means by a "fatally recurrent behaviour-pattern" in German politics. I might need to read an encyclopedia article on modern German history.

Step 3

CATEGORIZING MATERIAL

What categories should I divide my material into?

I am using the general categories for textual analysis.

Subject: What is the work about?

The relation between national character and national foods.

Structure: How is the work put together?

Brief introduction; one paragraph each on the foods of four different countries. Paragraphs arranged in order of ascending interest, from Germans' "obsession" with caraway to Austrians' mixture of charm and bitterness, Italians' "perfect . . . ardour," and Swedes' "robust" complexity.

Development: What are the details that give the work substance?

Examples of national dishes in each paragraph, linked to national character. No evidence to support his assertions about national character.

Style: How does the author use language?

Uses unusual words—("neophyte," instead of "inexperienced") and abstract terms to describe food ("abrupt incongruousness" of caraway, "divine harmonies" of Italian dishes, flavours "implicitly critical of each other," "masculine but not uneasily so" in Swedish smorgasbord). Long, complicated sentences, with a few short and straightforward ones.

Tone: What is the author's attitude towards the subject, as conveyed by the text?

Playful, doesn't try to sound scientific or serious.

Thesis: What is the central idea of the work?

States the opinion that national dishes reflect national character, but does not give a reason. Look for more complete thesis in Step 4.

Step 4

FINDING A THESIS

What is the nature (theme or thesis) of the thing I am analyzing?

MacLennan states a partial thesis, that national foods reveal national character, but since he doesn't give any reasons to support this opinion I should see what my analysis of the passage suggests his complete thesis is.

> **A.** What pattern of conflict does the work establish between sets of values?

According to MacLennan's description, the food of each country is a combination of simplicity and complexity. German food is simple on the surface but has a "fatal undertone"; Austrian pastries are complex and sweet, but the coffee is bitter; Italian pasta dishes are complex, but the wine is honest and rough, and the desserts of fresh fruit and nuts are simple; individually, Swedish foods are "robust," "blunt," and "fresh," but together they make "an immense variety of carefully thought-out detail enclosed within a single central idea." Furthermore, MacLennan's style is also a combination of simplicity and complexity. He states a simple idea about national character but describes national foods in unusual, abstract terms. His sentences also alternate between being long and complicated and being short and simple. The conflict in the passage, then, seems to be between simplicity and complexity.

> **B.** How is this conflict resolved?

Does MacLennan seem to prefer simplicity or complexity? I see that in my notes on the structure of the passage I had decided that the paragraphs were in an order of ascending interest. What is the relation between this order and the conflict between simplicity and complexity? MacLennan seems to prefer complexity that is direct and straightforward, like that of Italian and Swedish dishes, to complexity that is hidden (as in German and Austrian food). Similarly, he seems to prefer simplicity that is "strong," "robust," and "implicitly critical" to simplicity that is "heavy" (German food), "bitter" (Austrian coffee), or "delicate" (Italian food). The paragraph on Swedish food must come last, then, because MacLennan feels that Swedish food (and by implication Swedish people) combine a vigorous simplicity with an honest complexity.

> **C.** What is the work's theme or thesis?

My interpretation of the passage shows MacLennan's thesis to be something like this:

> National dishes allow us to evaluate national character by establishing the degree to which the country's food and people meet the ideal standard of vigorous simplicity and honest complexity.

Why does the thing I am analyzing have this particular nature?

What features of the work led me to this interpretation?

After consideration, it seems that my idea of MacLennan's thesis must come from his methods of development and tone. MacLennan uses examples instead of factual information to support his points about national character. His tone is playful; he is obviously not trying to persuade his readers by being serious and scientific. He certainly recognizes that the connections he makes between national food and national character merely reflect his personal preferences. His ideas are interesting, however, because he presents them in a complex yet fanciful way.

If I combine my ideas about what the passage says with my ideas about its manner of presentation, I will have a thesis like this for my essay:

> Because he realizes the impossibility of making "scientific" claims about the relation between national food and national character, Hugh MacLennan adopts a playful approach to the task of persuading us that a combination of vigorous simplicity and honest complexity is ideal in both food and character.

From this example, you have seen how the general categories of textual analysis can be used to analyze a work or performance as a whole. By following these four steps, you will arrive at a thesis about the relationship between the theme of the work or performance and the techniques used to convey that theme.

Using Special Categories to Analyze a Poem

As you become more accustomed to doing textual analysis, you are likely to find **special categories** more useful than general categories.

Perhaps an example will help to explain the relation of general categories to special categories. You can analyze the **structure** of any text, written or performed. This general category would not alert you, however, to the ways in which the structure of a poem might be different from the structure of an essay. The special categories give you the critical terms for analyzing particular forms of expression. You will find charts of questions to ask when you are analyzing various types of written works and performances in the Reference Section of this text.

To illustrate the use of special categories of textual analysis, we have chosen this topic:

> Write a 750-word essay analyzing Alden Nowlan's use of Christ symbolism in "The Bull Moose."

Step 1

CLARIFYING THE TOPIC

A. Do I understand the terms used in the topic?
B. Do I understand the directions the topic gives me?
   1. Am I asked to analyze, to compare, or to evaluate?
   2. Does this topic require content analysis or textual analysis?
C. Do I know what kind of material to use in my essay?
D. Do I know how to limit the topic if necessary?
E. Do I know how to choose a topic that fits my interest, knowledge, time, and writing skills?

A. I'm not sure what "Christ symbolism" means, so I'll check "symbol" and "symbolism" in a dictionary of literary terms. From the definitions in C. Hugh Holman's *A Handbook of Literature* (3rd edition; Indianapolis: Bobbs Merrill, 1972), it seems that a symbol combines a concrete, objective image with a more abstract level of meaning, and that "symbolism" is the use of such images. For example, a reference to a flag not only makes me think of a piece of material flying over public buildings, but also makes me think of meanings we attach to flags, such as patriotism. When I read "The Bull Moose," then, I should watch for images that have something to do with, or make me think of, the story of Christ.

B. The topic says to analyze, not to compare or to evaluate, and I'm obviously supposed to do textual analysis. Although the topic doesn't say so explicitly, I will have to show how the Christ symbolism relates to the theme of the poem as a whole.

C. This is a short essay, so I shouldn't need any material except the text itself, unless I need to look up words or allusions in reference books.

D. The topic is already limited.

E. No choice of topic. I should allow at least a week to read and analyze the poem, write my first draft, let it sit, and then revise it.

Step 2

GATHERING MATERIAL

What source or sources of material can I draw on?

A. What is my main source of information and ideas?

My main source of information and ideas will be Nowlan's poem:

THE BULL MOOSE[3]

Down from the purple mist of trees on the mountain,
lurching through forests of white spruce and cedar,
stumbling through tamarak swamps,
came the bull moose
5   to be stopped at last by a polefenced pasture.

Too tired to turn or, perhaps, unaware
there was no place left to go, he stood with the cattle.
They, scenting the musk of death, seeing his great head
like the ritual mask of a blood god, moved to the other end
10   of the field and waited.

The neighbours heard of it, and by afternoon
cars lined the road. The children teased him
with alder switches and he gazed at them
like an old, tolerant collie. The women asked
15   if he could have escaped from a Fair.

---

[3]Alden Nowlan, "The Bull Moose," in *The Things Which Are* (Toronto: Contact Press, 1962), pp. 25-26; reprinted in *The Evolution of Canadian Literature in English*: *1945-1970*, ed. Paul Denham (Toronto and Montreal: Holt, Rinehart and Winston of Canada, 1973), pp. 228-29. By permission of the author.

The oldest man in the parish remembered seeing
a gelded moose yoked with an ox for ploughing.
The young men snickered and tried to pour beer
19 down his throat, while their girl friends took pictures.

And the bull moose let them stroke his tick-ravaged flanks,
let them pry open his jaws with bottles, let a giggling girl
plant a little purple cap
23 of thistles on his head.

When the wardens came, everyone agreed it was a shame
to shoot anything so shaggy and cuddlesome.
He looked like the kind of pet
27 Women put to bed with their sons.

So they held their fire. But just as the sun dropped in the river
the bull moose gathered his strength
like a scaffolded king, straightened and lifted his horns
so that even the wardens backed away as they raised their rifles.
When he roared, people ran to their cars. All the young men
33 leaned on their automobile horns as he toppled.

B. Do I need additional material?

I'm not sure I understand all the parallels between the poem and the story of Christ. Both the moose and Christ were tortured and killed, but the only symbol that seems to link the two is the cap of thistles, which is similar to Christ's crown of thorns. I'll need to reread the story of Christ's crucifixion in the New Testament. A dictionary of the Bible might be a good place to start.

Why is the moose's head compared to the "ritual mask of a blood god?" I'll see what I can find in a dictionary of mythology. Maybe I should also check a dictionary of symbols to see whether some of the other images in the poem have symbolic meanings. I'll also look up "musk" and "scaffolded" in my dictionary to make sure I know what those words mean.

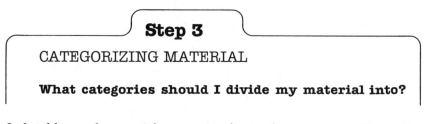

Step 3

CATEGORIZING MATERIAL

What categories should I divide my material into?

I should use the special categories for analyzing poetry. Since the topic asks me to focus on Christ symbolism, I will have more material

in the category "Images and Symbols" than in other categories. I will
have to show how the Christ symbolism relates to the theme of the
poem, however, and so I have made brief notes on the poem under
all the special categories for analyzing poetry.

SPECIAL CATEGORIES FOR ANALYZING POETRY

Subject: What is the poem about?
The moose's journey down the mountain to a human settlement,
the reactions of people in the community, and the killing of the
moose.

Poetic Structure: (1) What is the principle behind the selection and
arrangement of events, ideas, and/or feelings in the poem?
(2) How does this principle relate to the form of the poem, the
units or stanzas into which it is divided?
     Events follow a chronological order. The first two stanzas
describe the moose's descent; the next four describe people's reactions; the last describes the killing.

Setting: What is the time, place, and social environment within
which the events of the poem take place?
     Shifts from the mountain to the pasture. No specific time or
place, but seems to be a modern farming community.

Characterization: What are the characters like? What techniques
are used to portray them?
     The moose is described at first as "lurching," "stumbling,"
"tired." Cattle move away because they scent death. When he is
teased, he behaves "like an old, tolerant collie." People think
of him as a pet or stuffed toy, "shaggy and cuddlesome." When
he roars, however, he seems strong, powerful, and threatening.
     The onlookers' actions show them to be insensitive, cruel,
or patronizing at first, then frightened by the moose's strength.

Diction: What do the general level of usage and particular word
choices tell me about the speaker or the characters?
     Most of the vocabulary is that of everyday speech. Diction is
most important in relation to characterization and images/symbols.

Images and Symbols: What do I learn about the speaker, the
characters, or the situation from **images** (figures of speech, such
as metaphors, similes, personification; or, more generally, descriptions of sensations, such as sight, sound, touch, smell, taste) or
from **symbols** (objects, actions, gestures, or patterns of images
used to express an emotion or an abstract idea)?
     Since this is the category on which the topic asks me to focus,
I have lots of notes on symbolism. I'll organize them according
to the stages in the events of the poem.

Descent

Image/ Symbol	Meaning	Moose	Christ
Purple	royalty, power	"purple mist"	Son of God, King of the Jews
White	purity, inno- cence	"white spruce"	without sin
Mountain	home of the gods	home of moose	home in heaven
Fence	barrier	stops moose	comes to earth
Blood-god	sacrificial god	?	sacrifices him- self

Torture

Switches	suffering	teased with alder switches	scourged by Roman sol- diers
Beer	humiliation	beer poured down its throat	given vinegar on the cross
Cap of thistles	humiliation	cap of thistles	crown of thorns

Death

Cross	sacrificial death	"like a scaf- folded king"	Christ as King on cross
Setting sun	disappearance of source of life; death	sun "dropped in the river" as moose shot	darkness at crucifixion

Rhythm, Metre, Patterns of Sound: How do these devices contribute to the meaning of the poem?

No fixed metre or rhyme. The rhythm of the first stanza reinforces the sense of movement. The pauses in the second stanza (indicated by commas) slow the movement to reinforce the idea that the moose has "no place left to go." The rhythm of the four middle stanzas is conversational, as attention shifts to different people. In the last stanza, the short line emphasizes the moment of change: "the bull moose gathered his strength."

Speaker's Attitude: (1) From whose point of view is the poem written? (2) How does this point of view affect the way the poem is written? (3) What is the tone of the poem? (4) How does this tone reflect the speaker's attitude towards the characters or the situation?

Third-person limited omniscient: indicates how moose and cattle think or feel, but presents humans only through their actions. This point of view encourages readers to empathize with the moose and discourages empathy with the onlookers. Readers are therefore likely to judge the onlookers' actions more harshly.

Theme: What is the central idea of the poem?

I can define the theme of the poem once I have worked out why Nowlan uses so many parallels between the story of the moose and the story of Christ's crucifixion.

Step 4

FINDING A THESIS

This is the stage at which the procedures for this type of topic differ most from the procedures for analyzing the work as a whole. Instead of defining the theme at this point, you first define the nature of the part or parts you are analyzing and then show how this part (or these parts) are related to the theme.

What is the nature of the thing I am analyzing?

A. What is the nature of the part I am analyzing?

To answer this question, I should look at all the parallels between the moose and Christ and decide what generalization I can make about them. My statement would be something like this:

> The images and symbols of the poem suggest that the moose's descent from the mountain, treatment by the onlookers, and death are like Christ's descent from heaven, reception on earth, and crucifixion.

B. What is the relation between the part I am analyzing and other features of the work?

Now I must see whether my generalization about the nature of Christ symbolism in the poem fits with my other material. The subject and structure of the poem definitely emphasize parallels between the killing of the moose and the crucifixion of Christ. The characterization of the moose as patient and tolerant of his tormentors suggests Christ's forgiveness of those who put him to death; the point of view further encourages us to sympathize with the moose and to be critical of the onlookers' actions.

I can state this relationship between the Christ symbolism and other features of the poem like this:

> The symbolic parallels between the killing of the moose and the crucifixion of Christ are reinforced by the structure, characterization, and point of view.

Why does the thing I am analyzing have this particular nature?

Since the Christ symbolism is such a central element of the poem, it must embody the theme. To arrive at a statement of the poem's theme, I must consider the nature of the conflict in the poem. The conflict is between the moose and the onlookers who finally kill him. What sets of values do these two sides represent? Which values "win," and why?

Perhaps it will help if I think about the parallel with Christ. Christ represented the realm of the spirit. He was crucified when the religious and political leaders of Jerusalem began to see him as a threat to their authority. Since Christ was put to death, it might seem that earthly power "wins" over heavenly power. According to the New Testament, however, Christ was resurrected from the dead, thus showing that spiritual power ultimately triumphs over earthly power.

What does the moose represent? The first images and symbols in the poem identify his natural habitat with Christ's power, purity, and divinity. Furthermore, his head is like "the ritual mask of a blood-god." Together these symbols suggest that the moose represents the world of nature. The conflict in the poem, then, is between the natural world and the human desire to control that world. When the onlookers no longer feel in control of the situation, they kill the moose. Unlike the crucifixion of Christ, however, the destruction of the natural world may be final, since the sounding of the horns in the final line suggests Judgment Day. Nowlan therefore seems to suggest that by destroying the natural world, human beings will bring about their own destruction.

By combining my generalization about the nature of Christ symbolism and its relation to other aspects of the poem with this statement of the poem's theme, I can write a thesis that explains how and why Nowlan uses Christ symbolism in "The Bull Moose":

> Nowlan uses symbolic parallels between the killing of the moose and the crucifixion of Christ, reinforced by the poem's structure, characterization, and point of view, to suggest that human attempts to control the natural world, like human attempts to control the spiritual world, will ultimately fail because they are self-destructive.

Once you have a thesis, you are ready to write your first draft. You will find suggestions for writing and revising analysis essays in Chapter 5.

SUMMARY

The basic process for analyzing texts consists of these four steps:
1. Making sure you understand the requirements of the topic
2. Gathering material by reading or viewing the work you are analyzing, looking up unfamiliar words and literary and historical allusions, and, if necessary, consulting other writers on your subject
3. Categorizing details of the work under appropriate headings of textual analysis
4. Finding a thesis for your essay by (a) using the material in your categories to arrive at your interpretation of the work's theme or thesis (or your interpretation of the relation between one or more parts and the work's theme or thesis) and (b) defining your reason(s) for your interpretation.

This chapter should provide you with a framework for your study of written and performed texts and with specific guidelines for preparing to write essays of textual analysis.

EXERCISES

Save your responses to the following exercises for possible use in the exercises for Chapter 5.

A. Follow the steps outlined in this chapter for preparing to write an essay on this topic:

> What point about the nature of escape does Eli Mandel make in the poem "Houdini"?

1. Clarifying the Topic
a. Do you understand the terms used in the topic?
b. Do you understand the directions? (i) Are you asked to analyze, to compare, or to evaluate? (ii) Does this topic require content analysis or textual analysis?

c. Do you know what kind of material to use?

d. Do you need to limit the topic?

e. What difficulties might you experience with this topic because of factors such as interest, knowledge, time, and writing skills? How much time should you allow to complete the assignment?

2. Gathering Material

a. What source or sources of material can you draw on? Your main source of information and ideas will be Mandel's poem.

> HOUDINI[4]
>
> I suspect he knew that trunks are metaphors,
> could distinguish between the finest rhythms
> unrolled on rope or singing in a chain
> and knew the metrics of the deepest pools
>
> I think of him listening to the words
> spoken by manacles, cells, handcuffs,
> chests, hampers, roll-top desks, vaults,
> especially the deep words spoken by coffins
>
> escape, escape: quaint Harry in his suit
> his chains, his desk, attached to all attachments
> how he'd sweat in that precise struggle
> with those binding words, wrapped around him
> like that mannered style, his formal suit
>
> and spoken when? by whom? What thing first said
> "There's no way out"?; so that he'd free himself,
> leap, squirm, no matter how, to chain himself again,
> once more jump out of the deep alive
> with all his chains singing around his feet
> like the bound crowds who sigh, who sigh.

b. What additional material do you need? Are there words or references you will need to look up?

3. Categorizing Material

Use the general categories for textual analysis (Subject, Structure, Development, Style, Tone, Theme) to make notes on the poem.

4. Finding a Thesis

a. What is the nature of the poem you are analyzing? (i) What pattern of conflict does the poem establish between sets of values? (ii) How is this conflict resolved? (iii) What is the poem's theme?

b. Why does the poem have this particular nature? Define the features of the work which led you to your interpretation.

---

[4]Eli Mandel, "Houdini," in *An Idiot Joy* (Edmonton: Hurtig, 1967), p. 31; reprinted in *The Evolution of Canadian Literature in English: 1945-1970*, ed. Paul Denham (Toronto and Montreal: Holt, Rinehart and Winston of Canada, 1973), p. 145.

B. Use the steps outlined in the sample topic on using special categories to complete the preparation process for an essay on this topic:

> Write an essay of about 750 words on the symbolism of the penny in Ernest Buckler's short story "Penny in the Dust."

Here is the story.

PENNY IN THE DUST[5]

My sister and I were walking through the old sun-still fields the evening before the funeral, recalling this or that thing which had happened in this or that place, turning over memories after the fashion of families who gather again in the place where they were born—trying to disclose and identify themselves with the strange children they must have been.

"Do you remember the afternoon we thought you were lost?" my sister said. I did. That was as long ago as the day I was seven.

"We searched everywhere," she said, "up in the meeting-house, back in the blueberry barrens—we even looked in the well. I think it's the only time I ever saw Father really upset. He didn't even stop to tie up the horse's reins. He raced right through the chopping where Tom Reeve was burning brush, looking for you—right through the flames almost. They couldn't do a thing with him. And you up in your bed, sound asleep!

"It was all over losing a penny or something, wasn't it?" she went on, when I didn't answer. It was. She laughed indulgently. "You were a crazy kid, weren't you?"

I was. But there was more to it than that. I had never seen a brand-new penny before. I thought they were all black. This one was bright as gold. And my father had given it to me.

You would have to understand about my father and that is the hard thing to tell. If I say that he worked all day long, but I had never seen him hurry, that would make him sound like a stupid man. If I say that he never held me on his knee and that I never heard him laugh out loud in his life, it would make him sound humorless and severe. If I said that whenever I'd be telling mother some of my fancy plans and he'd come into the kitchen I'd stop, like someone hiding the pages of a foolish book, you'd think that he was distant and that in some kind of way I was afraid of him. None of that would be true.

There's no way you can tell it to make it sound like anything more than an inarticulate man a little at sea with an imaginative child. You'll have to take my word for it that there was more to it than that. It was as if his sure-footed way in the fields forsook

[5]Ernest Buckler, "Penny in the Dust," *Maclean's*, December 15, 1948; reprinted in *Canadian Anthology*, 3rd ed., ed. Carl F. Klinck and Reginald E. Watters (Toronto: Gage Educational Publishing Ltd., 1974), pp. 331-34. Reprinted by permission of Curtis Brown, Ltd. Copyright 1948 by Ernest Buckler.

him the instant he came near the door of my child's world and that he must wipe off his feet before he stood inside, awkward and conscious of trespass; and that I, sensing that but not understanding it, felt, at the sound of his solid step outside, my world's foolish fragility.

He would fix the small spot where I planted beans and other quick-sprouting seeds before he prepared the big garden, even if the spring was late; but he wouldn't ask me how many rows I wanted and, if he made three tiny rows and I wanted four, I couldn't ask him to change them. If I walked behind the load of hay, longing to ride, and he walked ahead of the oxen, I couldn't ask him to put me up and he wouldn't make any move to do so, until he saw me trying to grasp the binder.

He, my father, had just given me a new penny, bright as gold.

He took it from his pocket several times, pretending to examine the date on it, waiting for me to notice it. He couldn't offer me *anything* until I had shown some sign that the gift would be welcome.

"You can have it if you want it, Dan," he said at last.

I said, "Oh, thanks." Nothing more.

I started with it to the store. For a penny you could buy the magic cylinder of "Long Tom" popcorn, with Heaven knows what colored jewel on the ring inside. But the more I thought of my bright penny disappearing forever into the black drawstring pouch the Assyrian merchant kept his money in, the slower my steps lagged as the store came nearer and nearer. I sat down in the road.

It was that time of magic suspension in an August afternoon. The lifting smells of leaves and cut clover hung still in the sun. The sun drowsed, like a kitten curled upon my shoulder. The deep flour-fine dust in the road puffed about my bare ankles, warm and soft as sleep. A swallow-tailed butterfly clung to the road, its bright-banded wings spreading and converging like the movements of breathing. The sound of the cowbells came sharp and hollow from the cool swamp.

I began to play with the penny, postponing the decision. I would close my eyes and bury it deep in the sand and then, with my eyes still closed, get up and walk around and then come back to search for it, tantalizing myself each time with the thrill of discovering afresh its bright shining edge. I did that again and again. Alas, once too often.

It was almost dark when their excited talking in the room woke me. It was mother who had found me. I suppose when it came dusk she thought of me in the bed other nights and I suppose she looked there without any reasonable hope, but as you do when the search has become desperate, in every place where the thing lost has ever lain before. And now suddenly she was crying.

"Danny!" she cried, with the pointlessness of sudden relief, *"where* have you been!"

"I lost my penny," I said.

"You lost your penny—? But what made you come up here and hide?"

If my father hadn't been there, I might have told her. But when I looked up at my father, standing there like the shape of everything sound and straight, it was like daylight shredding the memory of a foolish dream. How could I bear the shame of repeating before him the soft twisting visions I had built in my head in the magic August afternoon when almost anything could be made to seem real, as I buried the penny and dug it up again? How would I explain that pit-of-the-stomach sickness which struck through the whole day when I had to believe, at last, that it was really lost? How could I explain that I wasn't really hiding from them? How, with the words and the understanding I had then, that the only possible place to run from that awful feeling of loss was the soft, absorbing, dark safeness of bed? That I had cried myself to sleep?

"I lost my penny," I said. I looked at father and turned my face into the pillow. "I want to go to sleep."

"Danny," my mother said, "it's almost nine o'clock. You haven't had a bite of supper. Do you know you almost scared the *life* out of us!"

"You'd better git some supper," my father said. It was the only time he had spoken.

I knew mother would talk about it and talk about it, but I never dreamed of father ever mentioning it again. But the next morning when we had the forks in our hands, ready to toss out the hay, he seemed to hold up the moment of actually leaving for the field. He stuck his fork in the ground and brought in another pail of water, though the kettle was chock-full. He took out the shingle nail that held his broken brace together and put it back in exactly the same hole. He went into the shed to see if the pigs had cleaned up all their breakfast.

"Ain't you got no idea where you lost your penny?" he said suddenly.

"Yes," I said, "I know just about."

"Let's see if we can't find it," he said.

We walked down the road together, stiff with awareness. He didn't hold my hand.

"It's right here somewheres," I said. "I was playin' with it in the dust." He looked at me, questioningly, but he didn't ask me what game anyone could possibly play with a penny in the dust.

I might have known that he would find it. In making a whistle he could tap alder bark with his jack knife just exactly hard enough so it wouldn't break but so it would twist free from the wood beneath, though I couldn't believe he had ever made a whistle for himself when he was a child. His great fingers could trace loose the hopeless snarl of a fishing line that I could only succeed in tangling tighter and tighter. If I broke the handle of my wheelbarrow ragged beyond sight of any possible repair, he could take it and bring it back to me so you could hardly see the place if you weren't looking for it.

He got down on his knees and drew his fingers carefully through the dust, like a harrow; not clawing it frantically in heaps as I had done, covering even while I uncovered. He found the penny almost at once.

He held it in his hand, as if the moment of passing it to me were a deadline for something he dreaded to say, but must. Something that could not be postponed any longer if it were to be spoken at all.

"Dan," he said, "You needn'ta hid. I wouldn'ta beat you."

"*Beat* me? Oh, Father! You didn't think that was the reason—?" I felt almost sick.

Do you know how I felt then? I felt as if I had beaten him. His face looked like I had seen it of an evening when mother wasn't speaking and he would pick up a schoolbook or a paper and follow the lines patiently, though he never read any other time at all. I had to tell him the truth then. Because only the truth, no matter how foolish it was, would have the unmistakable sound of truth, to scatter that awful idea out of his head.

"I wasn't hidin', father," I said, "honest—I was—I was buryin' my penny and makin' out I was diggin' up treasure. I was makin' out I was findin' gold. I didn't know what to *do* when I lost it, I just didn't know where to *go*—" His head was bent forward, like mere listening. I had to make it truer still.

"I made out it was gold," I said desperately, "and I—I was making out I bought you a mowin' machine so's you could get your work done early every day so's you and I could go into town in the big automobile I made out I bought and everyone'd turn around and look at us drivin' down the streets—"

His head was perfectly still, as if he were only waiting with patience for me to finish.

"—*laughin'* and *talkin'*—" I said, louder, smiling intensely, compelling him, by the absolute conviction of some true particular, to believe me.

He looked up then. It was the only time I had ever seen tears in his eyes.

I wondered, though, why he hesitated and then put the penny back in his own pocket.

Yesterday I knew. I never found any fortune and we never had a car to ride in together. But I think he knew what that would be like, just the same. I found the penny again yesterday, when we were getting out his good clothes—in an upper vest pocket where no one ever carries change. It was still shining. He must have kept it polished.

I left it there.

Chapter 5

Writing Analysis Essays

You've chosen a topic for analysis in accordance with the suggestions made in Chapter 2; you've gathered material and worked out a thesis, following the procedures outlined in Chapter 3 or 4. There you sit, pencil poised over paper or hands poised over the keyboard.

What do you do next?

You won't get much further by simply sitting and thinking about your subject. Now is the time to write a draft in order to stimulate new ideas and insights. When you revise this draft, revision can become re-vision, a matter of "seeing again," of reworking your material so that it supports the more complex understanding of your subject you have reached through the process of writing.

Writing a first draft benefits you as writer; revising your draft benefits your readers. There are two kinds of revisions you are likely to need to make: (1) revisions in structure and development and (2) revisions in style and tone. This chapter will take you through the process of writing the first draft of an analysis essay and revising it for structure and development. The next chapter, "Final Editing," will remind you of the kinds of revisions you may need to make in style and tone. You can ensure that you are communicating your ideas effectively by evaluating your drafts with the reader's eyes and revising carefully.

BASIC PROCEDURES FOR WRITING AND REVISING ANALYSIS ESSAYS

Although we focus in this chapter on the process of writing and revising analysis essays, the procedures we outline below are basic to all college and university essays. In later chapters we will examine the special considerations that would apply to writing and revising comparison, evaluation, and research essays.

Writing the First Draft

In this draft, your main purpose is to translate your notes into sentences and paragraphs. Once you have a piece of writing in front of you, you can evaluate and revise it.

Here are the steps you can follow in writing a first draft.

Step 1

SELECTING MATERIAL

Which categories of my analysis best support my thesis?

You may often have more material in your notes than you need for your essay. Rather than trying to cram every point and detail into your first draft, take a few minutes to decide which categories best support your thesis.

If your thesis statement defines the features that led you to your generalization, examine the categories that correspond to those features. In a short essay (up to 1000 words or so), you only have room to explain three to five points adequately. If you have more categories than that, see whether you can eliminate those that seem less important or that contain little specific detail. For a longer essay you may use most of the material you have gathered. It is still better to cover a few major points in depth, however, than to lose your reader in a sea of minor points.

Step 2

ORDERING MATERIAL

In what order should I arrange points in the body of the essay?

A. Should I arrange points in chronological order?

If the sequence in which events occur is integral to your topic, arrange your points in **chronological order**. In the simplest case, this means starting with events furthest away in time and ending with events closest in time. This arrangement would be appropriate for describing the steps in a process, the stages in a person's life, or the actions leading up to or following a major historical event.

B. Should I arrange points in spatial order?

Spatial order is another basic principle of organization. Depending upon the effect you wish to achieve, you might describe an object, a scene, a country, a galaxy, or a universe by moving from near to far or far to near, top to bottom or bottom to top, left to right or right to left. Or you might describe objects in the order in which a particular observer perceives them.

C. Should I arrange points in logical order?

If the relationship among ideas is more important than the sequence of events or the arrangement of objects, then you will arrange your points according to a **logical order**.

Your chain of reasoning might follow the structure of the syllogism in philosophy, as in this familiar example:

> All men are mortal.
> Socrates is a man.
> Therefore Socrates is mortal.

Or it might set out a series of causes and effects, either real or hypothetical:

Because A happened, B happened.	If A happens, B will happen.
Because B happened, C happened.	If B happens, C will happen.
Because C happened, D happened.	If C happens, D will happen.

In setting out a chain of reasoning, you have little choice about the order in which you present material; the order is determined by your need to establish one point so that it will serve as the basis for the next.

Is the order I've chosen an order of ascending interest?

When you arrange your points according to the effect you want to make on your reader, you are considering **rhetorical** principles. The principles of rhetoric tell us that the most emphatic position in an essay, as in a sentence, is at the end. That means you can build your reader's interest by putting your points in an **order of ascending interest**, from least to most important. If your essay does not suggest an order of ascending interest, it may seem haphazard or anticlimactic.

You can usually accommodate a chronological, spatial, or logical order within an order of ascending interest. Since a **logical** ordering of material always leads up to the conclusion to be drawn, this order would correspond to an order of ascending interest. In the case of a chronological or spatial arangement, you can choose your starting and ending points so that you lead up to your most interesting or most persuasive material.

In some cases, the rhetorical principle of presenting your points in a **order of ascending interest** is the only one you will need to consider. If you were examining three causes of traffic accidents, for instance, you would order your points so that you would begin with the least important and end with the most important.

How do you decide which order to use? The categories you have used for your analysis usually provide the framework of your essay. Once you have selected the categories to use in your first draft, decide which principle of organization best fits your material; then see whether you can put your categories in an order of ascending interest.

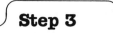

Step 3

WRITING THE DRAFT

Now write a draft. Don't labour over your introduction; you will easily be able to revise it once you are sure about the overall structure of your essay. Put your thesis at the end of your introduction to remind yourself of the points to cover. Then write the body of the essay, using each of your categories as the topic of a middle paragraph. Add ideas that occur to you as you write. Although these new ideas may seem fuzzy, they may turn out to provide the links you need between points in your notes. Let your conclusion follow your train of thought to a logical end, instead of forcing it to conform to a preconceived pattern. Often by the time you reach the conclusion of a first draft, you have discovered a better thesis than the one you began with. The main thing is to get your ideas on paper.

Revising the First Draft

After you have written a first draft, leave it for a day or two. You will find it hard to revise something as soon as you have written it, because you will see what you intended to say rather than what is actually on the page. After a day or two you will be better able to see what you have written as it would appear to another reader.

Until you become familiar with the process, you will probably find revising your work easier if you do it systematically. The following steps will show you how.

Step 1

REVISING THE THESIS

Since your thesis sets out the main idea you will develop in your essay, it is the first part you should check for possible revision. If you have prepared to write your essay according to the guidelines in Chapters 3 and 4, your first draft should have a good thesis. If you hurried through the preparation process, or you added new ideas as you wrote your first draft, however, you may need to adjust your thesis.

Does the thesis state an opinion and support it?

If you are not sure whether your thesis both states an opinion and gives one or more reasons to support that opinion, check it against the examples of weak thesis statements below. The examples illustrate the kinds of problems students encounter when they have not gone through an adequate preparation process. The examples are based on these sample topics from Chapters 3 and 4:

EDUCATION 200
Keep a journal over the term about your experiences as a student or the experiences of some member of your family in an educational setting. At the end of the term, you will use your entries to write a 1000-word essay on what you have learned about some aspect of the educational system.

ENGLISH 101
Analyze the given passage from Hugh MacLennan's essay " 'By Their Foods. . . .' "

A. Does the thesis merely restate the topic?

"I have learned many things about the educational system by observing a privately run day-care centre."

"In this essay I will analyze a passage from Hugh MacLennan's essay " 'By Their Foods. . . .' "

B. Does the thesis merely state facts or summarize information?

"During the last three months the day-care centre lost its kindergarten teacher and reduced its programmes."

"In his essay MacLennan discusses the foods of four countries."

C. Does the thesis merely state a general opinion, without supporting reasons?

"Day-care centres are inadequately funded."

"MacLennan's essay is playful and entertaining."

D. Does my thesis merely state the theme or thesis of the work I am analyzing?

"In this essay MacLennan shows that national dishes allow us to evaluate national character by establishing the degree to which the country's food and people meet his ideal standard of vigorous simplicity and honest complexity."

E. Is the thesis stated in a confusing or pretentious way?

"The quality of education, like the quality of mercy, is strained when the guardians of public funds do not open their purses to provide rich educational experiences for their wards in institutions of education."

"MacLennan's investigation of the secret affinity between the dark recesses of the national psyche and the viands on the table of its people is a playful attempt to cozen his readers into accepting his preference for a combination of vigorous simplicity and honest complexity in national cuisine and national character."

If your thesis has any of these problems, see the suggestions below on how to work out a better thesis.

Do I need to work out a better thesis from my first draft?

In some cases, you will be able to revise your thesis fairly easily. If your thesis is confusing, you can rewrite it for clarity. If it states only a general opinion or the theme or thesis of the work you are analyzing, you can define your reasons by returning to the last question for finding a thesis, "What has led me to this generalization?"

In other cases you may need to work out a new thesis from your first draft. If you have merely restated the topic or summarized information, you don't actually have a thesis; if you added new ideas as you wrote your draft, the thesis you began with may not adequately explain your material. In these circumstances, reread your draft, especially the conclusion, to see what you have actually said. Then return to Step 4 of the preparation process, using the material in your middle paragraphs as the basis for asking questions.

If you revise the weak thesis statements above in accordance with these suggestions, you will have theses that are both complete and comprehensible:

> The deterioration I observed in a privately run day-care centre because of lack of government funds suggests that the quality of education we can offer students in any educational setting is dependent upon adequate public funding for teachers, programmes, and facilities.

> Because he realizes the impossibility of making 'scientific' claims about the relation between national food and national character, Hugh MacLennan adopts a playful approach to the task of persuading us that a combination of vigorous simplicity and honest complexity is ideal in both food and character.

Step 2

REVISING ESSAY STRUCTURE

Once you have revised your thesis, your next step is to re-examine your middle paragraphs to see how adequately they explain and support the point you are now making. If your revised thesis is substantially different from the one with which you began, you may find that you need to add or delete, expand or condense points in your first draft.

> **Do my paragraphs correspond to the analytical categories I selected for writing the first draft? If not, is there a good reason?**

The first question to ask about the overall structure of your essay is whether your paragraph divisions are logical. In writing your draft you may have divided material into two or more paragraphs when it belongs in one; or you may have combined material that needs to be separated; or you may have forgotten to put in paragraphs at all.

A good rule of thumb for writing a first draft of a short essay is to use each of your analytical categories as the topic of a separate paragraph. If your categories for a short essay on alcoholism were its social, psychological, and physical effects, for example, each of these effects would be the topic of a separate paragraph. In checking your draft, you would make sure that your paragraph divisions corresponded to these categories or that you had a good reason for paragraphing differently.

What would be good reasons for paragraphing differently? You might discover, for example, that you had very little material on the psychological effects of alcoholism, and therefore decide to combine that paragraph with the one on physical effects, since both pertain to the individual rather than to society. Or you might find that your discussion of social effects of alcoholism runs to two pages, and so you need to break it into shorter paragraphs, based on subcategories such as effects on family, effects on friends, and effects on co-workers.

Outlining your draft to show the topics you have used in each paragraph is a good way of checking whether your paragraph divisions are logical. If they are not, make an outline of what the structure should be as a guide for your revisions.

Have I arranged points in an appropriate order?

You can also use your outline of paragraph topics to determine whether you have followed the order you intended (chronological, spatial, or logical order, if appropriate, as well as an order of ascending interest) and whether that order still seems the most appropriate. If you have changed your thesis or your paragraph divisions, you may need to adjust the order as well. Indicate any proposed changes on your revised topic outline.

Step 3

REVISING MIDDLE PARAGRAPHS

The next step is to look carefully at the structure and development of each of your middle paragraphs. As you revise, you may be working back and forth between your original draft, revised thesis and outline. At this point the main question is this: Have I developed each point fully and clearly enough so that a reader could understand it?

Does each middle paragraph have a topic sentence?

Topic sentences are the bridge between the generalization you make in your thesis and the specific details you give in your middle paragraphs. In college and university essays, topic sentences generally come at the beginning of the paragraph so that the structure of the essay will be clear to the reader.

Each topic sentence should not only identify the topic of the paragraph but, more important, state the point to be developed. In this way, the topic sentence acts as a mini-thesis for the paragraph. One topic sentence for the essay on alcoholism, for example, might be something like this: "Although the physical effects of advanced alcoholism are well known, many people are unaware of the early symptoms of physical dependency." This sentence identifies the topic of the paragraph, physical effects, but also makes a point about these effects.

A. Does each topic sentence serve as a mini-thesis for the paragraph?

You can use the same questions to check your topic sentences that you use to check your thesis:

QUESTION	EXAMPLE
Does it merely state the topic of the paragraph?	"Another factor in alcoholism is its physical effects."
Does it merely state facts or summarize information?	"Alcoholism may cause malnutrition and cirrhosis of the liver."
Does it merely state a general opinion?	"Alcoholism has harmful physical effects."
Is it stated in a confusing or pretentious way?	"The well-known ravages of advanced alcoholism conceal the subtle onslaught of symptomatic debilitation."

Revise your topic sentences to ensure that they both identify the topic of the paragraph and make a point that relates the paragraph to the thesis.

B. If a single aspect occupies more than one paragraph, have I used an "umbrella" topic sentence?

As we noted in talking about essay structure, you may sometimes have more material on a particular aspect of your subject than you can put into one paragraph. You can tie a series of related paragraphs together by using what is called an "umbrella" topic sentence. If you divided your material on the social effects of alcoholism into paragraphs on family, friends, and co-workers, for example, each of these paragraphs would have its own topic sentence; but the first would also have an "umbrella" topic sentence mentioning all three topics, as in the following example:

"Umbrella" Topic Sentence	Because of the erratic behaviour it produces, alcoholism may have devastating social effects on family, friends, and co-workers. Family violence, for example,
Point 1	is strongly associated with excessive drinking.
Topic Sentence: Point 2	The alcoholic's behaviour may cause frustration, embarrassment, or injury to friends.
Topic Sentence: Point 3	Co-workers may suffer because of the alcoholic's lateness, absenteeism, or carelessness.

Does the material in each middle paragraph adequately support the point made in its topic sentence?

Once you have revised your topic sentences, you can re-examine each of your middle paragraphs to see whether they adequately support the points made in the topic sentences.

Most middle paragraphs contain material that is on three different levels of generality. The point made in the topic sentence is at the highest level of generality. At the lowest level are the specific details supporting that point. In between is material explaining the topic sentence or the details. A middle paragraph lacking in material at any one of these levels is likely to be inadequately developed.

When you examine the middle paragraphs in your first draft, consider this relationship between topic sentence, explanation, and detail rather than merely length. A paragraph two sentences long is almost surely undeveloped, but so is a long paragraph that offers a series of points without giving any specific details to support them.

Begin your revision of middle paragraphs by eliminating any material that is irrelevant to your topic sentences. Then consider the questions below.

A. Does each paragraph provide sufficient detail to support its point?

What kinds of details can you use to provide evidence for your point? There are three major kinds:

> 1. Factual information: specific names, dates, places, statistics, incidents, objects, and so on.
>
> 2. Examples, real or hypothetical. Real examples are better evidence than hypothetical ones. One example will illustrate a point, but will not prove a point.
>
> 3. Quotations from authorities in the field or from the text you are analyzing. For suggestions on how to incorporate quotations into your essay, see Section 8 of the "Handbook for Final Editing."

Giving specific details is important whether your focus is content analysis or textual analysis. You would no doubt recognize the need for details in history essays; but you may think there's no need for them if you are writing on something your reader has read or seen. Not all readers/viewers notice the same things, or interpret what they do notice in the same ways, however. The details you use help your reader to understand your interpretation of the work.

B. Does each paragraph provide enough explanation of the point made in the topic sentence and of the detail offered?

If your middle paragraphs are full of details but you do not explain how those details support your topic sentences (and therefore your thesis), you will seem to be merely summarizing the data, historical events, or literary work you are writing about. Consider, for example, this paragraph from an essay on the development of abstract painting in Canada.

> While the Plasticien fervour was in full swing in Montreal, a small revolution took place in Saskatchewan, where the Emma Lake Workshop was set up. It was organized in 1956 by the School of Fine Arts at the University of Saskatchewan and was supported by the Saskatchewan Art Board and the Canada Council. It resulted in a workshop program that occurs every

August. The original idea was conceived by Ken Lochhead, who became one of the "Regina Five," and it was he who injected the spark of enthusiasm. The first workshops were led by Jack Shadbolt and other well-established Canadian abstract artists.

This paragraph is full of specific details, but there is little explanation of how the Emma Lake Workshops contributed to the development of abstract painting in Canada. The impression is that the writer has gathered historical information without thinking about its meaning. Unless you attempt to explain the details you have collected, your writing is likely to seem superficial.

Step 4

REVISING INTRODUCTIONS AND CONCLUSIONS

When you write a first draft, you are more concerned with getting your ideas straight than you are with presenting them to a reader. As a result, your introduction and conclusion are likely to be sketchy. Once you have revised your thesis and middle paragraphs so that your main idea is clear and your points are fully developed, you can consider how to introduce and conclude your essay. Since the introduction and conclusion are responsible for your reader's first and last impressions, you will want to take some care with them.

Does the introduction establish an appropriate context for the essay?

Your introduction gives your reader a chance to prepare, emotionally and intellectually, for the essay that is to follow: to find out what your subject is, how you feel about it, and what you intend to say. In most college and university essays, you will be writing seriously about serious subjects, and the tone you adopt in your introduction will convey this attitude to your reader. For specific suggestions about tone, see Handbook Section 1. Here we will focus on what you say in an introduction.

A. Does the introduction give readers enough background to understand the thesis?

Don't say anything in your introduction that you do not intend to support in your essay. If you are writing on blindness in *King Lear*, for example, don't feel that you have to start by saying something like "Shakespeare is the greatest dramatist that ever lived." In the first sentence or two, give your readers the specific details they need in order to understand what you are writing about, such as authors and titles of written works, factual information about historical events, or the theoretical framework of a concept you plan to discuss.

B. Does the introduction as a whole, or the thesis itself, outline in order the points covered in the essay?

Indicate the structure of your essay by mentioning, in the order you plan to discuss them, the main topics you will cover. If, for example, your middle paragraphs examine the social, psychological, and physical effects of alcoholism, your introduction should let your reader know to expect these topics in this order. These points are usually part of your thesis statement when you go through the preparation process we've outlined. Trying to fit all this information into one sentence is sometimes cumbersome, however, and so you may want to outline your points before you come to your thesis proper.

C. Does the introduction end with the thesis?

In most college and university essays, the thesis comes at the end of the introduction. There are two reasons. First, if you state your thesis before you have established the limits of your discussion, you may encourage your reader to think of objections; whereas if you give background information first, you will have prepared your reader for your thesis. Second, both you and your reader will find it easier to focus on your main idea if your thesis comes at the beginning of your essay rather than at the end. Writers sometimes save their thesis for the conclusion, or leave it implied rather than stated. Unless the writer is very skilful, however, this method of presenting material is likely to seem confusing and chaotic.

Does the conclusion tie together the points made in the essay?

The conclusion is an opportunity for both you and your reader to step back from the specific points made in the body of the essay in order to get a better view of the overall pattern of thought you have developed and the larger issues raised by your treatment of the topic.

For this reason, you should not merely repeat in your conclusion the points you have made in your thesis and topic sentences; you should attempt to clarify their significance. In the material below, you will find suggestions for revising your conclusion to achieve this purpose.

A. Does the conclusion restate the thesis in different words?

You can avoid merely repeating your thesis by (a) using material in your middle paragraphs to make your thesis more specific; (b) using synonyms for some key terms and repeating others; (c) changing the structure of the thesis sentence; (d) beginning with a transitional phrase that links your middle paragraphs to your thesis (not "in conclusion" or "thus we have seen"). If you were writing on economic conditions on the prairies during the Depression, for example, your thesis and its restatement in the conclusion might look like this:

Thesis   During the Depression, no group of Canadians suffered more hardships than the prairie farmers, who had to contend with drought as well as the economic problems besetting the rest of the country.

Restatement   Since the prairie farmers thus depended upon the land for both their livelihood and their food, the drought plunged them into even greater suffering than the Depression itself.

B. Does the conclusion summarize the points made in the middle paragraphs in order to clarify the thesis?

Because of the points and evidence you present in your middle paragraphs, the full meaning of your thesis should be more apparent to your readers by the time they reach the conclusion than it was when they began the essay. You can help to make this fuller meaning more explicit by the way you tie together the points you've made. You can avoid merely repeating your topic sentences as a summary of your points by (a) combining several points into one or two sentences and, more important, (b) emphasizing the common principle that ties the separate points together. A summarizing sentence for the Depression essay, for instance, might read like this:

Canadians on the coasts could turn to the sea; those in central Canada could turn to gardening and raising livestock; but for farming families on the drought-parched prairies there was nowhere to turn.

This sentence clarifies the significance of the thesis by presenting the circumstances of various groups in concrete terms instead of the more abstract terms of the thesis and topic sentences.

C. Does the conclusion suggest the wider implications of the analysis, if any?

It is not a good idea—indeed, it is a bad idea—to end every essay with a sweeping generalization about the overwhelming importance of the text or subject you have discussed. Nevertheless, you may sometimes feel that your analysis raises important issues that are beyond the scope of your essay. In these cases, you can suggest the broader significance of your topic in one of these ways:

1. Identifying the causes or effects of events or processes. You might end an essay on prairie farmers during the Depression, for example, with a sentence like this:

> Together, drought and depression taught prairie farmers two lessons they have never forgotten: to conserve their land and to distrust the economic policies of the federal government.

2. Moving from the specific case you have discussed to the general category to which it belongs. You might move from an analysis of a sonnet by Wordsworth, for example, to a reference to Wordsworth's place among other writers of sonnets or among other Romantic poets.

3. Briefly comparing your subject with one more familiar to your readers. For instance, you might suggest the similarity between the "gold fever" of 1979-1980 and the "gold fever" of 1849.

As you will see in the case of the sample topic below, you can greatly improve the first draft of your essays by revising systematically.

SAMPLE TOPIC: AN ESSAY ANALYZING FICTION

In this section we will follow the steps for preparing, writing, and revising an analysis essay for structure and development. We have chosen a topic requiring textual analysis because essays of this type often present more difficult problems of structure and development than essays based on content analysis. As you will see, the revised draft with which the chapter ends is far from perfect. We have not corrected problems of expression because we will use the revised draft in Chapter 6 to discuss the second stage of revision, final editing.

Preparing to Write

Let's suppose that one of the texts for your Canadian literature course is Margaret Laurence's novel *The Stone Angel*, and that you have chosen the following topic for your second essay:

> Choose a passage from Margaret Laurence's *The Stone Angel* and write an essay of 750-1000 words in which you discuss the significance of the passage in the work as a whole.

Step 1

CLARIFYING THE TOPIC

I've gone through the list of questions about essay topics, and I've decided that this topic contains no unfamiliar terms, requires textual analysis, and does not require further research. Since I must read the novel before I can begin my essay, I will allow ten days for completing this assignment.

Step 2

GATHERING MATERIAL

Now that I've read the novel, I know that Hagar Shipley, the narrator and main character, tells her life story in sections that alternate between the present, in which she seems to be a cantankerous, almost senile ninety-year-old, and the past, in which she describes her childhood, her marriage, her escape from that marriage, and the deaths of her husband and her favourite son, John. One of the major concerns of the novel seems to be how Hagar's childhood influences the type of person she becomes. I'll choose a passage that will allow me to focus on this issue.

This passage from the first chapter, in which Hagar remembers herself as a young girl walking through the cemetery in which her mother lies buried, will be my main source of information and ideas.

> I used to walk there often when I was a girl. There could not have been many places to walk primly in those days, on paths, where white kid boots and dangling skirts would not be torn by thistles or put in unseemly disarray. How anxious I was to be neat and orderly, imagining life had been created only to celebrate tidiness, like prissy Pippa as she passed. But sometimes through the hot rush of disrespectful wind that shook the scrub oak and the coarse couchgrass encroaching upon the dutifully cared-for habitations of the dead, the scent of cowslips would rise momentarily. They

were tough-rooted, these wild and gaudy flowers, and although they were held back at the cemetery's edge, torn out by loving relatives determined to keep the plots clear and clearly civilized, for a second or two a person walking there could catch the faint, musky, dust-tinged smell of things that grew untended and had grown always, before the portly peonies and the angels with rigid wings, when the prairie bluffs were walked through only by Cree with enigmatic faces and greasy hair.[1]

I have checked the meanings of unfamiliar words ("unseemly," "disarray," "enigmatic," "musky") and tracked down the allusion to Robert Browning's poetic drama, *Pippa Passes*. The most famous lines of the poem are from the song Pippa sings as she passes through the streets in the morning:

> God's in His heaven—
> All's right with the world!

I'll need to consider why Hagar is described as being like "prissy Pippa."

Step 3

CATEGORIZING MATERIAL

I have made the following notes about the passage, using the special categories for analyzing fiction.

Subject: What is the passage about?
Hagar's memories of herself as a young girl walking through the cemetery where her mother is buried.

Narrative Structure: What is the principle behind the selection and arrangement of events ("plot")?
   Flashback ("used to walk," "when I was a girl," "in those days"). One of many shifts from present (when Hagar is ninety) to past, as she remembers her life.

Setting: What is the time, place, and social environment within which the events take place?
TIME: 80-85 years before narrative present ("when I was a girl"); references to "white kid boots," "dangling skirts," and Pippa suggest late 19th century (1880s-1890s).
PLACE: Cemetery where Hagar's mother, who died when she was born, is buried. The stone angel over her mother's grave dominates the landscape. The cemetery is outside a small town earlier identified as Manawaka, Manitoba.

---

[1]   All extracts from *The Stone Angel* by Margaret Laurence are reprinted by permission of the Canadian Publishers, McClelland and Stewart Limited, Toronto.

SOCIAL ENVIRONMENT: Emphasis on tidiness, duty ("dutifully cared-for habitations of the dead"); civilized behaviour (keeping the plots "clear and clearly civilized"); need to protect this way of life.

Characterization: What are the characters like? What techniques are used to portray them?

Hagar describes herself as walking "primly," as "anxious . . . to be neat and orderly"; she is concerned about her boots and skirts and therefore careful to keep "on paths."

She also comments on the fact that "a person walking there would catch the faint, musky, dust-tinged smell of things that grew untended and had grown always," but does not identify herself with that "person." She contrasts her walk through the cemetery with the time when "the prairie bluffs were walked through only by Cree with enigmatic faces and greasy hair."

Suggests a conflict between "civilized" settlers and native inhabitants. Note that her husband, Bram Shipley, is "uncivilized."

Diction: What do the general level of usage and particular word choices tell me about the narrator or about individual characters?

Hagar's language in this passage is that of a well-educated person; slightly formal because of the many multi-syllable words ("unseemly disarray," "habitations," "encroaching," "enigmatic").

Reference to "prissy Pippa" indicates both her familiarity with Browning's poem and her scorn of the naive optimism represented by "God's in His heaven—All's right with the world!"

Vocabulary establishes opposition between what is "clearly civilized" and what is "wild," "gaudy" and "disrespectful."

Images and Symbols: What do I learn about the narrator or about individual characters from **images** (figures of speech, such as metaphors, similes, personification; or, more generally, descriptions of sensations, such as sight, sound, touch, smell, taste) or **symbols** (objects, actions, gestures, or patterns of images used to express an emotion or an abstract idea)?

Many visual images, especially plants (contrast "portly peonies" and "wild and gaudy" cowslips); "uncivilized" life also associated with smells. Cemetery a symbol of death. Clothes symbolic in later parts of the novel.

Sentence Structure: What do sentence patterns and length tell me about the narrator or about individual characters?

Mainly long, complex sentences, consistent with formal diction in showing Hagar as educated, in control.

Point of View: From whose point of view is the story told? How does this point of view affect the way the story is told?

Hagar is the first-person narrator in this scene, as she is throughout the novel. How accurate is her perception of herself?

Tone: What attitude does the narrator adopt towards the story or the characters?

Hagar does not seem to feel any sympathy for her younger self. She seems critical of the values represented by the cemetery, with its "portly peonies" and its "angels with rigid wings." She seems to find more life in the "disrespectful wind" and the "wild and gaudy" cowslips, but these lively things are also associated with the Cree and their "enigmatic faces and greasy hair," an unpleasant image. The tone is critical, detached.

Theme: What is the central idea of this passage? How does it relate to the theme of the novel as a whole?

Tentative ideas: conflict between the "civilized" and the "uncivilized." How does this relate to conflicting impulses in Hagar's character? I'll explore these ideas more thoroughly in the next stage of my analysis.

Step 4

FINDING A THESIS

My analysis of setting, characterization, style, and tone suggests that the passage sets up a conflict between order (represented by the carefully tended cemetery and the carefully groomed girl who walks there) and disorder (represented by the untamed elements of nature and by the native inhabitants). This conflict is not resolved in the passage; Hagar clearly rejects her "prissy" younger self and the rigid, deadening order that the cemetery represents. But while she describes the "disorder" of the "uncivilized" prairie and its native inhabitants in terms that make them seem more "alive," she still judges them by the very values she rejects, as indicated by the emphasis on the Crees' "greasy hair."

In considering how this passage relates to the novel as a whole, I realize that this conflict between order and disorder recurs throughout Hagar's life. She is attracted to Bram Shipley's wildness and she prefers her wild son John to her respectable son Marvin. Nevertheless, she evaluates Bram and others by the conventional standards of her childhood, and so she can never really give her heart to them. Like the stone angel in the cemetery, she remains blind and rigid to all around her. This passage, then, illuminates the theme of the novel.

I can therefore use a thesis like this for my essay:

> The passage from <u>The Stone Angel</u> in which Hagar describes her younger self walking through the cemetery helps to establish the central theme of the novel as a whole: that even though people may feel the attraction of a life beyond the order and conventions of their upbringing, they may never be able to escape from the rigidity and blindness to others that this early emphasis on respectability encourages.

Now that I've completed the preparation process, I'm ready to write my first draft.

Writing the First Draft

Before I begin to write, I should decide which major points to make and in what order to present them.

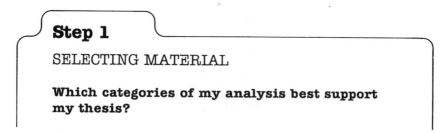

Step 1

SELECTING MATERIAL

Which categories of my analysis best support my thesis?

I have lots of material on setting, characterization, diction, images and symbols, tone, and theme. I have to talk about the theme; I can relate the diction, images and symbols, and tone to setting and characterization, since the passage tells us a great deal about Hagar and the kind of environment in which she grows up. I should try to link these elements in the passage to other parts of the novel, especially to her relationships to her husband and sons.

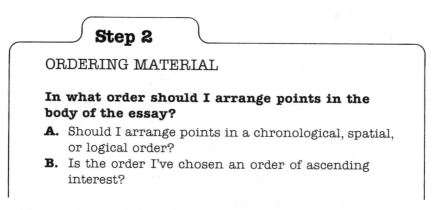

Step 2

ORDERING MATERIAL

In what order should I arrange points in the body of the essay?
A. Should I arrange points in a chronological, spatial, or logical order?
B. Is the order I've chosen an order of ascending interest?

Although the novel shifts back and forth between the past and the present, it has a basic chronological structure that begins with Hagar's childhood and ends with her death. Since my essay deals with the whole novel, I think I'll use that chronological order to discuss Hagar's relationship with Bram, Marvin, and John in order to show how the conflict in the passage is central to the novel as a whole. I'll work out a more systematic presentation of this analysis when I revise my first draft.

Step 3

WRITING THE DRAFT

Here is my first draft:

THE STONE ANGEL

Introduction

Thesis

The Stone Angel is Margaret Laurence's masterpiece, and the passage I have chosen to discuss shows why. The passage in which Hagar describes her younger self walking through the cemetery helps to establish the central theme of the novel as a whole: that even though people may feel the attraction of a life beyond the order and conventions of their upbringing, they may never be able to escape from the rigidity and blindness to others that this early emphasis on respectability encourages.

Middle Paragraph 1

The cemetery in the passage suggests that the emphasis on order and respectability is deadening, and the Cree represent the wilderness that is encroaching on the cemetery. These images reappear in the description of Hagar's first meeting with Bram Shipley. When Hagar meets Bram at a dance, she is intensely attracted to him because he is the exact opposite of the life her father has forced her to accept. Hagar is attracted to him because he seems to offer an escape from the deadening life that she has been living.

> We spun around the chalky floor, and I reveled in his fingernails with crescents of ingrown earth that never met a file. I fancied I heard in his laughter the bravery of battalions. I thought he looked a bearded Indian, so brown and beaked a face. The black hair thrusting from his chin was rough as thistles. The next instant, though, I imagined him rigged out in a suit of gray soft as a dove's breast-feathers. (p. 45)

Middle Paragraph 2

Hagar marries Bram to escape from her father's notions of respectability and yet she uses these standards to judge Bram. Hagar complains about Bram's language and manners and Bram becomes more offensive to spite her. As the novel progresses Hagar and Bram become increasingly distant. Bram escapes Hagar's constant criticism by going to the bar, and Hagar furiously cleans their unpainted house in an effort to maintain the standards of respectability.

Middle Paragraph 3

The passage also describes respectability in terms of the clothes the young Hagar wears: "There would not have been many places to walk primly in those days, on paths, where white kid boots and dangling skirts would not be torn by thistles or put in unseemly disarray" (pp. 4-5). Hagar's concern with social status and respectability eventually make it impossible for her to live with Bram. Her concern with clothes as the symbol of respectability is relevant here, for when she realizes she looks like the egg-woman she has become, she decides to leave Bram. When she is living in Vancouver as Mr. Oatley's housekeeper, however, Hagar's black uniform suggests the cemetery, and she says, "I never thought of Bram in the days any more, but I'd waken, sometimes, out of a half sleep and turn to him and find he wasn't beside me, and then I'd be filled with such a bitter emptiness it seeemed the whole of night must be within me and not around or outside at all" (p. 160). Hagar has the orderliness and respectability she says she wants, and yet "the image of Bram's heavy manhood" (p. 160) disturbs her.

Middle Paragraph 4

As might be expected, Hagar's ambivalent attitudes also affect her relationships with her sons. Although Marvin, who is solid, respectable, and hard-working, is a much better example of middle-class values, Hagar prefers her second son, John, who like his father cares nothing for conventions and respectability. Her concern for respectability eventually leads to his death.

Middle Paragraph 5

The reference in the passage to "prissy Pippa" suggests that civilized life represents a view of religion in which "God's in his heaven—All's right with the world." But when John dies, Hagar seems to lose her belief in God. Hagar is too proud to cry in front of neighbours, but can't cry even when she is alone: "The night my son died I was transformed to stone and never wept at all" (p. 243). This image reminds us of the stone angel over her mother's grave.

Middle Paragraph 6

As we have seen, the symbols, ideas, and characterization of Hagar in this passage are important to the novel as a whole. The diction is also carefully chosen, the multi-syllable words ("unseemly," "disarray," "habitation," "encroaching," "enigmatic") gives the impression of a well-educated person. Later we see her constantly correcting her children's grammar and criticizing Bram's crude language. The long complex sentences in this passage are consistent with the formal diction and help to give a sense of control. The critical, detached tone of the passage shows Hagar's lack of sympathy with her younger self and her inability to reconcile the conflicting values symbolized by her description of the cemetery.

Conclusion   Hagar's tragedy is that she can't accept a life of order and respectability, because that life feels dead, like the cemetery. On the other hand, she can't accept a life of disorder such as the wilderness represents either. When Hagar lives on the farm with Bram, she is cut off from her father and the respectable and civilized life of the town. Her isolation is intensified because she clings to the values of her childhood and withdraws from Bram. When she lives with Marvin and Doris, she judges them by what she imagines Bram would have said. When Mr. Troy visits her in the hospital, she regrets that she has not enjoyed life more. But she is never able to reconcile these conflicting ways of life. This shows how strong the influence of our early lives can be.

Revising the First Draft

It's been two days since I wrote my first draft, so I should be able to evaluate and revise it.

Step 1

REVISING THE THESIS

Does the thesis state an opinion and support it? Do I need to work out a better thesis from my first draft?

My thesis does state and support an opinion, but I notice that my draft suggests a slightly different focus. In my notes I had characterized the conflict in the passage as being between order and disorder. Now that I have explored the relation of the passage to the book more thoroughly, I would say that "respectability"—keeping up appearances—better describes what the cemetery represents, and the fact that it is a cemetery, and that Hagar eventually feels herself turn to stone like the angel over her mother's grave, emphasizes the deadening effect this emphasis on respectability can have.

Can I find a better term than "disorder" for the opposite set of values? The neatly tended cemetery seems in danger of being over-run by things that have vitality and freedom of movement, like the wind, the "encroaching" plants, and the Cree who used to walk there. Bram represents this vitality, but when Hagar responds to him sex-ually, she decides not to let him know. This decision is typical of her tendency to stifle her emotional responses (as at John's death). The song Mr. Troy sings at the hospital makes her realize, "I must always, always have wanted that—simply to rejoice" (p. 292). The desire to respond emotionally, then, would be the opposite of the desire to appear respectable. This ability to respond emotionally would make her feel "alive," in contrast to the "deadening" effect of respectable life.

I'll revise my thesis to include this more precise way of describing the conflict and to show that all people are strongly influenced by their upbringing, not just those with backgrounds like Hagar's.

> I think this passage describing Hagar walking through the cemetery is important because Hagar's inability to resolve the conflict between deadening respectability and emotional re-sponsiveness illustrates the theme of the novel as a whole. This theme is that the values that shape our early lives con-tinue to govern us despite our desire for something different.

Step 2

REVISING ESSAY STRUCTURE

Do my paragraphs correspond to the categories I selected for writing the draft? If not, is there a good reason? Have I arranged points in an appropriate order?

A. Have I used a chronological, spatial, or logical order, if appropriate, as well as an order of ascending interest?

B. Does the order I have used still seem the best way of organizing my material?

There are serious problems with the structure of this draft. In the first middle paragraph I mention the images of the cemetery and the wil-derness, and in the third I mention the clothing, but most of what I say is about Hagar's relationships with Bram and her sons. The last midddle paragraph sounds as though I know I've drifted off topic, and so I've crammed in everything about diction, sentence structure, and tone. I can't tell whether I've used all the categories I intended to use or not. I'll make an outline of my draft, noting the main point I make about the **passage** and the main point I make about the **book** in each paragraph, so that I can see whether I have linked the treatment of each aspect of the novel.

OUTLINE OF DRAFT

Middle Paragraph 1	Passage—images of cemetery and Cree (mentioned) Book—images used to describe Hagar's meeting with Bram
Middle Paragraph 2	Passage—nothing Book—H's and B's fights over language, manners
Middle Paragraph 3	Passage—clothes as symbol of respectability (mentioned) Book—clothes (coat, uniform); contrast with Bram's physicality
Middle Paragraph 4	Passage—nothing Book—H's attitude towards sons
Middle Paragraph 5	Passage—allusion to Pippa Book—H's loss of belief at John's death
Middle Paragraph 6	Passage—diction, sentence structure, tone Book—correcting Bram's and children's grammar

From this outline I can see that I have discussed primarily the images, symbols, diction, sentence structure and tone as they relate to characterization and theme in the passage and in the book as a whole, so I will use these categories as paragraph topics. The paragraph on Hagar's loss of belief doesn't really seem to fit, so I'll drop it.

I need to discuss the conflict set up in the passage more thoroughly at the beginning of the essay. That will probably require a whole paragraph. I should put the discussion of the language used in the passage with my discussion of the fights over grammar. To keep a better balance between the passage and the book and to make it easier to see how the two are connected, I should examine one aspect of the passage and of the novel as a whole within each paragraph (except for the first point). I'll use this as my revised outline:

REVISED OUTLINE

Middle Paragraph 1	Passage—*images* that establish conflict between respectability and responsiveness
Middle Paragraph 2	Book—recurrence of these *images* in H's meeting with Bram
Middle Paragraph 3	Passage—clothes as *symbol* of respectability Book—clothes vs. physicality

Middle **Paragraph 4**	Passage—*language* (diction and sentence structure) Book—conflict over language
Middle **Paragraph 5**	Passage—*tone* Book—H's isolation from others as a result of her critical, detached attitude

This order will allow me to follow the chronology of the book and also end with my general point about the isolation that results from Hagar's lack of emotional responsiveness.

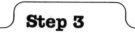

REVISING MIDDLE PARAGRAPHS

Does each paragraph have a topic sentence?
A. Does each topic sentence serve as a mini-thesis for the paragraph?
B. If my analysis of a single aspect of my subject occupies more than one paragraph, have I used an "umbrella" topic sentence?

All of my paragraphs have topic sentences that make a point, but the first ("The cemetery . . . suggests . . . and the Cree represent . . .") is too limited to serve as a mini-thesis for the paragraph as it stands, since it says nothing about Bram. Even when I divide this material into two paragraphs, I will need a better topic sentence to define the conflict. Several topic sentences contain quotations. To separate points from supporting evidence more clearly, I should probably put the quotations in the body of the paragraph.

When I revise the body of the essay, I'll have to make sure that my topic sentences identify the topic of the paragraph and make a point that shows the relation between that aspect of the passage and the book as a whole. I may need an "umbrella" topic sentence for the first two paragraphs.

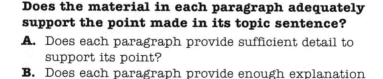

Does the material in each paragraph adequately support the point made in its topic sentence?
A. Does each paragraph provide sufficient detail to support its point?
B. Does each paragraph provide enough explanation of the point made in its topic sentence and of the detail offered?

I will need to rewrite all my middle paragraphs to conform to my revised outline. The first will require the fewest changes in material, so it's a good place to begin.

All that I say about the passage in my first middle paragraph is that the cemetery represents the deadness of respectability and the Cree represent the wilderness. These points lack support; I'm assuming my readers know the passage as well as I do. I will need to analyze the passage more fully to show this conflict. In discussing Hagar's meeting with Bram, I mention that "he is the exact opposite of the life her father has forced her to accept," but I don't give the **details** of what that life is. Later I give the quotation that links Bram with the Cree and thistles of the cemetery passage, but I don't **explain** the point of the quotation adequately.

As I decided when I made my revised outline, I'll divide this material into two paragraphs, one to show how the images in the passage set up the conflict between respectability and responsiveness, and one to show how these same images are used to characterize Hagar's expectations of Bram. Here is my revised first paragraph.

Topic Sentence	The conflict between respectability and responsiveness is evident in this passage in the images used to describe the setting.
Details	But sometimes through the hot rush of disrespectful wind that shook the scrub oak and the coarse couchgrass encroaching upon the dutifully cared-for habitations of the dead, the scent of cowslips would rise momentarily. They were tough-rooted, these wild and gaudy flowers, and although they were held back at the cemetery's edge, torn out by loving relatives determined to keep the plots clear and clearly civilized . . . (p. 5).
Explanation **Detail** **Explanation** **Detail**	It could hardly be more obvious that Laurence intends us to see that the cemetery represents the life of deadening respectability, and the wilderness (wind, scrub oak, couchgrass, cowslips) represents the potential for a freer life, one like that of the Cree who in the younger Hagar's imagination had walked "with enigmatic faces and greasy hair" through the place where she now walks.

As I write each new paragraph, I'll check to make sure it includes enough explanation and detail to explain my point fully. I may need to integrate my quotations better when I do the final editing.

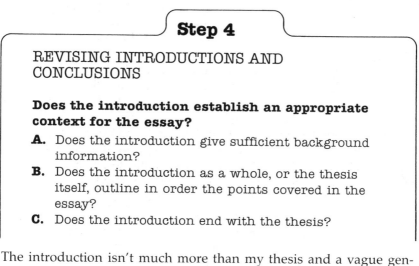

Step 4

REVISING INTRODUCTIONS AND CONCLUSIONS

Does the introduction establish an appropriate context for the essay?

A. Does the introduction give sufficient background information?

B. Does the introduction as a whole, or the thesis itself, outline in order the points covered in the essay?

C. Does the introduction end with the thesis?

The introduction isn't much more than my thesis and a vague generalization about "Margaret Laurence's masterpiece," a statement I don't intend to support by comparing *The Stone Angel* with everything else Laurence has written. There isn't any background information on the novel that will help my readers understand the context of this passage. I could bring in the structure and point of view of the book, as well as indicating where the passage I'm analyzing comes in the novel, like this:

> The narrative structure of Margaret Laurence's The Stone Angel consists of a series of shifts between the present and the past in which the narrator and main character, Hagar Shipley, who is now ninety, describes her past and present life. The novel begins with a description of the stone angel Hagar's father had placed over her mother's grave, who had died at her birth. Immediately following, is a passage in which Hagar described herself as a girl walking through the cemetery outside the small prairie town of Manawaka where she grew up.

I'm not entirely satisfied with the way I've expressed myself here, but I'll examine my sentences more closely during the final editing process. I still need to complete my introduction by mentioning in order the specific topics I will discuss (images, symbols, language, and tone) and ending with my revised thesis.

Does the conclusion tie together the points made in the essay?

A. Does the conclusion restate the thesis, in different words?

B. Does the conclusion summarize the points made in the middle paragraphs in order to clarify the thesis?

C. Does the conclusion suggest the wider implications of the thesis, if any?

Since I've changed my thesis and middle paragraphs so much, I'll need to rewrite my conclusion. My revised thesis is that Hagar's inability to resolve the conflict between deadening respectability and emotional responsiveness shows that the values that shape our early lives continue to govern us despite our desire for something different. I have argued that this conflict leads to Hagar's emotional isolation. I can therefore restate and clarify my thesis like this:

> Hagar's emotional isolation, which results from her inability to resolve the conflict between respectability and responsiveness, suggests that we may not be able to escape from the values that have formed us, even though we are aware of their limitations. The images and symbols Laurence uses to describe the setting and to characterize Hagar in this early passage makes us aware of the values she swings between throughout the novel. Her need for respectability, conveyed in this passage by her concern for her clothes, is stronger than her dream of a freer emotional life. The educated, controlled language and critical, detached tone show that she could not accept herself, therefore she could not really accept anyone else or any set of values. So the passage describing her younger self walking through the cemetery foreshadows the concerns of the novel as a whole.

Can I say anything about the wider implications of my analysis? I don't know enough about Laurence's other writing or modern fiction generally to put the book into a wider literary context. The conclusion sounds complete, so I'll leave it as it is.

Writing the Revised Draft

If you were making basic changes in essay structure such as those indicated for the essay on *The Stone Angel*, it might well take a third or fourth draft before you could work out your ideas as carefully as in the draft presented below. This draft, as you will see, contains problems with quotations, format, grammar, and punctuation that will be explained and revised in the following chapter on final editing.

THE STONE ANGEL

The narrative structure of <u>The Stone Angel</u> consists of a series of shifts between the present and the past in which the narrator and main character Hagar Shipley who is now ninety describes her past and her present life. The novel begins with a description of the stone angel Hagar's father had placed over her mother's grave, who had died at her birth. Immediately following, is a passage in which Hagar described herself as a girl walking through the cemetery outside the small prairie town of Manawaka where she grew up. The images, diction, and tone used in the passage seem to me to set up a conflict between two opposite approaches to life which I will describe as deadening respectability and emotional responsiveness. The conflict between these two approaches dominates the novel. I think this passage describing Hagar walking through the cemetery is important because Hagar's inability to resolve this conflict between deadening respectability and emotional responsiveness illustrates the theme of the novel as a whole. This theme is that the values that shape our early lives continue to govern us despite our desire for something different.

The conflict between respectability and responsiveness is evident in this passage in the images used to describe the setting.

> But sometimes through the hot rush of disrespectful wind that shook the scrub oak and the coarse couchgrass encroaching upon the dutifully cared-for habitations of the dead, the scent of cowslips would rise momentarily. They were tough-rooted, these wild and gaudy flowers, and although they were held back at the cemetery's edge, torn out by loving relatives determined to keep the plots clear and clearly civilized... (p. 5).

It could hardly be more obvious that Laurence intends us to see that the cemetery represents the life of deadening respectability, and the wilderness (wind, scrub oak, couchgrass, cowslips) represent the potential for a freer life, one like that of the cree who in the younger Hagar's imagination had walked "with enigmatic faces and greasy hair" through the place where she now walks.

Laurence shows us the conflict these images set up is an internal conflict that Hagar experiences in her first description of her meeting with Bram Shipley:

> We spun around the chalky floor, and I reveled in his fingernails with crescents of ingrown earth that never met

a file. I fancied I heard in his laughter the bravery of battalions. I thought he looked a bearded Indian, so brown and beaked a face. The black hair thrusting from his chin was rough as thistles. The next instant, though, I imagined him rigged out in a suit of gray soft as a dove's breast-feathers (p. 45).

One of the reasons their marriage fails is because Hagar cannot accept Bram's limitations, she cannot accept his inability to become the cultured gentleman as well as the wild Indian. Another reason it fails is that she hides her sexual response from Bram, and so cuts herself off from the one way they might have been able to communicate.

The emphasis on clothing as the symbol of respectability is conveyed here by the gray suit, but it is first introduced in the cemetery passage: "There could not have been many places to walk primly in those days, on paths, where white kid boots and dangling skirts would not be torn by thistles or put in unseemly disarray" (pp. 4-5). After almost twenty years of marriage, Hagar suddenly realizes how she looks delivering eggs in her older son Marvin's cast-off coat. This prompts her to take her younger son John and leave Bram. Yet the conflict between the desire for respectability and the desire for emotional responsiveness remain. Living in Vancouver as Mr. Oatley's housekeeper, dressed in her black uniform, "I never thought of Bram in the days any more, but I'd waken, sometimes, out of a half sleep and turn to him and find he wasn't beside me, and then I'd be filled with such a bitter emptiness it seemed the whole of night must be within me and not around or outside at all" (p. 160). Hagar has the orderliness and respectability she says she wants and yet "the image of Bram's heavy manhood" (p. 160) remains a disturbing memory.

As the language of the passage describing the cemetery suggests, however, Hagar never gives up the deeply ingrained middle-class values that the cemetery represents. The many multi-syllable words ("unseemly," "disarray," "habitation," "encroaching," "enigmatic") and the long, complex sentences illustrate Hagar's attempts to understand and control her experience through language. But language is also an important tool in maintaining her sense of superiority. Initially, Hagar finds Bram's coarse speech attractive; later it becomes a source of annoyance. Hagar's snobbery about language also becomes a means to avoid contact with her older son. An example of this is where Marvin, eager for her approval, announces, "I brought them long pieces from the new woodpile," and Hager says, "And for pity's sake say <u>those</u> pieces, not <u>them</u>" (p. 113). Although Hagar never gives up these values, she never totally accepts them either. Marvin, as we come to see, is a much better example of middle-class values than his rebellious brother John, but Hagar prefers John and dismisses Marvin as a "Shipley through and through."

Hagar's inability to resolve this conflict is foreshadowed by the critical, detached tone of the cemetery passage. As a narrator, she seems contemptuous of the girl who was anxious "to be neat and orderly." The girl who imagined "that life had been created only to celebrate tidiness" (p. 5). On the other hand, her description of the wilderness with its disrespectful wind, encroaching scrub-oak, coarse couchgrass, and dust-tinged cowslips that smell like musk suggest that the wilderness is disrespectful, hard to control, unclean, and musky (a word that suggests animals and mating). These words make the wilderness seem equally unattractive. Because the emphasis falls on the Crees' "greasy hair" suggests that Hagar will finally not be able to surrender herself to the values that the wilderness represents. When she is in the hospital, dying, the minister sings a hymn that makes her realize, "I must always, always have wanted that—simply to rejoice" (p. 292). But because she has denied her opportunities to respond to the world, she has become a bitter, critical old woman.

Hagar's emotional isolation, which results from her inability to resolve the conflict between respectability and responsiveness, suggests that we may not be able to escape from the values that have formed us, even though we are aware of their limitations. The images and symbols Laurence uses to describe the setting and to characterize Hagar in this early passage makes us aware of the values she swings between throughout the novel. Her need for respectability, conveyed in this passage by her concern for her clothes, is stronger than her dream of a freer emotional life. The educated, controlled language and critical, detached tone show that she could not accept herself, therefore she could not really accept anyone else or any set of values. So the passage describing her younger self walking through the cemetery foreshadows the concerns of the novel as a whole.

This revised draft demonstrates the significant improvements in structure and development that you can make by systematic revisions of the kind outlined in this chapter.

SUMMARY

These are the steps to remember when you are writing and revising a first draft.

1. From the material you gathered during the preparation process, select the categories that best support your thesis.

2. Decide on an appropriate order to present this material in your essay.

3. Write a first draft, using the categories you have selected as the topics for your middle paragraphs.

4. Check your thesis, essay structure, middle paragraphs, introduction, and conclusion for problems in structure and development. Revise as necessary.

When you have completed these steps, use the Checklist for Final Editing to determine whether you need to make changes in areas such as format, grammar, punctuation, and tone. You will find an example of this last stage of revision in the next chapter, "Final Editing," where we will use the revised draft of the essay on *The Stone Angel* to demonstrate how to proofread for specific problems in these areas. For your convenience, the checklist is reprinted in the reference section.

EXERCISES

A. Checking Thesis Statements

Decide whether each of the following is a good or a weak thesis for an analysis essay and explain the reasons for your decision.

1. For an essay analyzing Jacob Bronowski's essay "On the Reach of the Imagination":

> The main point of Bronowski's essay is that the imagination is a unique human gift which helps man discover new techniques.

2. For an essay analyzing the role of multi-national corporations during World War II:

> Several political incidents, seen in the light of the economic impetus behind them, enforce a conviction that historians have ignored the role of multi-national corporations in promoting and maintaining the economic base upon which the prosecution of the war depended.

3. For an essay on the role of environmentalist groups:

> Society must maintain a balance between its needs and the preservation of the environment.

4. For an essay asking students to choose and analyze a single aspect of the relationship between inflation and unemployment:

> There are many factors to take into consideration when one is considering the relationship between inflation and unemployment.

5. For an essay asking students to analyze the steps by which Faustus damns himself in Christopher Marlowe's play *Dr. Faustus*:

> First Faustus sells his soul to the devil; next he misuses his magical powers; then he refuses to repent when he has a chance.

B. Planning Essay Structure

Suppose that you have been asked to write an essay analyzing the treatment of moral issues in American films from the early days of film-making through World War II. On the basis of the material you have gathered, you have arrived at the following thesis:

> The history of American film-making from the early days through the end of World War II shows that, for the most part, audiences liked a simple confrontation in which good triumphs over evil.

1. From the notes given below, select the points that seem to support this thesis best.[2]

a. Movies made immediately after World War I show a temporary disillusionment with violence as a solution.

b. The gangster movies of the thirties offered simple (i.e., violent) solutions to complex problems, and thus reflected the frustrations of Depression-era viewers who felt a sense of betrayal and disillusionment with the traditional American belief that goodness would eventually be rewarded with material success.

c. The early westerns made before World War I depicted a simple confrontation between good and evil in which the good guys were very good and the bad guys were very bad.

d. *Citizen Kane*, made in 1941, reflected a profound disillusionment with the belief that might equals right and that goodness is rewarded with material success.

e. In the twenties, Chaplin's comedies reaffirmed the traditional belief that self-reliance and goodness would triumph even in the face of a new and more complex society.

f. The war movies made during and shortly after World War II reverted to simpler moral concepts in which might and right were once again on the same side.

g. The comedies made immediately after World War I were of the escapist slapstick sort.

---

[2]This information on American film history has been taken from *Teacher's Guide to Film: A Reflection of American Values* (White Plains, N.Y.: The Center for Humanities, Inc., 1974), pp. 10-18.

2. List the points you have selected to show how you would accommodate the chronological order to an order of ascending interest.

C. Checking Middle Paragraphs

Read the two paragraphs below. Then answer the questions that follow.

Paragraph 1. From an essay on the treatment of the criminally insane.

> Canadians are presently providing help for mentally ill criminals. The man who murdered the Peterson family in Saskatchewan several years ago, for example, has been spending time at the psychiatric institute in North Battleford, where he is getting help. With luck he can be cured and will be able to live a normal life at some time. Many mentally ill people are known to be "dangerous" because they cannot control their emotions.

Paragraph 2. From an essay on Mordecai Richler's novel *The Apprenticeship of Duddy Kravitz*.

> When Duddy goes to borrow money from Dingleman, Dingleman asks him to go to New York with him. In New York, Duddy attends a party where he becomes the centre of attention when he does his imitation of Mr. Friar and explains his ambition to become a producer. Everyone laughs at Duddy, mainly because of his crude, unrefined manner. When Duddy asks Dingleman to be a silent partner, Dingleman changes the topic, never taking the time to consider the young man's ambition seriously, thinking nothing would ever become of Duddy. When Duddy went to Mr. Calder to beg that Lennie not be expelled, Mr. Calder asked him to dinner, the main reason being that Duddy's manner amused Calder—such a young Jew with big ambitions trying to pull himself out of the gutter. Duddy himself states how sick he is of people who think it is funny to see someone struggle to improve his lifestyle.

Answer these questions for each paragraph.
1. Does the paragraph have a topic sentence that acts as a mini-thesis?
2. Does the paragraph give enough detail to support the point made in the topic sentence?
3. Is there enough explanation of the point and of the detail?
4. Does everything in the paragraph serve to support its point?

D. Planning Introductions and Conclusions

You have been asked to determine the theme of Earle Birney's poem "Bushed" and to show how Birney develops the theme. Read the poem and then answer the questions that follow:

BUSHED[3]

He invented a rainbow but lightning struck it
shattered it into the lake-lap of a mountain
so big his mind slowed when he looked at it

Yet he built a shack on the shore
learned to roast porcupine belly and
wore the quills on his hatband.

At first he was out with the dawn
whether it yellowed bright as wood-columbine
or was only a fuzzed moth in a flannel of storm
But he found the mountain was clearly alive
sent messages whizzing down every hot morning
boomed proclamations at noon and spread out
a white guard of goat
before falling asleep on its feet at sundown

When he tried his eyes on the lake, ospreys
would fall like valkyries
choosing the cut-throat
He took then to waiting
till the night smoke rose from the boil of the sunset

But the moon carved unknown totems
out of the lakeshore
owls in the beardusky wood derided him
moosehorned cedars circled his swamps and tossed
their antlers up to the stars
Then he knew though the mountain slept, the winds
were shaping its peak to an arrowhead
poised

But by now he could only
bar himself in and wait
for the great flint to come singing into his heart.

1. From the following list, select material for an introduction to an essay analyzing the poem. Select your thesis first. Then select the material appropriate to introduce it and write the introduction.
a. Poetry is always simultaneously auditory and visual.
b. At the beginning of the poem, the man builds a shack on the lake side and roasts procupines.
c. Earle Birney was born in Calgary in 1904. His best-known poem is "David."

---

[3]From *The Poems of Earle Birney*, by Earle Birney (1969), p. 11. Reprinted by permission of The Canadian Publishers, McClelland and Stewart Limited, Toronto.

d. Birney is a recognized Chaucerian scholar and a Canadian pioneer in university education in creative writing.

e. At first the man lives in harmony with nature.

f. Stanza by stanza the poem goes through the man's alienation from nature, moving from anxiety to terror.

g. Later in the poem he locks himself in his cabin and waits for the mountain to kill him.

h. Birney's theme is not so much that nature is a monster, but that nature is so powerful and strange that it can become a monster to a man who dares to confront it.

i. Margaret Atwood argues in *Survival*, a thematic study of Canadian literature, that the Canadian attitude to nature on the whole is one of distrust.

j. In "Bushed," Birney shows how apparently idyllic surroundings—a mountain, a lake, a cabin away from it all—destroy a man whose initial trust in nature turns into terror.

2. State in a few sentences why you chose the information you did and omitted the rest.

3. From the following list, select material suitable for a conclusion to an essay analyzing "Bushed," and then write the conclusion.

a. This combination of hostility and helplessness presented in "Bushed" is part of the victim psychology evident in much of Canadian literature.

b. "Bushed" is a good example of the kind of poetry that helped Earle Birney win the Governor-General's medal for poetry in 1942 and 1945.

c. In all Canadian poetry, nature is a monster out to get you.

d. In "Bushed," we see the violent clash between the romantic idealization of nature and the realities of the Canadian landscape.

e. Thus, stanza by stanza, Birney's "Bushed" presents the perceptions and feelings of a man to whom nature is becoming increasingly monstrous.

f. The man who retreats to his cabin is very different from the man who roasted porcupine belly on the shore of a mountain lake.

g. "Bushed" is a very powerful poem and I enjoyed reading it very much.

h. All in all, "Bushed" supports Margaret Atwood's thesis about Canadian literature.

i. Earle Birney is probably one of Canada's greatest poets.

j. By barricading himself in his cabin, he shows that he has succumbed to the helpless feeling that nature is out to get him and that it will win because it is bigger and stronger.

4. State in a few sentences why you chose the information you did and omitted the rest.

E. Printed below is a first draft of an essay on the problems of adolescence. Using the steps in the revision process in this chapter as a guide, write a paragraph outlining which parts of the draft would need revising and why.

THE PROBLEMS OF ADOLESCENCE

Adolescents have a lot of problems. They are often unhappy because they feel that they are too old to be children but too young to be adults.

Many adolescents feel that they are treated unfairly by adults. They can get a driver's licence at sixteen, but they pay higher insurance rates because statistically they are more likely to have an accident. Human rights legislation should protect people from being discriminated against on the basis of age.

Children know that they are supposed to love the things that society has created especially for them. These things include television programmes like <u>Sesame Street</u> and <u>Mr. Rogers</u>, anything with a Walt Disney character on it, and songs like "Alligator Pie."

Adolescents create their own world with its own food, books, movies, and television programmes. They have their own rigid standards for dress. You have to wear exactly the right kind of jeans. Jeans are such a status symbol in Russia that they sell for hundreds of dollars on the black market. Teens don't trust anyone their age who fails to conform or anyone outside their age group.

Adults, on the whole, have an unfavourable image of adolescents. They think all adolescents are clumsy, sullen, rebellious, selfish, lazy, and irresponsible. Some teens work to help support themselves or their families, and some are volunteers. A friend of mine coaches a hockey team of six- and seven-year-olds. None of the adults in the community would help with the team. Adolescents must get the consent of their parents before they can marry, and they cannot vote until they are eighteen.

So you can see that adolescents have a lot of problems. Maybe all we can do about it is wait for them to grow up!

F. Write a first draft of an essay for which you have completed the preparation process. Choose a topic from the exercises in Chapter 3 or 4 (on smoking, Mandel's poem "Houdini," or Buckler's story "Penny in the Dust"), or use another topic you have been assigned. Check and revise your draft according to the suggestions made in this chapter.

Chapter 6

Final Editing

In the previous chapter you saw how to revise the first draft of an essay in order to improve its structure and development. The next stage in the process of revision is that of final editing: checking your essay for tone and diction, sentence structure, grammar, punctuation, and format. You may find that you eliminate some problems in these areas as you revise your first draft. Good writers, however, invariably give their work a final polishing because they know that even small mistakes in expression can ruin the effect of a well-constructed essay.

To make these final revisions, you obviously need to know what to look for. We will therefore begin by setting out a Checklist for Final Editing that will alert you to the most common problems. This checklist is keyed to the sections of the handbook so that you can easily find explanations and examples of specific kinds of revisions. In the next part of this chapter we will briefly show how you might use this checklist to identify and make changes in an actual sample draft: the revised draft of the essay on *The Stone Angel* from Chapter 5.

When you do final editing, you are not merely concerned with correcting errors; you also consider whether you can make your writing more concise and more precise, and thus communicate your ideas more effectively. So that you can judge for yourself the improvement in quality that this stage of revision makes possible, we conclude the chapter with the final draft of the essay on *The Stone Angel*.

CHECKLIST FOR FINAL EDITING

Each question represents a summary of matters discussed in the designated section of the handbook. Common marking symbols are indicated in parentheses.

HANDBOOK SECTION **1**

TONE

Is my tone appropriate for the subject and reader of my essay?

(*P Add*) Have I used appropriate pronouns of address for referring to myself, my subject, and my reader?

(*Dic*) Is my diction appropriate in level, clear in connotation, and correct in meaning?

HANDBOOK SECTION **2**

SENTENCE PROBLEMS

Are my sentences grammatically complete and structurally unambiguous?

(*Frag*) Are there any sentence fragments?
(*cs*) Are there any comma splices?
(*R-O*) Are there any run-on sentences?
(*MM, DM*) Are there any misplaced or dangling modifiers?
(*Mix*) Are there any mixed constructions?
(*//ism*) Is there any faulty parallelism?

HANDBOOK SECTION **3**

SENTENCE EFFECTIVENESS

Are my sentences concise, varied, and effectively linked?

(*Rep*) Have I eliminated wordy constructions and unnecessary repetition from my sentences and paragraphs?

(*Emph*) Have I altered sentence patterns to distinguish among main points, explanations, and details?

(*Trans*) Do I use words, phrases or clauses to provide transitions and to maintain continuity?

HANDBOOK SECTION **4**

VERBS

Are my verbs correct in regard to agreement, tense, and voice?

(*Agr*) Does each verb agree with its subject?
(*Tense*) Are there any unnecessary shifts in tense?
(*Pass*) Have I used the passive voice unnecessarily?

HANDBOOK SECTION **5**

PRONOUNS

Is my use of pronouns consistent, correct, and clear?

(*P Shift*) Are there unnecessary shifts in pronouns of address?
(*P Agr*) Are there errors in pronoun agreement?
(*P Ref*) Are there problems with ambiguous pronoun reference?

HANDBOOK SECTION **6**

PUNCTUATION

Is my punctuation a correct and reliable
guide to my meaning?

(˄, ⁄) Have I used **commas** to separate independent clauses and items in a series (list)? Have I used **commas** to set off from a sentence's main clause all the clauses, phrases, modifiers, and other expressions not essential to its meaning?
(˄; ⁄) Have I used **semicolons** to separate independent clauses not joined by a conjunction?
(˄: ⁄) Have I used **colons** to introduce an expansion of what has already been said?
(˄() ⁄) Have I used **parentheses** to enclose non-essential explanatory material?
(⌒ ⁄) Have I used **dashes** to set off interruptions in thought or sentence structure?
(˄" ⁄) Have I used **quotation marks** for direct speech, quotations from a text if not indented, and titles of works contained within larger works?

(△   ⟋) Have I used **italics** (underlining) for titles of separately published works and for foreign words or phrases?

HANDBOOK SECTION **7**

SPELLING AND CAPITALIZATION

Is my spelling, use of apostrophes, and capitalization correct?

(Sp) Have I checked my **spelling** to eliminate careless errors, common misspellings, and non-Canadian spellings?

(Apos) Have I used **apostrophes** to indicate contractions and possessives?

(Cap) Have I used **capitalization** to distinguish proper nouns from common nouns?

HANDBOOK SECTION **8**

QUOTATIONS

Have I used quotations effectively to support and illustrate my points?

(Quot) Am I right to quote rather than to explain or to paraphrase?

(Quot) Are my quotations introduced effectively?

(Quot) Are my quotations precise, accurate, and set out in the appropriate format for long or short quotations from prose, poetry, or drama?

HANDBOOK SECTION **9**

FOOTNOTES AND BIBLIOGRAPHY

Have I used footnote and bibliographical references accurately to indicate references to ideas, information, and words from other sources?

(Source?) Have I used a footnote or endnote to identify the source of every idea, piece of information, or sequence of words that is neither my own nor common knowledge?

(⨍oot) Have I set out my footnotes or endnotes according to an accepted format?

(Bib) Have I set out my bibliography according to an accepted format?

HANDBOOK SECTION **10**

ESSAY FORMAT

Is my essay set out in the appropriate general format?

(EF) Have I followed conventions as to paper, ink, spacing, margins, page numbering, and presentation?

(EF) Does my title page contain the required information, presented in an appropriate format?

THE PROCESS OF FINAL EDITING: EDITING A SAMPLE DRAFT

The best way to use the Checklist for Final Editing is to refer to the questions as you go through your revised draft. Each time you find a possible problem, mark it with the appropriate correction symbol. When you finish, check the handbook section to see what the problem is and how to correct it, and then make your revisions. Here is the revised draft of the essay on *The Stone Angel* from the previous chapter, marked with correction symbols. Explanations and revisions of selected problems, indicated by the correction symbol, appear after the essay.

Second Draft

EF   The Stone Angel

The narrative structure of The Stone Angel consists

of a series of shifts between the present and the past

in which the narrator and main character Hagar Shipley, Pn

Pn   who is now ninety describes her past and her present

life. The novel begins with a description of the stone an-

gel Hagar's father had placed over her mother's grave,

P Ref   who had died at her birth. Immediately following is a   Pn

Tense   passage in which Hagar described herself as a girl walk-

ing through the cemetery outside the small prairie town

of Manawaka where she grew up. The images, diction,

and tone used in the passage seem to (me) to set up a con- **P Add**
flict between two opposite approaches to life which (I)
will describe as deadening respectability and emotional
responsiveness. The conflict between these two approaches dominates the novel. (I) think this passage describing Hagar walking through the cemetery is
important because Hagar's inability to resolve this conflict between deadening respectability and emotional
responsiveness illustrates (the theme of the novel as a **Rep**
whole. This theme) is that the values that shape our early
lives continue to govern us despite our desire for some-
Middle thing different.

Paragraph 1: The conflict between respectability and responsiveness is evident in this passage in the images used to
describe the setting.

Quot   But sometimes through the hot rush of disrespectful
wind that shook the scrub oak and the coarse couchgrass encroaching upon the dutifully cared-for habitations of the dead, the scent of cowslips would rise
momentarily. They were tough-rooted, these wild and
gaudy flowers, and although they were held back at
the cemetery's edge, torn out by loving relatives
determined to keep the plots clear and clearly civi-
Source? lized ... (p. 5).

Dic   (It could hardly be more obvious) that Laurence intends us
to see that the cemetery represents the life of deadening
respectability, and the wilderness (wind, scrub oak,
couchgrass, cowslips) represents the potential for a freer
Cap life, one like that of the (c)ree who in the younger Hagar's
imagination had walked "with enigmatic faces and greasy
hair" through the place where she now walks.

Rep   Laurence shows us the conflict these images set up
Trans is an internal conflict that Hagar experiences in her first
description of her meeting with Bram Shipley:

Quot   We spun around the chalky floor, and I reveled in his
fingernails with crescents of ingrown earth that

never met a file. I fancied I heard in his laughter the bravery of battalions. I thought he looked a bearded Indian, so brown and beaked a face. The black hair thrusting from his chin was rough as thistles. The next instant, though, I imagined him rigged out in a suit of gray soft as a dove's breastfeathers (p. 45).

mix   One of the reasons their marriage fails is because Hagar cannot accept Bram's limitations; she cannot ac-   *CS* cept his inability to become the cultured gentleman as well as the wild Indian. Another reason it fails is that she hides her sexual response from Bram, and so cuts herself off from the one way they might have been able to communicate.

The emphasis on clothing as the symbol of respectability is conveyed here by the gray suit, but it is first   *P Ref*
Quot introduced in the cemetery passage: "There could not have been many places to walk primly in those days, on paths, where white kid boots and dangling skirts would not be torn by thistles or put in unseemly disarray" (pp. 4-5). After almost twenty years of marriage, Hagar suddenly realizes how she looks delivering eggs in her older
P Ref son Marvin's cast-off coat. This prompts her to take her younger son John and leave Bram. Yet the conflict between the desire for respectability and the desire for
agr emotional responsiveness remain. Living in Vancouver as Mr. Oatley's housekeeper, dressed in her black uni-
Quot form, "I never thought of Bram in the days any more, but I'd waken, sometimes, out of a half sleep and turn to him and find he wasn't beside me, and then I'd be filled with such a bitter emptiness it seemed the whole of night must be within me and not around or outside at all" (p. 160). Hagar has the orderliness and respectability she says she wants and yet "the image of Bram's heavy manhood" (p. 160) remains a disturbing memory.

As the language of the passage describing the ceme-
Pn tery suggests, however, Hagar never gives up the deeply   *Sp*

ingrained middle-class values that the cemetery represents. The many multi-syllable words ("unseemly," "disarray," "habitations," "encroaching," "enigmatic") and
the long, complex sentences illustrate Hagar's attempts
to understand and control her experience through language. But language is also an important tool in maintaining her sense of superiority. Initially, Hager finds **Sp**
Bram's coarse speech attractive; later it becomes a source **Pn**
of annoyance. Hagar's snobbery about language also becomes a means to avoid contact with her older son. An
example of this is where Marvin, eager for her approval, **mix**
announces, "I brought them long pieces from the new
Quot woodpile," and Hagar says, "And for pity's sake say <u>those</u>
pieces, not <u>them</u>" (p. 113). Although Hagar never gives
up these values, she never totally accepts them either.
Marvin, as we come to see, is a much better example of
middle-class values than his rebellious brother John, but
Hagar prefers John and dismisses Marvin as a "Shipley
through and through" (p. 64).

Hagar's inability to resolve this conflict is foreshadowed by the critical, detached tone of the cemetery passage. As a narrator, she seems contemptuous of the girl
who was anxious "to be neat and orderly." The girl who **frag**
imagined "that life had been created only to celebrate
tidiness" (p. 5). On the other hand, her description of the
wilderness with its disrespectful wind, encroaching scrub
oak, coarse couchgrass, and dust-tinged cowslips that **Rep**
smell like musk suggest that the wilderness is disres- **agr**
pectful, hard to control, unclean, and musky (a word that
suggests animals and mating). These words make the
wilderness seem equally unattractive. Because the em-
mix phasis falls on the Crees' "greasy hair" suggests that Hagar will finally not be able to surrender herself to the
values that the wilderness represents. When she is in the
hospital, dying, the minister sings a hymn that makes
her realize, "I must always, always have wanted that—

simply to rejoice" (p. 292). But because she has denied her opportunities to respond to the world, she has become a bitter, critical old woman.

Hagar's emotional isolation, which results from her inability to resolve the conflict between respectability and responsiveness, suggests that we may not be able to escape from the values that have formed us, even though we are aware of their limitations. The images and symbols Lawrence uses to describe the setting and to characterize Hagar in this early passage makes us aware of the values she swings between throughout the novel. Her need for respectability, conveyed in this passage by her concern for her clothes, is stronger than her dream of a freer emotional life. The educated, controlled language and critical, detached tone show that she could not accept herself therefore she could not really accept anyone else or any set of values. So the passage describing her younger self walking through the cemetery foreshadows the concerns of the novel as a whole.

Comments on the Revisions

HANDBOOK SECTION **1**

TONE

Is my tone appropriate for the subject and reader of my essay?

For the most part, the tone seems to be about right—I sound like one reasonable person speaking to another. In a couple of places, however, I sound too apologetic or too assertive.

(*P add*) I could improve the introduction, for example, by removing the references to myself. Using three first-person pronouns in one paragraph diverts attention from my subject.

(*Dic*) I could also improve the tone of the first middle paragraph by taking out the phrase "It could hardly be more obvious." I need to give evidence to support my point, not merely to assert that it is obvious.

HANDBOOK SECTION **2**

SENTENCE PROBLEMS

Are my sentences grammatically complete and structurally unambiguous?

(Frag) The third sentence in my fifth middle paragraph ("The girl who imagined . . .") is a sentence fragment, since there is no main verb. I will correct the error by attaching this fragment to the previous sentence, so that it reads like this:

> As narrator she seems contemptuous of the girl who was "anxious to be neat and orderly" and who imagined "that life had been created only to celebrate tidiness."

(CS) In my second middle paragraph, I have used just a comma to join two independent clauses in the sentence immediately after the long quotation ("Hagar cannot accept Bram's limitations, she cannot accept his inability . . ."). It would be simple to correct this error by putting a semicolon or a period between the clauses, but I can achieve greater conciseness by eliminating the repetition:

> Their marriage fails, in large part, because Hagar cannot accept Bram's limitations, his inability to become the cultured gentleman as well as the wild Indian.

(Mix) In my fifth middle paragraph, the sentence about the "Crees' 'greasy hair'" starts with a dependent clause ("Because the emphasis falls . . .") and then continues as though I were writing the main clause (". . . suggests that"). To make the structure of this sentence clear, I'll take out the dependent clause and rewrite the main clause: "The emphasis on the Crees' 'greasy hair' suggests . . . ."

HANDBOOK SECTION **3**

SENTENCE EFFECTIVENESS

Are my sentences concise, varied, and effectively linked?

(Rep) My draft seems wordy and repetitious in a number of places, notably in the opening sentence to my second middle paragraph. First, this sentence is repetitious; if the conflict is internal, then of course Hagar must experience it. Second, my wordiness makes it unclear whether Laurence or Hagar is describing the meeting with Bram. To be more concise, I will have to clarify my point. Since my point is that the images in the cemetery passage are used elsewhere to describe a conflict in Hagar herself, I will rewrite my sentence like this:

> The repetition of these images from the cemetery passage in Hagar's description of her first meeting with Bram Shipley emphasizes their function as symbols of Hagar's internal conflict.

(*Trans*) My revision of this sentence also makes it a more effective **transition** from the previous paragraph. The original sentence did not make clear that the "internal conflict" was a development from the externally conflicting images in the cemetery scene; now this connection is quite clear.

HANDBOOK SECTION **4**

VERBS

Are my verbs correct in regard to agreement, tense, and voice?

(*agr*) There is an error in subject-verb agreement in my third middle paragraph. The subject of the fourth sentence is "conflict," and so the verb should be "remains."

(*tense*) There is a slip in verb tense in the introduction. In writing about texts, I should use the present tense unless there is a good reason for using another tense. "Hagar described herself as a girl . . ." should therefore be "Hagar describes herself as a girl. . . ."

HANDBOOK SECTION **5**

PRONOUNS

Is my use of pronouns consistent, correct, and clear?

(*P Ref*) My main problem with pronouns is that I have used several that do not clearly refer to a specific noun. In the introduction, for instance, the "who" in "who died at her birth" should refer to Hagar's mother, but instead it seems to refer to her mother's grave. Similarly, "it" in the opening sentence of the third middle paragraph appears to refer to "gray suit," but really refers to clothing as a symbol. In the third sentence of the same paragraph, I need to make clear that "this" refers to Hagar's sudden realization of how she looks delivering eggs. I can correct these problems either by moving the pronoun closer to the noun or by rewriting to leave out the pronoun. I need to check the rest of this draft carefully to make sure every pronoun refers to a specific noun.

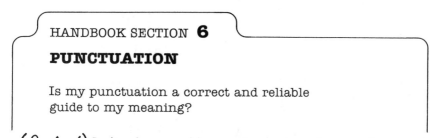

HANDBOOK SECTION **6**

PUNCTUATION

Is my punctuation a correct and reliable guide to my meaning?

(Pn ⌃ ⁄) I often have problems using **commas** because I am confused about which modifiers or other expressions are essential to the meaning and which are not. Looking carefully at the first sentence of my introduction, I can see that when I identify the narrator and main character as "Hagar Shipley who is now ninety," I am giving additional information, and so I should set off both the name and the clause with commas. In the third sentence ("Immediately following, is a passage . . .") I have used a comma to separate essential elements, and so I will take it out. I will need to check my use of commas throughout the draft.

(Pn ⌃) I have used a semicolon before "however" in the first sentence of middle paragraph 4. But I see now that the first half of the sentence is a dependent clause, not an independent clause. I should therefore use a comma instead of a semicolon.

HANDBOOK SECTION **7**

SPELLING AND CAPITALIZATION

Is my spelling, use of apostrophes, and capitalization correct?

(Sp)   I see that I have carelessly misspelled the author's name in the conclusion and the main character's name in the fourth middle paragraph.

(Cap)   In my first middle paragraph I need to capitalize "cree," since this is the proper name of a tribe.

HANDBOOK SECTION **8**

QUOTATIONS

Have I used quotations effectively to support and illustrate my points?

(Quot) From checking the handbook, I can see that my use of quotations in the draft could be improved considerably. For example, the long quotation in my first middle paragraph is ineffective. I need to quote here to show that the conflict between respectability and responsiveness is conveyed through Laurence's choice of particular words and their connotations. But I need to pick out and explain which terms convey each side of this conflict, rather than expecting the reader to pick them out of my long quotation. So I should use a mixture of quotation, summary, and explanation. For example, I can describe the cemetery as a symbol of respectability as follows:

> The plots, described as the "dutifully cared-for habitations of the dead," are kept "clear and clearly civilized" by "loving relatives" determined to maintain order and respectability....

I will check my use of quotations in the rest of the draft in the same way, to see if I am using quotations to support my points, rather than relying on quotations to make my points for me.

HANDBOOK SECTION **9**

FOOTNOTES AND BIBLIOGRAPHY

Have I used footnote and bibliographical references accurately to indicate references to ideas, information, and words from other sources?

(Source?) Because I am using only one text, I was not sure whether to footnote every quotation or whether to put the page numbers in parentheses after the quotation. According to the handbook, I should use a blanket note giving full bibliographical information the first time I quote, and thereafter put page numbers in parentheses in the body of my essay. I'll add the note to the end of the first sentence in which I quote from the text.

HANDBOOK SECTION **10**

ESSAY FORMAT

Is my essay set out in the appropriate general format?

(E F)   I'm not satisfied with my title since it gives the reader no indication of what my essay is about. I should use a short form of my thesis for my title. Since my main point is about the conflict between conventional respectability and emotional responsiveness both in the passage and in the novel as a whole, I'll title my essay "The Conflict Between Respectability and Responsiveness in *The Stone Angel.*"

WRITING THE FINAL ESSAY

This is the essay that results from the revisions outlined above and other revisions made as a result of using the Checklist for Final Editing.

The Conflict Between Respectability and Responsiveness in
The Stone Angel

The narrative structure of The Stone Angel consists of a series of shifts between the past and the present in which the narrator and main character, Hagar Shipley, now ninety, describes her past and present life. The novel begins with a description of the stone angel her father had placed over the grave of her mother, who had died at Hagar's birth. Immediately following is a passage in which Hagar describes herself as a girl walking through the cemetery outside the small prairie town of Manawaka where she grew up. The images, diction, and tone used in this passage to describe the setting and to characterize Hagar set up the conflict between deadening respectability and emotional responsiveness that dominates the novel. Hagar's inability to resolve this conflict illustrates the theme of the novel as a whole: that the values that shape our early lives continue to govern us, despite our desire for something different.

The conflict between respectability and responsiveness is evident in this passage in the images used to describe the setting. The cemetery represents the life of deadening respectability. The plots, described as "the dutifully cared-for habitations of the dead," are kept "clear and clearly civilized" by "loving relatives" determined to maintain order and respectability, both out of duty and out of a desire to subdue the wilderness they have settled.[1] The "portly peonies" they have planted are contrasted with the gaudy, dust-tinged, musky, tough-rooted cowslips they ruthlessly tear out. The cowslips are one image of the wilderness and the enlivening responsiveness it represents. Other images are those of the encroaching scrub oak and coarse couchgrass, the disrespectful wind, and the Cree who in the younger Hagar's imagination had walked "with enigmatic faces and greasy hair" through the place where she now walks.

The repetition of these images from the cemetery passage in Hagar's description of her first meeting with Bram Shipley emphasizes their function as symbols of Hagar's internal conflict. When, after three years of serving tea to her father's friends and avoiding any contact with unworthy suitors, Hagar meets Bram at a dance, he seems to offer a way of escape from deadening respectability. Images from the cemetery passage are used to convey Hagar's romantic notion that through Bram she could have both the danger and excitement of the wilderness and the gentility of "civilized" life, without the limitations of either:

> We spun around the chalky floor, and I reveled in his fingernails with crescents of ingrown earth that never met a file. I fancied I heard in his laughter the bravery of battalions. I thought he looked a bearded Indian, so brown and beaked a face. The black hair thrusting from his chin was rough as thistles. The next instant, though, I imagined him rigged out in a suit of gray soft as a dove's breastfeathers (p. 45).

Their marriage fails, in large part, because Hagar cannot accept Bram's limitations, his inability to become the cultured gentleman as well as the wild Indian.

The emphasis on dress as the symbol of respectability, conveyed here by the gray suit, is first introduced in the cemetery passage. Explaining why she chose to walk in the cemetery, Hagar comments, "There could not have been many places to walk primly in those days, on paths, where white kid boots and dangling skirts would not be torn by thistles or put in unseemly disarray." After almost twenty years of marriage, it is Hagar's realization of how she looks, delivering eggs in her older son Marvin's cast-off coat, that prompts her to take her younger son, John, and leave Bram. Yet the conflict between the desire for respectability and the desire for emotional

---

[1] Margaret Laurence, The Stone Angel (Toronto: McClelland and Stewart, 1964), pp. 4-5. All other quotations, unless identified by page number in the text, are from this passage.

responsiveness remains, for when she is living in Vancouver as Mr. Oatley's housekeeper, dressed in her black uniform, she bitterly misses "Bram's heavy manhood" (p. 160).

As the language of the passage suggests, however, Hagar never gives up the deeply ingrained middle-class values that the cemetery represents. The many multi-syllable words ("unseemly," "disarray," "habitations," "encroaching," "enigmatic") and the long, complex sentences illustrate Hagar's attempts to understand and control her experience through language. But language is also an important tool in maintaining class distinctions. Initially, Hagar finds Bram's coarse speech attractive; later it becomes a source of constant annoyance. Hagar's snobbery about language also becomes a means to avoid emotional contact with her older son. When Marvin, eager for approval, announces, "I brought them long pieces from the new woodpile," Hagar ignores his emotional needs and concentrates on correcting his grammar: " . . . say <u>those</u> pieces, not <u>them</u>" (p. 113). Although Hagar never gives up these values, she never totally accepts them either. Marvin, as we come to see, is a much better example of middle-class values than his rebellious brother John; but Hagar dismisses Marvin as a "Shipley through and through" (p. 64).

Hagar's inability to resolve this conflict between respectability and emotional responsiveness is foreshadowed by the critical, detached tone of the cemetery passage. As narrator she seems contemptuous of the girl who was "anxious to be neat and orderly" and who imagined "that life had been created only to celebrate tidiness." On the other hand, her description of the wilderness as disrespectful, controlled only with great difficulty, unclean, and musky (a word that suggests animals and mating) makes this alternative seem equally unattractive. The emphasis on the Crees' "greasy hair" suggests that Hagar will finally not be able to surrender herself to the values the wilderness represents.

Hagar's emotional isolation, which results from her inability to resolve the conflict between respectability and responsiveness, suggests that we may not be able to escape from the values that have formed us, even though we are aware of their limitations. The images and symbols Laurence uses to describe the setting and to characterize Hagar in this early passage make us aware of the values she alternates between throughout the novel. Her need for respectability, conveyed in this passage by her concern for her clothes, is stronger than her dream of a freer emotional life. The educated, controlled language and critical, detached tone show that she cannot accept herself. As a consequence, she is never really able to accept anyone else or any set of values. The passage describing her younger self walking through the cemetery thus foreshadows the concerns of the novel as a whole.

EXERCISE

Use the Checklist for Final Editing to identify necessary revisions in
the following essay, and then make as many of these revisions as
you can. Consult the appropriate handbook section if you need help.

<u>"Black Orpheus"</u>

    In this essay, I am going to discuss the meaning of the
visual imagery in the film "Black Orpheus" (<u>Orfeo Negro</u>). It
was made in 1958 and it was directed by Marcel Camus[1]. It is
a modern-day treatment of the myth of Orpheus and Eurydice.
This was originally a Greek myth. According to this myth,
Orpheus was a terrific lyre player. He married his wife Eurydice who was a Dryad. Dryads were wood nympths. After the
marriage, Eurydice, when she was fleeing from the unwelcome
attentions of Aristaeus, who was the god of husbandry, stepped
on a snake, was bitten, and died. Orpheus, who was nearly
out of his mind with grief, followed Eurydice into Hades. Hades
being the greek word for the underworld containing both
heaven and hell. He used his music to persuade Persephone
who was the goddess of the underworld to let Eurydice go.
Persephone agree, but she made Orpheus promise that he
would not look back as she followed him to the world of the
living. Orpheus looked back and Eurydice was lost to him forever. Through its visual images, the film makes this pattern
of death and rebirth clearer and emphasizes its psychological
meaning. The film achieves its effects primarily through visual
images that lift the events of the plot from the world of reality
to the world of myth.

    The film is set in modern Rio. It takes place during the
three days (a symbolic number I think) of preparation for,
celebrating, and the period in which the city recovers from
the Carnival which turns the whole city into a swirling phan-
tasmagoria (sort of like a magic lantern show in which
there are alot of optical allusions in which things seem to
change size and blend into each other) of surrealistic-type
images. The main characters of the film, "Black Orpheus," are
Orfeu, a bus driver who plays a guitar and who is to be the
Sun King in the dance his barrio is preparing for the carnival.
There are also Mira, his brassy fiancee, who is to be Queen of
the Day and Eurydice, a peasant girl. Eurydice comes to her
cousin who lives in Rio because she is trying to escape from a
man who is trying to kill her and she takes her cousins place
in the dance as the Queen of the Night. The events in the
film symbolize Orfeu's coming to consciousness through his
love for Eurydice.

---

[1]Camus, Marcel, dir. Orfeu Negro/Black Orpheus (New Cinema,
1958).

The opening scene at the beginning of the film is a symbolic foreshadowing of what is to follow. Benedetto, a young boy who becomes Eurydice's guardian spirit, is flying a yellow kite from a cliff. The cliff overlooks the harbour. As the kite rises and then falls towards the water, you see Eurydice coming into the harbour. An example of the visual imagery in the film is that the yellow kite is a visual image of Orfeu in his role as the Sun King in the festival and we also see him causing the sun to rise by playing on his guitar everyday. Throughout the film you see that Orfeu is completely immersed and submerged in his collective identity because he is aware that there was an Orfeu before him and that there will be an Orfeu after him. It is only in the brief speech which he makes before the stones of his angry fiancee knock him off of the cliff where he falls to his death below that you could see that a new awareness of himself as an individual was born in him through his love for Eurydice.

Eurydice is the anima or soul figure who comes to him upon the waters of the unconscious. An example of how this is visually represented in the film is when she crosses the harbour in the boat. She is the anima as spiritual guide. Her simple white dress and her braids make her stand out among the city dwellers with their surface polish. When the crowds around her seem posessed with the holiday spirit—an affect Camus emphasizes with the insistent rhythms of the dance dominating the sound track and often the scene and there is a blur of bodies which emphasizes the lack of differentiation within and among people. Eurydice remains self-possessed.

The viewer knows that Eurydice is an anima figure because Orfeu is so fascinated by her. After their first brief meeting on the bus, his eyes follow her even as his fiancee talks to him about getting married and when he is in the marriage office and he discovers from a chance remark by the clerk that "Orpheus love Eurydice because that is the story" that he feels impeled to be with her, dancing with her, and finally he rescues her when she is frightened by the appearance of the man (appropriately dressed as death) from whom she had fled to the city in the first place. Their love is consummated amid all the symbols of rebirth in Orfeus shack. Their is a cock, a puppy, and various other animals. It is during this evening, the night before the carnival, that Eurydice gives Orfeu her scarf bearing the signs of the houses of the zodiac. This scarf identifies her house as that of the Ram, which as we know is the symbol of the rising sun. It is Orefeu's house as well. This constellation further identifies the carnival as the spring festival of rebirth.

The conflict between the Queen of the Day and the Queen of the Night for Orfeu culminates when Mira discovers that

Eurydice has taken her cousins place as the Queen of the Night in the dance. She reveals this fact to the man dressed as death. Chased by death, Eurydice makes it to the bus terminal, the end of the line for her, and the shots of her under the streetcar tracks are another example of how Camus visually represents the underworld to us. In the chase, Eurydice looses the lucky charm given to her by Benedetto and it is crushed underfoot by the dancers. This is a clear signal of her fate. However, it is not death who kills her but Orfeu, who then searches for her in the modern-day equivalents of the under-world, the hospital, the Missing Person's Bureau, which is located in a skyscraper filled with scraps of useless paper, and finally he is led to the cemetery which is guarded by a german shepherd which you recognize as a representation of Cerberus, the dog with three heads who guarded the gates of hell accord-ing to mythology. In the film, the dog is called Cerberus. Open-ing a door in the wall of the cemetery that leads him into a small chapel, a man tells him that Eurydice will answer if he calls. When she replies, he disobeys the order he had been given before by his guide not to turn around. When he turns around he sees an old woman talking in her voice. Finally Orfeu accepts the fact that Eurydice is dead and he claims her body from the morgue. Carrying it through the streets to the cliff and there meeting his own death.

However, we see that Orfeu's descent into the underworld (ie. his subconsciousness) has not been in vane. His final speech demonstrates that he can now seperate his ability to think from the mass of sensations and feelings in which he has always before this time lived. What he says subtly trans-forms the film into a political film. He tells us that he and his poor working class friends work hard all year and then spend all their money on costumes for the carnival. Although they dance, and sing, and generally have a great time, their living conditions (ie. poverty) and their ways of life remain the same because they like the awareness to change these condi-tions or even to see that they should be changed.

The film does not insist on this point. Instead it reaffirms the cycle of death and rebirth as Benedetto urges his young friend, who was Orfeu's apprentice, to play the guitar so that the sun will rise. Thus we can see that Orfeu is reborn as the new Eurydice dances to his music and the eternal cycle con-tinues over and over.

PART 2

Preparing and Writing: Special Types of Essays

Chapter 7

Preparing to Write: Making Comparisons

There's an old saying that you can't compare apples with oranges. But old sayings are not necessarily true.

You could, in fact, learn a great deal by comparing apples and oranges. First, you would pay much more attention than usual to the particular features of the two fruits: their similarities or differences in size, shape, texture, smell, taste. Second, you would learn something about "fruitness," that is, the characteristics that fruits share.

The things you compare in college and university courses will probably be more complex than apples and oranges. In making these comparisons, however, you will have the same goal: to understand more clearly (1) the similarities and differences between individual things, and (2) the general category to which the things belong.

Topics for comparison essays in your college and university courses may look like these:

SOCIAL ANTHROPOLOGY 101
On the basis of material presented in your textbook, compare the social organization of the !Kung San and Mutayr.

ENGLISH 100
Compare the Raymond Souster poems "The Cry" and "Killing a Bat."
Discuss the attitudes towards the imagination in two of the following essays: Isaac Asimov's "The Eureka Phenomenon," Carl Sagan's "The Abstraction of Beasts," Jacob Bronowski's "The Reach of the Imagination."

MECHANICAL ENGINEERING 210
How are the principles of solar heating systems similar to/different from the principles of geothermal heating systems?

ECONOMICS 233
Discuss 'supply-side' economics in the context of another economic theory covered in this course.

> HISTORY 275
> Compare and contrast the accounts of the clash between the U.S. Cavalry and the Northern Cheyenne Indians at Dull Knife's village in 1876 as presented in Ernest Wallace's *Ranald S. Mackenzie on the Texas Frontier* and Dee Brown's *Bury My Heart at Wounded Knee*.
>
> SOCIOLOGY 150
> How have sexual stereotypes in the mass media changed since the beginning of the Women's Movement?
>
> POLITICAL SCIENCE 214
> Compare the U.S. and Soviet positions in the negotiations over nuclear arms control.
> How did the political organization of Athens differ from that of Sparta?

As we pointed out in Chapter 2, the comparison essay is a special form of the analysis essay. Instead of dividing one thing into its parts, you divide two or more things into matching parts and then determine the meaning of their similarities and differences. In this chapter we will first examine the general principles involved in preparing to write comparison essays. Then we will look at two common types of assignments involving comparison: (1) comparing texts and (2) comparing sets of data.

BASIC QUESTIONS AND PROCEDURES FOR MAKING COMPARISONS

Here is a list of the most important questions for preparing comparison essays. For a full list of preparation questions, see Chapters 3 and 4.

Step 1

CLARIFYING THE TOPIC

Do I understand the directions the topic gives me?

A. Am I asked to analyze, to compare, or to evaluate?

Topics for comparison generally ask you to compare, to compare and contrast, or to discuss similarities and differences between two or more things. Comparison always asks you to take into account both similarities and differences, whether or not the topic says so explicitly. Some topics may ask you to compare when the instructor wants you to evaluate as well as to compare. If you are unsure, ask your instructor.

B. Does this topic require comparison of content or comparison of texts?

Comparisons of content ask you to compare causes, effects, or features of an event, a concept, a theory, or a set of data. Comparisons of texts ask you to compare two or more works or performances or to compare specific features in two or more works or performances. In the topics at the beginning of this chapter, three require textual comparison: the comparison of two poems by Souster, the comparison of two essays, and the comparison of two historical accounts. The others call for comparison of content.

C. Is the basis of comparison given?

Topics that can be put in the form "Compare X and Y in terms of Z" specify the basis of comparison. The basis of comparison, Z, tells you which features of the things you are comparing are relevant, and thus gives you a focus for gathering material and writing your essay. Most of the sample topics at the beginning of the chapter specify a basis of comparison: social organization in two cultures; attitudes towards the imagination in two essays; principles of two heating systems; the positions of U.S. and Soviet negotiators.

If the basis of comparison is not given, you may want to establish one before you begin the preparation process. Otherwise, you may find that you are trying to cover too much ground, particularly if you are writing a short paper on a large subject. For example, you might limit the topic "Discuss supply-side economics in the context of another economic theory covered in this course" by using as your basis of comparison a key issue such as government debt or taxes. Before you limit a topic this way, however, check with your instructor to make sure you will not be reducing your coverage unacceptably. Then follow the suggestions for narrowing topics in Chapter 2.

If you are unsure about an appropriate basis of comparison, begin by gathering as much material as possible. The first sample topic below will show you how to use your material to arrive at a basis of comparison.

Do I know what kind of material to use in my essay?

The main question at this point is whether or not your topic requires research. If it does, make sure that you collect equivalent information for each of the things you are comparing. You will find an example of preparing to write a research paper on a comparison topic in Chapter 11.

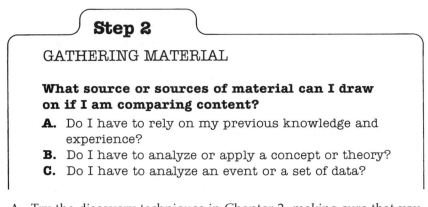

Step 2

GATHERING MATERIAL

What source or sources of material can I draw on if I am comparing content?

A. Do I have to rely on my previous knowledge and experience?

B. Do I have to analyze or apply a concept or theory?

C. Do I have to analyze an event or a set of data?

A. Try the discovery techniques in Chapter 2, making sure that you generate the same kind of information for all the subjects you are comparing.

B. Review discussions of the concept or theory in your class notes, textbook, or other reference material. Check to see whether the concept or theory is used in the same way by each writer. If you need to generate your own examples to illustrate the concept or theory, use the discovery techniques in Chapter 2.

C. Collect information from appropriate sources: textbooks, reference materials, interviews, questionnaires, experiments. Make sure that you have matching information for each of the things you are comparing. Otherwise you will have nothing to compare.

What source or sources of material can I draw on if I am comparing texts?

A. What is my main source of information and ideas?

B. Do I need additional material?

A. As in all textual analysis, your main source of information and ideas will be the written works or performances themselves. Make sure you ask the same questions about each of the works you are comparing.

B. Consult dictionaries and specialized reference books as necessary. If your topic requires research, look for books and articles that address a similar range of issues about each text. For an essay on Dickens' treatment of women in *David Copperfield* and *Bleak House,* for example, you would likely find two discussions of Dickens' techniques of characterization more useful than one article giving a Freudian interpretation of the role of women in *David Copperfield* and one article giving a Marxist interpretation of the role of women in *Bleak House.*

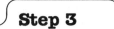

Step 3

CATEGORIZING MATERIAL

What matching categories should I divide my material into?

You will need to end up with your material arranged in matching categories because you can only compare equivalent aspects of your subject.

If you know from the beginning what your categories will be, use parallel columns so that you can easily see the similarities and differences between the things you are comparing. Taking notes this way is particularly easy when you are comparing texts because you can use the appropriate general or special categories of textual analysis. In comparing two stories, for example, you would establish parallel columns for Subject, Narrative Structure, Setting, Characterization, Style (diction, images and symbols, sentence structure), Point of View, Tone, and Theme.

If you are comparing content (events, theories, concepts, or sets of data), you may be less sure about appropriate categories of analysis. In that case, you would first need to categorize information separately for each of the things you are comparing, and then rearrange your material into matching categories. If some of your categories don't match, you will have to decide whether to omit information, find new information, or combine information under a broader category. Since your purpose is to compare, you will have no use for information on one subject that is not matched by information on your other subject or subjects.

You may end up with much more material in your notes than you will need for your essay. You will only know which material is relevant when you have worked out the central likeness or difference between the things you are comparing.

Step 4

FINDING A THESIS

What generalization can I make about the nature of the things I'm comparing?

A. What is my basis of comparison?

If no basis of comparison is specified in your topic, this is the point at which you will need to establish one. Let's suppose you have been asked to compare cigarette ads of the 1960s with present-day cigarette ads. In your initial analysis, you may have discovered differences in graphics, in types of models, and in the attitudes conveyed. When you review your material, however, you may decide that these changes reflect a more basic change in the stereotypes associated with sex roles. You may therefore decide to make sexual stereotyping your basis of comparison.

B. What pattern(s) do I perceive in my material?

Examine your material on each of your subjects in light of your basis of comparison to see what patterns you can identify. In investigating sexual stereotyping in the mass media, for example, you may have decided to focus on magazine advertisements for cigarettes. Your analysis might reveal that in the cigarette ads of the 1960s the graphics, models, and attitudes combine to present a stereotype of men who smoke as strong, handsome, and adventuresome, whereas women who smoke are stereotyped as glamorous and seductive. You would then identify the sexual stereotypes in present-day cigarette ads.

C. What is the central likeness or difference between these patterns?

The patterns you have noted will allow you to make a statement about the basic similarities or differences between your sets of material. Your statement comparing cigarette ads, for example, might be something like this:

> In the cigarette ads of the 1960s, men who smoke are portrayed as strong, handsome, and adventuresome, whereas women who smoke are portrayed as glamorous and seductive. Cigarette ads today continue to use these stereotypes, but they also show women as strong and adventuresome and both men and women as fun-loving and athletic.

> **Why are the things I'm comparing similar or different?**

Complete your thesis by defining the causes, effects, or features that led you to your generalization. The reason(s) you give here will provide the initial support for the opinion you stated in the previous step.

You might complete the thesis about cigarette ads, for example, in one of these ways:

> **Causes**: These changes are a result of changes in our conception of sex roles, changes that cigarette companies have had to respond to in order to appeal to a wide market.
>
> **Effects**: These changes may make smoking seem more acceptable to those who reject traditional sexual stereotyping.
>
> **Features**: These changes are most evident in the slogans and the poses used.

These are the basic steps to follow when you are making comparisons.

SAMPLE TOPICS: MAKING COMPARISONS

In this section you will find two examples of the preparation process for comparison essays: (1) a comparison of two poems (texts); and (2) a comparison of two sets of data (content). These examples demonstrate the efficiency with which you can organize your material and find a thesis for a comparison essay, even if your topic is complex.

Comparing Texts: Two Poems

If you have read Chapter 4 on textual analysis, you should have a good basic understanding of how to analyze texts. When you compare texts, you use the same analytical techniques. You have the additional task, however, of showing how the texts illuminate each other and other texts of the same kind.

To illustrate the steps in preparing to write a comparison essay on two texts, we will use two poems as the objects of comparison. You would use the same procedures for comparing any texts, literary or non-literary, written or performed (plays and films, for example). Only the special categories into which you divide your material would be different.

Let's assume, then, that the instructor in an introductory literature course has spent several class periods analyzing poetry. To see whether you can analyze poems that have not been discussed in class, your instructor has given you this assignment:

> Write a 750-word essay comparing two poems by Raymond Souster, "The Cry" and "Killing a Bat."

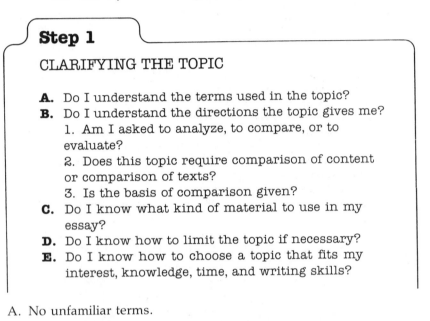

Step 1

CLARIFYING THE TOPIC

A. Do I understand the terms used in the topic?

B. Do I understand the directions the topic gives me?
  1. Am I asked to analyze, to compare, or to evaluate?
  2. Does this topic require comparison of content or comparison of texts?
  3. Is the basis of comparison given?

C. Do I know what kind of material to use in my essay?

D. Do I know how to limit the topic if necessary?

E. Do I know how to choose a topic that fits my interest, knowledge, time, and writing skills?

A. No unfamiliar terms.

B. Comparison of texts (no mention of evaluation). No basis of comparison given. That means I will have to establish one.

C. Poems given. The topic does not mention research and asks for a short essay, so probably no research is required.

D. No need to limit the topic further.

E. No choice. 750-word essay, due next Monday. The poems are short, but I haven't had much practice analyzing poetry, or writing comparison essays, so I'd better allow time to write several drafts of my essay.

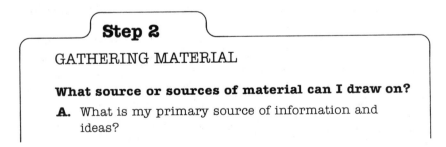

Step 2

GATHERING MATERIAL

What source or sources of material can I draw on?

A. What is my primary source of information and ideas?

These two poems by Raymond Souster:[1]

THE CRY	KILLING A BAT

THE CRY

In the third small hour
from our roof overhead
an almost human cry
4 of bird or animal.

I closed the window hard
against that unearthly scream,
then stood hard-rooted there
until the wail died, freeing
8 blood to run on again,
ears to rewind quietness

So back to bed, finding
all too soon the sleep
'of the righteous
12 and the just',

while for all I knew
something up on that roof
still waited an answer
to its cry.

KILLING A BAT

You don't get rid
of a bat by simply
flushing him swiftly
4 down the nearest toilet:

he'll swoop and swerve
through your head for days,
a torn-loose piece
8 of blackest night,

who was perfectly content
before being roused,
to rest on the curtains
12 of this upstairs room.

But a thing unclean,
unfit to live, to those
who swinging out wildly
16 with soaked towels, attempt

the one thing instinct
hammers in their heads,
kill him, kill:
20 while his wings fight the air

in a hopeless chance
to escape, stay alive.
But there's none, he died,
24 and they die a little too.

B. Do I need additional material?

Both of these poems use a simple vocabulary; neither contains obvious
references to literary, historical, or mythological figures. The phrase
"of the righteous and the just" in "The Cry" is in quotation marks,
and so it must be an allusion to something. There's a saying about
"sleeping the sleep of the righteous"; it sounds biblical, but I don't
know exactly where it comes from. If the source seems important
later on, I'll look for it.

---

[1]Reprinted from *The Evolution of Canadian Literature in English: 1945-70*, ed. Paul
Denham (Toronto and Montreal: Holt, Rinehart and Winston of Canada, 1973),
pp. 129, 130.

Step 3

CATEGORIZING MATERIAL

What matching categories should I divide my material into?

Since we have been studying poetry in class, I should use the special categories for analyzing poetry: Subject; Poetic Structure; Setting; Characterization; Diction; Images and Symbols; Rhythm, Metre, and Patterns of Sound; Speaker's Attitude; and Theme. The topic does not give a basis of comparison, and so I should begin by using all the categories. I will set up matching columns of notes on the poems.

	THE CRY	KILLING A BAT
Subject	Speaker's response to unidentified cry in the night	People's response to discovering bat in house
Structure	Chronological order. Speaker hears the cry in stanza 1; closes window in stanza 2; returns to bed and sleep in stanza 3, speculates that "something ... still waited an answer."	Flashback. Memory of bat emphasized in stanzas 1 & 2; shifts to bat in stanza 3; killing in stanzas 4, 5, & 6; ends with effect on killers
Setting	Bedroom, night-time	Upstairs room (of house?), time not given
Characterization	Cry "almost human"; speaker seems frightened, then relieved to go back to sleep, but still uneasy	Bat described as "perfectly content" before attack, then fighting hopelessly to stay alive; humans panic on finding the bat, feel driven to kill it, but are then haunted by it
Diction	Faintly biblical ("third small hour," "sleep 'of the righteous and the just'")	Ordinary speech except for image of bat; biblical echoes in "a thing unclean"?

Images, Symbols	Combination of night and disembodied cry suggests the unknown, alien	Bat described as "torn-loose piece / of blackest night" (7-8); bats often associated with vampires, madness
Rhythm, Metre, Sound	Free verse; short lines. Is this significant?	Same
Speaker's Attitude	First person ("I"). Tone serious; becomes more emotional in 2nd stanza, distanced in 3rd; ends on note of uncertainty	Second person ("you") suggests a general statement that includes both the speaker and reader. Tone melancholy, as though recalling nightmare; reinforces ending ("they die a little too").
Tentative Theme	Something like "I only look out for myself"	Something like "Killing harms those who do it as well as those who are killed"

Step 4

FINDING A THESIS

What generalization can I make about the nature of the things I'm comparing?
A. What is my basis of comparison?

The themes in the two poems seem similar, and I can explain other aspects of the poems in relation to their themes. I will make the theme my basis of comparison.

B. What pattern(s) do I perceive in my material?
  1. What pattern of conflict does each poem establish between sets of values?
  2. How is the conflict resolved?
  3. What is the theme of the poem?

THE CRY	KILLING A BAT
1. The conflict seems to be between the peace that comes from lack of awareness (sleep) and the pain that comes from awareness of others' distress (cry).	The conflict seems to be between the need to protect oneself from what is "unclean," "unfit to live," and the guilt that comes from doing so.
2. There is no real resolution. The last lines suggest the speaker should have acted differently, but don't say how or why.	No resolution. The line "they die a little too" (24) suggests there's no escaping from the guilt of such an action.
3. Human beings try to shut out others' pain because it frightens them; they nevertheless feel guilty about their unwillingness to help.	The guilt people feel when they destroy something in order to protect themselves can be more harmful than the thing they destroyed.

> **C.** What is the central likeness or difference between
> these patterns?

To compare the themes of these two poems, I must say what their basic similarities or differences are. The themes are more alike than different, because they both stress human guilt. In "The Cry," this guilt comes from failing to act when something or someone is in pain; in "Killing a Bat," this guilt comes from action that causes pain. Can I make a more general statement about theme that will include both poems?

In both poems, the imagery suggests that humans feel isolated from the natural world, which therefore seems alien and frightening. Their guilt suggests they are aware of this isolation and of their failure to show empathy for other living things. Their attempt to protect themselves has the opposite effect, because they "die a little too." To be alienated from nature, then, is to be diminished as a human being. The weight of emotion these poems attach to the characters' seemingly trivial actions may imply that these actions also reflect the way the characters behave towards other human beings.

I could emphasize these similarities by a statement of theme such as this:

> In both poems, Souster suggests that people's attempts to
> protect themselves, both from the natural world and from the
> human world, are self-defeating because those actions increase
> their isolation.

> ### Why are the things I'm comparing similar or different?

Since I am comparing whole poems, with theme as my basis of comparison, I must define the features of the work that led me to my generalization about the theme. If I knew enough about Souster's poetry or contemporary Canadian poetry in general, I could also put these poems into a broader context.

The most relevant categories are those of Structure, Characterization, Images/Symbols, and Speaker's Attitude (point of view and tone). If I show how these features relate to the theme, I will have a thesis for my essay:

> Although the structure and point of view in these two poems are somewhat different, their images, tone and characterization point to similar themes: that people's attempts to protect themselves, both from the natural world and from the human world, are self-defeating because those actions increase their isolation.

Once you have arrived at a thesis, you are ready to write your first draft. You will find suggestions for writing and revising an essay comparing two texts in Chapter 8.

Comparing Content: Two Sets of Data

If you look again at the list of essay topics at the beginning of this chapter, you will see that many of them ask you to compare sets of data. In writing on topics such as the social organization of the !Kung San and the Mutayr, the principles of solar and geothermal heating systems, two economic theories, or the political organization of Athens and Sparta, you would use secondary sources—textbooks or library materials—for the information you need. Your focus is on the information itself, rather than on the way the information is presented by a particular author.

Your purpose, you will recall, is to understand more clearly both the individual things you are comparing and the general category to which they belong. Comparing the political organization of Athens and Sparta, for example, will enable you to learn much more about those societies. More important, you will learn something about the characteristics of all political systems. You will be able to bring this awareness to bear on your thinking about a wide range of issues long after you have forgotten the details of Athenian and Spartan political organizations. Working with specific cases thus gives you a means of increasing your understanding of the concepts of a particular discipline.

Let's assume that you are taking an anthropology course in which your instructor has been lecturing on social organization in a Malaysian society. To see whether you understand the *concept* of social organization and the importance of social organization in all societies, your instructor has given you this topic for a 1000-word essay:

> On the basis of material presented in your textbook, compare the social organization of the !Kung San and the Mutayr.

Step 1

CLARIFYING THE TOPIC

A. Do I understand the terms used in the topic?
B. Do I understand the directions the topic gives me?
  1. Am I asked to analyze, to compare, or to evaluate?
  2. Does this topic require comparison of content or comparison of texts?
  3. Is the basis of comparison given?
C. Do I know what kind of material to use in my essay?
D. Do I know how to limit the topic if necessary?
E. Do I know how to choose a topic that fits my interest, knowledge, time, and writing skills?

A. Yes. We discussed social organization in class; the textbook also defines and illustrates the concept.

B. To compare content. The focus is on the information the text presents; I'm not asked to consider the manner in which the text is written. The basis of comparison is social organization in the two societies.

C. Text only. No further research allowed.

D. The topic is already limited.

E. No choice of topics. 1000-word essay, due in two weeks. I'll have to read and take notes on about 40 pages of material, and organizing a comparison essay may take a lot of time. I'd better start my paper right away so that I will have plenty of time to revise.

Step 2

GATHERING MATERIAL

What source or sources of material can I draw on?

A. What is my main source of information and ideas?
  — Previous knowledge and experience?
  — Discussions of a concept or theory?
  — Sets of data?

I am comparing sets of data from my text. Here are my notes on the two cultures, using the categories that my reading of the course text has suggested:[2]

!KUNG SAN

Environment
About 45 000 !Kung San live in and around the fringes of the Kalahari Desert. Grassy plain, with no permanent rivers; rainfall varies between 7 and 46 inches per year. The area is very rich in vegetation. The !Kung San have named 500 local plants and animals and use about 150 plants and 100 different animals for food. Many varieties of both hard and soft woods are available for weapons, fire, and shelter.

Physical Appearance, Language
The !Kung San are small—men about 5'2", women about 5'. Their language includes various popping noises and clicks, indicated in transcriptions by typographical symbols (e.g., !,#).

Work Organization
They are a hunting and gathering people, but have no difficulty in finding food. Look for food only 2-3 days most weeks, and can be quite choosy. Game makes up 20-50% by weight of diet.

  On food gathering days members leave camp in the morning and work through the surrounding range. In the late afternoon they return to camp and pool their resources. The women usually go out in groups of 3-5 to get a particular species of plant. The men hunt singly or in pairs. They use poisoned arrows and average one kill in four days of hunting.

---

[2]From *The Study of Anthropology* by David E. Hunter and Phillip Whitten: Summary of Richard B. Lee's "The !Kung San: A Hunting and Gathering Community" (pp. 468-84) and Summary of Federico S. Vidal's "Mutayr: A Tribe of Saudi Arabian Pastoral Nomads" (pp. 468-505). Copyright © 1976 by Harper & Row, Publishers, Inc. Reprinted by permission of the publishers.

Living Arrangements

The camps, located at waterholes, usually contain between 10 and 30 people but composition changes from month to month and day to day. Much time is spent visiting other camps and each year about 15% of the camp shifts permanently. 35% divide their time evenly between camps. Movements may appear random but are actually based upon underlying principles of association.

The camp is basically a unit of sharing. If the sharing breaks down, people will disperse and seek another camp where relations are more cordial.

Huts are used to store possessions, but eating, socializing, sex, and sleeping take place outside.

Political Organization

No hereditary leadership. Leadership based upon demonstrated ability, and changes frequently. The centre of each camp is a core of siblings (brothers and sisters) and their spouses and offspring. They all share a claim to the ownership of the waterhole. The genealogical structure of the camp is thus a chain of spouses and siblings radiating from the core. The society is strongly bilateral, with no strict rule of descent from either male or female line.

All disputes are settled by verbal confrontations. The !Kung San discourage both sullen withdrawal and boastful arrogance.

Family Structure

The kinship system, involving a complex network of shared names, is also important in maintaining the cohesiveness of the !Kung San. There are 35 men's names and 34 women's names. There are no surnames. The first-born male is named after the father's father, the first-born female after the father's mother; the second-born male after his mother's father and the second-born female after her mother's mother. (Rarely more than two children.) Bearers of the same name are thought to have descended from the same ancestor. They thus share affectionate connections with one another regardless of biological ties.

A man may not marry his cousin or a girl with the same name as his mother or sister or, in the case of a second marriage, a girl with the same name as his sister or mother-in-law. Similarly, a girl may not marry a man whose name is the same as that of her father, brother, son, or father-in-law. Men marry between 20-30; women at about the age of puberty, 14-16. There is no bride-price or dowry. Divorce is common and is initiated as often by women as by men. Children always remain with the mother.

Religion

The !Kung San believe in a high god #quean!a who is thought to be a remote force, creator of the world, and the ultimate source of misfortune and death. //gangwa is a trickster god, the protagonist of a series of myths about the past. The //gangwasi are ghosts of the recent dead and are thought to bring sickness and death to the community. The shamen (medicine men) drive the ghosts out and pull sickness out of people. The !Kung San believe that the dead live in a society that exactly duplicates their own. The dead may long for the living to join them and so send ghosts and sickness to them. Death is the struggle between two groups of loving relatives. The fact that sick people can be cured proves that the forces of the dead are not all-powerful.

MUTAYR

Work

The Mutayr, a tribe of about 25 000, are Bedouins, desert nomads who own and breed camels.

Environment

Every Bedouin tribe in Arabia owns a **dirah**, a tribal grazing ground over which it travels throughout the year in search of pasture and water for the camels. The Mutayr dirah is in NE Saudi Arabia, an interior desert subject to extreme variations in temperature.

Trade Economics

The Mutayr must trade to survive. Most of the tent furnishings and clothing are not made in the desert but are obtained by trading tent cloth, livestock, and skins. Even the staples of their diet, rice and dates, are obtained by trade.

Work Organization

Labour is unending, and is divided along sexual lines. The Mutayr get up at dawn and go to bed at sunset. The men look after the animals and the women look after the children, cook, and weave tent cloth from camel hair.

Living Arrangements

In the winter the tribe splits up into camping groups, usually composed of a single family: the head of the household, his wife, their married sons with their wives and children, and any unmarried sons or daughters. In the summer when water is scarcer, the Mutayr congregate at available water. Summer is a bad time of the year: both people and camels are short-tempered and the tribe is more easily found by its enemies and by Saudi Arabian tax collectors.

Family Structure

Arabian women are less secluded in the desert than they are in the city, but they are still subordinate to men. Mutayr women must eat separately from the men and after them. A Mutayr woman may join in the men's discussions, but she must sit at the farthest corner of the tent. When the women are left alone all day in the winter camps, they are expected to deal with problems and to be hospitable to strangers.

Political Organization

The Mutayr are a patrilineal rank society. The Mutayr consider themselves to be a noble tribe and differentiate themselves from non-noble tribes. The head of a group of families is the sheik. The sheik's position is inherited by a member of his patrilineage, but not necessarily by his first-born son. The grand sheik is head of all groups of Mutayr.

Religion
The Mutayr are devout Moslems, although desert conditions make the strict observance of some Muslim rituals, such as washing before prayers and travelling to Mecca, impossible.

Social Rules
The Mutayr have very strict rules governing the hospitality that must be shown to a stranger or even to an enemy who seeks shelter. These rules reflect their awareness that a person alone in the desert is sure to die.

B. Do I need additional material?

Not unless I need to look up words in the dictionary.

Step 3

CATEGORIZING MATERIAL

What matching categories should I divide my material into?

I have taken notes under headings related to social organization, such as the organization of work, family structure, and political structure. Now I need to arrange my notes in matching categories so that I can compare them. I'll begin by making a list of the categories I have used for each culture.

!KUNG SAN	MUTAYR
Environment	Environment
Physical Appearance, Language	– – –
Work Organization	Work Organization
Living Arrangements	Living Arrangements
Political Organization	Political Organization
Family Structure	Family Structure
Religion	Religion
– – –	Work
– – –	Trade Economics
– – –	Social Rules

Four of my categories don't match. Since I can only compare features of the two cultures on which I have the same kinds of information,

I will have to decide whether to find new material, omit material, or reorganize it. Since physical appearance and language aren't really relevant to social organization, I'll drop that category for the !Kung San instead of adding information on the Mutayr. My notes under "Work" and "Trade Economics" would fit under "Work Organization." I'll put the information on social rules into "Living Arrangements."

Now I'll summarize my notes and arrange them in matching columns so that I can see the similarities and differences more easily.

	!KUNG SAN	MUTAYR
Environment	living area: grassy plain; many varieties plants, animals, woods	living area: desert; extreme variations in temperature
Work Organization	food easy to find; women gather, men hunt. Resources pooled.	breed camels; have to trade to live. Work hard; men look after animals, women cook, weave.
Living Arrangements	camps based on kinship but much movement; camp a sharing unit; all activities occur outside huts	camping groups based on family ties; gather in larger groups in summer; strict rules for hospitality.
Family Structure	names give children collective ties, not family ones; divorce common; no dowries.	Arabian women subordinate to men.
Political Organization	no hereditary leadership; bilateral descent. Disputes settled verbally.	patrilineal rank society; leadership inherited.
Religion	belief in variety of gods; world of dead same as world of living.	strict Moslem beliefs

Step 4

FINDING A THESIS

What generalization can I make about the nature of the things I'm comparing?

A. What is my basis of comparison?

Social organization in the two societies.

B. What pattern(s) do I perceive in my material?

What qualities characterize each of these societies? My notes on the work organization, family structure, and living arrangements of the !Kung San show that both men and women go out for food and share their resources; that there is a wide network of social relations available to both men and women; and that camps are units for sharing. The social organization of the !Kung San seems to be characterized by flexibility and equality.

My notes on work organization, family structure, and living arrangements among the Mutayr show that the men tend the camels, the principal means of subsistence; that men are dominant within the family and within the culture; and that families operate as individual units except when the scarcity of water and need for protection brings them together. The social organization of the Mutayr seems to be rigid and hierarchical.

C. What is the central likeness or difference between these patterns?

Since social organization within these societies is so obviously different, all I have to do is to combine my statements like this:

> Social organization among the !Kung San is flexible and egalitarian, whereas social organization among the Mutayr is rigid and hierarchical.

Why are the things I'm comparing similar or different?

To answer this question, I should consider the causes, effects, or features that support my generalization. The most relevant question here is that of causes: What has caused the difference in social organization between these two societies?

Looking at my notes, I see that the environments in which these two groups live are totally different: the !Kung San live in a region where food is plentiful and easily obtained, whereas the Mutayr struggle for survival under extremely harsh conditions. How would these environments influence the social organization of the two cultures?

Where food is plentiful, a society does not need a leader and strict rules to ensure equitable distribution of resources, and so the society can afford to be egalitarian and flexible. Where survival is an issue, however, those who control the means of subsistence, such as water and camels, are likely to be dominant, and the rules governing access to resources will be rigidly enforced.

Putting these ideas together, then, I would have a thesis like this:

> The !Kung San have developed a flexible, egalitarian social organization because of the easy availability of the means of subsistence in their environment. The rigid, hierarchical social organization of the Mutayr, on the other hand, is a logical outgrowth of their dependence on males for subsistence in a harsh environment.

The purpose of comparison, you will recall, is to illuminate both the objects being compared and the general category to which they belong. Writing an essay on a topic such as this one should help you learn a good deal not only about the specific societies you study, but also about the forces that shape social organization in all cultures.

SUMMARY

Here are the steps to remember when you are preparing to write comparison essays:

1. Collect equivalent information about each of your subjects and divide your material into matching categories.
2. Determine the central similarity and/or difference between the things you are comparing.
3. Write a thesis that explains the central similarity and/or difference.

Once you have a thesis, you are ready to write a first draft. You will find suggestions for writing and revising comparison essays in Chapter 8.

EXERCISES

The following exercises will give you practice in systematically carrying out the steps in preparing to write a comparison essay. Save your responses to the following exercises for possible use in the exercises for Chapter 8.

A. Work out a thesis for an essay comparing the social organization of the society with which you are most familiar and that of either the !Kung San or the Mutayr.

1. Use any four of these categories to develop matching sets of information: environment, work organization, living arrangements, family structure, political organization.

2. Examine your categories of material to see what pattern(s) you discover within your own society and within the !Kung San or Mutayr society. Formulate a generalization about these patterns that shows the central likeness or difference between the two societies.

3. We have already seen that one explanation for the flexible, egalitarian social organization of the !Kung San and the rigid, hierarchical structure of the Mutayr is the difference in the environments in which they live. What accounts for the central likeness or difference between the two societies you are comparing?

4. Combine your statement of the central likeness or difference and the reason(s) for it into a thesis statement comparing the two societies.

B. Use the material on either "The Cry" or "Killing a Bat" from this chapter and gather matching information about John Newlove's poem "By the Church Wall," reprinted below, in order to arrive at a thesis comparing the two poems.

BY THE CHURCH WALL[3]

The mocking faces appear in the churchyard,
appear as I curl on the hard ground
trying to sleep—trying to sleep
as the voices call me, asking why
must I always be frightened and dreaming?

I have travelled this road many times,
though not in this place, tired
in the bones and the long blistered feet
beneath a black mass of flat clouds,
dry in a damned and useless land.

Frogs croak hollowly, the loons cry
their thin bewildered song on a far-off lake,
the wind rises and the wet grass waves;
by the wall of the white rural church
I count a thousand to go to sleep.

But it will not happen. The faces
float before me, bloated and grinning,
succubus and incubus, a child
screams in a house across the road;
I turn and turn in my fear.

---

[3]John Newlove, "By the Church Wall," from *Moving in Alone*, Contact Press, 1965 (pp. 56-57), new edition Oolichan Press, 1977, copyright John Newlove, 1965, 1977. Reprinted in *The Evolution of Canadian Literature in English: 1945-1970*, ed. Paul Denham (Toronto and Montreal: Holt, Rinehart and Winston of Canada, 1973), pp. 249-50.

There is nothing to hurt me here,
and I know it, but an ancient dread
clenches my belly and fluttering heart,
and in the cold wet grass I count
what may happen and what has.

All the mistakes and desires are here,
old nameless shame for my lies,
and the boy's terrible wish to be good and
not to be alone, not to be alone,
to be loved, and to love.

I remember a letter a friend sent,
trivial and gossiping, quite plain,
of no consequence to him, casually typed
and then signed easily by hand,
All our love, and wish I could say that.

But I lie alone in the shadowed grass,
fond only, incapable of love or truth,
caught in all I have done, afraid
and unable to escape, formulating
one more ruinous way to safety.

Chapter 8

Writing Comparison Essays

You've completed all the steps in preparing to write a comparison essay, confident that your thesis explains the central likeness and/or difference between the things you are comparing. But when you sit down to write the essay, you realize you are not sure how to present comparisons clearly and effectively. Do you say everything you have to say about one of the things you're comparing, and then everything you have to say about the other? Or do you move back and forth? If you move back and forth, won't your reader be confused?

These are the kinds of questions we'll answer in this chapter. We'll start by outlining the basic questions you can ask yourself when you're writing and revising, focusing on the questions particularly relevant to comparison essays. Then, so that you can see the process of writing comparison essays from start to finish, we will examine the steps involved in comparing two texts, from clarifying the topic and gathering material to revising the first draft. We will cover the steps of preparing to write in less detail than in the previous chapter, since our purpose is to focus on the process of revision.

BASIC PROCEDURES FOR WRITING AND REVISING COMPARISON ESSAYS

Writing the First Draft

Step 1

SELECTING MATERIAL

Which matching categories of material best support my thesis?

If you have completed the preparation process for your topic, you should have a thesis derived from matching categories of material on the things you are comparing. Decide which of your categories were most useful in helping you arrive at your thesis. Make sure that you use the same categories for each of the things you are comparing. You will also need to consider the amount of material demanded by the length of the essay and to adjust the number of categories you use accordingly.

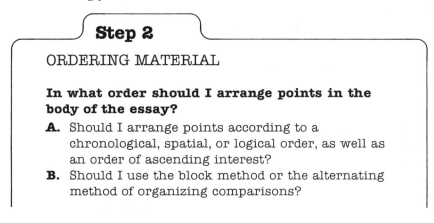

Step 2

ORDERING MATERIAL

In what order should I arrange points in the body of the essay?

A. Should I arrange points according to a chronological, spatial, or logical order, as well as an order of ascending interest?

B. Should I use the block method or the alternating method of organizing comparisons?

When you have decided which of your categories from the preparation process you want to make into points to develop your thesis, you need to decide the order in which these points will appear in your draft. For comparison essays, you need to consider not only the ordering principles we discussed in Chapter 5 (chronological, spatial, logical, and ascending interest), but also the main ways of organizing comparisons: (1) the block method and (2) the alternating method.

Block Method   When you use the block method of comparison, you write everything you have to say about one of the things you are comparing, and then everything you have to say about the other. The block method is appropriate if you are writing brief comparisons of fairly straightforward material, such as character sketches of two people, descriptions of two places, or the meanings of two words.

Alternating Method   When you use the alternating method of comparison, you discuss the things you are comparing category by category in order to bring the features you are comparing closer together. Suppose, for example, that you are writing a 1000-word essay comparing the social organization of the !Kung San and Mutayr, and you have decided that the matching categories of family structure, political organization, and work organization, in that order, best support your thesis. In each middle paragraph, you would write on one of these categories, using material on both societies.

Step 3

WRITING THE DRAFT

When you have decided which matching categories of your material to use as paragraph topics, the order in which to use them, and the basic method of organizing your comparison, write your first draft and put it away for a day or two. When you come back to it, you will more easily see how to revise it.

Revising the First Draft

Once you have had some practice in writing comparison essays, you will likely find it fairly easy to plan the structure of your essay and to stick to your plan. Your first few comparison essays may need quite a lot of revision, however, particularly if you are writing on complex subjects. You can make the revision process more efficient by following these steps.

Step 1

REVISING THE THESIS

Does the thesis state an opinion and support it?
Does the thesis explain the central likeness or difference between the things I'm comparing?
Do I need to work out a better thesis from my first draft?

First check your thesis to make sure that it does not have any of the general problems outlined in Chapter 5: (1) merely restating the topic; (2) merely stating facts or summarizing information; (3) merely stating a general opinion without supporting reason(s); (4) merely stating the theme or thesis of the works you are comparing; (5) stating the thesis in a confusing or pretentious way. If your thesis has any of these problems, return to steps 3 and 4 in the preparation process and rethink your material until you have a clearly stated thesis that contains both an opinion and one or more reasons to support it.

Then check that the thesis in your draft is truly a comparison thesis. Does your thesis comment on **one** similarity or difference (or similarity and difference) between the things you are comparing? Is this similarity and/or difference at a higher level of generality than the comparisons discussed in the middle paragraphs? For example, if your first draft comparing imagery, tone, and characterization in Raymond Souster's poems "The Cry" and "Killing a Bat" has a thesis that only mentions characterization in "The Cry," the thesis will need revision. If you revise it to show that imagery, tone, and characterization all point to similar themes (a higher level of generality), you will have an effective comparison thesis.

Even if your draft has a good thesis, you may find that in the act of writing you added new ideas and insights about your subject, and that by the time you reached your conclusion, you understood the essential likeness or difference between the things you were comparing in a more complex way. Check your conclusion to see whether it contains a better thesis than the one you started with, and, if so, use the new thesis as the basis for the rest of your revisions.

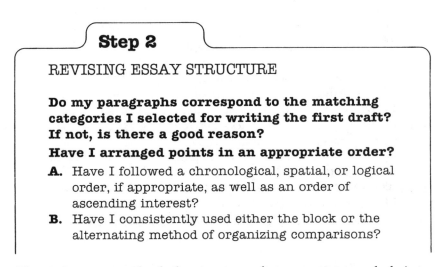

Step 2

REVISING ESSAY STRUCTURE

Do my paragraphs correspond to the matching categories I selected for writing the first draft? If not, is there a good reason?

Have I arranged points in an appropriate order?

A. Have I followed a chronological, spatial, or logical order, if appropriate, as well as an order of ascending interest?

B. Have I consistently used either the block or the alternating method of organizing comparisons?

The easiest way to check the structure of your essay as a whole is to make a brief outline of the topics you have discussed in each paragraph. This outline will tell you whether you have included all the matching categories you had planned to use; whether your paragraph divisions correspond to those categories; and whether you have included equivalent material on each of the things you are comparing. Furthermore, you can use this outline to determine whether you have followed the order you intended, whether this order is still the best one, and whether you have been consistent in your use of either the block or alternating method of organizing comparisons.

If you need to revise the structure of your essay, you may find it useful to make a second outline to remind you of the changes you intend to make.

Step 3

REVISING MIDDLE PARAGRAPHS

Does each middle paragraph have a topic sentence?

A. Does each topic sentence serve as a mini-thesis for the paragraph?

B. If I am using the alternating method, does each topic sentence compare a single aspect of the things being compared?

C. If my comparison of a single aspect occupies more than one paragraph, have I used an "umbrella" topic sentence?

To serve as a mini-thesis for the paragraph, you remember, a topic sentence must both state an opinion and give a reason, just as the thesis does. The topic sentence will make a point that the rest of the paragraph will develop. For comparison essays in which you are using the alternating method, the topic sentence will make a point about the similarities and/or differences between one aspect of the things you're comparing.

When you need to break your discussion of a particular point into two or more paragraphs for your reader's convenience, remember to use an "umbrella" topic sentence to help tie all the related paragraphs together. You could unify two paragraphs comparing the environments of the !Kung San and the Mutayr, for example, by providing an umbrella topic sentence (underlined):

> The environments of the !Kung San and the Mutayr are at the opposite ends of the scale of hospitality to human life. The environment of the !Kung San, who live in a grassy, fertile plain on the fringes of the Kalahari desert, is extremely hospitable. Though rainfall varies from seven to forty-six inches a year, water is plentiful, and the area is rich in plants and animals. The !Kung San use about one hundred fifty different species of these plants and animals for food.
>
> In contrast, the environment of the Mutayr, who live in the interior desert of northeast Saudi Arabia, is very harsh. Temperatures in the area vary widely, and the Mutayr must travel continually in search of pasture and water for their camels. The staples of the Mutayr diet, rice and dates, can only be obtained by trade.

Does the material in each middle paragraph adequately support the point made in its topic sentence?

A. Does each paragraph provide sufficient detail to support its comparison?

B. Does each paragraph provide enough explanation of the point made in its topic sentence and of the detail offered?

C. If I am using the alternating method, does each paragraph provide all the explanation and detail about one of the things being compared before shifting to the other?

Whether you are using the block or the alternating method of organizing comparisons, your middle paragraphs should support and develop the point made in their topic sentences. You develop your point by providing **details**, such as factual information, examples, and quotations from primary sources, and by giving **explanations** of what the topic sentence means and what the detail shows.

As with any essay, everything in the paragraph should serve the purpose of proving the point. In addition, there are two special considerations for paragraph development in comparison essays. The first is that you should give roughly the same amount of detail and explanation for each thing you are comparing. If you develop one side of a comparison in much greater depth or scope than another, your comparison will seem unfair or "loaded." The second consideration is that when you are comparing aspects of things, you should give all the detail and explanation about one side of the comparison before you move to another. Otherwise, the paragraph will seem to "ping-pong."

To see how lack of balance and "ping-ponging" can affect middle paragraphs, consider this version of the comparison between the environments of the !Kung San and the Mutayr:

> The environments of the !Kung San and the Mutayr are at the opposite ends of the scale of hospitality to human life. The environment of the !Kung San, who live in a grassy, fertile plain on the fringes of the Kalahari desert, is extremely hospitable; the environment of the Mutayr, who live in the interior desert of northeast Saudi Arabia, is very harsh. Though rainfall in the !Kung San environment varies from seven to forty-six inches a year, water is plentiful and the area is rich in plants and animals. In contrast, temperatures in the Mutayr environment vary widely and pasture and water for the

camels is hard to find. Of the five hundred or so plants and animals for which the !Kung San have names, they use about 150 for food. Gathering the plants and hunting the animals takes very little of their time.

You can see that this paragraph is unbalanced because there is more detail on the !Kung San than on the Mutayr, and also that it "ping-pongs" between the two societies. As a result, it is hard to keep in mind the main point that the explanation and detail are supporting.

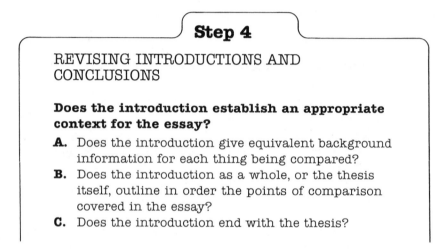

Step 4

REVISING INTRODUCTIONS AND CONCLUSIONS

Does the introduction establish an appropriate context for the essay?

A. Does the introduction give equivalent background information for each thing being compared?

B. Does the introduction as a whole, or the thesis itself, outline in order the points of comparison covered in the essay?

C. Does the introduction end with the thesis?

The principle of balance that applies to explanation and detail in comparison essays also applies to introductions. If your comparison is not to seem "loaded," you must give equivalent background information about all the things you are comparing. You can often achieve an effective, balanced context by making a general comment about the subject to be discussed and then introducing the things to be compared. For example, you might begin your essay on arms negotiations this way:

> The frequent breakdowns in U.S.-Soviet negotiations on nuclear arms reduction remind us of the precariousness of the present nuclear "peace." Comparing the positions of the American and the Russian negotiators is a useful way of gaining insight into why these negotiations have been relatively unproductive.

In analysis essays, the introduction outlines the main divisions of the essay and ends with the thesis. In comparison essays, the introduction has the same structure. You suggest the specific areas of comparison you plan to discuss in your essay, and end with your comparison thesis. The introduction thus provides an effective lead-in to the first point in your middle paragraphs. The thesis in the essay comparing positions on nuclear arms reduction, for example, might read like this:

> A review of their positions on the quantity of nuclear weapons reductions, on the kind of weapons preferred for reduction, and on the possibilities for surveillance reveals each side's desire to maintain the advantage.

Notice that each of the three areas of comparison indicated, as well as the overall opinion about attitudes ("desire to maintain the advantage"), applies equally to both things being compared.

Does the conclusion tie together the points made in the essay?

A. Does the conclusion restate the thesis in different words?

B. Does the conclusion summarize the comparisons made in the middle paragraphs in order to clarify the thesis?

C. Does the conclusion suggest the wider implications of the comparison, if any?

Your conclusion, you will recall, gives you an opportunity to reaffirm your thesis and to clarify its significance. Check your conclusion, as you checked your thesis, your middle paragraphs, and your introduction, for balance. In your restatement and development of the thesis, do you refer equally to the things being compared? Have you considered the wider implications of your comparison as a whole, not just of one of the things you are comparing?

To see how you might put these suggestions into practice, consider this conclusion for the essay comparing U.S. and Soviet positions on nuclear arms reduction:

> Comparing the American and Russian negotiating positions on nuclear arms reduction reveals quite clearly that the two sides are locked in a struggle for advantage in which the other side is always urged to disarm first. What the comparison further reveals is that even the key terms defining the areas of arms reduction I have discussed are in dispute. The two sides cannot agree on what would constitute an equal quantity of reductions, what kinds of weapons to limit, or what effective surveillance would consist of. This lack of agreement points to a lack of desire for substantial reductions in nuclear weapons. It sometimes seems as if it will take a nuclear catastrophe before serious talks take place.

The basic steps in revising comparison essays, as you can see, are the same as those for revising analysis essays. In addition, you make sure at each stage of the process—revising your thesis, essay structure, middle paragraphs, introduction and conclusion—that you have maintained a balance between the things you are comparing.

SAMPLE TOPIC: AN ESSAY COMPARING TWO PASSAGES OF PROSE

Knowing how something should be done is one thing: being able to do it is another. Even if you have followed all the steps for preparing to write a comparison essay, and you have attempted to use the alternating method for organizing material in your first draft, you may still run into difficulties. To see what these problems might be and what you could do about them, let's go through the procedure you would follow for writing an essay comparing two texts, from clarifying your topic to writing the final draft.

In textual comparison you are, of course, comparing not only the ideas and themes of particular writers but also the way they present those ideas or themes. To show you that the principles of textual comparison extend beyond literary material, let us assume that in your history class you have been discussing the fact that historians are interpreters, not merely recorders, of events. So that you can see for yourself that historians convey a particular point of view by the way in which they organize their material, by the kinds of evidence and specific details they use, and by their style, your instructor has asked you to write a 750-word essay on this topic:

> Compare the accounts reprinted below of the clash between the U.S. Cavalry and the Northern Cheyenne at Dull Knife's village in 1876.

Preparing to Write

Step 1

CLARIFYING THE TOPIC

The requirements of the topic are clear; no research is necessary. I have one week to write and revise my paper. Since this is my first comparison essay, I'll start right away.

Step 2

GATHERING MATERIAL

The two accounts will be my main source of information and ideas. Here is Ernest Wallace's version of the incident, taken from *Ranald S. Mackenzie on the Texas Frontier:*[1]

> With the reservation quiet, General George Crook, commanding the Department of the Platte, placed Mackenzie in command of a winter campaign, known as the Powder River Expedition, against a large band of Northern Cheyennes under Chief Dull Knife, who had fled the Red Cloud Agency in time to participate in the slaughter of Custer's troops. In a blinding snowstorm on November 14, Mackenzie with 1,552 men, 6 surgeons, almost 400 Indian scouts, and 168 supply wagons rode out of Fort Fetterman on the upper North Platte for the Powder River, one hundred miles to the north. Eight days later scouts located Dull Knife's camp on the Red Fork of the Powder River. Packing rations for ten days and taking 363 Indian scouts and 818 troops, including his tough and reliable 4th Cavalry, Mackenzie in subzero temperature marched for the village. When he attacked soon after daylight on the 25th, the surprised warriors rushed to a sheltered spot surrounded by an open stretch of level prairie. After Dull Knife refused to surrender, Mackenzie ordered his men to burn the village, with its 173 lodges, huge quantities of hides and robes, and "tons" of buffalo meat, and then with Cheyenne bullets flying all around him led the dangerous assault against the Indian stronghold. One officer, at least, concluded that Mackenzie deserved the star of a brigadier general for the courage and skill he demonstrated on that day. The band escaped, but in the fight it lost twenty-five known dead and about five hundred ponies, while Mackenzie in turn lost one officer and five enlisted men killed, twenty-six men wounded, and fifteen cavalry horses killed. General Crook reported that he could not commend too highly Mackenzie's "brilliant achievements"; his victory would be a terrible blow to the hostiles.

The second description is from *Bury My Heart at Wounded Knee* by Dee Brown:[2]

> The soldiers were looking for Crazy Horse, but they found a Cheyenne village first, Dull Knife's village. Most of these Cheyennes had not been in the Little Bighorn battle, but had slipped away from Red Cloud agency in search of food after the Army

---

[1] Lubbock, Texas: West Texas Museum Association, 1964, pp. 172-73.

[2] Copyright © 1970 by Dee Brown. Reprinted by permission of Holt, Rinehart and Winston, Publishers

took possession there and stopped their rations. General Crook sent Three Fingers Mackenzie against this village of 150 lodges.

It was in the Deer Rutting Moon, and very cold, with deep snow in the shaded places and ice-crusted snow in the open places. Mackenzie brought his troopers up to attacking positions during the night, and struck the Cheyennes at first daylight. The Pawnee mercenaries went in first, charging on the fast ponies Mackenzie had taken from the reservation Sioux. They caught the Cheyennes in their lodges, killing many of them as they came awake. Others ran out naked into the biting cold, the warriors trying to fight off the Pawnees and the onrushing soldiers long enough for their women and children to escape.

Some of the best warriors of the Northern Cheyennes sacrificed their lives in those first furious moments of fighting; one of them was Dull Knife's oldest son. Dull Knife and Little Wolf finally managed to form a rear guard along the upper ledges of a canyon, but their scanty supply of ammunition was soon exhausted. Little Wolf was shot seven times before he and Dull Knife broke away to join their women and children in full flight toward the Bighorns. Behind them Mackenzie was burning their lodges, and after that was done he herded their captured ponies against the canyon wall and ordered his men to shoot them down, just as he had done to the ponies of the Comanches and Kiowas in Palo Duro Canyon.

Step 3

CATEGORIZING MATERIAL

After I made notes on the two passages, using the general categories for analyzing texts (set out in Chapter 4 and in the reference section), I arranged my material in matching categories for easy comparison:

	WALLACE	BROWN
Subject	The battle at Dull Knife's village, 1876	Same
Structure	Begins with a long section on preparations for battle. Ends with commendation of Mackenzie.	Fewer preliminaries. More focus on the battle. Ends with Mackenzie killing the ponies.
Development	Precise details of numbers and quantities: 1,552 men, 6 surgeons, etc.	Few precise details; more evocative, sensory descriptions of "biting cold," "furious moments" experienced by Indians.

Style	Vocabulary is that of a military expert: "the hostiles"; Mackenzie's "brilliant achievement." Long detailed sentences.	Vocabulary is Indian: "Deer Rutting Moon," "Three Fingers Macken-zie." Sentences empha-size action.
Tone	Mackenzie presented as leading a dangerous assault against well-armed Cheyenne, taking just revenge for the slaughter of Custer's troops.	Mackenzie presented as finding the village by accident, attacking with unfair surprise, taking brutal retribution; brave warriors "sacrificed their lives."
Thesis	The battle consisted of a well-planned, justified, and successful attack.	The battle consisted of a brutal, unheroic attack upon less well-equipped and defenceless Indians.

Step 4

FINDING A THESIS

Since the assignment does not tell me on what basis I am to compare the accounts, I must find one. This is not difficult, as it has become increasingly clear that the **attitudes** conveyed in the two accounts are in sharp contrast. This basis of comparison also makes it easy to see the pattern in each writer's choice of structure, development, style, and tone.

In my notes on Wallace's account, structure, tone, and thesis emphasize Mackenzie's achievement, while development and style reinforce this emphasis by using details and language that reflect the priorities of the military. In my notes on Brown's account, structure, tone, and thesis emphasize the contrast between the brutality of the attack and the nobility of the defence, while development and style reinforce this contrast by focusing on the Indian experience. My generalization about the central likeness and/or difference between these two accounts, then, is that Wallace's account is favourable to Mackenzie and unfavourable to his foes, whereas Brown's is hostile to Mackenzie and favourable to the Indians.

What are the features, causes, or effects that have led me to this opinion? Clearly my generalization is based on the features of structure, development, style, and tone. Here then is my thesis:

> If we compare their use of structure, development, style, and tone, it becomes very clear that Wallace's account presents

a favourable attitude towards Mackenzie and an unfavourable attitude towards the Indians, whereas Brown's account presents the opposite attitude.

WRITING THE FIRST DRAFT

Now that I have a thesis and a list of similarities and differences between the two accounts, divided into appropriate categories, I can write my first draft.

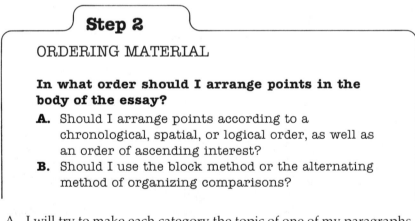

Step 1

SELECTING MATERIAL

Which matching categories of material best support my thesis?

I have found relevant material in all the general categories of textual analysis. However, it seems clear that structure, development, and style all contribute to the two writers' attitude to the subject, or tone. So I will try to focus my middle paragraphs on these three aspects and discuss tone in my conclusion.

Step 2

ORDERING MATERIAL

In what order should I arrange points in the body of the essay?

A. Should I arrange points according to a chronological, spatial, or logical order, as well as an order of ascending interest?

B. Should I use the block method or the alternating method of organizing comparisons?

A. I will try to make each category the topic of one of my paragraphs. The order of the categories as I took notes on them seems as good as any, since it leaves the category most concerned with attitude, the category of tone, until the end. Again, this is a decision I can reconsider after I have written my draft.

B. I know my comparison is going to be too long and detailed to use the block method, so I will try to use the alternating method. But I know I may have trouble organizing so much detail without making blocks of it.

Step 3

WRITING THE DRAFT

Here is my first draft:

TWO VIEWS OF THE BATTLE AT POWDER RIVER

Introduction   Ernest Wallace's <u>Ranald S. Mackenzie on the Texas Frontier</u> is an historical study of General Mackenzie's expeditions against the Indians. One of these expeditions was the Powder River expedition of 1876 in which Mackenzie and his cavalry attacked Dull Knife's village. I will compare Wallace's account of this attack with Dee Brown's <u>Bury My Heart at Wounded Knee</u>.

Thesis   If we compare these authors' use of structure, development, and style, it becomes very clear that Wallace's account presents a favourable attitude towards Mackenzie and an unfavourable attitude towards the Indians, whereas Brown's account presents the opposite attitude.

Middle Paragraph 1   Wallace's account stresses the justification for the battle: the necessity of punishing the Indians who "participated in the slaughter of Custer's troops." According to Wallace, Mackenzie's march is difficult, for it is in "subzero temperatures." He describes the battle as "hard": the Indians are in a "sheltered spot" and "Cheyenne bullets" are flying all around Mackenzie and his men. Wallace's account ends with praise for Mackenzie's abilities as a military leader.

Middle Paragraph 2   Brown's account claims, on the other hand, that "most of these Cheyenne had not been in the Little Bighorn battle." Brown suggests that Mackenzie's attack was unfair because the Cheyenne were only just waking. Brown emphasizes the courage of Dull Knife and Little Wolf. He ends his account with Mackenzie killing the Indian ponies.

Middle Paragraph 3   Wallace's account has lots of details about exactly how many troops were in the battle, how many lodges were burnt, and so on. Brown mentions only one figure: 150 lodges. Wallace uses the language of the military historian. Brown uses the language of the Indians ("Deer Rutting Moon").

Middle Paragraph 4   Wallace speaks of the Indians "fleeing" the government agency to take part in the slaughter of Custer's troops. Brown describes the actual experience of the battle in more detail. He talks about the "ice-

Concluding Sentence crusted snow" and "biting cold." Wallace is more concerned with numbers. These two accounts are very different because Wallace and Brown have different attitudes towards the Army and the Cheyenne. Both accounts are interesting, but they are very different.

Revising the First Draft

I was fairly pleased with my first draft when I finished it yesterday. I wonder how it will seem today? I'll check it part by part.

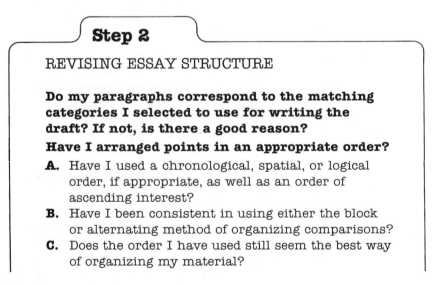

Step 1

REVISING THE THESIS

Does the thesis state an opinion and support it?

Does the thesis explain the central likeness and/or difference between the things I'm comparing?

Do I need to work out a better thesis from my first draft?

My thesis clearly states an opinion about the two authors' attitudes and supports that opinion by referring to the features of structure, development, style, and tone. The thesis also compares the two accounts in terms of their central difference, the attitudes towards the two sides in the battle. It still seems to be an effective thesis for my essay.

Step 2

REVISING ESSAY STRUCTURE

Do my paragraphs correspond to the matching categories I selected to use for writing the draft? If not, is there a good reason?

Have I arranged points in an appropriate order?

A. Have I used a chronological, spatial, or logical order, if appropriate, as well as an order of ascending interest?

B. Have I been consistent in using either the block or alternating method of organizing comparisons?

C. Does the order I have used still seem the best way of organizing my material?

When I examine the middle paragraphs of my draft, I find that I have dealt with the matching categories in which I gathered material, but that as the draft progressed I have failed to keep each paragraph focused on a single category. The first two middle paragraphs discuss the structure of the two accounts; the third discusses development (use of detail) and style (use of language); and the fourth discusses development (use of detail) and tone (writers' attitudes). I've managed to use the alternating rather than the block method of organization, but I need to straighten out the order. There's too much material on structure to put it all in one paragraph, but development and style should each have a separate parargraph, leading up to the conclusion on tone.

I'll revise the structure of my essay according to this plan:

Middle Paragraph 1.   Structure in Wallace's account
Middle Paragraph 2.   Structure in Brown's account
Middle Paragraph 3.   Development in both accounts
Middle Paragraph 4.   Style in both accounts

Step 3

REVISING MIDDLE PARAGRAPHS

Does each paragraph have a topic sentence?

A. Does each topic sentence serve as a mini-thesis for the paragraph?

B. If I am using the alternating method, does each topic sentence compare a single aspect of the things being compared?

C. If my comparison of a single aspect occupies more than one paragraph, have I used an "umbrella" topic sentence?

There's a real problem with my topic sentences. None of them compares the two accounts, and only the third one suggests the category I'm talking about ("details"). Furthermore, since the third and fourth paragraphs deal with two aspects of the material, not one, their topic sentences do not act as a mini-thesis. Middle paragraphs 1 and 2 are both on structure, and so they need an "umbrella" topic sentence.

First I'll check my revised plan for the structure of the essay. Then I can work out a topic sentence comparing the two accounts for each of the paragraph topics in my revised outline.

Here are my revised topic sentences, with the original ones for comparison.

TOPIC SENTENCES

	First Draft	Revised
Paragraph 1	Wallace's account stresses the justification for the battle: the need to punish the Indians who "participated in the slaughter of Custer's troops."	(Umbrella) The structure of Wallace's account emphasizes the justice and courage of Mackenzie's expedition, while the structure of Brown's emphasizes the injustice and cowardice of the attack.
Paragraph 2	Brown's account claims, on the other hand, that "most of these Cheyenne had not been in the Little Bighorn battle."	Brown's account, on the other hand, begins by disputing the justice of the expedition.
Paragraph 3	Wallace's account has lots of details about exactly how many troops were in the battle, how many lodges were burnt, and so on.	The choice of detail in the two accounts helps develop the attitudes established by the structure, since Wallace's detail reflects military precision while Brown's reflects the Indians' experience of the battle.
Paragraph 4	Wallace speaks of the Indians "fleeing" the government agency to participate in the slaughter of Custer's troops.	The contrast between an emphasis on military precision and an emphasis on Indian experience is also apparent in the two historians' styles.

Does the material in each paragraph adequately support the point made in its topic sentence?

A. Does each paragraph provide sufficient detail to support its point?

B. Does each paragraph provide enough explanation of the comparison made in its topic sentence and of the detail offered?

C. If I am using the alternating method, does each paragraph provide all the explanation and detail about one of the things being compared before shifting to the other?

Now that I have revised my topic sentences, I need to see whether each paragraph adequately develops the point made in the topic sentence.

In the first two middle paragraphs of my first draft, I explain the structure of the two accounts adequately and give examples to illustrate my point. But the last two middle paragraphs, as I can see now, are quite confusing:

> Wallace's account has lots of details about exactly how many troops were in the battle, how many lodges were burnt, and so on. Brown mentions only one figure: 150 lodges. Wallace uses the language of the military historian. Brown uses the language of the Indians ("Deer Rutting Moon").
>
> Wallace speaks of the Indians "fleeing" the government agency to participate in the slaughter of Custer's troops. Brown describes the actual experience of the battle in more detail; he talks about the "ice-crusted snow" and "biting cold." Wallace is more concerned with numbers. These two accounts are very different because Wallace and Brown have different attitudes towards the Army and the Cheyenne. Both accounts are interesting, but they are very different.

In paragraph three I mention the two authors' methods of developing their material and then their style, but I don't explain either point thoroughly; similarly, paragraph four mixes sentences on style and tone with a concluding sentence. Both paragraphs alternate too quickly between Wallace's account and Brown's. I need to reorganize the detail in these two paragraphs to support the points in my revised topic sentences.

If I go back to my new topic sentence for this paragraph, I see that I should focus on the contrast between military precision and the Indians' experience of the battle. The sense of military precision, I now realize, comes from Wallace's use of precise numbers. This will be my **explanation** of the Wallace side of the comparison. To find more **details** to support this point, I will have to provide examples from the passage. Brown conveys the sense of the Indians' experience of the battle, I see, through the use of sensory images. This will be my **explanation** of Brown's side of the comparison. I will need to add details to illustrate this point.

Now I have the explanation and detail for both sides of the comparison, as well as the topic sentence that links the two sides. All I have to remember is to avoid the "ping-pong" effect by finishing my discussion of one account before I switch to the other. My revised paragraph on the authors' means of developing their accounts will read like this:

REVISED MIDDLE PARAGRAPH

Topic Sentence providing transition from previous paragraph and comparing one aspect of both accounts	The choice of detail in the two accounts helps develop the attitudes established by the structure, since Wallace's detail reflects military precision while Brown's reflects the Indians' experience of the battle.
Explanation of point in relation to first author	The military precision of Wallace's account appears most obviously in the focus on exact numbers.
Details supporting point from first author's account	Mackenzie, according to Wallace, starts out with "1552 men, 6 surgeons, almost 400 Indian scouts, and 168 supply wagons."
Details	For the actual expedition he takes "363 Indian scouts, and 818 troops."
Details	During the battle he burns 173 lodges and loses one officer, five enlisted men, and fifteen cavalry horses.
Explanation of point in relation to second author, with transition indicating similarity or difference	Brown, on the other hand, is much more concerned with recounting the sensory impressions the Indians would likely have experienced.
Details supporting point	His description of the setting emphasizes images of coldness: "the deep snow" in the shaded places and the "ice-crusted snow" in the open places.
Details	In his description of the battle itself, he stresses the "biting cold" the Indians face and the "furious moments of fighting."
Summary of both accounts	Although their emphasis is different, both authors use only observable detail; neither says what those involved are thinking or feeling.

I can now go through the same process to write my revised paragraph on style.

Step 4

REVISING INTRODUCTIONS AND CONCLUSIONS

Does the introduction establish an appropriate context for the essay?

A. Does the introduction give equivalent background information for each thing being compared?

B. Does the introduction as a whole, or the thesis itself, outline in order the points of comparison covered in the essay?

C. Does the introduction end with the thesis?

Since my essay is a comparison of two accounts of a battle, I need to make sure that I've given the authors and titles of both accounts and that I've given enough historical information to identify the time, place, and participants. I have given most of this information in the introduction to my first draft, but I introduce the details primarily in terms of Wallace's account rather than giving equivalent background for both accounts. I'll revise the first three sentences of my first draft.

FIRST DRAFT	REVISION
Ernest Wallace's <u>Ranald S. Mackenzie on the Texas Frontier</u> is an historical study of General Mackenzie's expeditions against the Indians. One of these expeditions was the Powder River Expedition of 1876 in which Mackenzie and his cavalry attacked Dull Knife's village. I will compare Wallace's account of this attack with Dee Brown's in <u>Bury My Heart at Wounded Knee</u>.	Both Ernest Wallace's <u>Ranald S. Mackenzie on the Texas Frontier</u> and Dee Brown's <u>Bury My Heart at Wounded Knee</u> give accounts of the Powder River Expedition of 1876 in which the U. S. Cavalry led by Mackenzie attacked a Northern Cheyenne village.

The rest of the introductory paragraph seems all right. The opening of the thesis statement ("If we compare the use of structure, development, and style in the two accounts . . .") indicates the three points of comparison I will cover, in the order I will cover them. The thesis statement comes at the end of the introduction, after the new sentence establishing the context.

> **Does the conclusion tie together the points made in the essay?**
>
> **A.** Does the conclusion restate the thesis, in different words?
>
> **B.** Does the conclusion summarize the comparisons made in the middle paragraphs in order to clarify the thesis?
>
> **C.** Does the conclusion suggest the wider implications of the comparison, if any?

One of the major problems in my first draft is that it has no conclusion. The final paragraph briefly discusses development and tone, and then the last sentence says, "Both accounts are interesting but they are very different." This sentence is little more than a vague restatement of the topic.

To revise for a good conclusion, I need to restate and develop my thesis by showing its relation to my main points, and then suggest why my topic is important. At the same time, I should be careful to maintain a balance between the two accounts.

I'll begin by putting my thesis in more definite terms, like this:

> We can conclude that the structure, development, and style in the two accounts all contribute to conveying quite different attitudes towards the two sides in the battle at Dull Knife's village.

The evidence I've presented in my middle paragraphs should allow me to *extend* my thesis as well as restate it. If I look back at my main points of comparison, I see that what ties them together is that the authors seem to have accepted the values of the two sides in the battle. This point can constitute the development of my thesis.

Finally I can consider whether my comparison of these passages has any wider implications. The purpose of this assignment was to alert me to the ways in which historians' attitudes may shape historical accounts. If this is true about historians, it is probably also true of other writers, including journalists and others on whose records historians depend for their material. Noting this possibility at the end of my conclusion would constitute a statement of wider implications.

Writing the Revised Draft

Having checked my thesis, my essay structure, my middle paragraphs, and my introduction and conclusion, I am now ready to write the revised draft, incorporating the changes I made.

TWO VIEWS OF THE BATTLE AT POWDER RIVER

Both Ernest Wallace's Ranald S. Mackenzie on the Texas Frontier and Dee Brown's Bury My Heart at Wounded Knee give accounts of the Powder River expedition of 1876, in which the U.S. cavalry led by Mackenzie attacked a Northern Cheyenne village. If we compare the use of structure, development, and style in the two accounts, it becomes clear that Wallace's conveys a favourable attitude towards Mackenzie and an unfavourable attitude towards the Indians, while Brown's account conveys the opposite attitude.

The structure of Wallace's account emphasizes the justice and courage of Mackenzie's expedition, while the structure of Brown's account emphasizes the injustice and cowardice of the attack. Wallace's account begins by pointing out that the attack is justified, in the military's eyes, because this band had left their reservation "in time to participate in the slaughter of Custer's troops." As the expedition gets underway, Wallace's account focuses on the courage of the cavalry. The march is undertaken in a "blinding snowstorm" and in "subzero temperatures." The large number of lodges and hides destroyed in the battle helps to suggest the strength of the Indian forces in their "stronghold." Wallace's account ends on a note of justice: the commendation that Mackenzie receives from his superior reinforces the idea that the whole expedition was just.

Brown's account, on the other hand, begins by disputing the justice of the expedition. He says that "most of these Cheyenne had not been in the Little Bighorn battle" and points out that they had left the reservation because the army had "stopped their rations." Brown emphasizes the cowardice and brutality of the attack. According to his account, many of the Cheyenne warriors were killed "as they came awake." He describes other Indians struggling to protect the women and children. His description implies that the soldiers and their Indian mercenaries are cowardly enough to attack these helpless members of the tribe. This image of a cowardly attack upon the helpless is repeated in the final image of the account: Mackenzie's destruction of the trapped ponies. This image reinforces both the cowardliness and the injustice of the attack from the Indians' point of view.

The choice of detail in the two accounts helps develop the attitudes established by the structure, since Wallace's detail emphasizes military precision while Brown's detail focuses on the Indian experience of the battle. The military precision of Wallace's account appears most obviously in the focus on exact numbers. Mackenzie, according to Wallace, starts out with "1552 men, 6 surgeons, almost 400 Indian scouts, and 168 supply wagons." For the actual expedition he takes "363 Indian scouts and 818 troops." During the battle he burns 173 lodges and loses one officer, five enlisted men, and fifteen cavalry horses. Brown, on the other hand, is much more concerned with recounting sensory impressions of the kind the Indians would likely have experienced. His description of the setting, for example, emphasizes images of coldness: the "deep snow in the shaded places and the ice-crusted snow in the open places." In his description of the battle itself, he stresses the "biting cold" the Indians face and the "furious moments of fighting." Although their emphasis is different, both authors use only observable detail; neither says what those involved are thinking or feeling.

The contrast between an emphasis on military precision and an emphasis on the Indians' sensory experience is also apparent in the two historians' styles. Wallace's style is a style for recording precise factual information. He uses long sentences to accommodate his details about the preparations for the expedition and its consequences. His vocabulary, with its "participate," "conclude" and "commend," is the vocabulary of the military. Brown's style, in contrast, focuses the reader's attention on the Indians' experience. His sentences emphasize action: Mackenzie brings his troops and strikes the Cheyenne, the Pawnee mercenaries go first, the Cheyenne warriors run out, and so on. To convey this experience from the Indian point of view, Brown uses their sense-oriented vocabulary: "Three Fingers Mackenzie" and the "Deer Rutting Moon," for example.

We can conclude then that structure, development, and style in the two accounts all contribute to conveying quite different attitudes towards the two sides in the battle at Dull Knife's village. In Wallace's account we have a well-planned, just, and courageous attack against deserving foes; in Brown's we have a careless, unjust, and brutal attack against heroic but helpless victims. This difference in attitude is conveyed not only by obvious choices in structure, development, and style, but more subtly by the way these elements combine to reflect the values of one of the sides in the battle. If historians' accounts are shaped in these ways, we must consider the possibility that so are the seemingly objective reports of journalists and other writers, upon whom later historians will depend for the records from which history is written.

Ordinarily when you have completed your revisions for structure and development, you will still need to do final editing. Since we demonstrate final editing only once, this revised draft has already been checked for sentence structure, grammar, punctuation, and format. For help in spotting and correcting problems in these areas, use the Checklist for Final Editing and the handbook.

SUMMARY

When you are revising comparison essays, keep in mind these three questions:

> 1. Do the points I make in my thesis and topic sentences illuminate the similarities and/or differences between the things I'm comparing?
> 2. Is my method of organization (either block or alternating) appropriate for my material and my readers?
> 3. Have I maintained an appropriate balance between the things I'm comparing?

The procedures demonstrated in this chapter will enable you to evaluate your first drafts and to revise them so that your comparison essays have a clearly defined structure and provide adequate support for your points.

EXERCISES

A. Checking Thesis Statements

Decide whether each of the following is a good or a weak thesis for a comparison essay and explain the reasons for your decision.

1. For an essay comparing Sigmund Freud's view of dreams with C. G. Jung's:

> In developing a theory of dreams that emphasizes their prophetic and compensatory functions, Jung departed from the view of the unconscious upon which his mentor, Freud, had built his theory of dreams.

2. For an essay comparing attitudes towards the imagination in Isaac Asimov's essay "The Eureka Phenomenon" and Carl Sagan's essay "The Abstractions of Beasts":

> In his essay Asimov makes the point that imagination is at least partly a function of the unconscious, whereas Sagan shows that humans are not the only animals with the ability to think.

3. For an essay comparing the principles of solar and geothermal heating systems:

> Although solar and geothermal heating systems are similar in some respects, in others they are different.

4. For an essay discussing Keynesian and 'supply-side' economics:

> In Keynesian economics, money is given to consumers to create a demand for goods. Supply-side economic theories advocate giving money directly to suppliers so that they can invest in factories and other capital.

5. For an essay comparing the political organization of Athens and Sparta:

> Athenian society was more democratic than that of Sparta.

B. Printed below is a first draft of an essay comparing Raymond Souster's poems "The Cry" and "Killing a Bat." Using the notes on the poems in Chapter 7 and the steps in the revision process in this chapter as a guide, write a paragraph or two outlining which parts of the essay would need revising and explaining why.

"THE CRY" AND "KILLING A BAT"

> Both "The Cry" and "Killing a Bat" present human beings who feel threatened by something from the world of nature. The two poems treat this situation in similar ways.
>
> In "The Cry" the speaker seems to be unfamiliar with the natural world. The speaker is not sure whether the cry came from a bird or an animal. He seems to be more interested in his own feelings than anything else. The longest stanza in this four-stanza poem is devoted to describing his physical reactions to this cry. Once he has recovered from his fear, he finds it easy to ignore the cry and go back to sleep.
>
> In "Killing a Bat" humans are also disturbed by an animal. The bat arouses superstitious fear and hatred in them. Flushing the dead bat down the toilet doesn't get rid of it, because they keep remembering the incident. In killing the bat, the narrator of the poem says, they have killed part of themselves too.
>
> Both of these poems deal with the same subject—the reactions of people when they feel threatened by something from the world of nature. Both are quite depressing.

C. Choose one of the topics from Chapter 7, or another comparison topic for which you have completed the preparation process, and write a first draft of the essay. Then check and revise your draft according to the suggestions made in this chapter.

Chapter 9

Preparing to Write: Making Evaluations

When you write analysis and comparison essays, you demonstrate your understanding of the material you are analyzing or comparing by developing a point of view, a thesis about it. Other topics ask you to develop a point of view about the **value**, the strengths and weaknesses, of an idea or a text. These assignments call for an **evaluation** essay.

Here are examples of assignments that ask you to evaluate:

Topics for Content Evaluation

1. Discuss the advantages and disadvantages of building a rapid transit system in our city.

2. Should universities be government controlled so as to provide a closer link between the programmes students pursue and the employment opportunities available to them when they graduate?

3. Write an essay agreeing or disagreeing with the position Christopher Lasch takes on the value of spectatorship in sports in the following passage from *The Culture of Narcissism*.

4. Richard Leakey, the paleontologist, highly values the cultures of pre-agricultural, nomadic societies, while Jacob Bronowski, the scientist and social critic, sees these cultures as impoverished precursors to true civilization. Which view seems to you to be more valid?

Topics for Textual Evaluation

1. How effective is Dee Brown's attempt to convey the native American point of view in *Bury My Heart at Wounded Knee*?

2. *The Stone Angel* is a more popular novel than *The Diviners*. Is it also a better novel? Write an essay justifying your judgment.

3. How successful is the film *Ordinary People* in showing ordinary people trying to cope with extraordinary situations?

　　　　　OR

　　Both *Ordinary People* and *Missing* show ordinary people trying to cope with extraordinary situations. Compare the movies in order to assess the strengths and weaknesses of each.

Each of these assignments, as you can see, asks you to take a position on some issue: a proposed action, such as building a transit system or putting universities under government control; a point of view, such as the value of spectatorship in sports or the value of pre-agricultural societies; or a text, such as an historical account, a novel, or a film. In order to take a position, you must evaluate the strengths and weaknesses of your subject, whether or not these terms appear in the topic.

ANALYSIS, COMPARISON, AND STANDARDS OF EVALUATION

Evaluation and Analysis

The first stage in the process of evaluation is **analysis**. Before you can evaluate something, you must divide it into its parts so that you can establish its strengths and weaknesses. For example, a hockey coach might evaluate offensive players by dividing their performance into categories such as scoring, play-making, and forechecking. Then the coach would evaluate each player's strengths and weaknesses in each of those categories.

As this example suggests, evaluation essays commonly require a two-part analysis: division of the subject into appropriate categories, and division of the categorized material into strengths and weaknesses. In evaluating you consider both strengths and weaknesses (just as in comparing you consider both similarities and differences) for two main reasons. First, looking for both strengths and weaknesses will encourage you to explore your subject more thoroughly, and therefore result in a better thesis. Second, your essay will be more persuasive if you present a balanced view than if you discuss only the strengths or only the weaknesses of the thing you are evaluating.

Evaluation and Comparison

To determine what something's strengths and weaknesses are, you will have to **compare** the thing you are evaluating with something else, for it is impossible to establish strengths and weaknesses in a vacuum. For example, if you were trying to sell a ten-year-old car, the fact that it had been driven only 50,000 kilometres would be an advantage, since most cars that age would have been driven many more kilometres; but if you were trying to sell last year's model, an odometer reading of 50,000 kilometres would be high in comparison to other cars of that year, and therefore a disadvantage.

Standards of Evaluation

To assess strengths and weaknesses, then, you compare your material with something. This something may be one or more things of the same kind; or it may be a **standard of evaluation**, a set of criteria based upon accumulated judgments of things of the same kind. The hockey coach, for example, might compare offensive players with each other or with other players in the league. The coach will likely also have in mind a standard of excellence based on the performances of great hockey players, past and present.

What standards might you use in evaluating? Let us imagine that three students have been asked their opinion about the university's plan to build an innovatively designed staircase in the new Arts Building. The first student might find the proposed staircase beautiful; the second might find the open design dangerous; the third might argue that the proposal should be dropped because the design competition was unfair. These responses illustrate three of the most common standards of evaluation. The first student is judging the staircase by an **aesthetic** standard; the second student is using the standard of **practicality**; the third student is evaluating the plan itself in **ethical** terms.

A fourth common standard of evaluation is that of **logical consistency**, the standard concerned with the internal strengths and weaknesses of a line of reasoning. If you were evaluating two articles on capital punishment on logical grounds, for example, you might conclude that the first offered better reasons and stronger evidence in support of its position, even if you disagreed with its point of view.

To make sure that your own essay is logically consistent, you need to think about which standards of evaluation you are using and to make sure that those standards are appropriate for your subject. For instance, the student who argues that the staircase is dangerous cannot logically say that it is therefore ugly.

This chart of sample questions will help you decide which standard or standards of evaluation may be appropriate to your subject.

STANDARD OF EVALUATION	SAMPLE QUESTIONS
Aesthetic	1. Do the features of the work fit together effectively? 2. How effectively does form convey content? 3. Is this a good work of its kind?
Logical	1. Can the conclusions in this work be validly inferred from the premises and evidence presented?

2. Does the reasoning in this text conform to accepted conventions of argumentation?
3. What is the quality of thought in these ideas or this text?

Practical	1. Will this idea work?
	2. How useful is this?
	3. How wide or narrow is the application?

| Ethical | 1. Is this idea right or wrong? |
| | 2. Should we follow the course this text recommends? |

BASIC QUESTIONS AND PROCEDURES FOR MAKING EVALUATIONS

Here is a list of questions to ask yourself when you are preparing evaluation essays. Some of the standard questions for clarifying the topic have been omitted; for a full list, see "Questions to Ask about Essay Topics" in the reference section.

Step 1

CLARIFYING THE TOPIC

Do I understand the directions the topic gives me?

A. Am I asked to analyze, to compare, or to evaluate?
B. Does the topic require content evaluation or textual evaluation?
C. Is the standard of evaluation given or implied?

A. Topics for evaluation may contain words such as evaluate, assess, or judge; they may ask you to agree or disagree, to discuss strengths and weaknesses or advantages or disadvantages, or to compare two things to say which is better.

B. Content evaluation usually asks you to evaluate an idea, position, argument, or viewpoint. Textual evaluation usually asks how effective the presentation of a theme or thesis is.

C. Some topics may spell out or imply the standard(s) by which you are to evaluate your material. For example, the topic "Discuss the claim that Paolo Freire's methods of teaching literacy cannot work in a North American context" implies an evaluation in terms of practicality. Other topics may give less guidance; to deal with these you will usually have to assemble your material and work out an appropriate standard of evaluation later.

Do I know how to limit the topic if necessary?

If you are given a broad topic such as "What are the advantages and disadvantages of computers?" you may want to narrow it by deciding on a standard of evaluation and by asking, "Advantages and disadvantages for whom or for what?"

Do I know how to choose a topic that fits my interest, knowledge, time, and writing skills?

If you have a choice, pick a topic on which you have an opinion, but avoid topics on which your mind is so firmly made up that you will have trouble seeing both strengths and weaknesses.

Step 2

GATHERING MATERIAL

What source or sources of material can I draw on?

A. What is my main source of information and ideas?

Am I evaluating an issue (such as nuclear disarmament) on a personal basis?	Use brainstorming, tree diagramming, and listing of arguments and details on all sides of the issue. Consider causes, effects, and features. (See Chapter 2.)
Do I have to agree or disagree with someone else's position on an issue?	Analyze the person's position and make a list of the arguments he/she uses. Add points of your own that support that position. Then make a list of arguments against that position.
Am I evaluating a text or a performance?	Read/watch/listen carefully and if possible, more than once. Take notes according to the categories for textual analysis.

B. Do I need additional material?

If you need factual information to support your position, or if your assignment asks you to consider the evidence and evaluations offered by others, follow the procedures for research outlined in Chapters 11 and 12.

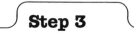

Step 3

CATEGORIZING MATERIAL

What categories should I divide my material into?

As we pointed out earlier, evaluation involves a two-part analysis: division into appropriate analytical categories, and division into evaluative categories. If you are evaluating content, organize your material (1) by using either the special categories provided by the discipline or the general categories of causes, effects, and features and (2) by further separating points and details into strengths and weaknesses, arguments for and against, advantages and disadvantages, or similar evaluative categories. For textual evaluation, organize your material under the general or special categories for textual analysis and into the evaluative categories of strengths and weaknesses.

Step 4

FINDING A THESIS

What generalization can I make about the nature of the thing(s) I'm evaluating?

A. What standard(s) of evaluation am I using?

To decide whether strengths outweigh weaknesses, advantages outweigh disadvantages, reasons for outweigh reasons against, or vice-versa, you must first know what standard(s) of evaluation you are using. Examine each point to see whether it is an aesthetic, logical, practical, or ethical argument.

B. What pattern(s) of strengths and weaknesses do I perceive in my material?

Your next step is to see how individual points relate to each other and to the standard(s) of evaluation they represent. Examine your categories to see what the strengths have in common; then do the same for the weaknesses. You might decide, for example, that the strengths of a particular dance performance in each of your categories (music, choreography, lighting, etc.) are linked to the successful creation of shifting moods, while the weaknesses of the performance result from a lack of technical skills. All of these points, as you would have determined in the previous step, reflect an aesthetic standard of evaluation.

In other cases you might discover that all the strengths in the thing you are evaluating pertain to one standard of evaluation while the weaknesses pertain to another. For instance, you might decide that the reasons for building a children's hospital are ethical and the reasons against are practical. Or the pattern might be less clear-cut, with a mixture of aesthetic, practical, and ethical arguments both for and against. Even in this case you would need to work out what was common to the arguments on each side. Do they reflect short-term versus long-term considerations, for example, or the interests of one group versus the interests of another?

C. What is my evaluation of the relationship between overall strength and overall weakness?

If you have made all of your judgments of strengths and weaknesses in terms of the same standard of evaluation, weigh the effect of the strengths and the weaknesses on the thing as a whole. In arriving at a final evaluation of the dance performance, for example, you would ask "Is this a good work of its kind?" You might decide the performance as a whole was a success, despite the flaws in technique; that it was a failure, despite its ability to convey shifting moods; or that its strengths and weaknesses were fairly evenly balanced.

If you find that you have used more than one standard of evaluation, you must weigh their relative importance. Do the practical advantages of building nuclear reactors outweigh the moral disadvantages? Do the logical inconsistencies in a passage of prose detract from its aesthetic value? Your final evaluation will reflect your sense of priorities.

Your statement about the relationship between strengths and weaknesses will constitute the opinion part of your thesis.

Why have I come to this evaluation?

Complete your thesis by defining the causes, effects, or features that led you to your evaluation. Include both the strengths and weaknesses you intend to discuss in your essay. Indicate the relationship between strengths and weaknesses by setting out your thesis in one of the following ways:

1. When strengths clearly outweigh weaknesses, or vice-versa, put the weaker position first:

> Despite minor flaws in execution, the dance performance was a success because the music, choreography, and lighting combined to create a strong sense of shifting moods.
>
>   OR
>
> Despite its success in conveying moods, the dance performance was disappointing because of technical flaws in the music, choreography, and lighting.

2. When strengths and weaknesses (advantages and disadvantages, reasons for and reasons against) are fairly equal, use a balanced sentence structure. Since the end of the sentence is the most emphatic position, the last statement will carry the most weight. You should therefore put the argument you favour at the end of the sentence.

> Genetic research raises ethical questions about the legal, social, and military consequences of further experimentation; however, it also promises practical benefits in industry, agriculture, and medicine.
>
>   OR
>
> Genetic research promises practical benefits in industry, agriculture, and medicine; however, it also raises serious ethical questions about the legal, social, and military consequences of further experimentation.

Note that in the first example, the thesis clearly implies an aesthetic standard of evaluation, and therefore the standard is not mentioned. In the second example, two standards are used, creating the possibility of confusion, and so both standards are mentioned explicitly.

SAMPLE TOPICS: MAKING EVALUATIONS

To show how you would apply these basic procedures to specific topics, we will use four examples: one extended and one brief demonstration each of evaluating content and evaluating texts.

Evaluating Content

Topics for content evaluation ask you to assess the strengths and weaknesses of an action, a set of ideas, or a text on ethical, practical, or logical grounds. The first sample topic demonstrates how you would evaluate a proposed action; the second suggests guidelines for evaluating a set of ideas.

Evaluating a Proposed Action   Let's suppose that you have chosen this topic for an evaluation essay:

> Discuss the advantages and disadvantages of building a rapid transit system in our city.

Step 1

CLARIFYING THE TOPIC

A. Do I understand the terms used in the topic?
B. Do I understand the directions the topic gives me?
   1. Am I asked to analyze, to compare, or to evaluate?
   2. Does this topic require content evaluation or textual evaluation?
   3. Is the standard of evaluation given or implied?
C. Do I know what kind of material to use in my essay?
D. Do I know how to limit the topic if necessary?
E. Do I know how to choose a topic that fits my interest, knowledge, time, and writing skills?

A. No unfamiliar terms.
B. Although the word "discuss" is ambiguous, the mention of "advantages and disadvantages" indicates that this is an evaluation essay. I am asked to evaluate the issue of rapid transit, not someone's writing on the subject. Therefore the topic requires **content** evaluation. The assignment doesn't specify a particular standard of evaluation. I will gather material first, and then see which standard(s) to use in Step 4.
C. The topic does not ask me to evaluate the arguments for and against rapid transit; if it did, I would have to do research. As the assignment is phrased, it seems to ask for an evaluation of the merits of rapid transit, based on my own experience, thoughts, and casual reading on the subject.
D. No need to limit the topic.

E. I've chosen this topic because I'm fed up with our inefficient bus system. Nevertheless, I'm not sure that rapid transit is the best alternative. Since this is a short essay that does not require reading or research, I should be able to write a rough draft in one day and then revise it later.

Step 2

GATHERING MATERIAL

What source or sources of material can I draw on?

A. What is my main source of information and ideas?

Since I am evaluating an issue on the basis of personal knowledge and casual reading, I'll begin by listing all the arguments I can think of for and against building a rapid transit system:

Arguments For

1. reduction of traffic congestion
2. reduction of air pollution
3. less land required for downtown parking facilities
4. conservation of energy
5. reduction of traffic accidents
6. stimulation of business downtown

Arguments Against

1. never be popular because inconvenient
2. rise in taxes to cover costs
3. lack of public interest

B. Do I need additional material?

These arguments seem enough to base my essay on. If I can't think of details for each, I can do some research later on.

Step 3

CATEGORIZING MATERIAL

What categories should I divide my material into?

All of my arguments fit into the general category of the **effects** that building a rapid transit system would have. I can categorize my material further by asking, "Effects on whom or what?" and by using the evaluative categories of advantages and disadvantages.

	ADVANTAGES	DISADVANTAGES
Personal Effects	• reduction of traffic congestion • reduction of traffic accidents	• lack of convenience • lack of public interest
Economic Effects	• less land required for parking • stimulation of downtown business	• rise in taxes
Environmental Effects	• reduction in air pollution • conservation of energy	

Step 4

FINDING A THESIS

What generalization can I make about the nature of the thing(s) I'm evaluating?

A. What standard(s) of evaluation am I using?

All the disadvantages I have listed are **practical** disadvantages of cost and convenience. The advantages could be considered **practical** ones as well. But reducing pollution and conserving energy seem to be **ethical** as well as practical issues because they concern what is good for future generations.

B. What pattern(s) of strengths and weaknesses do I perceive in my material?

When I consider my list of advantages and disadvantages, the disadvantages all seem to be matters of immediate or short-term inconvenience. Most of the advantages, however, such as stimulation of downtown business and conservation of energy, are long-term benefits. I could say then that building a rapid transit system may have short-term disadvantages but long-term advantages.

> **C.** What is my evaluation of the relationship between overall strength and overall weakness?

Which do I think is more important, long-term practical and ethical advantages or immediate practical disadvantages? Put this way, it seems obvious that I consider the long-term practical and ethical advantages to outweigh the short-term practical disadvantages.

> **Why have I come to this evaluation?**

To complete my thesis, I need to define the specific advantages and disadvantages of building a rapid transit system. Since I have decided that the advantages outweigh the disadvantages, I should put the advantages last.

> Although rapid transit systems are expensive to build and perhaps initially less convenient than driving a car, in the long run rapid transit will provide practical and ethical advantages in preserving the environment and its resources for future generations.

This thesis will serve as a good guide for what I should include in my rough draft.

Evaluating Ideas in a Passage of Prose.   At some point you are likely to have an exam, an in-class essay, or a longer assignment in which you are given a quotation and asked to agree or disagree with the ideas expressed, as in the third topic for content evaluation at the beginning of this chapter, the response to Christopher Lasch's ideas on the role of spectatorship in sports. Faced with this kind of assignment, you may be unsure whether to analyze the passage, or simply to respond to its thesis, or to do both. Here are some brief suggestions.

1. Analyze the quotation to determine the author's thesis (opinion and reasons). List the supporting evidence for each reason.
2. On the basis of your own experience, class discussion, reading for the course, and sense of logic, make a list of points for and against the author's position.
3. To arrive at a thesis, first decide which standard(s) of evaluation the author is using and which standard(s) your own points represent.

4. Then evaluate the validity of the author's argument by deciding whether its strengths, and the standard(s) of evaluation they represent, outweigh its weaknesses, and the standard(s) they represent.
5. Write a thesis in which you give your reasons for the evaluation you have reached.

By preparing in this way, you will demonstrate your understanding of the quotation and related material while having a clearly defined position of your own to use as the basis of your response.

Evaluating Texts

When you say to someone "I just read a good book" or "That was a good movie," you usually have in mind an **aesthetic** standard of evaluation. Your judgment suggests that the parts of the book or movie fit together effectively; that the form of the work was appropriate to its content; and that, in comparison with other books or movies of the same kind, the work was better than average.

These are the kinds of judgments we have in mind when we talk about **textual evaluation**. It is possible to evaluate written works and performances according to other criteria: you might object to an essay on logical or ethical grounds, for example, and still consider it well written. When you evaluate written works or performances according to standards other than the aesthetic, however, you are treating them as **content** rather than as **texts**. Textual evaluation, like textual analysis, is concerned with the relation between form and content, not with content alone.

In order to answer the question "Is this a good work of its kind?" you obviously need to know something about other works of the same kind. If you have been an avid reader of mysteries, for example, you have no doubt developed a good sense of "the rules of the game" by which mystery writers operate, and you are likely to be disappointed by books that violate those rules. When you read a new mystery novel, you may evaluate it by comparing it, directly or indirectly, with other mysteries you've read. In this way, you continually develop and refine your sense of what constitutes a "good mystery."

If you are not familiar with the kind of text you are evaluating, you will naturally have a less well-developed sense of what would constitute a good one of its kind. Since many students lack this familiarity, instructors often frame assignments so as to make the evaluation process more straightforward. Consequently, the two common kinds of assignments for textual evaluation are (1) assignments that ask you to assess how well a text treats a given subject, and (2) assignments that ask you to compare two texts, either to determine which is better, or to assess the strengths and weaknesses of each. We will demonstrate in detail the preparation process for the first kind, and make brief suggestions about the preparation process for the second.

Evaluating a Film. Let us assume that you have chosen the following topic for your first essay in a film studies course:

> How successful is the film *Ordinary People* in showing ordinary people trying to cope with extraordinary situations?

Step 1

CLARIFYING THE TOPIC

A. Do I understand the terms used in the topic?
B. Do I understand the directions the topic gives me?
   1. Am I asked to analyze, to compare, or to evaluate?
   2. Does this topic require content evaluation or textual evaluation?
   3. Is the standard of evaluation given or implied?
C. Do I know what kind of material to use in my essay?
D. Do I know how to limit the topic if necessary?
E. Do I know how to choose a topic that fits my interest, knowledge, time, and writing skills?

A. No difficult terms.
B. Since the topic asks "how successful" the film is in presenting a specific subject, textual evaluation is called for. That means using an aesthetic standard of evaluation. We haven't discussed film techniques very much, so I'll use the general categories for analyzing texts for my initial preparation.
C. I'm not asked to consider other people's opinions of the film, and so I won't need to do extensive research. I may look up one or two reviews to make sure I have the names of characters and actors right.
D. No need to limit the topic further.
E. I haven't written an essay on a film before, but I've discussed my views of *Ordinary People* with my friends, so I should not have too many problems with this assignment. I'll need to be careful not to write merely a plot summary, though.

Step 2

GATHERING MATERIAL

What source or sources of material can I draw on?

A. What is my main source of information and ideas?

Here are the notes I made after seeing the film twice.

ORDINARY PEOPLE

SUBJECT
The attempts of the Jarrett family to come to terms with the older son's death and the younger son's attempted suicide.

DEVELOPMENT

Main Characters
Calvin Jarrett (Donald Sutherland)—successful businessman. A "nice guy" caught between his loyalty to his wife and his recognition of his son's needs.
Beth Jarrett (Mary Tyler Moore)—Calvin's wife, an immaculately turned out woman who is so intent on maintaining her image of herself and her family that she is insensitive to the emotional needs of her husband and son.
Conrad Jarrett (Timothy Hutton)—their teenage son, who has recently been released from a mental hospital after attempting suicide because he felt responsible for the death of his brother Buck in a boating accident.
Dr. Berger (Judd Hirsch)—the psychiatrist who helps Conrad come to terms with his feelings about the accident and about his mother.

Setting
Lake Forest, a wealthy suburb of Chicago. Time is the present; the film begins in the fall, just after school starts, and ends soon after New Year's Day. Holidays mark passage of time: Halloween, Thanksgiving, Christmas.

STRUCTURE
The film focuses on the aftermath of Buck's death and Conrad's attempted suicide. It begins with shots of the lake, the Jarretts' large two-storey house, Conrad singing in the school choir, and his parents at the theatre, where Calvin has fallen asleep. The parents' relation to Conrad is established early. When they return from the play, Calvin sees the light under Conrad's door and goes in to talk to him, while Beth goes straight to their bedroom. We discover Conrad's problem gradually, as though we have walked into a situation that everyone else knows about. Parts of the past are presented in flashbacks: we see Conrad's suicide attempt and a younger Beth from Calvin's point

of view, and we see the relationship between Beth and Buck, and later the boating accident, from Conrad's point of view. Beth, who is intent on trying to forget the past, has no flashbacks.

Most of the scenes are very short, and most depict characters attempting to communicate, initially with little success. As Conrad, with Dr. Berger's help, learns to accept rather than deny his feelings, he gradually makes friends with a girl in the choir and attempts to improve his relationship with his mother. At the same time, Calvin faces the fact that his feelings for Beth have changed as a result of her coldness towards Conrad. Determined to maintain her image of what the family should be rather than take their problems to Dr. Berger, Beth packs her bags and leaves. The film ends with Calvin and Conrad sitting together on the front steps, with patches of snow around them, after Beth's cab has pulled away.

STYLE   The film is mainly realistic and low-key, but the imagery often conveys characters' emotional states. There is an early scene in which Conrad, riding to school with friends, sees images of a cemetery flashing between the cars of a train; we are not sure whether these images are real. A later scene in which Calvin is running with a friend begins realistically, but then as Calvin runs alone he hears the conflicting voices of Conrad and Beth growing louder and louder. When he falls, we realize that he can no longer run away from this conflict. The plate Beth breaks after the fight over picture-taking seems to symbolize her brittleness, and her insistence that she can mend the plate so that the crack won't show emphasizes her need to keep up appearances.

The short, disconnected scenes reinforce the idea of the lack of communication between characters.

Close-ups are used to register characters' moods.

TONE   I'm not quite sure what to put here. My general impression, especially at the beginning of the film, is of stiffness, people walking on eggshells, keeping their feelings under tight control, not really talking to each other, as in the breakfast scene where Conrad insists he's fine but not hungry, and Beth takes his unwillingness to eat as a personal rejection. Towards the end of the film, Conrad and Calvin try to say what they feel, sometimes clumsily, but Beth won't. Her struggle not to lose control is most evident in the scene where she gets her suitcase from the closet. Though the final scene shows the love between father and son, there is a feeling of melancholy at Beth's leaving.

TENTATIVE
THEME
The theme seems to concern the need to accept one's own feelings and mistakes in order to have emotionally satisfying relations with other people.

B. Do I need additional material?

I forgot to note the name of the director. I'll see if I can find it.

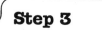

Step 3

CATEGORIZING MATERIAL

What categories should I divide my material into?

Since I've already used the general categories for textual analysis in gathering material, all I have to do now is to arrange my notes according to the film's strengths and weaknesses in portraying "ordinary people confronting extraordinary situations."

	STRENGTHS	WEAKNESSES
DEVELOPMENT Characterization	Calvin and Conrad are convincingly portrayed as ordinary people. Calvin seems bored with his life, but unlikely to change it. Conrad has the normal interests and insecurities of a teenager; he is not just a "looney," as someone calls him. Their reactions (Calvin's fleeting expressions, Conrad's mood changes) are realistic for middle-class people who are neither sophisticated and witty nor loud and brutal.	Dr. Berger remains a helping figure rather than a fully developed character, even though his clumsiness in his first scene and his rumpled clothes are designed to make him seem ordinary. Although Beth's rigidity is very well portrayed by Mary Tyler Moore, she seems monstrous because the reasons for her coldness are not explored (Calvin says she can't stand messes).
Setting	The various settings (houses, school, church, park, etc.) build up a life appropriate for "ordinary people."	The Jarretts have a higher standard of living than most "ordinary people," though they probably consider themselves ordinary.

STRUCTURE "Extraordinary situations" are present in the psychological issues characters have to deal with: the memory of a dead brother, a mother's emotional frigidity. The structure of the film effectively focuses on Calvin's and Conrad's psychological development.

External events are not "extraordinary situations." Flashbacks minimize the impact of dramatic events such as the boating accident, attempted suicide. What we see in the present are mostly domestic scenes.

STYLE Effective use of images, camera angles to convey psychological states.

TONE Reinforces the film's realism, especially the ending, which conveys a feeling of loss without being sentimental.

Perhaps too harsh towards Beth, since she is not explained realistically.

THEME Convincing in its suggestion that in order to help someone in psychological pain, we must be sensitive to what is going on beneath the social surface.

Step 4

FINDING A THESIS

What generalization can I make about the nature of the thing(s) I'm evaluating?
A. What standard(s) of evaluation am I using?

Since this is textual evaluation, I am using the aesthetic standard of evaluation.

B. What pattern(s) of strengths and weaknesses do I perceive in my material?

Looking at my list of strengths, I would say that *Ordinary People* is effective in showing Calvin and Conrad as "ordinary people confronting extraordinary situations." The weaknesses lie in the characterization of Beth and Dr. Berger.

> **C.** What is my evaluation of the relation between overall strength and overall weakness?

The problems in characterization seem minor in comparison with the film's obvious strengths. We could see Beth's unexplained (or inadequately explained) coldness as part of the "extraordinary situation" with which Conrad and Calvin have to come to terms. Dr. Berger's functions in the film are to help them face their feelings and to help the audience understand the issues involved. His character does not need to be fully developed to serve these functions. In fact, except for the scene in which Conrad recalls the boating accident, the film deliberately minimizes the possible drama of the sessions with the psychiatrist. I would say, then, that despite minor flaws in characterization, *Ordinary People* effectively portrays ordinary people confronting extraordinary situations.

> **Why have I come to this evaluation?**

Now I need to define the features of the film that support my evaluation of its strengths and weaknesses. Are the film's structure, development, style, and tone consistent with its theme? I decided that the theme of the film is that in order to help someone in psychological pain, we must be sensitive to what is going on beneath the social surface. Calvin and Conrad learn to make contact with others by acknowledging their own feelings, whereas Beth clings to the surfaces of ordinary middle-class life. The film's undramatic method, then, is a precise demonstration of the need to examine apparently undramatic events very closely. By paying attention to the tiny details the film focuses on, we understand the subtleties of its characterization.

I can condense these insights into a thesis like this:

> Although <u>Ordinary People</u> contains minor flaws in characterization, the film's style and structure successfully capture the qualities ordinary people need to cope with extraordinary psychological situations.

Evaluating Texts by Comparison.   Comparing two texts in order to evaluate which treats a given subject or uses a given technique better might seem more complicated than evaluating a single text. Actually, as we suggested earlier, this kind of assignment often makes it easier for you to see the comparison process implicit in evaluation, since it highlights the features, strengths, and weaknesses of the texts you are comparing.

To show you how to proceed with a comparison of two texts, let's assume that instead of choosing to write your essay for your film studies class only on *Ordinary People*, you have chosen this alternative:

> Both Ordinary People and Missing show ordinary people trying to cope with extraordinary situations. Compare the movies in order to assess the strengths and weaknesses of each.

We will briefly outline the steps you would follow in preparing to write on this topic. These steps would be the same for any assignment that asked you to evaluate texts by comparing them.

Step 1. To make sure you understand the topic, ask the same questions you would if you were evaluating a single text. In addition, note whether a basis of comparison is given. This topic asks how successful *Ordinary People* and *Missing* are according to this basis of comparison: their treatment of ordinary people in extraordinary situations.

Step 2. Gather material as you would for a comparison essay, ensuring that you have matching information about the texts you are comparing. For this assignment, you would use either the general categories for analyzing texts or, if you were familiar enough with them, the special categories for analyzing films.

Step 3. Arrange your material into matching analytical categories and evaluative categories of strengths and weaknesses. This listing might show, for example, that *Ordinary People* is more effective than *Missing* in its characterization, but weaker in its use of setting.

Step 4. Decide what the overall strength and overall weakness of each text is in relation to its theme, and then define the features that led you to this evaluation. You may decide that both are effective, that neither is effective, or that both have strengths and weaknesses. Your thesis will compare the texts as well as evaluate them.

With this sample topic, for example, you might decide that both films are thematically strong because both focus on ordinary people who are capable of change and show these people confronting extraordinary situations (psychological situations in *Ordinary People*, dramatic situations in *Missing*) that demand a changed response.

Your thesis comparing and evaluating these two films, then, might be something like this:

> Ordinary People and Missing are equally successful in portray-
> ing ordinary people trying to cope with extraordinary situa-
> tions. Their treatments of this subject and their strengths are
> quite different, however. In Ordinary People complex charac-
> terization and low-key action effectively portray the confron-
> tation of psychological crises, while the dramatic action and
> less complex characterization of Missing effectively portray a
> confrontation with an extraordinary political situation.

SUMMARY

If you follow the steps we have outlined for preparing to write an evaluation essay, you will have a thesis that defines the relation be-tween strengths and weaknesses in the thing(s) you are evaluating and gives reasons to support that opinion. You will also have clearly defined categories of material to use as paragraph topics in developing that thesis. In Chapter 10 you will find suggestions for writing and revising a draft based on this preparation process.

EXERCISES

A. Write a sentence or two explaining which standard, or standards, of evaluation (aesthetic, practical, ethical, or logical) you would use to write an evaluative essay on each of the following topics.
1. Explain why you agree or disagree with the definition of adoles-cence given in Ann Sieg's essay "Why Adolescence Occurs":[1]

> Adolescence is the period of development in human beings that
> begins when the individual feels that adult privileges are due him
> which are not being accorded him, and that ends when the full
> power and social status of the adult are accorded to the individual
> by his society.

2. Do you agree or disagree with the proposition that universities should be government controlled so as to provide a closer link be-tween the programmes students pursue and the employment op-portunities available to them when they graduate?
3. Write a short essay in which you argue for or against the position Jerry Goodis presents in the following passage from *Have I Ever Lied to You Before?*:[2]

---

[1] *Adolescence*, 6 (1971), p. 337.
[2] Jerry Goodis, *Have I Ever Lied to You Before?* (1972), p. 135. Reprinted by permission of the Canadian Publishers, McClelland and Stewart Limited, Toronto.

Conventional Canadian media are not for the poor, the old, the young, the Indian, the Eskimo, the black. The opinions and furies of these minority groups are downplayed because, literally as well as symbolically, who needs them? That's hardly a healthy situation for a democracy. We don't have mass media, we have class media.

4. Richard Leakey, the paleontologist, highly values the cultures of pre-agricultural, nomadic societies, while Jacob Bronowski, the scientist and social critic, sees these cultures as impoverished precursors to true civilization. Write a 1000-word essay in which you show which view seems to you to be more valid.
5. Write a short essay evaluating a book, movie, play, or concert with which you are familiar.

B. Choose one of the topics above and complete the steps outlined in this chapter for preparing to write an evaluative essay. Save your material for possible use in the exercises for Chapter 10.

C. Complete the steps for preparing to write an essay on this topic:

How effectively do the authors' styles convey their attitudes towards time in the following passages?

Save your material for possible use in the exercises for Chapter 10.
Here are the passages. The first is a description of the fictional industrial city of Coketown from Charles Dickens' novel *Hard Times*:[3]

It was a town of red brick, or of brick that would have been red if the smoke and ashes had allowed it; but, as matters stood it was a town of unnatural red and black like the painted face of a savage. It was a town of machinery and tall chimneys, out of which interminable serpents of smoke trailed themselves for ever and ever, and never got uncoiled. It had a black canal in it, and a river that ran purple with ill-smelling dye, and vast piles of buildings full of windows where there was a rattling and a trembling all day long, and where the piston of the steam-engine worked monotonously up and down, like the head of an elephant in a state of melancholy madness. It contained several large streets all very like one another, inhabited by people equally like one another, who all went in and out at the same hours, with the same sound upon the same pavements, to do the same work, and to whom every day was the same as yesterday and tomorrow, and every year the counterpart of the last and the next.

---

[3] New York: Harper and Row (1958), p. 22.

In the second passage, Wallace Stegner describes the landscape near his boyhood home in southern Saskatchewan:[4]

> The drama of this landscape is in the sky, pouring with light and always moving. The earth is passive. And yet the beauty I am always struck by, both as present fact and as revived memory, is a fusion: this sky would not be so spectacular without this earth to change and glow and darken under it. And whatever the sky may do, however the earth is shaken or darkened, the Euclidean perfection abides. The very scale, the hugeness of simple forms, emphasizes stability. It is not hills and mountains which we should call eternal. Nature abhors an elevation as much as it abhors a vacuum; a hill is no sooner elevated than the forces of erosion begin tearing it down. These prairies are quiescent, close to static; looked at for any length of time, they begin to impose their awful perfection on the observer's mind. Eternity is a peneplain.

---

[4] *From Wolf Willow,* by Wallace Stegner (New York: Viking, 1955), p. 7. Copyright © 1962 by Wallace Stegner. Reprinted by permission of Brandt & Brandt Literary Agents, Inc.

Chapter 10

Writing Evaluation Essays

Let's suppose that your English instructor has asked you to write a five-page essay on the strengths and weaknesses of Margaret Atwood's novel *Surfacing*, or your psychology instructor has asked you to discuss the validity of Freud's theory of the death instinct. You have completed the process of preparing to write an evaluation essay by working out a thesis, but you are not sure how readers will react to your point of view.

You might wonder, for example, how can I convince someone of what is merely a personal opinion? What if my reader knows more than I do, or disagrees with the position I am taking? Should I include in my essay just the points and evidence that support my thesis, or should I bring in opposing points of view? If I do include opposing points and evidence, won't they tend to destroy my argument?

These are all reasonable questions. They reflect the attention you must give to being **persuasive** when you are writing evaluative essays. There is a persuasive element in all essay-writing, of course, since you are concerned with establishing the validity of your thesis. But when your purpose in writing is to analyze or to compare things, you persuade primarily by the way you organize and present your **knowledge** of your subject. Evaluation is a matter of **belief** as well as knowledge, however. Therefore when your purpose in writing is to evaluate, you must take into consideration the possibility that your readers' beliefs are different from your own. In this chapter we will focus on ways of persuading your readers to share your evaluation.

We will first outline the basic steps in writing and revising evaluation essays, and then examine the steps in preparing and writing a very common kind of evaluation essay, the evaluation of an argument on a topic of general interest.

BASIC PROCEDURES FOR WRITING AND REVISING EVALUATION ESSAYS

Writing the First Draft

If you have completed the preparation process for your evaluation essay, you will have a thesis that explains the relationship between strengths and weaknesses in the thing you are evaluating, together with notes on those strengths and weaknesses, arranged in systematic categories. Your first step is to decide what material to use in your draft.

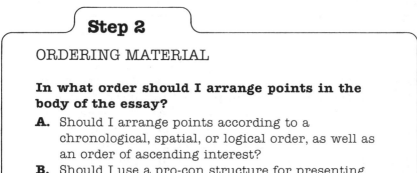

> ## Step 1
>
> SELECTING MATERIAL
>
> **Which categories of strengths and weaknesses best support my thesis?**

Since you can adequately cover only three to five points in a short essay, you may have to decide which of your categories to use and which to omit. Be sure to include the categories of strengths **and** weaknesses that support the evaluation you make in your thesis. Use these categories as the **topics** for your paragraphs.

> ## Step 2
>
> ORDERING MATERIAL
>
> **In what order should I arrange points in the body of the essay?**
> **A.** Should I arrange points according to a chronological, spatial, or logical order, as well as an order of ascending interest?
> **B.** Should I use a pro-con structure for presenting my points?

When you are writing evaluation essays, you should consider not only the general ways of ordering discussed in Chapter 5, but also the possibility of using the way of ordering that is particularly effective for evaluative essays: pro-con structure.

What is pro-con structure? In a pro-con argument, you consider the points **against** your position (con) as well as the points **for** your position (pro). You have used this strategy, in fact, whenever you have tried to persuade someone to give you what you want—a car, a $10 loan, skating lessons—by anticipating the arguments against your request as well as presenting your arguments in favour of it. When you are writing an evaluative essay, you will find that countering the most likely objections to your point of view is an extremely effective way of making your thesis persuasive. If you ignore contrary views or present only the evidence that supports your position, your reader is likely to think that your argument is simplistic or that you have stacked the evidence too much in your favour. Using a pro-con structure will help you develop a balanced, reasonable presentation of your thesis.

To keep arguments against your position from becoming too prominent in your essay and thus too prominent in your reader's mind, put the con material before your pro material. The arguments for your position will thus leave the final impression. This structure applies to the arrangement of material in individual paragraphs as well as to the sequence of middle paragraphs in the essay as a whole. If you have decided, for example, that the disadvantages of genetic engineering outweigh the advantages, the disadvantages would become the pro side of the argument—the side you feel is stronger— and the advantages would become the con side—the side you feel is weaker. In a paragraph on the use of genetic engineering in agriculture, you would therefore discuss the possible advantages first and then discuss the more serious disadvantages. You would also arrange your points so that you finish your discussion of advantages as early in the essay as possible, allowing you to end with your strongest arguments against genetic engineering.

If you are comparing as well as evaluating, you will need to consider how to accommodate the block or alternating method of organizing material within your pro-con structure.

As you can see, a pro-con structure is a way of refining the principle of arranging material in an order of ascending interest—the principle of ending both individual paragraphs and the essay as a whole with your strongest material—to fit the special demands of the evaluation essay.

Once you have decided on the paragraph topics to use and the order in which they should appear, you are ready to write your first draft.

Revising the First Draft

After leaving your draft for a day or two so that you can view it freshly, you can begin the process of revision by checking your thesis.

Step 1

REVISING THE THESIS

Does the thesis state an opinion and support it?

Does the thesis explain the relation between strengths and weaknesses in the thing(s) I'm evaluating?

Do I need to work out a better thesis from my first draft?

Besides checking for the common thesis problems (a thesis that is merely a statement, summary, opinion without support or description, or a thesis that is not clearly stated), you especially need to check that your thesis is genuinely evaluative. The thesis should refer to strengths and weaknesses, advantages or disadvantages, or use similar evaluative terms. It should also indicate the **relationship** between strengths and weaknesses. To say that a film's potentially interesting theme is destroyed by clumsy direction and bad acting is to indicate a relationship where weakness outweighs strength. To say that changes in the Criminal Code have made the sentencing of juvenile offenders more consistent but have not improved rehabilitation programmes is to indicate a relationship where strength and weakness balance each other.

Tone is an especially important consideration in evaluative essays. If you want your readers to consider your position, you need to present it as worthy of serious, thoughtful attention. Don't be apologetic, in the hope that your readers will find your thesis more acceptable; the result is more likely to be confusion or loss of interest. On the other hand, don't state your thesis so assertively that you alienate your readers (as in "Anyone who believes in capital punishment should have his head examined . . .").

Step 2

REVISING ESSAY STRUCTURE

Do my paragraphs correspond to the categories of strengths and weaknesses I selected for writing the first draft? If not, is there a good reason?

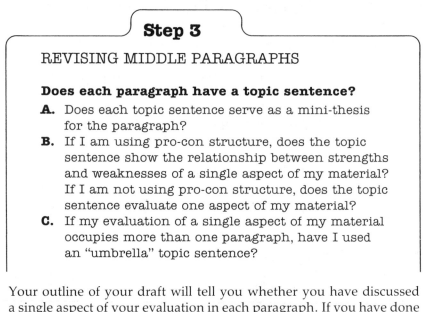

Have I arranged points in an appropriate order?

A. Have I followed a chronological, spatial, or logical order, if appropriate, as well as an order of ascending interest?

B. If I have used a pro-con structure, have I moved from con arguments to pro arguments?

Making a brief outline of the pro and con points in each paragraph is a good way of determining whether you have used all the categories you intended to and whether individual paragraphs and the essay as a whole move from con arguments to pro arguments. If your outline shows weaknesses in the overall structure of your essay, make a new outline to guide you when you revise.

Step 3

REVISING MIDDLE PARAGRAPHS

Does each paragraph have a topic sentence?

A. Does each topic sentence serve as a mini-thesis for the paragraph?

B. If I am using pro-con structure, does the topic sentence show the relationship between strengths and weaknesses of a single aspect of my material? If I am not using pro-con structure, does the topic sentence evaluate one aspect of my material?

C. If my evaluation of a single aspect of my material occupies more than one paragraph, have I used an "umbrella" topic sentence?

Your outline of your draft will tell you whether you have discussed a single aspect of your evaluation in each paragraph. If you have done so, check the topic sentences of your paragraphs to see whether each one makes an evaluative point about one aspect of your thesis and indicates the same relationship between strengths and weaknesses as the thesis. If your thesis says that a film's potentially interesting theme is destroyed by clumsy direction and bad acting, but your topic sentence for your paragraph on the acting suggests only minor weaknesses, you will need to revise either your topic sentence or your thesis. You may find that some of your topic sentences need revising or that you need to write new ones because of changes you have made in essay structure.

Effective topic sentences in evaluation essays often introduce the con point as a concession and then counter it with a stronger pro statement, as in the following example:

> While there were some good performances in minor roles, the limited emotional range of the two stars seriously undermined the film's portrayal of the subtle comprises that lead to political corruption.

This kind of topic sentence can also work as an "umbrella" topic sentence in cases where the con point, the concession, occupies one paragraph and the pro point occupies the next.

Does the material in each middle paragraph adequately support the evaluation made in its topic sentence?

A. Does each paragraph provide sufficient detail to support its point?

B. Does each paragraph provide enough explanation of the evaluation made in the topic sentence and of the detail offered?

C. If I am using pro-con structure within a paragraph, do I finish discussing one side before shifting to the other?

Since the evaluation essay lays more stress on persuasion, consider not only the **amount** of detail and explanation you have used to support each point but also the **kind** most suitable for your particular audience. Will this audience be receptive to statistics, or to personal experience, or to hypothetical cases? If you refer to authorities, do you need to explain who they are so that their relevance is clear? Have you explained your details fully enough to minimize the possibility that someone could reach a different conclusion from the same evidence?

If you are using pro-con structure within a paragraph, make sure that you do not move so rapidly between pros and cons that you create a confusing "ping-pong" effect, as in the following example:

> To use the intrinsic motivation of students so that they can learn at their own pace is a good idea. This approach is not practical for most teachers because of their full class loads and lack of preparation time. Using intrinsic motivation works well in individualized classrooms. There are other reasons, though, why intrinsic motivation is not sufficient....

The evaluation point the writer wants this material to support only becomes clear when the sentences are reorganized into con and pro groupings, with a transition indicating the shift:

> Using the intrinsic motivation of students so that they can learn at their own pace is an approach that works well in individualized classrooms. This approach is not practical for most teachers, however, because of their full class loads and lack of preparation time. There are also other reasons why intrinsic motivation is not sufficient. . . .

Step 4

REVISING INTRODUCTIONS AND CONCLUSIONS

Does the introduction establish an appropriate context for the essay?

A. Does the introduction give readers enough background to understand the purpose of the evaluation?

B. Does the introduction as a whole, or the thesis itself, outline in order the strengths and weaknesses to be covered in the essay and indicate the standard of evaluation?

C. Does the introduction end with the thesis?

At the beginning of an evaluation essay, readers first need to be persuaded that the thing being evaluated deserves attention, and then they need to feel their points of view are being taken into consideration. You can establish common ground with your readers by acknowledging the difficulty of judging the issue in question, by admitting the value in what will become your con argument, or by emphasizing the common values that both con and pro positions share. All three approaches are used in the following example:

> Parental censorship of school texts has been a hotly contested debate for several decades now. We should not see this debate as simply a struggle between enlightened teachers and reactionary parents, or between radical teachers and sensible parents, but rather as a difference of opinion over the best methods for student learning. There is some sense in the argument that young children need to be protected from things they cannot cope with, but there is even more sense in the argument that children learn best by eventually confronting reality in all its complexity.

Establishing common ground with your readers is one way of making your introduction persuasive. Another is setting out the limits of your discussion as clearly as possible, so that readers will know exactly what points you plan to include and what standards of evaluation you intend to apply. Indicating your standard(s) of evaluation is especially important when pro and con points are based on different standards. By the time your readers reach your thesis, they should be willing to consider your position.

Does the conclusion tie together the points made in the essay?

A. Does the conclusion restate the thesis, in different words?

B. Does the conclusion summarize the evaluations made in the middle paragraphs in order to clarify the thesis?

C. Does the conclusion suggest the wider implications of the evaluation, if any?

Since the thesis in a pro-con essay is about the relationship between strengths and weaknesses, the conclusion gives you an opportunity to say more about this relationship: why the strengths of A, taken together, are more important than its weaknesses, or vice-versa; or why A is of more value than B, or vice-versa. Noting more about this relationship may lead you to reflect on the standard of evaluation by which you have made your judgment and on its applicability to other cases, and thus lead you to discuss its wider implications. To extend your thesis in this way, you may need to reconsider the connections between the points in your revised middle paragraphs.

This conclusion to an essay on the issue of censorship of school texts will give you an example of how to put these suggestions into practice.

> Schools, with their captive audiences, are particularly vulnerable, as we have seen, to the use of censorship as a means of indoctrination. Well-intentioned or not-so-well intentioned parents and teachers may find the classroom an ideal forum in which to expound their own opinions on the desirability of nuclear weapons, or the advantages of solar energy, or the existence of a Zionist conspiracy. Thus the issue is not whether the schools ought to promote a particular version of reality by excluding all materials with opposing viewpoints, but whether both parents and teachers ought to support an approach to education that encourages students to think for themselves and provides them with the resources to do so.

Only in this way will students be prepared to respond effectively and responsibly to the competing views of reality they will encounter outside the school walls.

SAMPLE TOPIC: AN ESSAY EVALUATING IDEAS

A very common evaluation assignment is the evaluation of a proposed action. You might be assigned this kind of essay in a wide range of courses and disciplines, but whether the essay is for a sociology or for an education class, the steps for preparing, writing, and revising will be the same. To examine these steps in a detailed example, let us suppose that in your political science class you have been studying the relation between various levels of government and the institutions they fund. From a list of essay topics on this issue, you have chosen this one:

> The suggestion has been made that universities should be government controlled in order to provide a closer link between the programmes students pursue and the employment opportunities available to them when they graduate. Agree or disagree.

Preparing to Write

Step 1

CLARIFYING THE TOPIC

The requirements of the topic are clear. The last sentence indicates that I am to evaluate the suggestion, not simply analyze it. Since the assignment indicates no specific government proposal, it does not require research.

Step 2

GATHERING MATERIAL

I'm not very familiar with the arguments for and against this idea, but if I consider the general categories for analyzing content, it seems that the important question is what **effects** government control of the university might have. I'll list as many possible effects as I can think of.

Possible Effects of Government Control

1. The government might allocate money directly to faculties and programmes instead of giving money to the universities to allocate. This might mean more money for programmes with high employment opportunities, like business administration, engineering, and computer science, and less money for programmes with low employment opportunities, like the theoretical sciences and the liberal arts. Some programmes might even be eliminated.

2. The government might institute high quotas for preferred programmes and low quotas for others.

3. The government might change these quotas and allocations frequently to respond to the changing employment situation.

4. The government could restrict the optional courses taken by students in a particular programme.

5. Students would know they would have a job in their field when they graduate and thus could make plans for the future with more confidence.

6. Students who are in job-oriented programmes are likely to be more interested in the practical than in the theoretical aspects of the fields they are studying.

7. Students taking government-approved courses might find it easier to get loans and other forms of financial support.

8. By the use of financial pressure, the government could enforce more practical content in courses: report writing rather than Shakespeare in English courses, and behaviour management rather than Freudian psychoanalysis in psychology courses, for example.

9. Less emphasis on research and theoretical knowledge could result in fewer ideas being generated and thus diminish the universities' contribution to society.

10. Government control over both the kinds of courses offered and the content of those courses could result in an unwillingness on the part of the universities to offer criticism of society or government policies.

11. There would be fewer under-employed or unemployed university graduates.

12. Less security for faculty members, who could be hired and fired as job opportunities in their fields fluctuate.

13. More difficulty attracting and holding highly trained faculty.

 Step 3

CATEGORIZING MATERIAL

I know that I should divide my material into appropriate analytic categories and also into strengths and weaknesses. After considering several ways of categorizing these effects (long-term and short-term effects; financial and intellectual effects; effects on students, the university and society in general), I decide to group my points into effects on students, effects on the university, and effects on society. These categories seem to be the best ones to use because I can easily tell which points fit under which category, and therefore my readers are also likely to find these categories understandable.

Under each of these headings, I can further divide my points into the evaluative categories of advantages and disadvantages so that my final list looks like this:

EFFECTS ON STUDENTS

Advantages

1. more financial support for gov't approved field of study
2. job security upon graduation
3. more emphasis on information directly applicable to a job

Disadvantages

1. less freedom to choose a particular field of study
2. more difficulty in entering fields with low gov't priority and less financial support
3. fewer optional courses once a particular programme has been chosen.
4. fewer opportunities to gain knowledge not directly applicable to a given job

EFFECTS ON UNIVERSITIES

1. increased funding for job-oriented, practical courses and programmes

1. less freedom to determine the expansion or contraction of programmes and courses
2. less freedom to determine course content
3. less security in making long-range plans
4. more difficulty in attracting and holding highly trained faculty
5. less job security for faculty
6. less emphasis on research and theoretical sciences
7. decreased opportunity to pursue non-job oriented fields of knowledge and interest

EFFECTS ON SOCIETY

1. fewer unemployed or under-employed college graduates

1. loss of new ideas and an independent perspective
2. loss of social criticism and criticism of government policies

Step 4

FINDING A THESIS

When I look at the advantages of government control of the universities, I see gains in efficiency for both students and society in the area of employment. When I look at the disadvantages, I see losses in the university's ability to carry out its functions and in freedom for students, university, and society. Checking to see what standards of evaluation lie behind these assessments of advantages and disadvantages, I come up with the sense that I am weighing the **practical** advantages for students and society of employment-oriented education against the **practical** disadvantages for the university and the **ethical** disadvantages of loss of freedom in terms of student choice, university exploration, and social independence and criticism.

My consideration of the possible consequences has convinced me that I am against the idea of government control of universities. Some of my classmates who will be reading this essay are very much concerned about not getting jobs when they graduate, however, so I word my thesis cautiously:

> It seems to me (and this is only an opinion) that government control of university programmes and enrollment would have practical disadvantages for the university, and ethical disadvantages in terms of student freedom of choice, intellectual exploration, and social independence.

Writing the First Draft

Step 1

SELECTING MATERIAL

Which categories of strengths and weaknesses best support my thesis?

Since I mention in my thesis all three of the categories I used in the preparation process (effects on students, effects on universities, effects on society), I will use these as the paragraph topics for my middle paragraphs. I have several points in my first two categories, and I may not be able to include them all without confusing my readers. I'll decide which ones to eliminate as I write the draft.

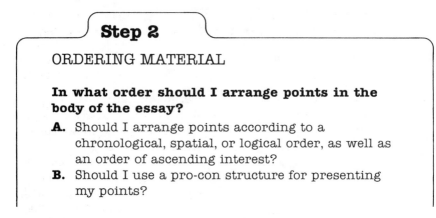

Step 2

ORDERING MATERIAL

In what order should I arrange points in the body of the essay?

A. Should I arrange points according to a chronological, spatial, or logical order, as well as an order of ascending interest?

B. Should I use a pro-con structure for presenting my points?

The order my categories are in seems as logical as any, since I'm moving from the smallest element in my subject (individual students), to a larger element (universities), to the largest element (society). This would also seem to be an order of ascending interest, since my readers may not have considered the contribution that universities make to society as a whole. So I will keep this order for my draft.

Considering the most likely objections to my points will make a more effective evaluation essay, so in each of the three paragraphs I will try to include material from the "advantages" column, which is now the "con" argument, the argument against my case.

Step 3

WRITING THE DRAFT

Having made these decisions I write my first draft, which looks like this:

WHY THE GOVERNMENT SHOULD NOT CONTROL UNIVERSITIES

Should the government control universities to make sure that the programmes students take will lead to jobs? There are lots of arguments on both sides of this question. The value of government control over universities depends on whether you are looking at it from a purely practical or an ethical viewpoint. It seems to me (and this is only an opinion) that government control of university programmes and enrollment would have practical disadvantages for the university and ethical disadvantages in terms of student freedom of choice, intellectual exploration, and independent social perspective.

If the government controlled university programmes and enrollment to bring them in line with the existing job market, then students attending university would be more assured than they are now of getting a job in their field when they graduate. This security would enable students to make long-range plans for the future with more confidence. If the government imposed low quotas on programmes that do not seem to have much job potential, it might be difficult for students to get into those programmes. This would limit the student's freedom of choice. But it would probably be easier for students who were entering high government priority programmes to get loans and other forms of financial assistance. Some students are interested in exploring ideas and experimenting with different fields of study in order to find the one or ones that are most personally satisfying. These students might be denied the opportunity to get a university education or end up taking courses they have no interest in and don't enjoy. It is true that even now students who enter a field such as engineering or pharmacy have few optional courses allowed to them. But government control would probably mean there would be fewer optional courses allowed for everyone and that most people would not take courses that were not directly relevant to the job they were training for. Government control would probably also mean that the content of existing courses would be changed to be more practical. So, in an English course, a student would take report writing, rather than Shakespeare. Some students, of course, would like this, but other students who enjoy literature would be frustrated.

Government-controlled universities would lose the freedom to determine the expansion or contraction of various fields of study. Government-controlled universities would also probably lose some of their power to determine the content of the courses they teach. In a government-controlled university there would probably not be much emphasis on knowledge and skills that could not be directly applied to an existing job. While this might mean that the courses taught were more practical and useful, it might also mean that the government could suppress information and ideas that it did not wish people to learn. This kind of control might be very bad for both individuals and society as a whole. Because a government-controlled university would not have much control over either the programmes it offered or the content of the courses taught, it would probably have a hard time attracting and keeping highly trained faculty—who would resent the fact that they would be hired or fired as job opportunities in their fields fluctuated. Research and the exploration of theoretical knowledge are valuable even if they do not seem to have any immediate application. Einstein's work led to the discovery of energy sources, for example. The practical advantage to the university of government control is that there would probably be more funding for job-oriented, practical fields of study.

Many people who are not students or part of a university would support the idea of a government-controlled university because they can see the practical advantages of having fewer university graduates either unemployed or under-employed. Employment is important, both for the individual and society as a whole. What people fail to realize, though, is that the really important ideas that have enormous long-range benefits for society usually occur when people are allowed to follow their own interests, although those interests may seem impractical at the time. Society also benefits from the social criticism and the criticism of government policies that a university free from government control can provide. A government-controlled university is more likely to suppress controversial ideas and attitudes and the suppression of freedom in a university suppresses the freedom of society as a whole.

So while it is true that a government-controlled university would ensure maximum employability of university graduates with maximum efficiency, the price that we have to pay for this efficiency, both as individuals and as a society, is too high. There is much more to university education than vocational training.

Revising the First Draft

As I revise my draft, I'll try to make sure that I have evaluated rather than merely summarized arguments, that I have used a pro-con structure effectively, and that the tone is persuasive.

Step 1

REVISING THE THESIS

Does the thesis state an opinion and support it?

Does the thesis explain the relation between strengths and weaknesses in the thing(s) I am evaluating?

Do I need to work out a better thesis from my first draft?

Looking at the thesis in my draft I see that I have stated an opinion and supported it. Nevertheless there's a problem, because in the essay I discuss both advantages and disadvantages of government control, but my thesis mentions only the disadvantages. I need to make the point that I consider the disadvantages more important than the advantages. I should also cut out the qualifications—"It seems to me (but this is only an opinion). . . ." I could revise my thesis like this:

> Although government control would have the practical advantage of ensuring maximum employment for university graduates, this advantage is outweighed by the practical disadvantages for the university and the ethical disadvantages in terms of student freedom of choice, intellectual exploration, and independent social perspective.

Step 2

REVISING ESSAY STRUCTURE

Do my paragraphs correspond to the categories of strengths and weaknesses I selected for writing the first draft? If not, is there a good reason?

Have I arranged points in an appropriate order?

A. Have I followed a chronological, spatial, or logical order, if appropriate, as well as an order of ascending interest?

B. If I have used a pro-con structure, have I moved from con arguments to pro arguments?

I intended to have one paragraph each on the effect of government control on students, on the university itself, and on society in general. My draft shows that the second middle paragraph includes material on the effects on society as well as material on the effects on the university. I'll have to move the material on society.

The problems with pro-con structure are more serious. My first and second middle paragraphs have a quite chaotic mixture of pro and con points. I'll make a quick outline so that I can see what I've put in each paragraph and how I should reorganize it.

OUTLINE OF FIRST DRAFT

Middle Paragraph 1. Effects of govt. control on students.
Pro and con points mixed, finishing with pro.

Middle Paragraph 2. Effects on university and society.
Pro and con points mixed, finishes on con.

Middle Paragraph 3. Effect on society.
Con points, then pro.

I know that I should give my pro arguments (on the disadvantages of government control) after the con argument. This won't be a problem with the second middle paragraph, which doesn't have much con material. There are quite a few points on the advantages of government control in the first middle paragraph, however. I'll divide this paragraph into two: the first con, the second pro. My third paragraph—effects on society—starts off with con material and then moves to pro material, and so fits my plan.

I'll make an outline to remind me of the changes I've decided on.

OUTLINE FOR REVISED DRAFT

Middle Paragraph 1. Effects on students—con
Middle Paragraph 2. Effects on students—pro
Middle Paragraph 3. Effects on university—con then pro
Middle Paragraph 4. Effects on society—con then pro

Step 3

REVISING MIDDLE PARAGRAPHS

Does each paragraph have a topic sentence?

A. Does each topic sentence serve as a mini-thesis for the paragraph?

B. If I am using a pro-con structure, does each topic sentence show the relationship between the strengths and weaknesses of a single aspect of my material? If I am not using a pro-con structure, does each topic sentence evaluate one aspect of my material?

C. If my evaluation of a single aspect of my material occupies more than one paragraph, have I used an "umbrella" topic sentence?

When I check my draft, I discover that the beginning sentences of my middle paragraphs make only con points (paragraphs 1 and 3) or only a pro point (paragraph 2). Thus they do not serve as a mini-thesis or show the relationship between advantages and disadvantages. I need to revise these sentences to reflect the pro-con structure of the essay, putting the pro point last for maximum effect.

From my revised outline I see that I have divided the first topic—students—into two paragraphs, and so I will need to start the first paragraph with an "umbrella" topic sentence. My con material is about the financial benefit for students, while my pro material is about the long-term effects of loss of freedom to choose and explore ideas.

I will put this con point in a qualifying clause and then move to the pro point in the main clause like this:

UMBRELLA TOPIC SENTENCE, PARAGRAPHS 1 AND 2

Although government control over university programmes and enrollment would bring about significant financial benefits for students, in the long run losing the freedom to choose courses and explore ideas would seriously reduce the value of university education for the individual student.

I'll follow the same procedure for each of the other topic sentences, making sure that I identify the paragraph topic and that I put the con point before the pro point.

Does the material in each middle paragraph adequately support the evaluation made in its topic sentence?

A. Does each paragraph provide sufficient detail to support its point?

B. Does each paragraph provide enough explanation of the evaluation made in the topic sentence and of the detail offered?

C. If I am using pro-con structure within a paragraph, do I finish discussing one side before shifting to the other?

The way I have developed my paragraphs seems reasonably good. Since the government does not actually control any universities right now, it is natural that the examples I use are hypothetical rather than concrete. To provide concrete examples, factual information, or quotations from authorities I would have to do research on countries in which the government does control the university, but this is not a research paper. So there is no problem with the kind of evidence I'm offering. I also give plenty of examples to support my points.

The main problem with my middle paragraphs is their structure. It's hard to follow my line of argument because my pro and con material is mixed together. As I revise each paragraph, I will put all my material on the con side first, and then discuss the pro argument with its explanations and details. The second middle paragraph, about the effects on the university, will be the hardest to revise, since it starts with pro material and ends with con material and also contains material belonging to the third topic (society). I should also change the Einstein example, since I'm not sure Einstein actually did his work at a university. I'll make a list to help me sort out the structure of this paragraph:

Con	Pro	Move to Para. 4
1. Practical and useful courses 2. More funding for job-oriented fields of study	1. University wouldn't control expansion and contraction of fields of study 2. University doesn't control content 3. Problems in hiring and keeping good faculty 4. Value of research and theoretical inquiry	1. Government suppression of information and ideas (more relevant to society) **Change Example** Einstein and energy sources

I can now rewrite this paragraph, adding details as necessary, so that it uses pro-con structure to support the points made in the revised topic sentence:

Topic Sentence   It is true that government control would have a limited financial advantage for the university, but this advantage would be greatly outweighed by the serious practical disadvantages for the organization of university affairs and the even more serious ethical problems regarding the university's fulfillment of its educational functions.

Explanation (con point)
Explanation (pro point)
Detail   The practical advantage of government control is that the university would likely receive increased funding for job-oriented programmes. We must recognize, however, that the demands of the job market are continually changing. If this market were to determine which educational areas should be expanded, maintained, or reduced, it would be impossible for the university to engage in any long-range planning, whether it be building construction, equipment purchases, or library allocations.

Explanation (pro point)
Detail
Explanation (pro point)   A government-controlled university would also have great difficulty attracting highly trained faculty, since it could make no promises about tenure or the kind or number of courses to be taught. It also could make no promise that faculty would fulfill what are surely the key educational functions of the university: the

Detail   pursuit of new areas of knowledge and the criticism of existing areas of knowledge through research and theoretical inquiry.

I will go through the same process of checking the structure and development of my other middle paragraphs, rewriting as necessary.

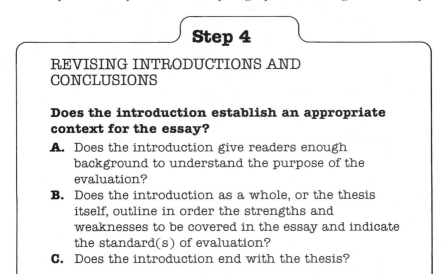

Step 4

REVISING INTRODUCTIONS AND CONCLUSIONS

Does the introduction establish an appropriate context for the essay?

A. Does the introduction give readers enough background to understand the purpose of the evaluation?

B. Does the introduction as a whole, or the thesis itself, outline in order the strengths and weaknesses to be covered in the essay and indicate the standard(s) of evaluation?

C. Does the introduction end with the thesis?

To persuade my readers to consider my evaluation, I need to catch their attention and establish some common ground as part of the context for my essay. The readers I need to include are those who take a very practical view of university control, since my own position eventually relies on abstract ethical arguments. The question at the beginning of my introduction is down-to-earth and attention-getting, so I think I'll keep it. My second sentence seems aimed at establishing common ground, since it refers to both sides of the question; my shift to the practical and ethical considerations is probably too rapid. I will elaborate briefly on the case for government control before I introduce my thesis refuting it, as follows:

FIRST DRAFT	REVISION
There are lots of arguments on both sides of this question and the value of government control depends on whether you are looking at it from a purely practical or ethical viewpoint.	Some people see the emphasis on vocational education that would result from government control over university programmes and enrollment as a desirable way of ensuring employment for university graduates.

The rest of my introductory paragraph consists of the thesis. I have already revised my thesis so that it reflects the pro-con structure of the essay and the standards of evaluation I am using, but it does not indicate very clearly the order of my points. I'll rewrite the thesis as follows:

> Although government control would have the practical benefits for students, the university, and society that result from an orientation to employment, these benefits would be outweighed by the practical and ethical damage to student freedom of choice, to the organization and exploration of knowledge in the university, and to independent thought in society.

Does the conclusion tie together the points made in the essay?

A. Does the conclusion restate the thesis, in different words?

B. Does the conclusion summarize the evaluations made in the middle paragraphs in order to clarify the thesis?

C. Does the conclusion suggest the wider implications of the evaluation, if any?

The conclusion in my draft is very disappointing, since it simply restates the thesis in the most general terms, without even referring to the specific areas of government control I discuss in the essay. My final sentence, "There is much more to university education than vocational training," is too vague to suggest the wider implications of my thesis.

I can revise the first part of my conclusion on the basis of my revised draft, but what can I add to clarify the thesis and explore the implications of government control? Is there a more profound relationship between student freedom of choice, intellectual exploration, and independent social thought? When I ask myself this question, I see that without some sense of free choice, intellectual exploration is inconceivable, and so is independent social criticism. Therefore when I discuss freedom in the universities, I am also discussing the conditions for independent thinking that all societies need. Realizing this, I can extend the essay's original thesis as follows:

> What should be clear by now is that these are not separate areas of concern. By allowing the individual some freedom of choice, we nurture the qualities that are necessary to produce new knowledge and valid criticism, the fruits of the university on which the creative growth of society itself finally depends.

Writing the Revised Draft

When I have made all the necessary revisions in structure and development and done the final editing, my revised draft looks like this.

WHY THE GOVERNMENT SHOULD NOT CONTROL
UNIVERSITIES

Should the government control universities to make sure that the programmes students take will lead to jobs? Some people see the emphasis on vocational education that would result from government control over university programmes and enrollment as a desirable way of ensuring employment for university graduates. Although government control would have the practical benefits for students, the university, and society that result from an orientation to employment, these benefits would be outweighed by the practical and ethical damage to student freedom of choice, to the organization and exploration of knowledge in the university, and to independent thought in society.

Although government control over university programmes and enrollment could bring about significant financial benefits for students, in the long run losing the freedom to choose courses and explore ideas would seriously reduce the value of university education for the individual student. It is true that an assured job would enable students to make plans for the future with greater confidence and that students willing to enter programmes with high government priority would probably be able to obtain loans and other forms of financial assistance more readily than at present. These practical benefits might seem very tempting until we examine the long-range implication of a government emphasis on vocational training in the university more closely.

Some students, no doubt, would find a vocational emphasis in university education quite congenial; however, other students will likely be less concerned that their education lead directly to a job and more concerned with the range and content of courses offered. Students who are interested in experimenting with different fields in order to find the most personally satisfying one may well, under a system of government control, find that low quotas in programmes such as fine arts and theoretical science deny them the opportunity of such experimentation. The choice may well be to take a programme with few or no options or to abandon the idea of a university education. Furthermore, the emphasis on vocational education would probably also mean a shift in the content of many courses. English courses, for example, would stress report-writing skills over an appreciation of Shakespeare. Behavioural management instead of Freudian psychoanalysis would be taught in psychology courses, and philosophy courses might cease to exist altogether. In order to process students with maximum efficiency, it is likely that government-controlled universities would provide students with fewer opportunities to gain information not directly relevant to an existing job.

It is true that government control would have a limited financial advantage for the university, but this advantage would be greatly outweighed by the serious practical disadvantages for the organization of university affairs and the even more serious ethical problems regarding the university's fulfillment of its educational functions. The practical advantage of government control is that the university would likely receive increased funding for job-oriented programmes. We must recognize, however, that the demands of the job market are continually changing. If this market were to determine which educational areas should be expanded, maintained, or reduced, it would be impossible for the university to engage in any long-range planning, whether it be building construction, equipment purchases, or library allocations. A government-controlled university would also have great difficulty attracting highly trained faculty, since it could make no promises about tenure or the kind or number of courses to be taught. It also could make no promise that faculty would fulfill what are surely the key educational functions of the university: the pursuit of new areas of knowledge and the criticism of existing areas of knowledge through research and theoretical inquiry.

Some people might argue that the pursuit and criticism of knowledge is less significant to society than training for employment, but the truth is that when vocational training is supported at the expense of research and the exploration of theoretical knowledge, society as a whole suffers. It is important to remember that the really important ideas with enormous long-range benefits to society usually occur when people are allowed to experiment and explore their own interests, however impractical those interests may seem. Highly theoretical research in chemistry, for example, led to the development of extremely useful new plastics. Criticism of existing knowledge is equally important to society. It is vital to realize that government control over course content means that the government could, if it wished, suppress ideas and information. The content of political science and history courses could be changed, for example, so that justice was redefined as the right of the powerful to take whatever they could get from everyone else, and democracy meant the right to vote for the one political party allowed to exist. Society benefits from the social criticism and the criticism of government policies that an independent university can provide. A government-controlled university is more likely to suppress controversial ideas and attitudes as well as to discourage free exploration of knowledge. This suppression limits the freedom of society as a whole.

When we examine how government control over university programmes and enrollment would affect not just students and universities, but the whole society, it seems clear that the practical advantages of such a proposal are outweighed by its massive disadvantages. The most immediate disadvantage is the practical impossibility of running a university worthy of the name under government control. Beyond this disadvantage lie the more profound disadvantages that would result: the disappearance of freedom of choice, intellectual exploration, and social independence. What should be clear by now is that these are not separate areas of concern. By allowing the individual some freedom of choice, we nurture the qualities that are necessary to produce new knowledge and valid criticism, the fruits of the university on which the creative growth of society itself finally depends.

Since this revised draft has already gone through the final editing process, it is in a more finished form than your own work may be. Use the Checklist for Final Editing and the handbook to ensure that your revised draft follows the conventions for format, sentence structure, punctuation, and grammar expected of college and university essays.

SUMMARY

These are the important points to remember when you are writing and revising an evaluative essay:

> 1. Maintain a tone appropriate to serious discussion between reasonable people.
> 2. Make your essay more persuasive by including both strengths and weaknesses or reasons for and against your position.
> 3. Use a pro-con structure to clarify the relationship between strengths and weaknesses.
> 4. Consider the interests and needs of your readers when you choose examples, factual information, and quotations to support your points.

If you follow these suggestions, you are likely to persuade your readers to take your position seriously, even if you don't persuade them to change their minds.

EXERCISES

A. Write a sentence or two assessing the strengths and weaknesses of the following thesis statements for evaluation essays. Use the questions below as a guide.

Does the thesis state an opinion and support it?

Does the thesis explain the relation between the strengths and weaknesses of the thing(s) being evaluated?

What standard(s) of evaluation (practical, ethical, logical, aesthetic) does the thesis suggest?

---

1. In *The Hazards of Being Male* Herb Goldberg argues that pressure to conform to a stereotyped image of masculinity forces many men to live like emotional zombies. This thesis seems valid, but the evidence Goldberg uses to support this thesis is seriously undermined by the fact that the men he refers to, for the most part, are already so unhappy with their lives that they have sought help from a psychotherapist.

2. Many of the people who object to the Canadian seal hunt on the grounds that it is wrong to kill defenceless animals are surprisingly indifferent to the plight of the seal hunters, who are economically defenceless without the money earned from the hunt.

3. Although coaches have a responsibility to develop the potential of individual athletes, this responsibility should not take precedence over their responsibility to the welfare of the team as a whole. Coaches should not allow their desire to help the individual athlete take precedence over their responsibility to their employers to produce winning teams.

4. Although it is true that much television programming for children is mere low-quality, time-wasting entertainment, it is still true that some programmes for children provide a valuable range of experiences and information that children would not have access to without television.

5. Restricting university enrollment to students with averages over 70 percent would have two important advantages: it would prevent the current overcrowding of university facilities and it would help to ensure jobs for university graduates. People who object to this restriction are probably too stupid to go to university in the first place.

B. This exercise is designed to give you practice in structuring a pro-con essay. You will be given a list of points, taken from Robert Cooke, *Improving on Nature: The Brave New World of Genetic Engineering* (New York: Demeter Press, 1977), that could be used to develop an essay on the topic "Should we encourage scientific research into genetic engineering?" Use this list to complete the following steps.

1. Label each of these points as pro or con arguments to support this thesis statement: "Although genetic engineering has a frightening potential for misuse by the unscrupulous, the benefits of this new science, both for the individual and for society as a whole, greatly outweigh the dangers."

_____ a. Some newly-created organism may accidentally be released into the environment, as is supposed in the case of the mysterious "Legionnaires' disease" that occurred in Philadelphia in 1976. (Cooke, p. 187)

_____ b. Because any one cell has all the genetic information necessary to produce all the other cells in the organism, it is possible to create a duplicate organism from one cell. Some gardeners, especially orchid and geranium growers, use the procedure regularly. (Cooke, p. 10)

_____ c. It may be possible to correct diseases caused by missing, incomplete, or scrambled genetic information, such as hemophilia, diabetes, and Tay-Sachs (which produces mental retardation, blindness, and early death), by inserting new genes into a cell. (Cooke, p. 6)

_____ d. Some destructive organism could be deliberately created, since many nations have departments of biological warfare. (Cooke, p. 189)

_____ e. New organisms, such as bacteria, could be created to facilitate the manufacture of medicines, hormones, and enzymes, which are now expensive to produce. (Cooke, p. 7)

_____ f. Toads have been reproduced in laboratories by cloning. It will be possible to clone human organs for transplant and even to clone complete individuals. (Cooke, p. 32)

_____ g. Scientists at General Electric have already produced a new bacterium that eats up oil. (Cooke, p. 7)

_____ h. Such common diseases as degeneration of the heart and blood vessels, lung diseases like emphysema, and cancer all seem to have genetic factors. (Cooke, pp. 6, 68-70)

_____ i. It is possible that the nitrogen-fixing ability of legumes (which enables them to make their own fertilizer from nitrogen in the air) could be transferred to cereal crops (corn, wheat, rice), which now require expensive fertilizers for maximum yield. (Cooke, p. 7)

_____ j. It is now possible to examine the genes of a foetus to see if the child will be normal, or if it will be physically disabled or mentally retarded. (Cooke, pp. 26, 48)

2. Group related points into matching pro and con categories and give each category a heading (e.g., "genetic diseases").

3. Work out a topic sentence for one of the categories you have established. Be sure that your topic sentence includes both the pro and con arguments for this section of the material.

C. Printed below are three possible introductions to an essay on the topic "What limitations, if any, are there to conventional methods of treating people who are emotionally disturbed?" Write two or three sentences assessing the strengths and weaknesses of each introduction, using the following questions as a guide.

Does the introduction give readers enough information to understand the purpose of the evaluation?

Does the introduction as a whole, or the thesis itself, outline in order the strengths or weaknesses to be covered in the essay and indicate the standard of evaluation?

Does the introduction end with a good evaluative thesis?

---

1. There are many methods of treating the emotionally disturbed. The conventional methods are drugs, shock treatments, and psychoanalysis. These methods of treatment have many limitations.

2. Many books have been written about the treatment of mental illness. In addition to scientific books on the subject, there have been many personal accounts by former mental patients. One of these books is *Too Much Anger, Too Many Tears*, by Janet and Paul Gotkin, a book that Doris Lessing has called one of the "classics in this field, like *I Never Promised You a Rose Garden*." *I Never Promised You a Rose Garden* has been made into a movie. The Gotkins live in Westchester, New York, where they have organized Mental Patients Resistance. In *Too Much Anger, Too Many*

Tears, Janet's account of her ten years as a mental patient alternates with Paul's account of their relationship during the last five of those years. As books like this show, conventional methods of treatment do not resolve deep-seated emotional problems; they simply create new dependencies that mask the patient's real needs.

3. Throughout the history of mankind, people have suffered emotional problems. Before Freud, the insane were locked away in attics or madhouses. Now there are an infinite number of ways of treating mental illness. Despite the vast sums of money spent on psychiatrists and mental hospitals, these modern methods of treatment offer patients no more help than they received in earlier times.

D. Write and revise an evaluative essay for which you have completed the preparation process. Use one of the topics from the exercises in Chapter 9 or another topic you have been given.

Chapter 11

Preparing to Write: Doing Research

In some high school courses and in many courses in college and university, you will be asked to write research papers. Research papers are basically extended versions of analysis, comparison, or evaluation essays. The special skills you need for preparing and writing research papers are those of searching for information and opinion and integrating this material into a coherent essay.

These are examples of assignments asking for a research essay:

1. Using several critical discussions of the play, explore the function of the graveyard scene in *Hamlet*.
2. From the relevant sources, compare the settlement of Red River and Fort Victoria.
3. Write a 3000-word essay comparing the use of the vampire myth in the films *Dracula* and *Nosferatu*.
4. Should students with physical disabilities be integrated into regular classrooms? Write an essay evaluating the arguments on both sides of the question.
5. Is the concept of adolescence useful for explaining human development? Evaluate two or more theories of the role of adolescence in human development.
6. It has been said that Dickens' novels were popular in his own day for reasons which would make him unpopular in ours. Do you agree or disagree? Focus on the popularity of one particular book if you wish.
7. Write a 2500-word essay discussing the effects of microcomputers on the automobile industry.
8. "Canadian art has always been derivative; it's all second-hand Cézanne, second-hand Mondrian." Discuss the development of Canadian abstract painting in the light of this quotation, taking into account the views of principal art critics.
9. Explain the development of the concept of narcissism in psychoanalytic theory with reference to at least three keynote discussions.

Some of these research assignments specifically ask you to consider sources other than your own reading or viewing; others are simply long essays that might or might not require research. If you are not sure whether to use secondary sources (books, articles, and other material **about** your subject), ask your instructor.

If the purpose of writing essays is to help you develop and communicate an opinion on a variety of subjects, what, you might ask, is the purpose of writing research papers using ideas and/or information from other people? Research papers serve three purposes.

1. To give you an opportunity to increase your understanding of a subject covered only briefly in class. A sociology instructor who has only one class period in which to discuss the social implications of family violence, for example, might assign research papers on various aspects of this subject.

2. To acquaint you with the procedures and categories, the general ways of working, of a particular discipline. In doing a research paper in psychology, for example, you would learn such things as how to use *Psychological Abstracts*; which journals to consult for research in a particular field; and, from reading those journals, how experiments in psychology are conducted and reported.

3. To synthesize information and integrate it with your own ideas. A research paper is not merely a summary of other writers' work; it is an essay in which you develop your own opinion on your subject and use your research material as part of your evidence to support that opinion.

In this chapter we will first consider the basic process of preparing to write research papers, paying particular attention to strategies for doing library research. Then we will show how to apply these procedures for preparing to write a research paper on a content topic: a comparison paper for a history course. In the next chapter we will demonstrate how to prepare and write a research paper requiring textual analysis.

BASIC PROCEDURES FOR PREPARING TO WRITE RESEARCH PAPERS

In doing research papers, you will find systematic preparation essential, both to ensure that you have enough material to work with and to prevent you from becoming lost in a mass of information. The following procedures will allow you to gather research material efficiently and to integrate that material with your own ideas to arrive at a thesis for your essay.

Step 1

CLARIFYING THE TOPIC

Do I understand the terms used in the topic?

Since research papers are usually on specialized topics, you should be alert to the specialized use of terms. The first step in writing on the development of the concept of narcissism (topic #9 in the list at the beginning of this chapter), for example, would be to look up narcissism in an appropriate dictionary, such as Charles Mycroft, *A Critical Dictionary of Psychoanalysis* (1968).

Do I understand the directions the topic gives me?
A. Am I asked to analyze, to compare, or to evaluate?
B. Does this topic require analysis, comparison, or evaluation of **content** or of one or more **texts**?

A. Answer this question as you would for any other essay, and refer to the appropriate chapter, if necessary, to remind yourself of the special considerations you will need to keep in mind as you prepare your research topic.

B. If your research topic asks you to analyze, compare, or evaluate content, you will likely have few ideas and little information of your own to begin with, and so your main focus will be on collecting and then interpreting material. If your topic requires textual analysis, comparison, or evaluation, on the other hand, you will basically be supplementing your initial interpretation of the text(s) by considering other writers' interpretations.

Do I know what kind of material to use in my essay?

Although you bring your own ideas to the topic, a research paper is not a research paper without references to other sources (books, articles, and other materials on your subject). Since one of the aims of doing research papers is to learn to evaluate and integrate different sources of information, you should be careful not to base your essay on a single author's point of view, a single experiment, or a single survey. The number of references considered adequate will depend on the discipline, the instructor, and the amount of material available on your topic. A good rule of thumb is to use at least six reference sources in the final draft of a short research essay; your working bibliography will likely contain two or three times as many entries as you actually use.

Do I know how to limit the topic?

Instructors often give broad topics for research papers in order to allow you to select your own focus. You might come to the decision to limit your topic in two ways. Your initial reading on a topic such as the causes of World War I, for example, might convince you that you would not be able to do justice to the subject in a short research paper unless you limited your discussion to economic causes or to conditions within a specific country. Or you might realize from the beginning that the topic should be narrowed, and use one of the discovery techniques in Chapter 2 to decide on a focus. Check your proposed change with your instructor to ensure that you are not limiting your topic inappropriately.

Do I know how to choose a topic that fits my interest, knowledge, time, and skills?

No matter how interested you are in your subject or how knowledgeable you are about it, research papers will always take more time for preparation and writing than other essays. Plan your time accordingly.

Step 2

GATHERING MATERIAL

What preliminary sources of material can I draw on?

You will save yourself a lot of time and potential confusion if you do some thinking about your topic before you start your research. If your research paper is on a content topic, you could use one or more of these ways of stimulating your thinking: (1) jot down what you already know and think about the subject, using one of the discovery techniques discussed in Chapter 2; (2) read an encyclopedia article for an overview of the subject; (3) discuss your subject with people who know something about it. If you can think of categories appropriate to your subject, using these categories will help you gather material efficiently.

If your research essay is on a text, read the text carefully, making notes according to the categories appropriate for the kind of text and for the topic.

What sources of reference material can I draw on to compile my working bibliography?

Although each research assignment will pose its own problems, the general search strategy outlined below will give you an efficient way to locate references, evaluate what you find, and take notes.

Your first task is to compile a working bibliography. A good rule of thumb is to collect two to three times as many references as you will need for the final draft of your essay. The reason for collecting more references than you are likely to use in your paper is to allow a margin of error for books and articles that are not in the library or that are less relevant than you thought they would be.

For each item in your working bibliography you will need to take down complete bibliographical details, in the form discussed below. You will need this information both to locate material in your library and to identify in your paper the sources you have used. If you record full publication data as you collect your initial references, you will save yourself the trouble of making return trips to the library. You will also protect yourself against unintentional plagiarism: the use of ideas and information from sources that are not identified.

Recording each reference on a separate file card will enable you to add or discard items easily. You will find a sample bibliography card below.

You will find references for your working bibliography in three places: (1) bound bibliographies; (2) periodical indexes and annual bibliographies; and (3) card and microfiche catalogues.

A. Is a bound bibliography available?

References to research in a particular area are often collected in books. These bound bibliographies are useful for several reasons. The most obvious is that they contain references that you might spend weeks compiling. Another advantage is that they may be annotated; that is, they may contain brief summaries of every item, or of selected items, and so make it easier for you to tell whether a particular reference fits your topic. Determining whether there is a bound bibliography on your subject is therefore a good place to start.

There are two ways of finding out whether there is a bound bibliography on your subject. The first is by consulting a bibliography of bibliographies. These works list under appropriate subject headings the various bibliographies that have been compiled. For example, if you were writing an essay on *King Lear*, you could look for bibliographies of criticism under the heading "Shakespeare" in *A World Bibliography of Bibliographies*, compiled by Theodore Besterman, with a supplement covering 1964-1974 compiled by Alice F. Toomey, 2 vols. Totowa, New Jersey: Rowan and Littlefield, 1977.

The second and simpler way, if you are doing a limited amount of research, is to check the subject heading in your card or microfiche catalogue under the subheading "Bibliography."

To make sure you are using the appropriate subject heading, consult the two-volume *Library of Congress Subject Headings*. This catalogue is especially useful for content topics that might appear under several different headings. If you are looking for information on vitamin deficiencies, for example, you might not find any references under that heading either in the card/microfiche catalogue or in the periodical indexes you consult. The *Library of Congress Subject Headings* catalogue would refer you to the appropriate headings, such as "Nutrition," for example.

If you have a choice of bibliographies, select the most recent or the most fully annotated.

Although bound bibliographies can be very useful, they also have at least one limitation: they will not contain the most recent work in the field. For current information, you will need to consult periodical indexes and annual bibliographies.

B. Is there a relevant periodical index or annual bibliography?

Although it may seem easier to take books off the shelf than to look up articles, there are several advantages to using articles as reference sources. One is that articles are more specialized than books, and therefore you are more likely to find articles directly related to specialized topics. Another is that current research in many fields appears in articles several years before it is available in books. Periodicals are therefore a much better source of information in new and rapidly developing fields such as computing science, genetics, astrophysics, and women's studies. A third reason is that if someone else has already checked out all the books on your topic, you can still find material.

To locate references to articles and to recently published books, consult a relevant periodical index or annual bibliography. Periodical indexes list, under appropriate subject (and sometimes author) headings, articles published in a selected range of magazines and/or scholarly journals during the preceding year. Annual bibliographies include books as well as articles. The following list suggests the wide range of periodical indexes and annual bibliographies you can choose from.

General Indexes

Canadian Periodical Index
Essay and General Literature Index
Readers' Guide to Periodical Literature

Specialized Indexes

Applied Science and Technology Index
Arts and Humanities Citation Index
Historical Abstracts
MLA International Bibliography (modern languages and literatures)
Philosopher's Index
Psychological Abstracts
Religious and Theological Abstracts
The Year's Work in English Studies

If you are not sure which periodical index or annual bibliography to consult for your topic, ask a reference librarian. Indexes with the word "abstract" in the title offer a summary of the books and articles they cite as well as giving publication details.

The most efficient way of using a periodical index or annual bibliography is to start with the most recent volume and work backwards until you reach the cut-off date of the bound bibliography you have used or until you have enough references. Copy down references exactly as they appear and then consult the key to abbreviations in the front of the volume to decipher the entries. If you were looking in the *1981 Applied Science and Technology Index* for references on industrial pollution of lakes, for example, you might come across this entry under the heading "LAKE sediments":

> Fluxes of arsenic, lead, zinc, and cadmium in Green Bay and Lake Michigan sediments. E.R. Christensen and N.K. Chian. bibl map Environ Sci & Tech 15:553-8 My '81

Checking the key to abbreviations for this index, you would discover that this article by E.R. Christensen and N.K. Chian was published in the periodical *Environmental Science and Technology*, volume 15, pages 553-558, in May 1981, and that the article includes a bibliography and map.

C. Can I find references through my library's card or microfiche catalogue?

The third step in compiling references for your working bibliography is to check your library's card or microfiche catalogue for books on your subject. Use the heading(s) you found in the *Library of Congress Subject Headings* catalogue. If you don't find any entries under a particular heading, ask a reference librarian where to look. Most libraries have some material on every subject imaginable; the trick is finding it.

Librarians may also be able to suggest other sources of information, such as government documents and newspaper files.

How do I choose, record, and track down references for my working bibliography?

With each of these sources of references—bound bibliographies, periodical indexes and annual bibliographies, and card or microfiche catalogues—you will have to decide which items to include in your working bibliography, how to record bibliographical information most efficiently, and how to find the relevant books and articles.

A. How do I choose which references to record?

The more you have thought about the topic and your approach to it, the easier it will be to pick out relevant references. Begin with the narrowest sections of bibliographies and indexes and the narrowest subject headings, working outward to more general headings if necessary. If you were doing a paper on attitudes towards marriage in Jane Austen's *Pride and Prejudice*, for example, you might begin by consulting the most recent *MLA International Bibliography*, turning first to the section "English Literature IX. Nineteenth Century" and then looking under the alphabetical listing of authors for "Austen." From the twenty or thirty articles and books on Jane Austen published the previous year, you would select only the two or three closest to your subject, marriage in *Pride and Prejudice*. For an author or subject on which very little is published each year, you would include titles of wider scope.

You may have only the title and date of publication by which to judge the relevance of some references; for others, you may find these

aids to evaluation: annotations, abstracts, recommendations by bib-
liographers (often indicated by asterisks), and, if you are somewhat
familiar with the field, the reputation of the journal or publishing
firm.

B. How can I record details of these references most
effectively?

For each reference you decide to include in your working bibliography, you will need to record complete bibliographical information
so that you can find the work in your library, and, if you use it in
your essay, put the reference in your footnotes and bibliography.
Using a separate file card for each item, record the following information, in the order given.

BOOKS
Complete name of author(s), last name first; title; place of publication, publisher, and date of publication.

ARTICLES
Complete name of author(s), last name first; title of article; magazine or journal in which the article appears; day, month, and
year of publication (for weekly and monthly magazines) or volume, issue number, and year (for journals); page numbers.

OTHER SOURCES
See Handbook Section 9 on footnotes and bibliography.

At the bottom of the file card, note the bibliography, index, or catalogue in which you found the reference, in case you discover you
have not recorded it accurately.

C. What procedures do I use to track down the
references I have recorded?

When you have collected two or three times the number of references
you will eventually need, you are ready to locate them in your library.
Begin by finding the **call numbers** of books and journals, the arrangement of letters and numbers that are your guide to the shelf locations
of your references. You will find the call number for books on each
author, title, and subject entry in the card or microfiche catalogue.

Some libraries include journal titles in card/microfiche catalogues;
others compile information about their periodical holdings in what is
called a **serials list**. The serials list is the most efficient way of determining whether your library has the articles you need, since you can

look up all the journal titles at the same time. Journal listings will indicate the volumes your library has; check to make sure the volume you need falls within its holdings.

Copy the call number for each book and journal you find onto the appropriate file card, and, if your college or university has more than one library, note the locations of copies. If you fail to find some of your references, note "not in library" or "volume missing" on your card.

Sample cards in your working bibliography, with a call number for the Library of Congress classification system, might look like this:

Sample Bibliography Cards

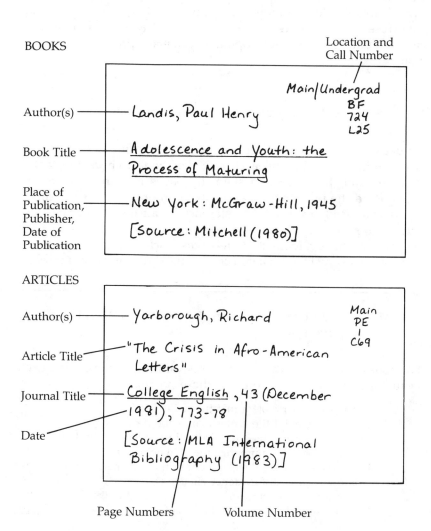

BOOKS   Location and Call Number

Author(s) —— Landis, Paul Henry   Main/Undergrad / BF / 724 / L25

Book Title —— Adolescence and Youth: the Process of Maturing

Place of Publication, Publisher, Date of Publication —— New York: McGraw-Hill, 1945

[Source: Mitchell (1980)]

ARTICLES

Author(s) —— Yarborough, Richard   Main / PE / 1 / C69

Article Title —— "The Crisis in Afro-American Letters"

Journal Title —— College English, 43 (December 1981), 773-78

Date —— [Source: MLA International Bibliography (1983)]

Page Numbers   Volume Number

These cards contain the information you need to find the book or journal on the shelves or to request it from closed stacks or from another library. If you discover that material is missing from the shelves, check with the circulation desk to see why and whether you can get hold of it within the time you need it.

How do I evaluate and take notes on the references I have found?

Even if several of your references are unavailable, you are still likely to have a fairly large working bibliography at this point. Instead of sitting down to take copious notes on every book and article, make your research time more efficient by eliminating material of only limited usefulness and by developing a systematic procedure for taking notes.

A. How do I evaluate the references I have found?

To decide which of your references are worth taking notes on, spend a few minutes evaluating each one. For books, check the table of contents and the index and skim the pages most relevant to your topic. Read the introductory and concluding paragraphs of articles.

If you decide to discard a reference because its focus seems different from your own, make a note on the file card saying so and indicating what its focus is. References discarded at this stage may prove to be useful later on if you change the direction of your research.

B. How do I take notes on the references I find to be worthwhile?

For books and articles that address relevant issues or provide useful factual information, take notes on these points:

1. The issue or problem that the writer identifies.
2. The main point the writer makes about the issue.
3. The context of this issue. Does this writer give background information or summarize the viewpoints of other writers?
4. Key points in the development of the explanation or argument and key pieces of evidence cited.
5. The writer's conclusion.
6. Your own reactions to and evaluation of the reference.

It is usually best to take notes in a mixture of summary or paraphrase, direct quotation, and commentary. Summarize or paraphrase (preferably in point form to avoid inadvertent plagiarism) when the point or detail is important but the way it is expressed isn't—as, for example, when you are collecting background material or factual information. Include the page reference for each item of information.

Use direct quotation when the precise wording may be important to your discussion, as in definitions of concepts or particulary effective ways of identifying a problem or suggesting a solution. Try not to quote more than a sentence at a time (it's very easy to decide that everything is important); quote the whole sentence so that the context will be clear (you can shorten quotations when you edit); copy the quotation **exactly** as it appears in the original (including spelling and punctuation); put quotation marks around everything you quote; indicate the exact page on which each quotation occurs. If a quotation is continued from one page to another, use a slash mark to indicate the page break in case you decide to use only part of it.

Conclude your notes on each reference with your own evaluation of the ideas and evidence it presents, your comments on its relation to other references, and/or your notes on its place in your essay. To avoid possible confusion, put your own comments in square brackets or use some other consistent way of identifying them.

What should I do if I have to change my original research direction?

The reason for developing your own approach to the topic as the first stage of gathering material is so that you will not be tempted to change direction with each new reference you read. As you research your subject, however, your original sense of the issues often becomes clarified and modified. As a result, you may decide to restore references you have discarded. You can do so easily if you have noted your reason for rejecting each reference, as we suggested earlier.

Occasionally your original research direction may lead you to a dead end. Then you may have to return to the bibliographies, indexes, and catalogues to compile a new working bibliography.

Step 3

CATEGORIZING MATERIAL

What categories should I use for my combined preliminary material (if any) and research material?

As you start to combine your preliminary material and your research material, make sure you do not lose track of the source of your information and ideas. Give the author and page number after each item that you have taken from other sources.

A. Can I use the same categories I used for taking notes?

If you were somewhat familiar with the special categories of the discipline before you began your research, you may have used them to organize your note-taking, and you may find them equally useful for your combination of preliminary material and research material. In gathering information for a research paper comparing the social organization of the !Kung San and the Mutayr, for example, you would probably use the same special categories you used for gathering information from your textbook, and these would also be the categories used by most of the writers you consulted.

Even when you can use the same set of analytical categories you started with, however, you need to ensure that you also meet any special demands of your topic: using matching categories for comparison essays, as for the paper on the !Kung San and Mutayr; or using evaluative categories (strengths and weaknesses, advantages and disadvantages, etc.) for evaluation essays.

B. Do I need to work out new categories for my combined material?

Often when you use the general categories of features, causes, and effects to begin your research on a content topic, you will later need to work out more appropriate special categories for your material. In the course of your reading you may become aware that most writers on your subject use similar sets of terms and similar ways of organizing their material. You will likely be able to adopt, and adapt, these terms and procedures. You will see an example of this possibility in the sample topic for this chapter.

If you are researching a textual topic, you may have used special categories for textual analysis for your preliminary material, only to discover that these categories are not widely used in your research material. The problem then is to find a way of accommodating both sets of material. You may decide to use your initial notes on the text(s) as the framework, adding comments from other writers where they are appropriate. Or you may decide that the issues identified by the writers you have read are more profound than the issues highlighted by the categories you used in your preliminary notes; in this case you will need to fit your analysis into the broader conceptual framework these writers provide. You will see an example of this procedure in the next chapter.

Step 4

FINDING A THESIS

What is the nature of the thing I am researching?

The process of finding a thesis is the same for a research paper as for any other kind of essay. If you find it hard to see connections among your categories because of the quantity of your material, try asking yourself these questions: What issue or problem did I identify when I was first thinking about this subject? What issues or problems are raised in the research material? What are the connections between the issues or problems I identified and those mentioned by other writers? The answers to these questions will likely lead you to a generalization about the nature of your subject.

Why does the thing I am researching have this particular nature?

Your generalization about the nature of your subject may not differ from the views of other writers you have consulted. If you were researching Britain's entry into World War I, for example, you might conclude, along with the historians you consulted, that the British were disorganized and inefficient during the early years of the war. You might wonder, then, how your thesis can be any more than a summary of research on your topic.

The answer is that the reasons you give to support your opinion will be your contribution to the debate. In your reading on Britain's war efforts in World War I, for example, you may have found one historian who blames the slow start on Prime Minister Herbert Asquith's indecisiveness; another who blames the arrogance of Field Marshall Earl Kitchener; and a third who blames the British class system and capitalist economics. In order to give reasons for your opinion, you will have to reach your own conclusion about the relevance of each of these factors. Developing your own opinion and finding reasons to support it will thus enable you to provide the intellectual framework for your essay, instead of depending upon the framework provided by one of the sources you have used.

In the next section of this chapter you will see how the procedure we have outlined can be used in preparing to write a research paper on a content topic. The following chapter will illustrate the preparation and revision process for a textual topic.

SAMPLE TOPIC: DOING RESEARCH FOR A CONTENT TOPIC

As you have seen, the research paper is a special form of the analysis, comparison, or evaluation essay. The special requirement of the research paper is that you need to work out a thesis based on categories of material derived from other writers' points of view as well as from your own thinking. From the first part of this chapter you are familiar with the general steps of preparing to write a research paper. Now it is time to turn to a specific topic.

In the next chapter we will demonstrate how to do research on a subject about which a great deal has been written. For some subjects, however, you may have trouble finding enough material. The sample topic we have chosen for showing you how to do research for a content topic illustrates this difficulty.

Let's suppose, then, that from the list of possible research topics in your Canadian history course you have chosen this one:

> From the relevant sources, compare the settlement of Red River and Fort Victoria.

Step 1

CLARIFYING THE TOPIC

Do I understand the terms used in the topic?

Yes. The word "settlement," as I understand it from class discussions, includes both the founding and early development of the two colonies.

Do I understand the directions the topic gives me?

A. Am I asked to analyze, to compare, or to evaluate?

B. Does this topic require comparison of content or comparison of texts?

A. The topic clearly states that I am supposed to compare these two settlements. As I analyze their histories, I'll look for both similarities and differences. There is no mention made of evaluating the colonies or evaluating any factor that led to their development.

B. This topic requires a comparison of content, since I will have to gather information about the two colonies from a wide variety of sources rather than to compare two historians' accounts of their development. I need to remember, however, that the attitudes and purposes of historians affect the kinds of information they present and how they present it.

Do I know what kind of material to use in my essay?

Because this topic demands research, I know I should use ideas and information derived from other sources as well as my own ideas. There may be primary sources of material on these colonies, such as letters from settlers and official documents, but I don't have the time to track them down. I'll have to depend on secondary sources—books and articles written by historians. The early history of these colonies is not dramatic in the way that the Riel Rebellion and the Battle of the Plains of Abraham are dramatic, and so I may not be able to find many references. I doubt that there's a book or article that conveniently compares the two; I'll probably have to collect information on each and then make the comparisons myself.

Do I know how to limit the topic?

The topic is already quite specific, but it does not say exactly what time period I should cover. It seems reasonable to begin with the founding of the two colonies and to trace their histories up to the point that each was securely established.

Do I know how to choose a topic that fits my interest, knowledge, time, and writing skills?

I chose this topic because I was born in Victoria but never learned anything about its history. I have written comparison essays, but I have not had much practice in writing research papers. I have three weeks to write this essay; I'd better start now so that I'll have enough time to collect my information and to revise the essay before I hand it in.

Step 2

GATHERING MATERIAL

What preliminary sources of material can I draw on? What categories can I use for gathering research material?

We haven't covered the history of these colonies in class, so I can't really do much thinking about the topic until I've done some research. I don't even know which special categories historians would use in discussing these settlements.

On the other hand, I need to have some idea of what to look for. I think I'll take notes according to the general categories for content analysis: **causes** (what caused the Red River settlement and Fort Victoria to be founded?; **effects** (how did the reasons for establishing them affect their development); and **features** (what were the settlements actually like?).

Within each category I'll need to look for matching information so that I can work out a central similarity or difference in the histories of the two settlements. I'll be able to work out more specific categories to organize my comparison after I've done some research.

What sources of reference material can I draw on to compile my working bibliography?

A. Is a bound bibliography available?

B. Is there a relevant periodical index or annual bibliography?

C. Can I find references through my library's card or microfiche catalogue?'

A. There is no bound bibliography available listing source material for this particular subject.

B. I checked the *Canadian Periodical Index* and discovered two articles in a magazine called *Beaver*, published by the Hudson's Bay Company. I also checked the *Social Sciences Index*, but there were very few references on Canadian history, and none on anything related to my topic.

C. As I looked through the subject section of the card catalogue under headings such as "British Columbia—History," "Canada—History," "Manitoba—History," and "The West—History," I paid particular attention to the titles of books that looked as though they might contain information about the Red River and Fort Victoria settlements. I found that index cards often contain a summary of the contents of the book, and, in some cases, a list of chapter headings. Using this information, I found eight books that should be useful. That gives me ten references.

How do I choose, record, and track down references for my working bibliography?

A. How do I choose which references to record?

B. How can I record details of these references most effectively?

C. What procedures do I use to track down the references I have recorded?

A. Since I have only ten references, I will need to try to find all of them.

B. Using a separate file card for each reference, I have recorded the name of the author, the title of the book, the place of publication, the publisher, date of publication, and call number. For the two articles I recorded the name of the author, title of the article, name and volume of the journal, date of publication, and page references.

C. First I consulted the serials list to see whether this library subscribes to *Beaver*. Unfortunately the library does not have any volumes of this journal. I then went to the library stacks with my file cards and located six of the eight books I had listed. Since two of the books were not on the shelves, I checked with the librarian and discovered that one is out on loan and the other is being rebound. I now have six books that look as if they might contain useful information:

> Begg, Alexander. *A History of British Columbia From Its Earliest Discovery to the Present Time* (Victoria: Ryerson Press, 1894 [reissued 1972]).
> Martin, Chester. *Lord Selkirk's Work in Canada* (Toronto: Oxford University Press, 1969).
> Morton, Arthur S. *A History of the Canadian West to 1870-71* (London: Thomas Nelson and Sons, n.d.).
> Morton, W.L. *Manitoba: A History* (Toronto: University of Toronto Press, 1967).
> Ormsby, Margaret A. *British Columbia: A History* (Vancouver: Macmillan of Canada, 1958).
> Rich, E.E. *The Fur Trade and the Northwest to 1857* (Toronto: McClelland and Stewart, 1967).

> ### How do I evaluate and take notes on the references I have folund?
>
> **A.** How do I evaluate the references I have found?

First I glanced through the tables of contents and the indexes of each of the books to see how much information they contained on the Red River and Fort Victoria settlements. I found that the books by E.E. Rich and Arthur S. Morton do not provide as much detailed information on the Red River settlement as the books by Chester Martin and W.L. Morton. Most of my information will therefore come from four books.

> **B.** How do I take notes on the references I find to be worthwhile?

I decided to read over the sections on Fort Victoria and the Red River settlement in each book before I start to take notes to see what issues these historians consider important.

I also read through the prefaces to see whether any of these books is written from a point of view that might affect the selection and interpretation of evidence. In doing so, I noticed that W.L. Morton says that his book is written primarily for Manitobans and that his history differs from others in that "it has agricultural settlements as its central theme. All else, the fur trade, social development, the play of politics, has been subordinated to that theme" (Morton, p. vii). As I take notes on Morton's book, I will watch for this bias.

SAMPLE NOTE CARD

Morton, W.L. *Manitoba: A History* (Toronto: University of Toronto Press, 1967).

Issue: Red River settlement: agriculture

Main Point: Difficulty in establishing farming

Context: Neglect of this subject by other writers (see Preface)

Evidence: (a) wilderness was "unbroken, undrained, uncontrolled" (p. 56)
(b) farms were "at the mercy of tempest, flood, or pest" (p. 56)
—When locusts stripped the crops, "Not only was no grain left for food, but little or none left for seed" (p. 56)

Conclusion: Crops improved after 1820, but for some years
" 'plains food' remained a large part of the Red River diet" (p. 57)

Comments: [Note Morton's focus on agriculture; check against other sources.]

What should I do if I have to change my original research direction?

When I first began my research, it seemed that the major difference between the two settlements was their relations with the Métis and Indians. Conflict between the white settlers and the Métis fur traders was a big factor in slowing the growth of the Red River settlement, whereas relations between the settlers and Indians at Fort Victoria were quite friendly.

I gradually began to realize, however, that the attitude of the Hudson's Bay Company was also an important factor, and so I paid closer attention to what my sources had to say about the Company's relations with the colonies.

Step 3

CATEGORIZING MATERIAL

What categories should I use for my combined preliminary material (if any) and research material?

A. Can I use the same categories I used for taking notes?

As I began to take notes, I found that the general categories for content analysis (causes, effects, and features) worked quite well as a place to start. I was able to find matching information on the reasons why the settlements were founded, how they developed, and the way of life established in each colony. By the time I finished taking notes, I had a much clearer idea of the issues surrounding the settlement of these two colonies, and so I decided to refine these categories.

B. Do I need to work out new categories for my combined material?

To establish new categories for my material, I began by making a list of topics that seemed to be important in the historians' discussions of each colony:

1. reasons for founding the colony
2. its economy
3. its relations with the British government
4. its government and the role played by specific governors
5. its relations with the Indians/Métis
6. its relationship with the Hudson's Bay Company.

This list helped me to arrive at five matching categories to organize my information: location and economy; attitude of the British government; government of the colony; relationships with Indians; role of the Hudson's Bay Company.

RED RIVER SETTLEMENT	FORT VICTORIA
Location and Economy Founded in 1812 in what is now southern Manitoba by Lord Selkirk (Martin, pp. 15-35) Economy based mostly on the fur trade (Martin, 36-63) Agriculture extremely difficult and slow to be established (Morton, pp. 56-57)	**Location and Economy** Founded in 1849 on Vancouver Island—a location ideal for trade with both the U.S. and Russia (Ormsby, p. 92) Agriculture quickly established and highly successful (Begg, p. 174)
Attitude of the British Little active support for the colony. No help in resolving conflict between Hudson's Bay Company and North-west Company. Antagonistic to all monopolies—HBC in particular (Martin, p. 47)	**Attitude of the British** Actively supported the colony in order to maintain British possession of Vancouver Island. Made Vancouver a colony in 1849 but unable to establish British government there without the active support of the HBC (Ormsby, p. 97)
Government of the Colony Authority of Miles Macdonell undermined by both NWC and HBC traders (Martin, pp. 55-56) Macdonell angered traders and Métis with Pemmican Proclamation: worsened colony's relations with the outside (Morton, pp. 50-51)	**Government of the Colony** Treatment of Richard Blanshard, the man Britain sent over as governor, shows determination of HBC to maintain control (Begg, pp. 190-195) Finlayson and Douglas extremely able administrators, working out good relations with Indians and establishing agriculture (Begg, pp. 174, 164)

Relationship with Indians
Very bad because NWC actively stirred up Métis antagonism to settlers (Martin, pp. 36-63)
Macdonell made no concessions to Métis and antagonized them (Morton, pp. 50-51)
Hostilities culminated in the Battle of Seven Oaks and a massacre of settlers (Morton, p. 54)

Relationship with Indians
Friendly for the most part; Indians quickly became part of the colony, aiding in agriculture and being paid the same as other employees of HBC (Begg, p. 174)
HBC adept at settling disputes with Indians quickly and peacefully (Begg, p. 164)

Role of the HBC
Red River settlement established through efforts of Lord Selkirk (Martin, pp. 15-35)
Selkirk depended on HBC to protect colony from hostility of NWC, but HBC traders indifferent to its survival (Martin, pp. 55-56)
HBC traders opposed to an agricultural settlement because it would interfere with quick profits from fur trade—actively attempted to undermine the colony (Martin, pp. 55-56)
Colony limped along with little growth and no security until Manitoba joined Confederation in 1870.

Role of the HBC
HBC actively supported colony but was determined to maintain control in Fort Victoria. Blanshard saw need for independent governor to break the HBC's stranglehold on the colony (Begg, p. 196)
HBC got rid of Blanshard and installed its chief factor, James Douglas, as governor (Begg, pp. 190, 195)
Independent settlers had great difficulty establishing themselves in Fort Victoria (Begg, p. 196)
Ultimately HBC control of colony was damaging, but initially its good management and support helped the colony to become firmly established and to make money for the HBC.

Step 4

FINDING A THESIS

What is the nature of the thing I am researching?

From my notes it seems clear that the attitude of the Hudson's Bay Company towards the two colonies should be my basis of comparison.

It seems equally clear that the HBC gave a great deal of support to the colony at Fort Victoria and very little to the Red River settlement.

> ### Why does the thing I am researching have this particular nature?'

To complete my thesis, I must explain why the HBC supported one colony and not the other. My notes indicate that the Hudson's Bay Company supported Fort Victoria because it could make money from the colony itself and because colonization was the best way to secure a valuable harbour. On the other hand, although the Hudson's Bay Company was theoretically in favour of a settlement in southern Manitoba, in reality the traders were opposed to the colony because they did not want the profitable fur trade to be disrupted by farming. In both cases, it seems clear that the Hudson's Bay Company was chiefly interested in making money. This point explains why the Company's attitudes to the two colonies were so different. Now I can formulate a thesis for my paper:

> The early success of Fort Victoria and failure of the Red River settlement were largely the result of the Hudson's Bay Company's attitude towards these two colonies, an attitude determined by how much immediate profit the Company felt it could make. Because Fort Victoria was profitable, the Company supported it fully; because the Red River settlement was unprofitable, the Company was indifferent, if not openly hostile, to its success.

This example demonstrates the process by which you would gather research material and use it as the basis for arriving at a thesis about a content topic. So that you can see the final form of a research paper of this type, we have included "The Effects of the Attitude of the Hudson's Bay Company on Fort Victoria and the Red River Settlement" in the reference section.

SUMMARY

If you have a clearly defined search strategy for finding what you need, you are less likely to be daunted by the wealth of material available in your college or university library. You can often get a better sense of what you need by clarifying your topic and gathering preliminary information. You can then follow the search strategy we have laid out for locating and recording library sources. Now that you are familiar with the purpose and procedures of library research, you can use the chart "Finding Research Material" in the reference section as a reminder of the steps to follow.

EXERCISE

If you do not summarize effectively when you take notes, you may fill your research paper with unnecessarily long quotations or take factual information out of context. This exercise is designed to give you practice in taking notes. Summarize each of the following selections, using this procedure:

1. State in your own words the issue or problem the author identifies.
2. State in your own words the author's main point about this issue.
3. List in point form the key points of evidence cited.
4. State the writer's conclusion in one sentence, using a few words of quotation, if appropriate.

A. Nothing Mickey Spillane has ever written can be compared in horror to some of the factual scenes in *Mutiny on the Bounty*. Few passages in literature describe more revolting episodes than those of the *Bounty* sailors being seized in the gangway and flogged until the flesh hung in strips from their backs. With our modern knowledge of neurology, we know that the agonies of these poor creatures did not end when the boatswain's mate ceased swinging the cat. Such beatings damaged the nerve roots along the spine and condemned the victims to permanent suffering. What makes those scenes of torture so unbearable to think about is the added realization that they were not the offshoots of a psychopathic movement like Naziism, but were standard practice in one of the most stable and reflective societies that ever existed. Captain Bligh's cruelty had the weight and approval of his entire society behind it. When the mutineers were later court-martialled, the court had no interest in determining whether Bligh had been cruel or not. It was interested solely in whether the accused had obeyed to the letter the harsh laws of the British Navy.[1]

B. When, by chance, the neurosurgeon's electrode activates past experience, that experience unfolds progressively, moment by moment. This is a little like the performance of a wire recorder or a strip of cinematographic film on which are registered all those things of which the individual was once aware—the things he selected for his attention

---

[1] From Hugh MacLennan, "The Shadow of Captain Bligh" (in *Thirty and Three*, ed. Dorothy Duncan [Toronto: Macmillan of Canada, 1954], pp. 145-52; reprinted in *A Book of Essays*, ed. Robert Chambers and Carlyle King [Toronto: Macmillan of Canada, 1963], pp. 123-28).

in that interval of time. Absent from it are the sensations he ignored, the talk he did not heed.

Time's strip of film runs forward, never backward, even when resurrected from the past. It seems to proceed again at time's own unchanged pace. . . . As long as the electrode is held in place, the experience of a former day goes forward. There is no holding it still, no turning back, no crossing with other periods. When the electrode is withdrawn, it stops as suddenly as it began.

A particular strip can sometimes be repeated by interrupting the stimulation and then shortly reapplying it at the same or a nearby point. In that case it begins at the same moment of time on each occasion. The threshold of evocation of that particular response has apparently been lowered for a time by the first stimulus. . . .[2]

C. Almost all the income of all Canadian newspapers, magazines, radio and TV stations comes from selling pieces of their space and bits of their time to advertisers. Three-quarters of the money earned by newspapers and about ninety per cent of the income of broadcasting stations comes from advertising. The four-bits you pay to buy a magazine hardly helps the publication at all. Most publishers could save money by giving their magazines away, because it costs them more to get your subscription than you pay. Magazines such as *Maclean's* and *Chatelaine* charge for a subscription to reassure advertisers that people will indeed read the magazine and not throw it away unopened.

*   *   *

Because the dependence on advertising developed gradually, we think it's inevitable. When we're on the receiving end of radio, magazines, newspapers, TV we all sometimes wonder whether the dependence is that much of a blessing. Our media are schizophrenic because they have two distinct sets of customers: their audience and their advertisers. One pays a pittance; the other carries the load. Editors, reporters, and program producers work for the low-paying customers, the reader. Publishers and advertising salesmen look after the advertiser, the main bill-payer. Predictably, the high-paying dog wags the low-paying tail.

That doesn't mean that national advertisers apply pressure to twist and corrupt news and programs. They are too sophisticated to try that. Not one of our clients has ever asked us to try to influence program or editorial content.

---

[2]Wilder Penfield and Lamar Roberts, *Speech and Brain Mechanisms* (Princeton: Princeton University Press, 1959), p. 53. Copyright 1959 by Princeton University Press; reprinted by permission of Princeton University Press.

In twentieth-century Canada they don't have to. The competition for advertising dollars is so intense that each medium, like any good salesman, anticipates its advertisers' desires. Each knows how best to butter up the side its bread comes from.

The job of editorial and program people is to attract a special sort of audience that will appeal to an advertiser. They don't care whether they appeal to people with brains; they do care that they appeal to people with dollars. They know the advertiser is not interested in just anybody. He wants to reach people who buy things and especially people who have enough spare money that their choice is not dictated by necessity. When you sell Cadillacs, one rich reader is worth a hundred times as much as a hundred men on welfare. Hence labour newspapers don't get as much advertising as executives' magazines.[3]

---

[3]Jerry Goodis, *Have I Ever Lied to You Before?* (1972), pp. 134-35 (reprinted by permission of The Canadian Publishers, McClelland and Stewart Limited, Toronto).

Chapter 12

Writing
Research Papers

In Chapter 11 we introduced you to the procedures for preparing a research essay up to the point of finding a thesis. In this chapter we will go through the general procedures for writing and revising the research paper, and then demonstrate the complete process with a topic requiring textual analysis. What you will learn is that the most important issue when you prepare a research essay—developing a clear relationship between your own material and material from your sources—is also the most important issue when you write and revise.

BASIC PROCEDURES FOR WRITING AND REVISING RESEARCH PAPERS

Writing the First Draft

Step 1

SELECTING MATERIAL

Which categories of material best support my thesis?

When you are choosing categories of material to use as paragraph topics, remember that you do not have to include every bit of information you found in your references, any more than you have to include every idea of your own when you are writing essays that do not require research. Select material that best supports your own line of argument.

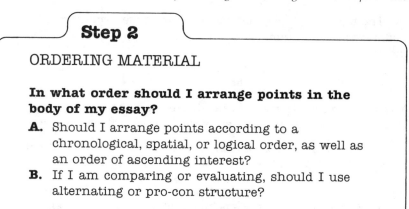

Step 2

ORDERING MATERIAL

In what order should I arrange points in the body of my essay?

A. Should I arrange points according to a chronological, spatial, or logical order, as well as an order of ascending interest?

B. If I am comparing or evaluating, should I use alternating or pro-con structure?

The structure of the research essay should be *your* structure, just as the thesis sets out *your* opinion and reasons. If you merely take over the organization used by one of your sources, you are likely to end up with an extended summary of that writer's position rather than a research essay. Thus you will ask yourself the same questions about the ordering of points in writing your research draft that you would ask in writing other drafts.

Revising the First Draft

At each stage of the revision process, check to make sure that you have presented your research material as support for your own ideas rather than merely summarizing other writers' views and information.

Step 1

REVISING THE THESIS

Does the thesis state an opinion appropriate to this kind of research essay and support that opinion?

Does the thesis reflect my own opinion, rather than merely summarizing the opinions of writers I have consulted?

Do I need to work out a better thesis from my first draft?

First check that your thesis meets the requirements for the kind of essay you are writing—analysis, comparison, or evaluation. Then make sure that your thesis clearly indicates *your* opinion and reasons, not merely those you found in your research materials.

The following thesis statement, for example, would suggest that you were merely summarizing research on the social aspects of smoking:

> Recent studies show that a great deal of smoking is stimulated by the smoking of others.

You could more clearly indicate the relation between the research studies and your own thinking by revising your thesis like this:

> Recent studies show that a great deal of smoking is stimulated by the smoking of others; this fact suggests that if we wish to reduce smoking among adolescents, we should not only refrain from smoking ourselves, but also educate our children about the dangers of smoking before they reach the age at which peer approval is more important than parental approval.

This would be an adequate thesis for an evaluation research paper on smoking.

If you find any problem with your thesis, return to your draft or to the preparation process to work out a better one.

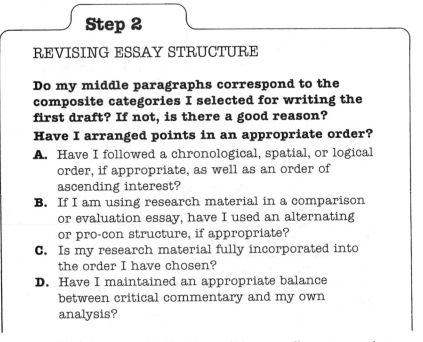

Step 2

REVISING ESSAY STRUCTURE

Do my middle paragraphs correspond to the composite categories I selected for writing the first draft? If not, is there a good reason?

Have I arranged points in an appropriate order?

A. Have I followed a chronological, spatial, or logical order, if appropriate, as well as an order of ascending interest?

B. If I am using research material in a comparison or evaluation essay, have I used an alternating or pro-con structure, if appropriate?

C. Is my research material fully incorporated into the order I have chosen?

D. Have I maintained an appropriate balance between critical commentary and my own analysis?

When you outline your draft to see if the overall structure of your research paper is satisfactory, you will need to pay special attention to whether you have integrated your research material. Your readers should be able to see how each paragraph relates to your thesis. To check that this relation is clear, ask yourself as you read each middle paragraph, "Which part of my thesis does this paragraph support?" If you are not sure, your readers won't be either. If there are sections of your paper that seem like a random compilation of facts and ideas, make a revised outline to remind yourself of the point you intend each paragraph to make.

Another consideration when you are doing a research paper on a textual topic is the proportion of your own analysis to critical commentary. In trying to include the interpretations of other critics, have you lost sight of the text(s)? Remember that the research paper should primarily be your own interpretation, supplemented by your use of critical commentary to define the context of the problem, to support your position, and to provide alternative interpretations.

Step 3

REVISING MIDDLE PARAGRAPHS

Does each middle paragraph have a topic sentence?

A. Does each topic sentence serve as a mini-thesis for the paragraph?

B. Does each topic sentence for paragraphs using research material clearly indicate how this material relates to a single aspect of my thesis?

C. If a single aspect of my material occupies more than one paragraph, have I used an umbrella topic sentence?

Your readers depend upon your topic sentences to indicate how the material in each paragraph supports your thesis. When you are presenting historical information, or summaries of psychological research, or critical opinions about a text, it is sometimes easy to forget this function of your topic sentence. The following example, from a research paper on the origins of the English Civil War, illustrates the kind of relationship you need to establish between your thesis and your topic sentences.

> **Thesis** The English Civil War had its roots in the reign of James I, whose persecution of the Puritans and quarrels with Parliament reflected not only his belief in the divine right of kings but also his obsessive need for order.

> **Topic Sentence 1** Underlying James's ineffectiveness as a monarch was his belief in the divine right of kings.

Topic
Sentence 2

The Protestant Reformation had undermined belief in the divine right of kings by its insistence that each person, not only the king, could know the will of God.

Topic
Sentence 3

The Puritans' and Republicans' rejection of James's claim to rule by divine right challenged his control of both church and state.

Topic
Sentence 4

Because of his obsessive need for order, James was incapable of the flexibility and compromise that might have prevented the Civil War that broke out during the reign of his son, Charles I.

Check that each topic sentence makes a point, and that the point is clearly related to your thesis.

Does the material in each middle paragraph adequately support the point made in its topic sentence?

A. Does each paragraph provide sufficient detail to support its point? In the case of research detail, is there an appropriate mixture of summary and quotation?

B. Does each paragraph provide enough explanation of the point made in the topic sentence and of the detail offered?

Although not every paragraph in a research paper will include research material in it, it is likely that many will. These paragraphs should contain the same mixture of explanation and detail as paragraphs in any other kind of essay. You can use your research material most effectively by presenting it in a mixture of summary and quotation: summary for conciseness, quotation for the texture of the original.

To support the point you make in your topic sentence, you must provide your readers with the ideas that link your research material; you can't simply dump facts and ideas from various sources into the paragraph and leave your readers to figure out the connections, as the writer of this paragraph has done:

> The social causes of smoking have been established in a number of studies. According to B. Mausner and E. Platt, many smokers reported that they thought of smokers as daring and sophisticated and of non-smokers as sensible and careful (p. 7). According to Richard Olshavsky, advertising does not seem either to promote or to inhibit cigarette smoking (p. 98). In his study of the smoking habits of British schoolboys, J.M. Bynner discovered that "Boys who smoke thought of them-

> selves as being fairly tough but not as tough as they would like
> to be. They, more than any other group, saw non-smokers as
> completely lacking in toughness, and thus the act of giving up
> smoking involved identification with a group which had a
> very unattractive characteristic." (p. 93)

This paragraph provides adequate *detail* in a mixture of summary and
quotation. It is very confusing, however, because it does not provide
enough *explanation* of the relationship between the topic sentence and
the various studies; indeed, one of the studies seems to contradict
the others. Notice how the revised version of this paragraph links the
topic sentence with the research details, explains the apparent con-
tradiction in those details, and maintains the mixture of summary
and quotation:

> The social causes of smoking have been established in a
> number of studies. Although the image of smokers conveyed by
> advertising may not be important, since, as Richard Olshavsky
> notes, advertising does not seem either to promote or to in-
> hibit cigarette smoking (p. 98), there is good evidence that the
> image smokers have of themselves is very important. In his
> study of the smoking habits of British schoolboys, J.M. Bynner
> discovered that "Boys who smoke thought of themselves as
> being fairly tough but not as tough as they would like to be.
> They, more than any other group, saw non-smokers as com-
> pletely lacking in toughness, and thus the act of giving up
> smoking involved identification with a group which had a very
> unattractive characteristic." (p. 93) Adults seem to share this
> kind of thinking. According to B. Mausner and E. Platt, many
> smokers reported that they thought of smokers as daring
> and sophisticated, and of non-smokers as sensible and careful
> (p. 7).

When you add explanations in this way, you will of course need to
keep clear the distinction between your own comments and your
research material. Since you may continue to change or delete material
as you go through the process of final editing, you may find it useful
to identify sources by author and page number until you are ready
to write the final draft. Then you can refer to the handbook section
for the format to follow in preparing your footnotes and bibliography.

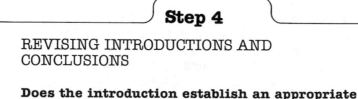

Step 4

REVISING INTRODUCTIONS AND CONCLUSIONS

**Does the introduction establish an appropriate
context for the essay?**

A. Does the introduction give the reader enough background to understand the thesis?

B. Does the introduction as a whole, or the thesis itself, outline in order the points covered in the essay?

C. Does the introduction as a whole, or the thesis itself, show the relation between my research material and my own line of thinking?

D. Does the introduction end with the thesis?

The principle of integrating your research material with your own line of analysis, comparison, or evaluation is one that you should put into practice right from the beginning of your essay. You can often indicate in your introduction that you are responding to the research, rather than merely summarizing it, by putting your reference to other writers (if appropriate) between your introductory sentence or two and your thesis, as in this example.

> The German painter Ernst Ludwig Kirchner (1880-1938) began his career as a representational artist when, as a youngster, he sat by the window to draw what he saw: people in the street, animals, the train station, and even the zoo. His style didn't remain representational, however. Critics have indentified four styles in his mature work: post-impressionism, expressionism, abstraction, and representational art. Because of his emphasis on inner feelings and experiences and his willingness to distort nature to convey his vision, Kirchner contributed most to the development of expressionism.

Your description of the research will often also serve, as in this example, to suggest the order of your points.

Does the conclusion tie together the points made in the essay?

A. Does the conclusion restate the thesis in different words?

B. Does the conclusion summarize the points about primary and secondary material made in the middle paragraphs in order to clarify the thesis?

C. Does the conclusion suggest the wider implications of the subject, if any?

Your conclusion should demonstrate that you have accomplished what you set out to do in your introduction: to provide evidence for your thesis by bringing in information and ideas from other sources. Your reflections on the adequacy of the research materials available on your subject might constitute your statement about "wider implications." But don't merely say (even if some of your sources do!), "More research is needed." A legitimate summing up of a research paper on the painter Kirchner, for example, might suggest the need for a new biography to help explain the reasons for the painter's greater achievements in the expressionist style than in any other.

Once you have finished revising your draft for content and structure, use the Checklist for Final Editing to spot and correct problems in style and tone. Be especially careful to provide full and accurate footnotes and bibliography. You will find detailed information on how to do so in the handbook.

SAMPLE TOPIC: A RESEARCH PAPER ANALYZING A TEXT

Let's suppose that from the list of topics for a 2000-word research paper in your first-year English course, you have chosen this one:

> Using several critical discussions of the play, explore the dramatic function of the graveyard scene in *Hamlet*.

Preparing to Write

Step 1

CLARIFYING THE TOPIC

A. Do I understand the terms used in the topic?
B. Do I understand the directions the topic gives me?
    1. Am I asked to analyze, to compare, or to evaluate?
    2. Does this topic require textual analysis or content analysis?
C. Do I know what kind of material to use in my essay?
D. Do I know how to limit the topic?
E. Do I know how to choose a topic that fits my interest, knowledge, time, and writing skills?

A. I'm asked to focus on the "dramatic function" of the graveyard scene. I'm not sure exactly what the term means. It seems to suggest that I should consider why the scene comes where it does in terms of the overall structure of the play, rather than to focus on the ideas. I'll need to keep this purpose in mind as I analyze the scene and read the critics.

B. The word "explore" is somewhat ambiguous, but the formula "Explain X (the part) in terms of Y (the whole)" indicates an *analysis* assignment; the topic obviously calls for textual analysis, since I'm asked to consider why the scene is presented as it is.

C. "Using several critical discussions of the play" clearly indicates that I am to use research material to clarify and extend my sense of the scene and the play. Six substantial references will probably be adequate for a 2000-word essay; thus I should aim for a working bibliography of about eighteen references.

D. and E. I don't need to limit the topic since it is precisely defined. This paper isn't due for six weeks, but I will have papers due for other courses about the same time, so I'll start now, before someone else has checked out all the reference material on *Hamlet*.

Step 2

GATHERING MATERIAL

What preliminary sources of material can I draw on?

Before I read the critics, I need to have some idea of what the play as a whole is about and to work out a preliminary analysis of the graveyard scene. Since we have discussed several definitions of tragedy in relation to other plays, I will also check my notes to see how *Hamlet* fits the definition of a tragedy.

When I first read the play, I find it puzzling, and so I skim Keith Sagar's *Hamlet (Shakespeare)* (Oxford: Basil Blackwell, 1969) for a scene-by-scene explanation of the action. On rereading the play, I get the sense that it is about Hamlet's search for the proper action to take in a world where his high standards for determining the truth come into conflict with the corrupt Danish court. At some point I'll have to consider how the graveyard scene fits this sense of the play as a whole.

Using the footnotes in my edition to explain difficult points, I then read the graveyard scene carefully and take notes on it under the special categories I have learned for the analysis of drama. (For a fuller explanation of these categories, see the reference section.)

Subject and Genre: What is the scene about? Does this play belong to a particular genre (kind) of drama?

Subject: death—conversation between two gravediggers about Ophelia's burial, Hamlet's jests with gravedigger about corpses and speculations about human mortality, Ophelia's funeral procession, Hamlet's quarrel with Laertes in the open grave, Claudius' decision to put his plot against Hamlet into action.

Genre: tragedy—according to my class notes, Shakespearean tragedy involves the fall of a hero of high estate as a result of both circumstances outside the hero's control and actions that stem from a flaw in his character. Because the flaw is also what makes the hero great, his death produces emotions such as sympathy, pity, fear, awe, and a sense of waste.

Dramatic Structure: What is the principle behind the selection and arrangement of events ("action")?

Structure of scene: two distinct episodes—gravediggers and confrontation with Laertes. Why does Shakespeare include the gravediggers? Why does he have Laertes and Hamlet leap into Ophelia's grave?

Relation of scene to play: Act V, scene i—only one more scene in play. Hamlet's last appearance was at the end of IV.iv., where he encounters Fortinbras' forces as he is leaving for England after killing Polonius. The intervening scenes focus on Ophelia's madness, Laertes' return to avenge his father, Claudius' plot for killing Hamlet, and the news of Ophelia's suicide. The graveyard scene thus sets the stage for the final confrontation between Hamlet and his foes.

Dramatic Setting: What is the place, time, and social environment within which the action takes place?

Place: church graveyard.

Time: day after Ophelia's death, news of Hamlet's return (see IV.vii.)

Social environment: Marked contrast in social position between the gravediggers and the court. The gravediggers conclude that Ophelia is to be given a Christian burial only because she is a gentlewoman; Hamlet contrasts the gravedigger's insensitivity with the "daintier sense" of those who don't work for a living (V.i. 65-66).

Relation of scene to play: graveyard setting connects this scene with others associated with death, such as Ghost's revelations, play within a play, murder of Polonius, Ophelia's death. The setting makes Hamlet's preoccupation with death part of the climax of the play.

Characterization: What are the characters like? How are various techniques, including dialogue and acting, used to portray them?

Hamlet: presented in the first half of the scene as philosophical about death, not morbidly obsessed as he was at the beginning of the play. Begins to rant in response to Laertes' lamentations about Ophelia, but also declares his love for her and for Laertes.

Other Characters: Laertes is the other major character in the scene. What is the purpose of his excessive show of grief?

Diction, Images and Symbols, Pacing: What do I learn from usage level and word choice? What do images and symbols convey? What is the rhythm of dialogue and action?

Diction: gravediggers' speech colloquial, comic, matter of fact; language of the court mainly informal, except for Laertes', which is formal and pretentious. Hamlet's language moves between these levels, sometimes in the same sentence: the lawyer's "fine pate" is "full of fine dirt" (V.i. 100); and the "noble dust of Alexander" can be found "stopping a bunghole" (V.i. 191-192).

Images and Symbols: many associated with death—skulls, grave.

Pacing: language shifts from conversational prose in gravedigger episode to blank verse in burial scene; verbal "fight" between Laertes and Hamlet is the most distinctive use of sentence structure. Action shows similar shift from slow pace of first half of scene to unexpected twist as Hamlet and Laertes fight in the grave. Doesn't this behaviour seem a bit ridiculous?

Tone: What attitude to subject or audience is evident?

The tone of the early part of the scene is playful, meditative, probing; the tone of the later part is emotional and dramatic.

Theme: What is the central idea?

The scene shows Hamlet reacting to death in two violently contrasting ways. He is playful and self-possessed, somewhat distant when he thinks of death in abstract terms; but he is much more emotional when death becomes personal (Yorick's skull, Ophelia). How does this conflict relate to his search for proper action?

Now that my preliminary analysis has given me some sense of the issues, it's time to look for critical discussions of the graveyard scene.

What sources of reference material can I draw on to compile my working bibliography?

A. Is a bound bibliography available?

A current bound bibliography of *Hamlet* would suit my purposes perfectly, but a current bound bibliography on Shakespeare with a section on *Hamlet* seems a likelier prospect. Looking in my library's subject catalogue under the general heading "Shakespeare," I find nine entries under the subheading "Bibliography." Of the nine, three are bibliographies of editions of Shakespeare's works and four others are out of date.

The last two entries both seem appropriate, since they are bound bibliographies of about 200 pages, published in the last 12 years. When I read the prefaces, however, I discover that the purpose of the more recent and more fully annotated bibliography is to identify resources for teaching Shakespeare, and so it excludes traditional literary criticism. The other bibliography, in contrast, aims to include all works of current relevance to the study of Shakespeare. So despite the fact that it is sparingly annotated, I choose this bibliography:

> Bevington, David. *Shakespeare* (Goldentree Bibliographies in Language and Literature). Arlington Heights, [Ill.]: AHM Publishing, 1978.

B. Is there a relevant periodical index or annual bibliography?

Bevington's cut-off date, I learn from the preface, is February 1977, and so I will miss much recent criticism if I use his book as an exclusive source. His bibliography contains a section on annual bibliographies and periodicals, however, and from it I discover that *Shakespeare Quarterly*, a periodical, has a comprehensive annual bibliography. I check the library's serials list (the list of periodical holdings) and see that the library has all the volumes of *Shakespeare Quarterly*. I can therefore look for references in its annual bibliography, starting with the most recent year and working back to 1977.

C. Can I find references through my library's card or microfiche catalogue?

Since recently published books may not yet have been included in *Shakespeare Quarterly*'s annual bibliography, I resolve to check the

"Shakespeare" section of the card catalogue to see if there are any titles that might be relevant to my discussion of the graveyard scene.

How do I choose, record, and track down references for my working bibliography?

A. How do I choose which references to record?

To choose references to books and articles, I begin with the most relevant section of Bevington's bibliography, that on *Hamlet*. Rather than reading this whole section, I focus on the "Particular Scenes and Passages" and "Language and Imagery" subsections. From these subsections I collect ten references whose titles indicate they focus on the graveyard scene, or the imagery of death, or both (e.g., "In Search of Yorick's Skull").

It is easier to choose references from the subsections on *Hamlet* criticism in the annual bibliographies in *Shakespeare Quarterly* because these bibliographies are annotated. I end up with four that look particularly relevant.

As the last step in compiling my working bibliography, I check my library's card catalogue under "Shakespeare: Criticism and Interpretation: Individual Plays: *Hamlet*" and discover titles of two books that might have some bearing on the issue of death and the graveyard scene, plus titles of two collections of essays on *Hamlet*. I now have eighteen references in my working bibliography.

B. How can I most effectively record details of the references I choose?

So that I can find the references I have chosen, I record, on separate file cards, the complete bibliographical information for each reference. For books I list the author, title, place of publication, publisher, and publication date:

> King, Walter N. *Hamlet's Search for Meaning*. Athens, Ga.: University of Georgia Press, 1982.

For each periodical I note the author, title, title of the periodical, volume number, date, and page numbers, like this:

> Cheadle, B.D. "Hamlet at the Graveside: A Leap into Hermeneutics," *English Studies in Africa*, 22 (1979), 83-90.

> **C.** What procedures do I use to track down the references I have recorded?

My next step is to check the card/microfiche catalogues and serials list for the call numbers of each item in my working bibliography and to see which ones I can find in the library. By the time I finish, I have discovered that the library does not carry two of the books and two of the journals; three books are out on long-term loan; and the volume I need of one journal is being bound. I now have ten references in my "active" stack of file cards and eight in my discard pile, with notes saying why I've discarded them (e.g., "not in library," "on loan").

> **How do I evaluate and take notes on the references I have found?**
>
> **A.** How do I evaluate the references I have found?

As I find each available item, I make a preliminary evaluation of its usefulness. For each book and collection of essays, I check the table of contents, skim the introduction, and look in the index for references to the graveyard scene; for each article, I read the introductory and concluding paragraphs. I decide that one collection of essays, one book, and one article are of no use to me. I now have seven references in my "active" stack.

> **B.** How do I take notes on the references I find to be worthwhile?

As I read each reference, I will try to keep before me the questions my initial analysis raised about the dramatic function of the graveyard scene: Why does the scene open with the gravediggers? In the first half of the scene, Hamlet seems a different character from our last view of him—why? Why does Shakespeare have Laertes and Hamlet fighting in Ophelia's grave?

Most of the critics I read are more concerned with the philosophical significance of the graveyard scene than with its dramatic function. They focus on the meaning of the change in Hamlet's attitude towards death. Some see Hamlet coming to a Christian acceptance of death as part of Providence's plan; others see him resigning himself to a stoic acceptance of the finality of death; others see an unresolved or unresolvable conflict between these views. I record these views and summarize or quote specific comments that may help to explain elements of the graveyard scene.

The article that seems most useful for discussing the scene's dramatic function is B.D. Cheadle's "Hamlet at the Graveside," which considers two ways of staging the confrontation between Hamlet and Laertes at Ophelia's grave and shows how the staging relates to the overall interpretation of the play. I therefore take careful notes on the article, using a mixture of summary, quotation, and commentary and recording page numbers for each bit of information.

Sample Notes

Cheadle, B.D. "Hamlet at the Graveside: A Leap into Hermeneutics," *English Studies in Africa*, 22 (1979), 83-90.

Issue in the criticism: Scene: Should Hamlet leap into Ophelia's grave or not? (pp. 85-86) Play: Christian interpretation or "deeply pessimistic" interpretation? (p. 88)

C's thesis: Scene: Whether to have Hamlet leap depends on interpretation of the play as a whole: if the play is about "the prince's striving for, and ultimately finding, an adequate role in terms of which to perform a called-for action," he should not leap. If the play is about "an infinitely painful and costly attempt to come to terms with the sickness at the heart of life," Hamlet should leap into the grave. (p. 87)

Play: The play as a whole "seems to tread a tightrope between the Christian possibility and an intense, weary disillusion. . . ." Cannot say that a Christian interpretation and a "deeply pessimistic" interpretation are equally valid: "the play forces us to contemplate both possibilities while yet retaining for itself a sort of 'negative capability.' " (p. 88)

Critical context: Harley Granville-Barker and others say that leaping into the grave compromises Hamlet's dignity; Cheadle argues, on basis of evidence for the way the scene was acted in Shakespeare's day, that with proper staging Hamlet can leap without compromising his dignity.

Points/evidence: H's declaration "this is I/Hamlet the Dane" is both an "assertion of identity and purpose" and a direct challenge to Claudius (only King had the right to refer to himself as "the Dane") (p. 86). Although overall interpretation (see above) may suggest interpretation of local details, it can also distort them (as in seeing "divine agency" implied by "Then, venom, to thy work" in V.ii.). Consideration of the immediate context suggests that (1) Laertes' ranting makes audience sympathetic to Hamlet; (2) bending over Ophelia in the grave gives Hamlet a chance to conclude his relationship with her "in a way that is appropriate both to the depth of his love and to his reaffirmed nobility as 'Hamlet the Dane.' " (p. 89)

C's conclusion: Leap into the grave should be staged so that it encompasses the possibility of both interpretations: the interpretation that stresses Hamlet's search "for an appropriate role or mode of action" would need to be "broad enough to include the tragic necessity of surrendering other more devoutly-to-be-wished roles (of royal lover, for example). . . ." (p. 89); the interpretation that stresses "Hamlet's coming to terms with the sickness at [the] heart of life" would need to be "broad enough to include the dignity of finding stature and purpose in the very heart of loss." (p. 90)

[Commentary: the question Cheadle quotes from Coleridge ("What reason does it contain within itself for being as it is and no other?") suggests a promising way of considering the dramatic function of the graveyard scene. I should also see whether Cheadle's comment on Shakespeare's engaging our sympathy for Hamlet has wider implications.]

What should I do if I have to change my original research direction?

Since there is so much critical disagreement about Hamlet's attitude towards death in the graveyard scene, it would be easy to focus on this issue. I'll have to keep reminding myself that my topic asks me to consider the scene's dramatic function. Perhaps by the time I write my first draft I'll have a better idea of how the two issues are related.

Step 3

CATEGORIZING MATERIAL

What categories should I use for my combined preliminary material (if any) and research material?

A. Can I use the same categories I used for taking notes?
B. Do I need to work out new categories for my combined material?

The special categories for analyzing drama gave me a good idea of what issues in the scene to pay attention to. Almost all of the critics I read focused on one part of the scene or another rather than discussing the scene as a whole, and so I don't have a very good sense of the categories they used. It seems a good idea, then, to continue to use the special categories for drama and to add material from the critics to these categories, making sure I identify the source and give the page number.

Step 4

FINDING A THESIS

What is the nature of the thing I am researching?

When I consider Cheadle's comment about Shakespeare's using the contrast with Laertes to make us more sympathetic to Hamlet, I begin to wonder whether other aspects of the scene serve the same dramatic function. The critics have a lot to say about the change in Hamlet. Does this change have a dramatic function? In the last scenes in which he appeared, Hamlet seemed cynical and cruel, full of loathing for almost everybody, including himself. The intervening scenes focus on the consequences of Hamlet's killing of Polonius—Laertes' desire for revenge, Ophelia's madness and death. If Hamlet on his return had not changed, would we have much sympathy for him? Probably not.

How does the scene engage our sympathy for Hamlet? The first half of the scene encourages a gradual shift from seeing events from the court's point of view to seeing them from Hamlet's point of view, beginning with the gravediggers' criticism of the court's using its power to ensure a Christian burial for Ophelia. When Hamlet enters, his first remark is a comment on the insensitivity of the gravedigger who sings as he works; this comment makes us feel that Hamlet is made of finer stuff. His exchanges with the gravedigger and his speculations about the dead seem almost comic, and yet we know, as Hamlet doesn't, that the grave being dug is Ophelia's. (If I remember right, this is called dramatic irony.) Our awareness of the situation would certainly make us more sympathetic to Hamlet.

What about the second half of the scene? Cheadle's interpretation suggests that we side with Hamlet in his initial confrontation with Laertes. How do we feel about Hamlet in the rest of the scene? His declaration of love for Ophelia and for Laertes would increase our sympathy, especially since we know that Laertes has agreed to Claudius' plot to kill Hamlet. Bringing Hamlet and Laertes together in the grave makes us fearful about their next encounter. Their grappling in the grave seems to symbolically foreshadow their duel and its outcome. This sense of impending doom would also make us sympathetic to Hamlet.

The generalization I come to about the nature of the scene, then, would be something like this:

> The dramatic function of the graveyard scene is to engage the audience's sympathy for Hamlet before his death.

> **Why does the thing I am researching have this nature?**

How have I come to this generalization? By considering the effects on the audience of Hamlet's relations with the gravediggers, with Ophelia, and with Laertes. I can complete my thesis by using these points to support my opinion about the dramatic function of the graveyard scene:

> The dramatic function of the graveyard scene is to engage the audience's sympathy for Hamlet before his death. The scene accomplishes this purpose in three ways: by using the grave-diggers as a means to shift the audience's perspective from the court to Hamlet; by clarifying Hamlet's relationship with Ophelia; and by symbolically foreshadowing the outcome of the duel between Hamlet and Laertes.

Now I can write my first draft.

Writing the First Draft

Step 1

SELECTING MATERIAL

Which categories of material best support my thesis?

All the categories I used for my analysis contain material relevant to my thesis. I'll choose the details to use as I write my draft. I'm not sure how many paragraphs to devote to each point or how thoroughly to discuss the criticism. I'll write the draft and then check the proportion of my own analysis to the critical commentary.

Step 2

ORDERING MATERIAL

In what order should I arrange points in the body of my essay?

Several of the critics seemed to discuss other interpretations of *Hamlet* first and then give their own. So I'll begin with my summary of critical views of the thematic significance of the graveyard scene and then discuss my three points about its dramatic function. I'll arrange my points to follow the chronology of the scene; this will also be an order of ascending interest, since I'll end with the point about foreshadowing Hamlet's death.

Step 3

WRITING THE DRAFT

Here is my draft:

THE FUNCTION OF THE GRAVEYARD SCENE IN <u>HAMLET</u>

Act Five, Scene One, commonly known as the graveyard scene, comes at an important point in William Shakespeare's tragedy <u>Hamlet, Prince of Denmark</u>. Up to this point, the play has focused on Hamlet's failure to avenge the death of his father. The graveyard scene, which marks Hamlet's reappearance after his interrupted voyage to England, presents a very different Hamlet from the cruel, cynical prince of Acts III and IV. The dramatic function of this scene is to engage the audience's sympathy for Hamlet before his death. The graveyard scene accomplishes this purpose in three ways: by using the gravediggers as a means to shift the audience's perspective from the court to Hamlet; by clarifying Hamlet's relationship with Ophelia; and by symbolically foreshadowing the outcome of the duel between Hamlet and Laertes.

Many critics have suggested that the episode with the gravediggers indicates a change in Hamlet's character, though they have not agreed about the meaning of that change. Some see Hamlet coming to a Christian acceptance of death; others see his attitude as that of fatalistic resignation; others argue that the scene is a mixture of both these ways of viewing death.

It is true that the graveyard itself, as the setting for the scene, makes a powerful statement about the inevitability of death. But our emotional response to the scene is shaped by the fact that it opens not with the funeral procession but with the gravediggers debating the decision to give Ophelia a Christian burial. After trying to figure out how a coroner might have reached a verdict of drowning in "self-defence," the gravediggers conclude that only her social position has secured Ophelia burial in consecrated ground, a burial that would have been denied a social inferior. The effect of this debate, as Peter Phialas points out, is to shift attention away from the religious question of salvation and damnation that had been so powerful in Hamlet's own considerations of suicide (Phialas, 231). The reduction of death from a metaphysical to a human concern is further emphasized by the first gravedigger's actions: he tosses skulls about and sings while he works.

But the function of the early part of this scene is not merely to reduce death from a metaphysical to a human concern. It is also to prepare us for a shift in our attitude towards Hamlet. We have seen little to admire in Hamlet since the early scenes of the play. As Knight points out, Hamlet "is cruel to Ophelia and his mother"; "exults in tormenting the King by the murder of Gonzago" and "takes a demoniac pleasure in the thought of preserving his life for a more damning death"; "murders Polonius in error" and then makes disgusting, callous comments to Claudius about the body (pp. 56-57). Furthermore, the scenes immediately before Hamlet's reappearance focus on Laertes' grief and anger over his father's death and on Ophelia's madness and suicide. Why would we mourn the death of a man who has caused such suffering?

The major function of the graveyard scene, then, is to restore our sympathy for Hamlet. This rehabilitation begins with Hamlet's first remark: "Has this fellow no feeling of his business, that 'a sings at grave-making?" To Horatio's response, "Custom hath made it in him a property of easiness," Hamlet replies, " 'Tis e'en so. The hand of little employment hath the daintier sense" (V.i. 62-66). By this exchange Shakespeare encourages us to forget Hamlet's earlier callousness and cynicism. Instead of asking us to identify with Hamlet immediately, however, Shakespeare shifts our perspective gradually. Hamlet's speculations about the identity of the skulls lead him from jests about the hypothetical politician, courtier, lawyer, to questions about who is about to be buried. By concealing Ophelia's identity from Hamlet and concealing Hamlet's identity from the gravedigger, Shakespeare increases the emotional tension while allowing us to maintain our distance from what is happening. The discovery of Yorick's skull brings death closer to Hamlet, and Hamlet closer to us, since we can identify with the mixture of fond memory, revulsion, and jest in Hamlet's comments. His final coment to the skull—"Now get you to my lady's chamber, and tell her, let her paint an inch thick, to this favor she must come" (180-182) again brings us dangerously close to Ophelia and Hamlet's jibe about women who paint their faces (III.i. 142-144). But we are drawn back again by Hamlet's playful fantasies about what might have happened to the "noble dust" of Alexander and Caesar. Our image of Hamlet at the end of this episode is that of a person who is neither morbidly preoccupied with death (as he was at the beginning of the play) nor overly sentimental about it (as Laertes and Gertrude will soon be). Instead, he has accepted its reality. The episode with the gravediggers thus prepares us to see the burial of Ophelia from Hamlet's point of view.

The second half of the scene continues the process of ennobling Hamlet in two ways: by resolving the ambiguity of Hamlet's feelings for Ophelia and by foreshadowing the final duel with Laertes. Mystery, as Maynard Mack points out, is one of the dominant elements of the play, and aside from the ghost nothing is more mysterious than Hamlet's relationship with Ophelia. We hear of Hamlet's attentions through Laertes' warnings to Ophelia in I.iii.; Polonius forbids those attentions in the same scene. When Ophelia reports Hamlet's wild dress and melancholy behaviour to Polonius in II.i., we are not sure whether his actions are motivated by blighted love or "mock-madness." (Footnote or discuss Knight). We do not actually see Hamlet and Ophelia together but twice: when she is acting as decoy for her father and Claudius in Act III scene i and when both attend the play-within-a-play in the following scene. The contempt and cruelty Hamlet exhibits on both occasions do little to convince us of his regard for her. But this mystery, which is at the heart of the Hamlet-Ophelia subplot, must be dispelled before the revenge plot is resolved. Hamlet's immediate recognition of the reason for the "maimed rites" (V.i. 206) and his identification of Laertes as "A very noble youth" (V.i. 211) contrast with Laertes' quarrel with the doctor of divinity and his curse upon Hamlet:

> O, treble woe
> Fall ten times treble on that cursed head
> Whose wicked deed thy most ingenious sense
> Deprived thee of!
> (V.i. 233-236)

This outburst, as B.D. Cheadle points out, "affords a contrast with Hamlet's initial self-control, such that our sympathies are with the watching and judging Hamlet rather than with the ranting Laertes" (Cheadle, p. 89). This incident, he adds, gives Hamlet "an opportunity for concluding his relationship with Ophelia in a way that is appropriate both to the depth of his love and to his reaffirmed nobility as 'Hamlet the Dane.'" (p. 89) Cheadle suggests staging the scene in this manner: "Hamlet advances and speaks his 'What is he . . .' speech in a way that gives equal balance to grief and dignity; after 'wonder-wounded hearers' he leaps firmly into the grave and bends firmly over Ophelia, speaking 'this is I' with all the intimacy that the use of the personal pronoun allows; then he rises to his full height within the grave, like an awesome 'embassage of death' fulfilling his father's will, and, looking straight at Claudius, . . . he delivers his affirmation and his challenge, 'Hamlet the Dane'" (p. 89). "This is I," in this reading, would be "an avowal to the dead Ophelia that had she lived and had things been different, she would have been Queen to the Dane"

(p. 87). A few lines later Hamlet says, "I loved Ophelia." (V.i. 256) The past tense marks not only Hamlet's acceptance of the end of the relationship but also his acceptance of the death of love. Earlier in the play he could not accept the fact that his mother, having once loved his father, could forget that love.

Laertes' grappling with Hamlet immediately after Hamlet's assertion of identity shifts attention to the bloody "fight" with which the play will end. Cheadle points out that Hamlet's calling himself "Hamlet the Dane" implies "an assertion of identity and purpose," since only the King has the right to call himself "the Dane." (p. 86) Laertes has allied himself with Claudius in order to avenge Polonius' death, and therefore assumes the role not only of Ophelia's grief-stricken brother but also of Claudius' champion. It is dramatically necessary for Shakespeare to bring them together before the duelling match so that each can recognize the justice in the other's actions and therefore "Exchange forgiveness," as the dying Laertes requests in the final scene. Their tussle in Ophelia's grave, initiated by Laertes and with Hamlet at first maintaining a cool control ("I prithee take thy fingers from my throat"—247) is thus a dramatic foreshadowing of the calm self-possession with which Hamlet is winning the duelling match until he urges Laertes to "pass with your best violence" (287). The grave itself foreshadows the death to which both will come.

In these ways, then, Shakespeare uses the graveyard scene to give Hamlet the qualities appropriate to his status as a tragic hero.

Revising the First Draft

Step 1

REVISING THE THESIS

Does the thesis state an opinion appropriate to this kind of research essay and support that opinion?

Does the thesis reflect my own opinion, rather than merely summarizing the opinions of writers I have consulted?

Do I need to work out a better thesis from my first draft?

My thesis does state an opinion and support it, and that opinion is based on my own thinking; nevertheless, my conclusion reminds me that I have not considered the question of *why* Shakespeare wants to engage our sympathy for Hamlet. I need to revise my thesis to link this purpose with Hamlet's role as a tragic hero:

> Without a change in character, Hamlet would not achieve the stature of a tragic hero, because his death would not arouse the pity, fear, and awe and the sense of waste common to Shakespearean tragedy.

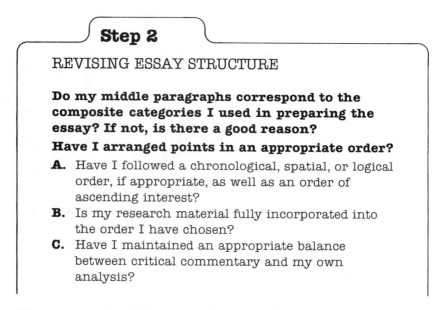

Step 2

REVISING ESSAY STRUCTURE

Do my middle paragraphs correspond to the composite categories I used in preparing the essay? If not, is there a good reason?

Have I arranged points in an appropriate order?

A. Have I followed a chronological, spatial, or logical order, if appropriate, as well as an order of ascending interest?

B. Is my research material fully incorporated into the order I have chosen?

C. Have I maintained an appropriate balance between critical commentary and my own analysis?

I have managed to follow the order I intended fairly well, and on the whole it still seems satisfactory. The fifth middle paragraph is far too long, however, and also contains a confusing mixture of points about Hamlet's relation to Ophelia and to Laertes. At the moment, I don't make much of a connection between the critical commentary on the meaning of the play and my analysis of its dramatic function. Bringing in the role of the tragic hero will help me make this link.

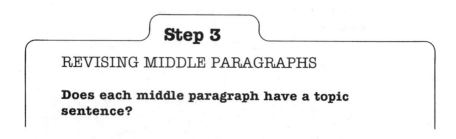

Step 3

REVISING MIDDLE PARAGRAPHS

Does each middle paragraph have a topic sentence?

A. Does each topic sentence serve as a mini-thesis for the paragraph?

B. Does each topic sentence for paragraphs using research material clearly indicate how this material relates to a single aspect of my thesis?

C. If a single aspect of my material occupies more than one paragraph, have I used an umbrella topic sentence?

I'll have to write new topic sentences to reflect my emphasis on the role of the tragic hero. Some of them were not very clear anyway. In the second middle paragraph, for example, the topic sentence says "But our emotional response to the scene is shaped by the fact that it opens not with the funeral procession but with the gravediggers debating the decision to give Ophelia a Christian burial." This sentence does not clearly make the point I intended about how the gravediggers serve as a bridge between the court's perspective and Hamlet's. I can make that point more clearly, and link it to Hamlet's role as a tragic hero, like this:

> The graveyard scene opens not with Hamlet's entrance but with the conversation between the gravediggers. This opening allows for a gradual shift in perspective from the court to Hamlet and humanizes him by making death a personal rather than a metaphysical concern.

Does the material in each middle paragraph adequately support the point made in its topic sentence?

A. Does each paragraph provide sufficient detail to support its point? In the case of research material, is there an appropriate mixture of summary and quotation?

B. Does each paragraph provide enough explanation of the point made in the topic sentence and of the detail offered?

Now that I've revised the topic sentence to my second middle paragraph, I can see that the whole paragraph is quite confusing. It's not clear how the dispute over Ophelia's burial or Phialas' explanation relates to my point. The last sentence seems to introduce a totally new point about "the reduction of death from a metaphysical to a human concern." I need to rewrite the paragraph so that it supports the point in my revised topic sentence and clarifies these connections. I may find that this point will take more than one paragraph to explain clearly.

I also need to expand my first middle paragraph to give more explanations and details about the three critical positions I discuss. This section also may expand into more than one paragraph. I'll make a note to use "umbrella" topic sentences as necessary.

As I revise the other middle paragraphs, I will check the balance between quotation and summary, my own analysis and critical commentary, and explanation and detail.

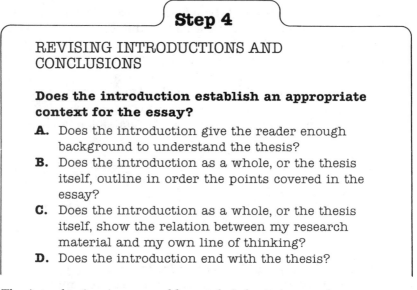

Step 4

REVISING INTRODUCTIONS AND CONCLUSIONS

Does the introduction establish an appropriate context for the essay?

A. Does the introduction give the reader enough background to understand the thesis?

B. Does the introduction as a whole, or the thesis itself, outline in order the points covered in the essay?

C. Does the introduction as a whole, or the thesis itself, show the relation between my research material and my own line of thinking?

D. Does the introduction end with the thesis?

The introduction is reasonably good. I don't suggest how my own analysis relates to the criticism, however. I will add a sentence before my thesis to make this point.

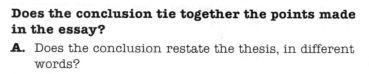

Does the conclusion tie together the points made in the essay?

A. Does the conclusion restate the thesis, in different words?

B. Does the conclusion summarize the points about primary and secondary material made in the middle paragraphs in order to clarify the thesis?

C. Does the conclusion suggest the wider implications of the subject, if any?

My first draft doesn't really have a conclusion, so I'll have to write one.

Writing the Revised Draft

When I finished revising my first draft for structure and development, I went through the Checklist for Final Editing to see what revisions I needed to make in tone, sentence structure, grammar, punctuation, and format. My biggest problem, I noted, was in using quotations, and so I consulted the handbook to find out how to make sure that each quotation was adequately introduced, as short as possible, and in the appropriate format. I also used the handbook to do my notes. (My instructor did not want a separate bibliography; if I had needed one, I could have used the suggestions in the handbook.) Here is my final draft, complete with a title that reflects my thesis.

THE MAKING OF THE TRAGIC HERO:
THE GRAVEYARD SCENE IN <u>HAMLET</u>

In William Shakespeare's tragedy <u>Hamlet, Prince of Denmark</u>, Act Five, Scene One, commonly known as the graveyard scene, marks Hamlet's reappearance after his interrupted voyage to England. The Hamlet we see in this scene is very different from the cruel, cynical prince of Acts III and IV. Most critics attribute this difference to a philosophical change in Hamlet's attitude towards death. In focusing on the thematic significance of this scene, however, they neglect its dramatic function: to engage the audience's sympathy for Hamlet before his death. Without a change in character, Hamlet would not achieve the stature of a tragic hero, because his death would not arouse the pity, fear, and awe and the sense of waste common to Shakespearean tragedy. The graveyard scene engages our sympathy for Hamlet in three ways: by using the episode with the gravediggers as a means to shift the audience's perspective from the court to a humanized Hamlet; by clarifying Hamlet's relationship with Ophelia; and by symbolically foreshadowing the outcome of the duel between Hamlet and Laertes.

Most interpretations of the play fail to consider the dramatic function of the graveyard scene; instead they focus on its philosophical significance. These interpretations fall into three main groups: those that see Hamlet coming to a Christian acceptance of death; those that see his attitude as fatalistic resignation; and those that argue that the scene is a mixture of both these attitudes.[1] Maynard Mack and Walter King are representative of those who favour a Christian interpretation. According to Mack, Hamlet by the last act of the play has "learned, and accepted, the boundaries in which human action, human judgment are enclosed" and therefore no longer assumes he must single-handedly set the world to rights.[2] Similarly, King argues that the graveyard scene presents "affirmation of life and love as a viable center of values in a God-created and God-centered universe," but within the context of a world in which these values "are perennially in danger of being snuffed out."[3]

The view that Hamlet's attitude is totally, or at least partially, fatalistic is propounded by G. Wilson Knight, Richard Levine, and Peter Phialas. Knight sees our sympathies as being divided between the members of the court, who for all their imperfections "assert the importance of human life," and Hamlet, whose philosophy is "inevitable, blameless, and irrefutable," but whose very existence asserts "the negation of life."[4] Far from admitting that there is a shift in our sympathies during the graveyard scene, he asserts that "Laertes and Hamlet struggling at Ophelia's grave are like symbols of life and death contending for the prize of love."[5] Unlike Knight, Levine sees a change in Hamlet but argues that the change is negative. In his view, Hamlet's "tragic flaw, his vacillating and faulty world view," is resolved by Hamlet's rejection of traditional religious belief in favour of "an attenuated stoicism."[6] Peter Phialas, while less negative in his assessment of Hamlet, reaches much the same conclusion. Focusing on the episode with the gravediggers, as most of the other critics do, he concludes that "the Christian framework of the play is profoundly qualified, though not replaced, by a strong fatalistic point of view" (p. 226).[7]

While these interpretations give us some insight into the philosophical issues raised by the play, they are not wholly satisfactory because they do not pay adequate attention to the scene's dramatic function. The danger of ignoring or distorting details in order to fit a particular interpretation is pointed out by B.D. Cheadle in "Hamlet at the Graveside: A Leap into Hermeneutics."[8] In his interpretation of Hamlet's confrontation with Laertes at Ophelia's grave, Cheadle uses Coleridge's question "What reason does it contain within itself for being as it is and no other?" as a guide.[9] Asking this question for the scene as a whole will enable us to see that the philosophical arguments about the change in Hamlet's attitude towards death do not adequately account for the presence of the gravediggers, Hamlet's farewell to Ophelia, or the struggle in the grave. If we consider the dramatic function of the scene, however, we will see that these elements are explained by their role in bestowing upon Hamlet the qualities of dignity, courage and deep feeling that make his death a waste of potential greatness.

The graveyard scene opens not with Hamlet's entrance but with the conversation between the gravediggers. This opening allows for a gradual shift in perspective from the court to Hamlet and humanizes him by making death a personal rather than a metaphysical concern. The shift in perspective has to be gradual because we have seen little to admire in Hamlet since the early scenes of the play. In the scenes preceding his exile, as Knight points out, Hamlet "is cruel to Ophelia and his mother"; "exults in tormenting the King by the murder of Gonzago" and "takes a demoniac pleasure in the thought of preserving his life for a more damning death"; "murders Polonius in error" and then makes disgusting, callous comments to Claudius about the body.[10] Furthermore, the three scenes from which Hamlet is absent focus on Laertes' grief and anger over his father's death and on Ophelia's madness and suicide. If we are to mourn the death of a man who has caused such suffering, we need to see him in a more favourable light.

The gravediggers serve as a means of detaching our sympathies from the court and transferring them to Hamlet. The dramatic goings-on and highly charged language of the court scenes seem excessive when contrasted with the matter-of-fact way in which the gravediggers go about their work. Emotional indulgence, like Christian burial for a suicide, seems a privilege accorded only to those of high social position. When Hamlet enters, however, his first comment is a criticism of the first gravedigger's singing at his work. His next is an assertion of the finer feelings of those with higher status: "The hand of little employment hath the daintier sense" (V.i. 66).[11] This exchange encourages us to forget Hamlet's earlier callousness and cynicism and to see him as a person of fine sensibility.

But the gravedigger episode does not merely shift the point of view from the court to Hamlet. It also humanizes Hamlet by making death a personal rather than a metaphysical concern. The gravediggers' debate over Ophelia's burial, as Peter Phialas points out, shifts attention away from the religious question of salvation and damnation that had been so powerful in Hamlet's own considerations of suicide to the social issues of power and status.[12] The reduction of death from a metaphysical to a human concern is further emphasized by the gravedigger's actions as he tosses skulls about and sings about the human cycle of love, age, and death.

Even more important in engaging our sympathy for Hamlet, however, is the dramatic tension created by his not knowing that the grave is for Ophelia. Although the discovery of Yorick's skull momentarily shows us Hamlet's deeper feelings and allows us to identify with the mixture of fond memory, revulsion, and jest in his response to this physical reminder of

mortality, his ignorance of Ophelia's death allows him to remain witty and self-possessed. As a result, our image of Hamlet
at the end of this episode is that of a person who is neither
morbidly preoccupied with death (as he was at the beginning
of the play) nor overly sentimental about it (as Laertes appears in the next part of the scene). Instead, he has accepted
its reality. The episode with the gravediggers thus prepares us
to see the burial of Ophelia from Hamlet's point of view.

The second half of the scene increases our sympathy for
Hamlet by revealing the depth of his feeling for Ophelia and by
bringing him face to face with the man we know will be the
instrument of his death. The simplicity of Hamlet's "I loved
Ophelia" (V.i. 256) dispels the mystery surrounding their relationship. Although we hear from Ophelia of her suitor's wild
dress and melancholy behaviour when his attentions are for-
bidden, we are not sure whether his actions are motivated
by "mock-madness" or, as Knight maintains, by blighted love.[13]
The only two times we see Hamlet and Ophelia together—
when she is acting as decoy for her father and Claudius in Act
III scene i and when both attend the play-within-a-play in
the following scene—Hamlet treats her with such contempt
and cruelty that we question his regard for her. B.D. Cheadle
suggests that Hamlet's leap into the grave should be staged
so that he says "This is I" (V.i. 244) as "an avowal to the dead
Ophelia that had she lived and had things been different, she
would have been Queen to the Dane."[14] When a few lines later
Hamlet says "I loved Ophelia," the past tense marks not only
Hamlet's acceptance of the end of the relationship but also his
acceptance of the death of love, a fact he could not accept in
his mother's remarriage. The ending of the Ophelia subplot in
this manner introduces, in a way sympathetic to Hamlet, the
sense of wasted lives and lost possibilities that will become
more pronounced in the final scene.

Interwoven with the burial of Ophelia is the confrontation
between Hamlet and Laertes. Although their behaviour seems
strange and inappropriate as an expression of grief for a
woman they both loved, it makes a very powerful dramatic
impact when considered as a prelude to, and symbolic foreshadowing of, their duel and deaths. Hamlet's dignity is enhanced by his initial self-control, a deliberate contrast, as
Cheadle points out, to Laertes' "ranting."[15] Furthermore, Hamlet's announcing himself as "Hamlet the Dane" is both "an
assertion of identity and purpose" and a direct challenge to
Claudius, since only the King has the right to call himself "the
Dane."[16] Claudius' plot against Hamlet makes Laertes not only
Ophelia's grief-stricken brother but also the King's champion.
The impact of the final duel would be much less, however, if
we saw Laertes only as Claudius' instrument. It is dramatically

necessary for Shakespeare to bring together Hamlet and Laertes, both of whom have vowed to avenge a father's death, so that each recognizes the justice in the other's actions and can "Exchange forgiveness," as the dying Laertes requests in the final scene. Their struggle in Ophelia's grave thus foreshadows the death blows they will deal each other and the sense of wasted nobility we will feel at their deaths.

This sense of waste, and the feelings of pity, fear, and awe that accompany it, would not be so pronounced at the end of the play without the graveyard scene to engage our sympathies. Interpretations of the scene's philosophical significance tend to overlook the dramatic impact of the gravedigger episode, of Hamlet's farewell to Ophelia, and of the struggle between Hamlet and Laertes. These critics forget, perhaps, that our response to the play, like Hamlet's to death, is personal as well as metaphysical, and equally shaped by the dramatist's art.

Notes

[1] This aspect of critial consensus is noted by Peter Phialas, "Hamlet and the Grave-Maker," Journal of English and German Philology, 63 (1964), 226.

[2] Maynard Mack, "The World of Hamlet," The Yale Review, 41 (1952), 521.

[3] Walter N. King, Hamlet's Quest for Meaning (Athens, Ga.: University of Georgia Press, 1982), p. 146.

[4] G. Wilson Knight, "The Embracing of Death: An Essay on Hamlet," in The Wheel of Fire (London: Oxford University Press, 1930); reprinted in Discussions of Hamlet, ed. J.C. Levenson (Boston: D.C. Heath, 1960), pp. 60-61.

[5] Knight, p. 64.

[6] Richard Levine, "The Tragedy of Hamlet's World View," College English, 23 (1962), 539, 543.

[7] Phialas, 226.

[8] B.D. Cheadle, "Hamlet at the Graveside: A Leap into Hermeneutics," English Studies in Africa, 22 (1970), 88.

[9] Cheadle, 89.

[10] Knight, pp. 56-57.

[11] William Shakespeare, Hamlet, Prince of Denmark, rev. ed., ed. Willard Farnham (New York: Penguin, 1970), V.i. 66. All further references to this text will be indicated in parentheses.

[12] Phialas, 231.

[13] Knight, 53.

[14] Cheadle, 87.

[15] Cheadle, 89.

[16] Cheadle, 86.

PART 3

Handbook for
Final Editing

Section 1

TONE

The word **tone** refers to the qualities in writing that the phrase "tone of voice" refers to in speaking. If you have read letters to the editor in a newspaper or magazine, for instance, you have no doubt encountered writers whose tone you would describe as "shrill," or "humorous," or "detached." Although these writers might be responding to the same issue—the foibles of politicians, perhaps, or the fate of the local hockey team—the general impression you formed about each writer would depend upon the **tone** of the piece. When we talk about tone, then, we mean the attitude the writer conveys about the subject and about the reader.

The tone that is appropriate for a particular piece of writing depends upon your audience and your purpose. If you were writing a column for your school newspaper, your tone might be witty and sarcastic. If you were writing a letter to your best friend, your tone would probably be casual and intimate. For the essays you write in college and university, you should aim for a tone that is confident but reasonable.

What determines the tone of a piece of writing? Although many aspects of style contribute to tone, you will be able to make appropriate choices if you consider only the two discussed below: (1) pronouns of address and (2) diction.

PRONOUNS OF ADDRESS

Personal pronouns in English are divided into first, second, and third persons.

PERSON	SINGULAR	PLURAL
1st	I, me	we, us
2nd	you, you	you, you
3rd	he, she, it, one	they, them
	him, her, it, one	

Each class of pronouns has its uses and its limitations as a way of referring to yourself, your subject, and your reader. When you are writing about your own experiences, you naturally refer to yourself as "I" and use first-person pronouns as appropriate. When you are explaining how to do something, you speak directly to your readers by using "you" (as in this book). When you want to focus attention on your subject, not on yourself or on your reader, you use third-person pronouns.

Notice how changing the pronouns affects the tone of the following statements.

> On the basis of my experiments, I think more Canadians are affected by mercury poisoning than we previously thought. (first-person pronouns)

> If you do these experiments, you will find that more Canadians are affected by mercury poisoning than you previously thought. (second-person pronouns)

> Scientists conducting experiments in the region have concluded that more Canadians are affected by mercury poisoning than they had previously thought. (third-person pronouns)

As you can see from these examples, first-person pronouns draw attention to the writer; second-person pronouns draw attention to the reader; third-person pronouns, by eliminating references to the writer and the reader, focus attention on the subject.

In most of your writing for college and university courses, your focus will be on your subject rather than on yourself or your reader. Consequently, you will use primarily third-person pronouns. Even so, there are likely to be situations in which you want to refer to yourself or to people in general, but feel uncertain about how to do so. Here are some suggestions.

How to Refer to Yourself

1. To express agreement or disagreement with another viewpoint, use a phrase such as "I think" or "I believe." Make such phrases inconspicuous by putting them inside a sentence rather than at the beginning.

> **NOT**   I think Jones is right when she calls *The Merchant of Venice* a flawed play.

> **BUT**   Jones is right, I think, when she calls *The Merchant of Venice* a flawed play.

2. When you are using an example from your own experience to support a point, use "I" instead of such awkward expressions as "this writer."

3. Avoid using "I" when you can express your thoughts and opinions in a more general way.

> **NOT**   I had a hard time figuring out what these two lines mean. (implies it's your own fault)

> **BUT**   The meaning of these two lines is hard to grasp. (implies that others would have the same difficulty)

4. Avoid using such "I" expressions as "this is only my opinion" and "I hope I will be able to show." Such expressions sound uncertain and apologetic and therefore weaken the force of your statement.

> **NOT**   I intend to prove that provincial governments should put more money into recreational facilities in order to attract tourists.

> **BUT**   Provincial governments should put more money into recreational facilities in order to attract tourists.

How to Refer to People in General

1. Use "we" sparingly to include your readers in your discussion. Make your "we" references as unobtrusive as possible. Often you can revise the sentence to omit "we."

> **NOT**   We have seen that Canada supplies a significant amount of the world's energy.

> **BUT**   Canada, as we have seen, supplies a significant amount of the world's energy.

> **OR**   Canada thus supplies a significant amount of the world's energy.

2. Use "we" sparingly to refer to people in general. Be careful that you are not overgeneralizing.

> **NOT**   We all remember our high school principals with affection.

> **BUT**   Many of us remember our high school principals with affection.

3. "One" is sometimes used in formal writing to mean "people in general, including the writer," as in "One might wish for better weather." Since "one" sounds stilted when used extensively, try to eliminate it, either by using "I" (if that is what you mean) or by using a noun.

> **NOT**   When one watches television, one is struck by the scarcity of good programmes.

> **BUT**   When I watch television, I am struck by the scarcity of good programmes.

> **OR**   Many television viewers are struck by the scarcity of good programmes.

4. Avoid using "you" to mean "people in general."

> **NOT**   This incident shows you that Duddy Kravitz is naive.

> **BUT**   This incident shows that Duddy Kravitz is naive.

5. Traditionally, masculine singular pronouns (he, him, his) have been used to signify a person of either sex in expressions such as "everyone bought his ticket" and "a student chooses his courses." Because many people feel that this usage contributes to stereotyped attitudes about the roles of women and men, you should try to avoid it.

Many writers find that when they attempt not to use the masculine singular pronouns in this way, they introduce errors in pronoun agreement (as in "Everyone bought their tickets"). Here are some suggestions for avoiding both problems.[1]

a. Reword the sentence to eliminate unnecessary gender pronouns.

> **NOT**   The average commuter drives his car fifty kilometres a day.
>
> **BUT**   The average commuter drives fifty kilometres a day.

b. Make the sentence plural.

> **NOT**   The enterprising business executive sends his managers to study European marketing practices.
>
> **BUT**   Enterprising business executives send their managers to study European marketing practices.

c. Alternate references to males and females in examples.

> **NOT**   Teachers sometimes make these complaints about their students: "he never does his homework"; "he constantly disrupts class"; "he never listens."
>
> **BUT**   Teachers sometimes make these complaints about their students: "she never does her homework"; "he constantly disrupts class"; "she never listens."

DICTION

The second aspect of tone you need to consider is the relationship you establish between yourself and your subject and between yourself and your reader through **diction**. Diction refers to the individual words you use in expressing your ideas. Together, these choices determine whether your writing sounds breezy or bureaucratic, superficial or supercilious, confident or cantankerous. We will focus on three possible problems with diction: (1) using an inappropriate level of diction; (2) using words with confusing connotations; and (3) using words with the wrong meaning for your context.

---

[1]These suggestions are among those contained in "Guidelines for Equal Treatment of the Sexes in McGraw-Hill Book Company Publications," in *The Norton Reader*, 4th ed., ed. Arthur M. Eastman et al. (New York: W.W. Norton, 1977), pp. 292-303.

Levels of Diction

The term **level of diction** or **level of usage** is used to describe the overall impression that a piece of writing creates about its writer and intended reader. At one end of the scale is the kind of casual, imprecise language characteristic of conversations among friends; at the other is the highly formal language characteristic of specialists writing to other specialists. In between is the language of informed discussion, that of newspapers and general interest magazines. The language of informed discussion is the level of diction appropriate for most college and university essays.

Identifying Problems with Your Level of Diction

Problems with your level of diction can be divided into two main types: (1) words and phrases that suggest an inappropriate attitude towards your subject and (2) words and phrases that suggest an inappropriate attitude towards your reader.

Attitude towards Your Subject. Your general level of diction may suggest that you take your subject either too seriously or not seriously enough. Suppose, for example, that you are writing an essay on the social and psychological effects of unemployment. If you fill your paper with ill-digested abstract concepts or sweeping generalizations about the human condition, you will seem to be putting yourself above the concrete reality of your subject. On the other hand, if your essay is full of slang words and colloquial expressions, or if your writing seems mechanical because you use only short, simple words and short, simple sentences, your level of diction will make your writing seem less serious and thoughtful than your subject deserves.

Attitude towards Your Readers. You may also use expressions that create an unflattering image of you as a writer. Apologetic expressions such as "I hope I will be able to show . . ." undermine your readers' confidence in your grasp of your subject, whereas argumentative expressions such as "Only a fool could believe . . ." raise the hackles of readers who believe that people of good will can have different views on a subject. Constant references to yourself and your own experiences (when these are not appropriate) can make you sound self-centred, whereas maintaining too much distance between yourself and your reader (by overusing constructions such as "It seems to this writer . . .") can make you seem stuffy and condescending.

The most appropriate tone to adopt for most college and university writing is that of a friendly, serious, but reasonable person writing to equally friendly, serious, and reasonable readers who might happen to be less well-informed or who might hold a different point of view. If your diction creates a different impression of your relation

to your subject and your readers, you can make the following kinds
of revisions.

Correcting Problems with Your Level of Diction

1. Eliminate inappropriate expressions.

> **NOT** I hope I will be able to show that many doctors over-
> prescribe medications because of their desire to live up to
> their patients' expectations. (too apologetic)

> **BUT** Many doctors over-prescribe medications because of their
> desire to live up to their patients' expectations.

> **NOT** Anyone with any sense can see that the number of nuclear
> weapons should be reduced in order to reduce the risk
> of nuclear war. (too argumentative)

> **BUT** The number of nuclear weapons should be reduced in
> order to reduce the risk of nuclear war.

> **NOT** In my experience, I have found that many good athletes
> also have other talents. (too personal)

> **BUT** Many good athletes also have other talents.

> **NOT** It was observed in the course of preparing this paper that
> little information is available in popular magazines on
> the use of fibre optics in medicine. (too stuffy)

> **BUT** Popular magazines do not contain much information about
> the use of fibre optics in medicine.

2. Rewrite sentences that are too colloquial, too abstract, too gran-
diose, or too mechanical.

> **NOT** This author has a real neat way of putting stuff. (too col-
> loquial)

> **BUT** This author has a lively, entertaining style.

> **NOT** The interpersonal interaction between counsellors and
> clients can provide the opportunity for both parties to gain
> a sense of self-worth and significance in the midst of our
> institutionalized society. (too abstract)

> **BUT** Meetings between clients and volunteer counsellors can
> help both parties feel more worthwhile.

> **NOT** Throughout history mankind has struggled to understand
> his place in the ever-changing world in which he was
> only one infinitesimal link in an infinite chain of existence.
> (too grandiose)

    BUT   Men and women have always tried to understand their place in the world.

    NOT   There are three aspects to this problem. The first is medical. The second is legal. The third is moral. (too mechanical)

    BUT   This problem has medical, legal, and moral implications.

Confusing Connotations

Even though your level of diction is appropriate, you may find that you occasionally use a word that is inappropriate because its connotations do not fit your context.

If you are not aware of the connotations of the words you use, you may unintentionally confuse your reader about your attitude towards your subject. For example, how would you decide whether to describe a character as thin, wiry, or scrawny? *Thin* is a more or less neutral descriptive word; *wiry* adds positive connotations of energy and strength to the idea of thinness; *scrawny* adds the negative connotations of weakness and insignificance to the idea of thinness. In deciding which to use, you would have to consider whether you wanted to convey a neutral, positive, or negative impression.

You should also be sensitive to the fact that your diction may arouse distracting associations in the minds of your readers. Since the Wife of Bath in Chaucer's "General Prologue" to *The Canterbury Tales* was married five times and also had numerous lovers, you would avoid describing her generosity and friendliness by saying that she was "open to everyone," just as you would avoid saying that the Cook was a "well-seasoned traveller," or that the language of the gravediggers in *Hamlet* is "down-to-earth."

Wrong Words

Sometimes you will use the wrong word not because you have succumbed to the lure of jargon or exotic words and not because you are unaware of a word's connotations, but simply because you think a word means one thing when it means another. Often these errors are essentially spelling errors: you write *principle* when you mean *principal*, *aisle* when you mean *isle*, *there* when you mean *their*, or *they're*. (For more on spelling, see section 7).

Other mistakes in word usage might occur because you confuse two meanings of a word. You might, for example, use *realize* in the sense of "making real" (as in *realize a profit*) when you mean *realize* in the sense of "understanding fully" (as in *to realize that he was wrong*). You can avoid confusing these two meanings of realize if you use *realize that* when you mean "understand fully."

NOT	He realized his mother's unhappiness.
BUT	He realized that his mother was unhappy.
NOT	She realized his failure.
BUT	She realized that he would fail.

You can find out if a word has more than one meaning by checking your dictionary.

On the other hand, you might occasionally slip up because a word means something altogether different from the meaning you have attached to it. Most of us, after all, learn words from seeing or hearing them, not from looking them up in a dictionary. As a result, we sometimes produce sentences like these:

1. We turned left, although Mary had **implicitly** (for **explicitly**) said to turn right.
2. The drug had **everlasting** (for **long-lasting**) effects.
3. The child was **enhanced** (for **entranced**) by the Christmas tree.
4. The neighbours were deeply **involved** in the scandal. (active participants) **for** The neighbours were deeply **engrossed** in the scandal. (absorbed onlookers).
5. They **partook** in the parade. **for** They **took part** in the parade.

There is no everlasting remedy for wrong-word-itis. Your best bet is to check your dictionary, both for spelling and for meaning, whenever you use a word outside your normal vocabulary. In the process you may increase the range of your word choices.

EXERCISES

A. Revise each of the following sentences to make the level of diction appropriate for a college or university essay and to replace wrong words and words with confusing connotations. You may need to use a dictionary.

1. Wielding his famous energy-mass conversion equation, $E = mc^2$, Albert Einstein excelled the modern physical scientific principles light years ahead of his time.

2. Pollutants sully the oceans by several methods. One of these methods is land drainage. Another of these means is precipitation from the heavens.

3. Engineers must realize every ecological niche, however tiny, they disturb.

4. Possibly the most legitimate reason, it seems to me, for halting genetic research is the possible religious overtones of such manipulations.

5. Canadian interest in the acid rain phenomena began by focusing in the metal smelting plants in southern Ontario.

6. Fibre optics have many inspiring advantages over traditional copper wire methods, especially for high-traffic and long-distance communication. Fibre optics are easy to install. They are also inexpensive to produce and cheap to maintain.

7. By now it should hopefully be obvious that acid rain is a serious problem affecting everyone.

8. Thermal gradient plants are comparative to offshore oil rigs in both size and technology.

9. The six-foot bear roamed the shoreline, pronouncing her superiority by randomly ripping our camp apart.

10. An undercurrent of respect for women had a modifying influence on Classical Greek thought, sponsoring a return to what were thought to be the primitive features of Athenian society.

B. Rewrite the following paragraph so that its tone (both pronouns of address and diction) is appropriate for a university essay. You may need to check your dictionary to find replacements for some words.

> I have actually found a variety of reasons for the bitching among the upper crust in Britain during the decades antecedent to the start of the civil war in 1642. The reigning monarchs, first James I and then his son Charles I, had abused Parliament for a long time. They had promulgated taxes without Parliamentary consent, they had stubbornly implemented unpopular political and ecclesiastical policies, and they had messed around with foreign trade. Any fool could see that the courts of James and Charles were absorbed in themselves, heedless of the welfare of the country and its citizens, and only into their own advancement and enjoyment. It seems to the author of this paper that this antagonism between court and country was the principal cause of the brutal and agonizing civil war that pitted brother against brother, father against son, but I could be wrong.

Section 2

SENTENCE PROBLEMS

In college and university courses, you may be expected to use a more formal level of writing than you are accustomed to. As a result, you may find that your usual patterns of sentence construction and punctuation are not satisfactory, or that in trying to write more formally, you create new problems for yourself. Sometimes a sentence may not sound quite right, but you may not be sure what the problem is or how to correct it.

This section should help you to understand the kinds of sentences that are appropriate for formal essay writing. The first part will show you how to identify and correct sentence fragments, comma splices, and run-on sentences. The second part will show you how to improve your sentence structure by eliminating misplaced and dangling modifiers, mixed constructions, and faulty parallelism.

Writing Complete Sentences

One of the main differences between formal and informal writing is the way sentences are punctuated. When you dash off a letter to a friend, your writing is likely to sound conversational because you use incomplete sentences and minimal punctuation. You don't worry about being misunderstood because your friend can fill in the gaps from his knowledge of you or he can ask you to explain. When you are doing formal writing, however, as in business letters, reports, and most college and university essays, you need to ensure that readers you may never meet understand what you have to say. Punctuating your sentences so that they are complete according to the conventions of formal writing is one way of ensuring effective communication.

A complete sentence is one that contains at least one **independent clause**: that is, it has a subject and a verb and it states a complete thought. If the sentence contains more than one clause, the punctuation indicates how the clauses are related. Here are some examples of complete sentences.

> The runners surged towards the finish line. (one independent clause)
>
> The runners surged towards the finish line, and the crowd cheered wildly. (two independent clauses)
>
> As the runners surged towards the finish line, the crowd cheered wildly. (one dependent clause and one independent clause)

Failure to punctuate clauses correctly may result in these types of sentence problems: (1) sentence fragments, (2) comma splices, and (3) run-on sentences.

SENTENCE FRAGMENTS

As its name implies, a sentence fragment is part of a sentence. A sentence fragment may lack a subject, a verb, or both, or it may be a dependent clause rather than a complete sentence.

Identifying Sentence Fragments

1. Silently, swiftly, crept down the mountain. (no subject)
2. Silently, swiftly, the soldiers down the mountain. (no verb)
3. Silently, swiftly, down the mountain. (no subject or verb)
4. When the soldiers silently and swiftly crept down the mountain. (dependent clause)

The last kind of sentence fragment—punctuating a dependent clause as if it were a complete sentence—is by far the most common kind of sentence fragment in student essays. Dependent clauses should not be punctuated as though they were complete sentences because their meaning is not complete unless they are attached to an independent clause. Independent clauses have both a subject and verb and can stand alone as complete sentences. Dependent clauses, on the other hand, describe either the verb or the noun in the independent clause and cannot stand on their own.

These examples illustrate the relation between dependent and independent clauses.

(When she completed her test),   the student felt exhilarated.
       dependent clause   independent clause

The student (who had completed her test) felt exhilarated.
                   dependent clause

As these examples demonstrate, dependent clauses cannot stand on their own as complete sentences, but must be attached to an appropriate independent clause.

Dependent clauses often begin with words that indicate logical relationships (because, although, if) or time relationships (after, before, during, while, when), or with the pronouns who, which, and that. When you are proofreading, double-check all sentences that begin with one of these words to make sure that they are complete sentences.

Correcting Sentence Fragments

To correct sentence fragments, supply the missing subject, verb, or both, or attach the fragment to the independent clause it refers to.

Fragment   Holden runs away. Soon realizing that the things he is running away from are the things he is running into.

Correct   Holden runs away. He soon realizes, however, that the things he is running away from are the things he is running into. (subject and verb added)

Fragment   Even though the students had been warned in advance that they would be expected to write an in-class essay. Many of them arrived late.

Correct   Even though the students had been warned in advance that they would be expected to write an in-class essay, many of them arrived late. (dependent clause attached to independent clause)

Fragment   Shakespeare's play *Richard III* deals with fundamental human problems. Such as the conflict between good and evil.

Correct   Shakespeare's play *Richard III* deals with fundamental human problems, such as the conflict between good and evil. (phrase attached to independent clause)

Using Sentence Fragments for Effect

Sentence fragments are generally considered inappropriate for formal essay writing. In less formal writing, however, you will sometimes find fragments used for emphasis. In an essay entitled "Intimations,"[1] for example, Bharati Mukherjee emphasizes the widespread concern for security in Calcutta by means of a sentence fragment (italics added):

> My mother likes to lock doors. *Also windows, cupboards, closets, trunks, valises.* Her closest friend in Chemur has installed a padlock and chain around her refrigerator.

Although sentence fragments can be used for stylistic effect, as in this passage, it is a good idea to avoid them unless your instructor has encouraged stylistic experimentation in a particular piece of writing.

EXERCISE

Revise the following sentences to correct any sentence fragments.
1. Many high school students decide not to hold part-time jobs. The reason being they need the time to study.
2. Although the benefits of pollution regulations do outweigh the costs. Every regulation has an effect on the Canadian economy.
3. The pollution of prairie waters is mainly due to agricultural insecticides and some industrial wastes. While the pollution of the St. Lawrence Seaway is due to the industrialization of southern Ontario.
4. Fibre cables, on the other hand, which require repeaters about every twenty kilometres depending on capacity demands.

---

[1] In *Days and Nights in Calcutta*, by Clark Blaise and Bharati Mukherjee (Garden City, N.Y.: Doubleday, 1977).

5. In the Classical Age Greek social life became dominated by the evolving institutions of the male social sphere. Excluding women, who were considered tied to nature and thus a lower order of being than men, from these institutions.

6. Kirchner placing prime emphasis on inner feeling and experiences and distorting nature in his paintings whenever this distortion was necessary.

7. Darwin's formulation of the theory of evolution had a profound impact on many areas of nineteenth-century thought. From history to economics to psychology.

8. People who want compensation for all the injustices they have endured and who will no longer accept the indifference of government bureaucracies.

9. Genetic manipulation could be useful in the treatment of some diseases. Such as diabetes, for example, which is caused by an error in genetic information.

10. In "My Last Duchess" where Browning criticizes the standards by which the Duke judges himself and others.

THE COMMA SPLICE

Instead of punctuating sentence fragments as though they were complete sentences, some students join sentences together with inadequate punctuation. The most common mistake is the **comma splice**: joining two independent clauses with nothing but a comma to hold them together.

Identifying Comma Splices

Each of the following sentences contains a comma splice.

1. The thinking behind the idea of the Divine Right of Kings is that God has invested the power of kingship in the king, whatever a king does is sanctioned by God.

2. Hagar and Rachel have very different personalities and live very different lives, both are enough like us and the people we know to be believable.

3. We have high expectations of our leaders, when they fail we are uncertain how to punish them.

4. He assumed the jewels were cheap fakes, therefore he must have thought his wife bought them with her household money.

5. She wanted so badly to win the prize, she practiced hours every day.

Correcting Comma Splices

Whenever you make two separate points, as the writers of these sentences are doing, you need more than a comma to show how your

points are related. There are five ways of correcting comma splices.
1. Separate the independent clauses with a period.

> The thinking behind the idea of the Divine Rights of Kings is that God has invested the power of kingship in the king. Whatever a king does is sanctioned by God.

2. Join the two clauses with a comma and one of the following co-ordinate conjunctions: **and, but, or, nor, yet, so, for, either . . . or, neither . . . nor, not only . . . but also**. Choose the conjunction that best shows how the ideas are related.

> Hagar and Rachel have very different personalities and live very different lives, but both are enough like us and the people we know to be believable.

3. Join the two clauses with a semicolon.

> We have high expectations of our leaders; when they fail, we are uncertain how to punish them.

4. Join the two clauses with a semicolon and one of the conjunctive adverbs. Put a comma after the conjunctive adverb if there is any danger of misreading.

Here is a partial list of conjunctive adverbs, with indications of how they are used:

> a) to signal that one idea follows as a result of another:
> *accordingly, consequently, therefore, thus, then, hence*
> b) to signal that one idea is being added to another
> *furthermore, moreover, besides, likewise*
> c) to signal a contrast in ideas
> *nevertheless, however, otherwise, still*

In order to choose the appropriate conjunction, you must consider how your ideas are related. In this sentence, the second idea follows as a result of the first:

> He assumed the jewels were cheap fakes; therefore he must have thought his wife bought them with her household money.

5. Make one of the clauses dependent. Note that when the dependent clause comes first, it is separated from the independent clause with a comma. .

> She wanted so badly to win the prize that she practiced hours every day.

> Because she wanted so badly to win the prize, she practiced hours every day.

EXERCISE

Choose the most appropriate method to correct the comma splices in the following sentences.

1. Holden wants to be like the ducks, no one seems to notice them.
2. The Premier met with his aides and advisors on several occasions, no word of their discussions reached the press.
3. The southern half of the province has received very little rain for the third consecutive year, poor crops are expected.
4. She was constantly late, her work was sloppy.
5. It is no surprise that autistic children do not want to participate in reality as they experience it, reality is garbled by their sensory perception.
6. The competition in Hong Kong high schools is intense, some students use alcohol as a way to escape from the pressure to succeed.
7. The decodable frequency range of copper is very small, it is quite economical to replace copper wiring with fibre optics.
8. Nuclear fusion is the power of the future, with it mankind may accomplish tasks never before dreamed of.
9. There is no need to sensationalize passion, Racine uses an elevated style to encourage his audience to examine his plays analytically.
10. He studied all night for the exam, he did poorly.

RUN-ON SENTENCES

Like the writer of comma splices, the writer of **run-on** (sometimes called **fused**) sentences tries to pack more information into a sentence than its grammatical structure can accommodate. Instead of having insufficient punctuation, however, run-on sentences have no punctuation to show how clauses are related.

Identifying Run-On Sentences

1. Television networks make money by selling advertising time therefore the programmes must appeal to people who can afford to buy the products advertised.
2. Jeans are a status symbol in Russia they sell for hundreds of dollars on the black market.
3. Some adolescents are sullen, rebellious, and lazy others work to support themselves and to help their families.

Correcting Run-On Sentences

Run-on sentences can be corrected in the same ways as comma splices. Make sure that you do not create a comma splice by merely putting a comma between independent clauses.

EXERCISES

A. Correct the following sentences by adding conjunctions and changing punctuation as necessary. Do not make any other changes.

1. It is easy to lose weight all you need is more will power and less starch.

2. The tasks of the secondary school are in confusion people both inside and outside the school system have different ideas on how the system should be run.

3. There are a number of problems with plurality voting in Canada there has recently been much pressure to change the system of electoral districts and to adopt its main alternative, proportional representation.

4. The practical use of Einstein's theories came about through the needs of the military although Einstein himself abhorred the thought of his work being used in this way it seems in the near future we may find more humanitarian uses for Einstein's concept of elementary particles.

5. Democratic institutions are slow to change because they respond to shifts in majority opinion they are a conservative force in the society.

B. First identify, and then correct, all sentence fragments, comma splices, and run-on sentences in the paragraph below.

> Various staging effects in Arthur Miller's play *Death of a Salesman* help the audience to understand Willy's thought. The music, for example, when it is used to indicate a change from the present to the past in Willy's mind. The musical instrument used is the flute, it prepares the audience to understand this shift. Time changes also indicated by changes in lighting. The town has expanded and become more densely populated towering apartment buildings have replaced the trees Willy remembers from the past. The lighting changes the scene from the present to the past. Fading out the apartment buildings and lighting up the trees. These staging effects help the audience to follow Willy's mental journey.

Improving Sentence Structure

Sometimes sentences are confusing or ambiguous because of the way they are put together. You can improve your sentence structure by learning how to recognize and to correct these problems: (1) misplaced and dangling modifiers, (2) mixed constructions, and (3) faulty parallelism.

MISPLACED AND DANGLING MODIFIERS

A **modifier** is a word, phrase, or clause that describes or explains another word in the sentence.

Identifying Modifiers

> The dog barked **furiously**.
> (**furiously** describes **barked**)
>
> The dog, **barking furiously**, attacked the stranger.
> (**barking furiously** is a phrase describing **dog**)
>
> The dog, **which had been barking furiously for hours**, went to sleep.
> (**which had been barking furiously for hours** is a clause describing **dog**)

For clarity, a modifier must be as close as possible to the word it modifies, and there must be a word in the sentence for it to modify. If these conditions are not met, the modifier is either **misplaced** or **dangling**.

MISPLACED MODIFIERS

Misplaced modifiers are single words (especially words such as *almost, even, hardly, just, merely, nearly, only, scarcely*), phrases, or clauses that are too far from the word they refer to for the meaning of the sentence to be clear.

Identifying Misplaced Modifiers

> 1. This film **only** runs fifty-eight minutes.
>   (Only this film runs fifty-eight minutes, or this film runs only fifty-eight minutes?)
> 2. She told him **on Friday** she was quitting.
>   (Did she tell him on Friday, or is she quitting on Friday?)
> 3. He **just** said that he would be a few minutes late.
>   (Did he say this very recently, or did he say that he would be only a few minutes late?)

Correcting Misplaced Modifiers

Misplaced modifiers can easily be corrected by moving the modifier as close as possible to the word it modifies.

> 1. This film runs **only** fifty-eight minutes.

2. **On Friday** she told him she was quitting.
   OR
   She told him she was quitting **on Friday**.
3. He said that he would be **just** a few minutes late.

DANGLING MODIFIERS

A dangling modifier is a phrase, often at the beginning of a sentence, which has no clear relationship to the rest of the sentence. The phrase "dangles" because there is no word in the sentence for it to modify.

Identifying Dangling Modifiers

1. **Bitterly regretting his misspent youth**, his days in jail seemed endless.
   The phrase "bitterly regretting his misspent youth" would have to modify "the prisoner" or an equivalent word; but there is no such word in the sentence.
2. **When empty**, return to the store.
   What does the phrase "when empty" refer to?

Correcting Dangling Modifiers

1. Expand the phrase into a dependent clause.

   Because he bitterly regretted his misspent youth, his days in jail seemed endless.

   When the bottles are empty, return them to the store.

2. Revise the independent clause so that it contains a word for the phrase to modify.

   Bitterly regretting his misspent youth, the prisoner endured seemingly endless days in jail.

   When empty, the bottles should be returned to the store.

EXERCISE

Revise the following sentences so that they do not contain misplaced or dangling modifiers.
1. He scarcely knew anyone at the party.
2. Even after studying all night, many of the questions on the exam were unfamiliar.
3. With versatility and mobility, there are few jobs the Soviet navy cannot undertake, whether in peace or in conflict.
4. By using a narrative introduction, the reader's attention can be caught.

5. Instead of working at a regular job, crime may seem an easier way to make a lot of money quickly.
6. When under-age, Louis XIV's ministers had charge of the government.
7. By regulating the disposal of technological waste products, the environment would be preserved.
8. In writing a successful magazine story, a happy ending is always desired by readers.
9. Countries such as Israel, Denmark, and Italy among others that use the list system have many parties and hence coalition governments.
10. To survive a jump from this height a special parachute was made for him.

MIXED CONSTRUCTIONS

If you try to combine two or more grammatically incompatible units within one sentence, you'll end up with a **mixed construction**.

Identifying Mixed Constructions

> 1. In *A Man for All Seasons*, Bolt shows that **the reason** Sir Thomas More becomes a martyr **is because** he is willing to die for his beliefs.
> 2. **An example** of her stubbornness **is when** she refuses to leave the party.

These sentences contain mixed constructions because the grammatical structures "the reason is" and "an example is" must be followed by nouns or noun phrases: the reason is **that**, an example is **her refusal**.

Correcting Mixed Constructions

Decide which of the two possible constructions best communicates your idea, and stick with it.

> 1. In *A Man for All Seasons*, Bolt shows that the reason Sir Thomas More becomes a martyr is that he is willing to die for his beliefs.
> > OR
>
> In *A Man for All Seasons*, Bolt shows that Sir Thomas More becomes a martyr because he is willing to die for his beliefs.
> 2. An example of her stubbornness is her refusal to leave the party.
> > OR
>
> She reveals her stubbornness when she refuses to leave the party.

FAULTY PARALLELISM

When you join parts of your sentence with a coordinate conjunction (**and, or, nor, but, yet, so, either** . . . **or, neither** . . . **nor, not only** . . . **but also**), you indicate that these parts are similar. To make this similarity more obvious to your reader, all the items that you join with the coordinate conjunction should have the same grammatical form. That is, all the items should be words, phrases, or clauses of the same type. This principle is known as *parallelism*. If sentence elements joined by a coordinate conjunction are not of the same type, they are not **parallel**.

Identifying Faulty Parallelism

1. She was lucky, intelligent, and a brave woman.
2. The riders made their way over the mountain, through the valley, and entered the town.
3. What we say, our thinking, and the way we do things are often at odds.
4. The cowardly fail because of their fear, but success comes to the courageous in spite of their fear.

Correcting Faulty Parallelism

You can make elements parallel by balancing word with word, phrase with phrase, and clause with clause.

1. She was lucky, intelligent, and brave. (parallel words)
2. The riders made their way over the mountain, through the valley, and into the town. (parallel phrases)
3. What we say, what we think, and what we do are often at odds. (parallel clauses)
4. The cowardly fail because of their fear, but the courageous succeed in spite of their fear. (parallel clauses)

EXERCISES

A. Revise the following sentences to correct mixed constructions and faulty parallelism. Be sure not to leave out any of the ideas.

1. Gandhi, as he is portrayed in Richard Attenborough's movie, is intelligent, brave, and he had a lot of personal integrity.
2. Bronowski tells his reader that scientists look for likenesses and then how their thinking progresses from these likenesses.
3. The reason for his absence was because he had a bad cold.
4. As a winner, not only will you have achieved success, but you have achieved respect.

5. Many children do poorly in school because of inadequate diet, poor instruction, and they are not very interested.

6. To prevent shock, cover the victim with a blanket, speaking re-assuringly.

7. The transition from adolescence to maturity is marked by the ac-quisition of certain qualities. These are being less self-conscious, to be able to manage one's affairs, and the ability to get along with people.

8. An example of her cunning is when she persuades her client not to consult another lawyer.

9. Yet another weakness of coalition governments in a multi-party system is when the centre parties form the government and there is no unified opposition.

10. By denying that the government intended to raise taxes increased the "credibility gap" between cabinet ministers and the public.

B. Rewrite the following paragraph to eliminate sentence fragments, comma splices, run-on sentences, dangling and misplaced modifiers, mixed constructions, and faulty parallelism. Do not omit any of the ideas.

> Although drugs seem to offer a quick and easy method of treating emotional problems and can be used effectively. Their long-range benefits are questionable. Prescribed by psychiatrists, patients often take drugs that alter their moods greatly. Patients cannot distinguish their real feelings from the feelings induced by the drugs they may think that their anxieties have been eliminated when they have been suppressed by only the drugs. An example of this is when a businessman who suffers from an overwhelming feeling of worthlessness takes psychic energizers. He may be capable under the influence of these psychic energizers of going to work regularly, running his business efficiently, and to fulfill his social obligations for a few months or even a few years. He be-comes more dependent on the drugs and the psychiatrist who prescribes them he becomes less and less aware of the misery within. These drugs have merely masked his underlying fears, they have not resolved them. These fears are likely to re-emerge, more overwhelming than before. Whenever the man is subjected to more stress than usual. Each breakdown leaves him more at the mercy of the drugs and to get help from his psychiatrist and others who treat the emotionally disturbed.

Section 3

SENTENCE EFFECTIVENESS

When you think of sentence structure, you may think only of the kinds of problems discussed in Section 2—sentence fragments, dangling modifiers, and the like. In formal writing, such as essays and reports, it is of course important to ensure that your sentences are complete and error-free. But there is more to using sentence structure effectively than merely avoiding errors.

In this section you will find a number of suggestions for increasing the effectiveness of your sentences. First we will examine techniques for making your writing more concise; then we will discuss two methods of using sentence structure to show how your ideas are related: (1) varying sentence patterns and (2) using transitions and other continuity devices.

WRITING CONCISELY

Most of us are in the habit of using a great many words to say very little. We use clumsy expressions such as *free up* instead of *free, at this moment in time* instead of *now.* We describe a small house as *small in size,* a yellow dress as *yellow in colour,* eleven marbles as *eleven in number,* his book as *his own personal book.*

The problem of wordy writing, however, includes more than unnecessary words within single sentences. Sometimes your whole essay may be wordy because you have not completely thought out your thesis, and so you keep circling around your ideas and repeating points. If so, you need to combine ideas spread out in four or five sentences into one or two. Don't be misled into padding your essay with unnecessary words and phrases (and even unnecessary sentences and paragraphs) just to reach the word limit. Such a strategy will only irritate your reader and weaken the force of your ideas.

Here are some suggestions for writing more concisely.

How to Condense Wordy Sentences

1. Choose exact nouns, verbs, and modifiers.

> **NOT**　We walked slowly and quietly in the direction of the run-down little house.
>
> **BUT**　We crept toward the hovel.

> **NOT** He pushed his brother roughly out of his way.
>
> **BUT** He shoved his brother aside.

2. Replace vague words such as *very, somewhat, really,* and *rather* with a more exact word.

> **NOT** He was very tired.
>
> **BUT** He was exhausted.

> **NOT** She was extremely happy.
>
> **BUT** She was ecstatic.

> **NOT** My cat is somewhat fat.
>
> **BUT** My cat is plump.

> **NOT** They were really frightened by the ghost.
>
> **BUT** They were terrified by the ghost.

3. Avoid carelessly repeating words and ideas. Notice how the following sentences become clearer as they become more concise.

> They learned to cooperate together inside of one short minute. (10 words)
> They learned to cooperate in a minute. (7 words)
> They quickly learned to cooperate. (5 words)

> Entries to this competition are restricted to students only; no one else need apply. (14 words)
> Only students may enter this competition. (6 words)

> The special difficulty in Zelnyk's case arises from the fact that he has no personal means of transportation. (18 words)
> Zelnyk's problem is that he has no car. (8 words)

4. Condense prepositional phrases to single words.

> She was dressed in a fashionable manner.
> She was dressed fashionably.

5. Avoid overusing the constructions **there is/are** and **it is . . . that** to introduce sentences.

> **NOT** There are many problems associated with laying the Mackenzie Valley pipeline.
>
> **BUT** Laying the Mackenzie Valley pipeline creates many problems.

NOT   It is often the case that we could organize our time more efficiently.

BUT   We could often organize our time more efficiently.

How to Combine Sentences

One good way of increasing the flow and complexity of your writing is to combine a series of short sentences into one longer sentence.

Perhaps you now write fairly short sentences something like this:

> The waiting room is full of people.
> I sit edgily.
> I tuck my cotton dress around my knees.
> I edge away from the woman.
> She is wearing a stout skirt.
> She is telling her five-year-old son something.
> She tells him to behave himself and hush.
> The boy is wearing spectacles.

Once you learn to combine short sentences such as these, your writing will look more like Margaret Laurence's original sentence:

> The waiting room is full of people and I sit edgily, tucking my cotton dress around my knees, edging away from the stout-skirted mother bidding a spectacled five-year-old to behave himself and hush.[1]

The following sentences illustrate similar procedures for making your writing more compact. In each example several short sentences are combined into one longer sentence by reducing sentences to clauses, clauses to phrases, and phrases to single words.

1. The car crashed into the telephone pole.
    The car screeched around the corner on three wheels.

    The car, which screeched around the corner on three wheels, crashed into the telephone pole.

    The car, screeching around the corner on three wheels, crashed into the telephone pole.

2. Television cameras filmed the demolition of the Regency Theatre.

    The Regency Theatre was one of the most ornate movie-houses in western Canada.

    Television cameras filmed the demolition of the Regency Theatre, which was one of the most ornate movie-houses in western Canada.

[1]   Margaret Laurence, *A Jest of God* (Toronto, McClelland and Stewart, 1966), p. 176.

Television cameras filmed the demolition of the Regency Theatre, one of the most ornate movie-houses in western Canada.

3. The patrol officer waved the car on.
The patrol officer was a cheerful young man.

The patrol officer, a cheerful young man, waved the car on.
The cheerful young patrolman waved the car on.

How to Revise Wordy Paragraphs

This is a paragraph from the first draft of a student essay on William Morris' utopian novel *News from Nowhere*. In this paragraph the student contrasts the economic system in Morris' utopia with the economic system in our society. This paragraph seems substantial because it is long; as you will see, however, it makes only two points: Morris' society, unlike ours, does not use money for business transactions; and people in Morris' society have more freedom in determining how, where, and when they work. Instead of supporting these points with specific details, however, the student merely repeats them:

> In Morris' society there is no monetary system or labour force. Everything is free. Nothing is paid for. A person works as an individual; in other words, he does whatever work he wants to do whenever he wants to do it. A person works as long and as hard as he wants to. A person may wish to do no work at all and just enjoy a life free of all care and obligations. Any labour position is open to a man or woman on an equal basis. Our society has a monetary system and a labour force. Money is the basis for the way we carry on our business transactions. Various work forces are organized for various occupations. A person employed in one occupation must conform to the guidelines that are set out for that type of work, such as hours of work and fulfillment of responsibility.

In order to make the paragraph as substantial as it seems, the student needs to eliminate the repetition and to add specific examples to illustrate the differences between the two societies.

EXERCISES

A. Revise the following sentences or groups of sentences to make them more concise.

1. A study has been done on smokers. This study revealed that much smoking is an automatic response to certain activities. These activities might be driving, typing, reading, or drinking coffee or alcohol.

2. The book *A Circle of Children* and its successor *Lovey* are stories

about a teacher of children who are emotionally disturbed. Mary MacCracken wrote an account of her experiences working with children with emotional problems and described her growth as a teacher. She began as a teacher's aide and gradually became a teacher who was fully qualified to work with emotionally disturbed children. The books show her development as a teacher.

3. Being a video game player, I find it my duty to give a good name to video games because I find them challenging and I would like to change people's attitudes towards video games by giving some information in the hopes that many people will discard their belief that these are mindless games and learn that these games require many years of practice and video games are played by millions of people all over the world.

4. A society that maintained a balance between the needs of the society and the preservation of the environment would be the kind of society in which I would like to live in.

5. He drove his car down the highway. He drove his car very fast. He was travelling about 150 kilometres an hour. Suddenly he hit a very icy section of the road. The car went out of control and slid quite quickly in the direction of the ditch.

B. Combine each of the following groups of sentences into one complete sentence. Use the fewest words possible, but do not omit any of the ideas.

1. Her first novel was a best seller.
   She had worked on it for ten years.
   The novel was praised by many critics.
2. Sylvester Stallone shot to stardom with *Rocky*.
   He was once an unknown actor.
3. They listened to the sounds coming from the other room.
   The radio was blaring.
   The vacuum cleaner was humming.
   The child was crying with complete abandon.

C. Rewrite the following paragraph to make it more concise. Add specific examples to illustrate points.

> Retirement for many people brings with it a reduction in the number of friends and acquaintances they socialize and share activities with. Since the friends they knew before they retired were often people they knew from work, retired people may not have so many friends after they quit working. People who have retired no longer share the same interests as people who are still working, and so they don't spend as much time together. If retired people don't have friends and acquaintances besides the people they worked with, they may feel very lonely when they quit working and have fewer contacts with people.

USING SENTENCE STRUCTURE TO CLARIFY IDEAS

You are more likely to communicate your ideas effectively, as we have seen, if your sentences are concise as well as correct. You can also make your meaning clearer by varying the structure of your sentences to indicate shifts among main points, explanations, and details, and by using transitions and other continuity devices.

Consider, for example, this discussion of the narrator in the "Prologue" to Geoffrey Chaucer's *The Canterbury Tales*.

> The narrator's weakness is his amazing tolerance of all types of people. This is his strength. His fellow pilgrims have weaknesses and oddities. He rarely criticizes them. He treats everyone in a kind, genial manner. He observes that the French spoken by the Prioress is not Parisian French. He is not condescending about her accent. He doesn't condemn the kind parson for an occasional harsh word. He kindly ignores the Wife of Bath's earlier amorous adventures. He does not make derogatory comments about the Pardoner's effeminacy. The narrator's tendency to adopt the standards of those around him springs from his desire to think well of others. He is not self-interested. His tolerance of their weakness seems a virtue.

This paragraph is difficult to understand for two main reasons.
1. All the sentences have the same basic structure and are about the same length. As a result, it is hard to distinguish explanations from examples.
2. There are no transitions; that is, there are no words, phrases, or clauses that establish relationships between sentences. As a result, it is hard to tell whether a particular statement is intended to reinforce, to qualify, or to contradict another, or whether a cause-and-effect relationship is implied.

If you discover when you evaluate your writing that you have not made your points clearly, consider the following suggestions about (1) varying your sentence structure and length, and (2) using transitions and other devices to ensure continuity.

Varying Sentence Patterns

The basic sentence pattern in English is subject-verb-object (Jack hit the ball). If all of your sentences follow this pattern, however, your writing will soon become as monotonous as a grade-one reader. Furthermore, your reader will have trouble distinguishing major points from minor ones and explanations from the details that support them. On the other hand, if every sentence follows a different pattern, your reader may find your paragraphs confusing.

Here are some guidelines for varying your sentence structure effectively.

1. Keep the structure of topic sentences fairly simple. When you are making major points, you don't want your readers to get lost in elaborate sentence patterns.

2. Change your sentence structure when you introduce an explanation. If your explanation takes more than one sentence, keep the sentences in similar patterns.

3. When you shift from explanation to details, change your sentence pattern.

4. Keep similar sentence patterns for all your details.

5. When you are ready to shift to a second explanation or to summarize, change your sentence pattern to match either your first explanation or, if you are summarizing, your topic sentence.

You will find that the length of your sentences will vary in accordance with your shifts in sentence structure. Generally, use shorter sentences for making main points and longer sentences for gathering together a number of details.

Unless you have experimented with writing different kinds of sentences over the years, you may find that you habitually use only a few sentence patterns. Perhaps the following list will remind you of other possibilities.

WAYS TO BEGIN SENTENCES

1. **With the subject:** John A. MacDonald was a colourful prime minister.

2. **With a prepositional phrase:** Before Confederation he had proved his skill as a politician.

3. **With single-word adjectives:** Bold, shrewd, and stubborn, he clung to power for over thirty years.

4. **With a participial phrase:** Drinking heavily, he nevertheless maintained a firm grip on his party and on the country.

5. **With a subordinate clause:** Because he helped to bring about the birth of the nation and presided over it during its infancy, he is known as the Father of Confederation.

6. **With an appositive:** A man of great historical importance as well as undeniable personal weaknesses, he continues to fascinate historians and biographers.

Using Transitions and Other Continuity Devices

Varying sentence structure and length is one way of increasing your reader's understanding of how your ideas are related. Another way is by using transitional words and phrases and other devices for achieving continuity both within and between paragraphs.

SECTION 3

Continuity Within Paragraphs

A. Sentence Hooks are words and phrases used to provide continuity between sentences: pronouns, demonstrative pronouns, synonyms and repeated words and phrases.

1. **Pronouns**. After the first reference by name, use pronouns and possessive pronouns to indicate a continuity of subject, so long as the reference is clear.

> **Margaret Atwood** has written several novels. **Her** most recent is . . . . **She** has also written . . . .

2. **Demonstrative pronouns**. To avoid repeating your last point, refer to it by using a demonstrative pronoun (*this, that, these, those*) and a noun that identifies the category to which you are referring.

> During the Depression, prairie farmers suffered because of the severe drought. **This problem** . . . .

> Macbeth murders Duncan and is responsible for the murder of Banquo and several others. **These acts of violence** . . . .

3. **Synonyms and repeated words and phrases**. Keep your readers' attention on your subject by repeating key words and phrases or using synonyms. Notice the repetition of **problem** and equivalent terms in the following paragraph.

> In the construction of the Imperial Hotel in Tokyo Frank Lloyd Wright had to solve several architectural problems. First, he had to solve the problem of earthquake tremors. Second, he had to correct for the weak soil base of the hotel site. Third, he had to keep the building from cracking. To solve the problem of cracking, he created a hotel of many sections with expansion joints; to provide a solid base and to prevent damage from earthquakes, Wright put concrete posts under the centre of each section of the hotel and then cantilevered the floor slabs from the centre in all directions.

B. Transitional Words and Phrases are means of indicating temporal, spatial, and logical relationships.

RELATIONSHIP	SAMPLE TRANSITIONAL WORDS AND PHRASES
TEMPORAL	before, after, meanwhile, as soon as, then
SPATIAL	on the right, near, farther away
LOGICAL addition	and, another, a second, also, too, furthermore, moreover, either-or, neither-nor, not only-but also, first, second . . .

contrast	but, in contrast, yet, however, on the other hand, nevertheless, otherwise
examples	for example, for instance, to be specific, in particular, to illusrate
cause and effect	therefore, thus, so, hence, consequently, as a result, accordingly
concession and qualification	although, despite, while it is true that
emphasis	most important, a crucial point, significantly, of overwhelming importance

Continuity Between Paragraphs

A.   Paragraph hooks are words and phrases used to provide continuity between paragraphs by recalling key ideas.

1. Single words, phrases, or synonyms carried over from the last sentence of one paragraph to the first sentence of the next.

> Last Sentence of Paragraph 1
> . . . . His pride thus leads him to reject his friends' offers of help.

> First Sentence of Paragraph 2
> His pride also prevents him from helping himself. . . .

2. Phrases, clauses, or occasionally whole sentences that briefly recall the ideas of one paragraph at the beginning of the next.

> First Topic Sentence:
> Mackenzie King, Diefenbaker, and Pearson. . . .
> Second Topic Sentence:
> These three prime ministers were not the only ones to favour such a policy. . . . .

B.   Transitional words and phrases indicate the structural or logical relationship between paragraphs. The same words and phrases are used to indicate transitions between paragraphs as to indicate transitions within paragraphs.

Sample Topic Sentences with Transitions

> Topic Sentence Paragraph 1
> Opponents of rapid transit are quick to point out that the present city bus system loses money each year, but they fail to point out that it does so because it is too inconvenient and inefficient to attract widespread use. . . .

SECTION 3

Topic Sentence Paragraph 2
> It is true that any rapid transit system is extremely expensive to build and thus for a few years our taxes will go up. . . .

Topic Sentence Paragraph 3
> But the most compelling arguments for rapid transit extend the context of the debate beyond our immediate needs and concerns to the future.

USING SENTENCE STRUCTURE EFFECTIVELY

As you can see, varying sentence structure and length and providing transitions are two ways of using sentence structure to help your reader see how your points are related. If you compare the paragraph on Chaucer's narrator at the beginning of this chapter with the paragraph the student actually wrote, you will see just how big a difference these simple changes make. In the student's original paragraph, the ideas are easy to follow because she varies her sentence structure and length to indicate the relation between main points and examples, and she also uses sentence hooks and transitional words and phrases to provide continuity.

SIMPLIFIED PARAGRAPH	STUDENT'S PARAGRAPH
The narrator's greatest weakness is his amazing tolerance of all types of people. This is his greatest strength. His fellow pilgrims have weaknesses and oddities. He rarely criticizes them. He treats everyone in a kind, genial manner. He observes that the French spoken by the Prioress is not Parisian French. He is not condescending about her accent. He kindly ignores the Wife of Bath's earlier amorous adventures. He does not make derogatory comments about the Pardoner's effeminacy. The narrator's tendency to adopt the standards of those around him springs from his desire to think well of others. He is not self-interested.	The narrator's greatest weakness, his amazing tolerance of all types of people, is also his greatest strength. Despite his awareness of his fellow pilgrims' weaknesses and oddities, he rarely criticizes, and treats everyone in a kind, genial manner. He observes, for example, that the French spoken by the Prioress is not Parisian French, yet he is not condescending about her accent. He kindly ignores the Wife of Bath's earlier amorous adventures, and does not make derogatory comments about the pardoner's effeminacy. Thus the narrator's tendency to adopt the standards of those around him springs from his desire to think well of others rather than from self-interest.

When you make final revisions, check to see whether you can help your reader understand the connections among your points by varying your sentence structure and length and by using transitional devices both within and between paragraphs.

EXERCISES

A. Use some or all of the following information to create sentences of the types listed below, in any order. See if you can make a paragraph from your sentences.[2]

> Psychologists and psychiatrists who have become interested in mental health as well as mental illness are studying groups of children known as "invulnerables" or "superkids."
> These children are at high risk for mental illness because of their backgrounds.
> Most of them come from families who have histories of mental illness or other severe problems, such as criminal behaviour, alcoholism, or chronic illness.
> These children may also live in slum conditions, have a physical handicap, or face other obstacles.
> The researchers discovered that the "invulnerables" nevertheless show an extraordinary capacity to prosper in extremely difficult conditions.
> They are socially at ease and able to attract the support of adults.
> They also have a sense of their own power to solve problems.
> They are capable of thinking and acting independently.
> Conditions for producing superkids include a warm relationship with an adult in infancy or early childhood; the opportunity to face and overcome obstacles; and a limited number of severe stresses at the same time.

1. A sentence beginning with the subject
2. A sentence beginning with a prepositional phrase
3. A sentence beginning with single-word adjectives
4. A sentence beginning with a participial phrase
5. A sentence beginning with a subordinate clause
6. A sentence beginning with an appositive

B. Rewrite the following paragraph to make the relationship among points clearer by (1) varying sentence structure and length; (2) providing sentence hooks and transitional words and phrases.

> Good classroom rapport depends upon the attitudes of teachers towards their students. Teachers are leaders. They set the goals

---

[2]This information is taken from Maya Pines, "Superkids," *Psychology Today*, January 1979, pp. 53-63.

and the pace for reaching those goals. Teachers should remember that they are dealing with people. They should be flexible. They should try to keep in tune with the needs and interests of their students. They should consider their students' limits. Teachers can establish friendly relationships. They can show a genuine understanding of their subjects and their students. They can show a commitment to both their subjects and their students. These attitudes create good classroom rapport. These attitudes make good human beings.

Section 4

VERBS

A verb is a word or group of words that express action, existence, possession, or sensation.

> He **plays** hockey. She **has been playing** hockey. (action)

> I **am** here. I **have been** here. (existence)

> You **have** the measles. Soon we **will have** the measles. (possession)

> The bread **smells** mouldy. Your hands **feel** cold. (sensation)

When you revise, check your final draft for these three common problems in the use of verbs:

1. Lack of agreement between subject and verb.
2. Unnecessary shift of verb tense.
3. Unnecessary use of passive voice.

SUBJECT-VERB AGREEMENT

Verbs must agree with their subjects in number: if the subject of the sentence is singular, the verb must also be singular; if the subject is plural, the verb must also be plural.

> The **engine is** hot. (singular subject, singular verb)
> The **engines are** hot. (plural subject, plural verb)

Identifying Subject-Verb Agreement Errors

By the time you reach college or university, you are not likely to make subject-verb agreement errors very often. When you do, it may be that you have lost track of the subject, as in the following cases.

1. Prepositional phrase between the subject and verb.

> **NOT**   The reaction to these incidents were quick and angry.

> **BUT**   The **reaction** (to these incidents) **was** quick and angry.

2. Phrases that imply a multiple subject when the actual subject is singular: *as well as, in addition to, including, like, together with, with.*

> **NOT**   The cost, including labour and parts, were far more than the estimate.

> **BUT**   The cost, (including labour and parts,) was far more than the estimate.

3. Words that always take a singular subject but whose meaning may seem plural:

anybody	anyone	anything	each (of)
everybody	everyone	everything	either (of)
nobody	no one	nothing	neither (of)
somebody	someone	something	

> **NOT**   **Everything** he ever wanted, books, pictures, records, **were** suddenly his.

> **BUT**   **Everything** he ever wanted, books, pictures, records, **was** suddenly his.

4. Multiple subjects joined by *or, either-or, neither-nor, not only-but also.* With these conjunctions, the verb agrees with the subject nearest to it.

> Neither John nor **his parents are** coming.
> Neither John's parents nor **John is** coming.

EXERCISE

A. Underline the subject with which the verb in parentheses should agree. Then circle the correct verb form.

1. There (doesn't/don't) seem to be any books or articles on this subject.

2. Banff National Park, with its breath-taking scenery, its nature programmes, and its plentiful campsites, (attract/attracts) millions of visitors every year.

3. Neither of the women (was/were) willing to vote for that candidate.

4. Not only the students but also the instructor (is/are) tired at the end of term.

5. Companies producing luxury goods are closing down because the demand for these products (is/are) decreasing.

UNNECESSARY TENSE SHIFT

Verb tenses indicate the time of existence, action, or occurrence. The basic tenses in English are present, past, and future. The tenses used in a sentence or series of sentences must accurately indicate the time relationships involved.

> She **walks** to the door. She **opens** her umbrella. She **leaves**. (all verbs in the present tense)

> She **walked** to the door, **opened** her umbrella, and **left**. (all verbs in the past tense)

> When she **finishes** her meal (present tense), she **will walk** to the door, **open** her umbrella, and **leave** (future tense). (change in tenses necessary to indicate time relationships)

Identifying Shifts in Tense

Unnecessary shifts in tense occur when the verb forms used do not correspond to the time relationships called for in the sentence or series of sentences. In the following sentence, the shifts from past to present to future tense are confusing because there is no reason for them.

> When she **finished** her meal, she **walks** to the door, **opens** her umbrella, and **will leave**.

Correcting Shifts in Tense

Shifts in tense usually result from inattention: caught up in the ideas you are trying to convey, you switch from present to past tense, or vice-versa, without noticing. These suggestions should help you keep your tenses straight.

1. When you are writing about literary works, keep your analysis and your account of events in the present tense:

> **NOT** In *Sons and Lovers*, D. H. Lawrence **describes** the poverty of English miners. The men's earnings **were determined** by the amount of coal they **mined** each week. If they **had** a poor spot, if they **were injured**, or if the mine **was shut down**, they **would not earn** enough to feed their families. Lawrence **shows** that because of the uncertainty about the men's wages, some women **earned** extra money

by knitting stockings and children often **went** to work at a very early age.

BUT In *Sons and Lovers*, D. H. Lawrence **describes** the poverty of English miners. The men's earnings **are determined** by the amount of coal they **mine** each week. If they **have** a poor spot, if they **are injured**, or if the mine **is shut down**, they **do not earn** enough to feed their families. Lawrence **shows** that because of the uncertainty about the men's wages, some women **earn** extra money by knitting stockings and children often **go** to work at a very early age.

2. Use the simple present or past tense in preference to *-ing* verbs.

NOT Freud is discussing the relation between the id, ego, and superego.

BUT Freud discusses the relation between the id, ego, and superego.

3. If you sometimes omit verb endings, writing "he learn" instead of "he learns" or "he learned," check each verb to make sure that you have not left off a necessary ending, especially *-s* and *-ed*. You may not hear these endings and so you will have difficulty knowing where they should go. Read your paper out loud to someone who does not share this problem, asking the person to listen particularly for verb endings.

4. If you know you have a problem with verb tenses, proofread your final draft a paragraph at a time, checking all the verbs to make sure that (1) they are in the same tense, or (2) changes in tense are justified by the time relationships.

EXERCISE

Underline all the verbs in the following paragraph. Then check to see whether there are any unnecessary shifts in verb tenses. Correct any tenses that need correcting. Do not make any other changes.

Planning for retirement while still at work can be done in several ways. The most common was through training programmes initiated by employers at least ten years before the employee's retirement. These programmes are providing information to the employees and help them to adopt a realistic view of the process of retirement. Most of these programmes will contain information pertaining to pension planning, leisure time, and other activities.

UNNECESSARY USE OF PASSIVE VOICE

Verbs have two voices: active and passive. In the active voice, the subject of the sentence performs the action. In the passive voice, the subject of the sentence is acted upon.

> Tom drove the car. (active)
> The car was driven by Tom. (passive)

Although there are legitimate uses of the passive voice, your writing will be more direct and concise if most of your verbs are in the active voice.

Uses of the Passive Voice

1. The passive voice is commonly used in reporting scientific experiments to focus attention on procedures and results rather than on the experimenter. The assumption is that the steps and outcome would be the same no matter who was performing the experiment.

> Ten milligrams of sodium chloride was placed in a glass of water.

2. The passive voice is also used in other circumstances where the agent of the action is understood, unimportant, or unknown.

> I was born in Saskatoon. (passive)
> The roads were sanded regularly. (passive)

3. The passive voice is sometimes used to emphasize the impersonality of actions. Compare these sentences:

> Their house was bombed during the war. (passive)
> Enemy planes bombed their house during the war. (active)

Misuses of the Passive Voice

1. Do not use the passive voice to avoid naming the agent responsible for an action or belief.

> NOT It is held that attractive people are also believed to be intelligent. (passive)
>
> BUT Psychologists have found that many people believe attractive people are also intelligent. (active)

2. Do not use the passive voice when the active voice would be more concise, more direct, or more emphatic.

> NOT It was reported to the president by the vice-president that an agreement was reached between the workers and the management. (passive)

BUT   The vice-president reported to the president that the workers and the management had reached an agreement. (active)

EXERCISES

A. Identify the verbs in the following sentences as active or passive. Then decide whether the active or passive voice is more appropriate. Revise those sentences in which the voice used is not appropriate or not effective.

1. The desire by Swift in "A Modest Proposal" for better food, better clothing, and better housing for the Irish is portrayed.
2. The government raised taxes on cigarettes and alcohol.
3. Skilled helicopter pilots lifted the terrified flood victims from their roof-tops.
4. The autopsy on the famous race horse was performed this morning.
5. The demand for better housing and more employment opportunities was forcefully expressed by the Métis in both Alberta and Saskatchewan.

B. Correct all problems with subject-verb agreement, tense shifts, and inappropriate use of the passive voice in the following paragraph.

> We were just getting used to the midnight sun and the lack of comforts in the bush camp when the animal came. We had no idea what was out there, but we knew it was coming towards us. Maybe a wolf or a small deer were foraging in the underbrush. A warning was given to us when the silence of the Arctic was broken by the crazed howling of our camp dog. With a sense of duty and pride, he flies into the bush towards the animal. Out of the thicket the dog came charging back, his eyes a picture of terror. He was refusing to leave his master's side, nor would he let us venture into the woods alone. This half-wild dog was trying to save us. Although we couldn't hear it, we could feel the thing coming closer. The wild howling was started by the dog again. The camp geologist took this warning and runs for his rifle, a World War II surplus Winchester 303 with a shaky sight. Sixteen shells were loaded into two clips. We were ready and so was it. Finally a large female grizzly bear and her cub was in sight. The grizzly had two massive forelimbs swinging six feet off the ground. The gray coat blended in with the charred trees as they were pushed over by her. The tiny gray cub playfully followed his fierce mother towards our camp. We had been seen by the huge bear, but she was not stopping. We were on the verge of panic, but we were ready, with the rifle having been loaded and aimed at her. The canoe was ready, the motor having been attached and the life jackets were thrown aboard. We could escape to the cold and windy lake.

Section 5

PRONOUNS

Pronouns are words that you can substitute for the names of things: you can refer to your friend as "she" instead of "Sally," for example, or to an office building as "it" instead of "Great Northern Life Building." When you are revising, check for these possible problems with pronouns:

Pronoun Shifts: Inconsistent use of personal pronouns
Pronoun Agreement: Lack of agreement between the pronoun and the word it refers to
Pronoun Reference: Lack of clarity about what the pronoun refers to

PRONOUN SHIFTS

Personal pronouns in English are divided into first, second, and third persons.

PERSON	SINGULAR	PLURAL
1st	I, me	we, us
2nd	you, you	you, you
3rd	he, she, it, one	they, them
	him, her, it, one	

In Handbook Section 1: Tone, we discussed how to choose the pronouns of address suitable for your subject and your audience. Once you have decided whether to use first, second, or third person pronouns as your basic mode, you need to check whether you have been consistent in using them. If you shift pronouns without good reason, you are likely to confuse or to jar your reader.

Identifying Pronoun Shifts

Although you may occasionally shift pronouns within a sentence, you are most likely to find this problem on the paragraph level. The following paragraph illustrates an extreme case. Here the writer begins with the pronoun "you," shifts to the third-person reference to "a student's marks" in the second sentence, and then to the third-person indefinite "one" in the last sentence.

Are you too tense to concentrate during exams? Inability to concentrate can lower a student's marks. One finds that one is con-
centrating on the clock instead of on the exam.

A more common problem is that of the inappropriate first- or second-
person pronoun in a piece of writing that is primarily in the third
person, as in the following example:

> Because of pressure from the administration, the student
> board that governs the residence hall recently approved the instal-
> lation of a security system designed to curb theft and vandalism
> by outsiders. With this system, *you* have locked doors, identifica-
> tion cards, security guards, and an obligatory sign-in procedure
> for visitors. Unfortunately, the system is ineffective because most
> damage is done by students who live in residence.

Correcting Pronoun Shifts

If you find that you have shifted pronouns unnecessarily, decide
whether you should be writing in the first, second, or third person,
and make changes accordingly. Depending on your audience and
purpose, you could rewrite a paragraph such as the first example
above either in the second or third person:

> Are *you* too tense to concentrate during exams? Inability to
> concentrate can lower *your* marks. *You* find that *you* are concen-
> trating on the clock instead of on the exam.
>
> OR
>
> Some students are too tense to concentrate during exams.
> Inability to concentrate can lower *their* marks. *They* find that *they*
> are concentrating on the clock instead of on the exam.

Where you have slipped into using a first- or second-person pronoun within a third-person context, revise to eliminate the inappropriate pronoun:

> Because of pressure from the administration, the student
> board that governs the residence hall recently approved the instal-
> lation of a security system designed to curb theft and vandalism
> by outsiders. *This system includes* locked doors, identification cards,
> security guards, and an obligatory sign-in procedure for visitors.
> Unfortunately, the system is ineffective because most damage
> is done by students who live in residence.

EXERCISE

Revise the following paragraphs to remove any unnecessary pronoun
shifts. If a paragraph could be revised in more than one way, choose
the one you consider most appropriate and explain your choice.

1. A well-balanced diet is necessary if you want to be healthy. Many people eat the wrong kinds of foods. You should be eating fewer heavily refined foods, such as white bread, frozen dinners, and candy. Instead, they should eat fresh fruit and vegetables; whole-grain bread and cereals; lean meat, fish, and poultry; and some eggs and dairy products. Such a diet may demand radical changes in one's eating habits. But once you try it, your body will like it.

2. I would rather drive a car to work than take a bus. In summer, people who have to wait for a bus get soaked in the rain; in winter, they freeze. By the time a bus gets to my stop it is always filled, and so a rider never has a place to sit. The buses are so hot and crowded that you can hardly breathe. I plan to save my money by walking to work until I can afford to buy a car.

3. Many people actually feel that it is simple enough to hang one's culture on the wall in the form of a native artifact. They forget that the native peoples are bitter and want compensation for the injustices done to us. Along with the loss of our land, why should one have to endure the needless discrimination inflicted on all the aboriginal peoples of the world?

PRONOUN AGREEMENT

Pronouns are either singular (*I, you, he, she, it, one*) or plural (*we, you, they*). Pronouns must agree with the word they refer to in **number**. That is, the pronoun must be singular if the word it replaces is singular, and plural if the word it replaces is plural.

> The player (singular) took off her (singular) gloves.
> The players (plural) took off their (plural) gloves.

> **A patient** wants **his** doctor to inform **him** about **his** condition. (all singular)
> **Patients** want **their** doctor to inform **them** about **their** condition. (all plural)

Identifying Pronoun Agreement Errors

If the pronoun does not agree in number with the word it refers to, there is an error of pronoun agreement. In most cases, pronoun agreement is a problem only when the sense of the sentence is plural, but the word that the pronoun refers to is singular.

> **The worker** wants to have some control over **their** working conditions.
> **Each** of the children had popped **their** balloon.
> **Everyone** wanted to have **their** picture taken.

Correcting Pronoun Agreement Errors

If you know you have a problem with pronoun agreement, read your final draft sentence by sentence, stopping whenever you come to a pronoun. Check to see what word each pronoun refers to. If the pronoun is taking the place of a singular word, the pronoun should be singular; if the pronoun is taking the place of a plural word, the pronoun should be plural.

Remember that you always use singular pronouns to refer to *each* and to words that end with *body, one,* and *thing: anybody, everybody, nobody, somebody; anyone, everyone, no one, someone; anything, everything, nothing, something.*

EXERCISE

Correct all errors in pronoun agreement in the following sentences.
1. When a firm meets government pollution emission standards, their expenses increase.
2. In a nuclear conflict, the submarine armed with ballistic missiles could maneuver into range to fire their warheads at whatever targets are deemed most vital.
3. A cancer patient may be misled by quack cures that seem to promise them miraculous results.
4. The House of Commons said that they will enforce new security measures. Everyone entering the building will be searched to see if they are carrying weapons.
5. Because it loses less energy than copper wire, fibres are being used to transmit thousands of signals at once in enormous bandwidths.

PRONOUN REFERENCES

A pronoun is said to be **ambiguous** when it does not clearly refer to a specific noun or pronoun.

Identifying Ambiguous Pronoun References

In the following sentences, either the pronoun(s) could refer to more than one noun, or there is no noun to which the pronoun refers.

> 1. Mary passed Susan on the street, but **she** ignored **her**.
> 2. In Shakespeare's plays **he** presents us with a picture of English society.
> 3. He did not know whether she would leave or wait for him, **which** made him anxious.

Correcting Ambiguous Pronoun References

Here are three ways of correcting ambiguous pronoun references.
1. Keep the pronoun close to the noun to which it refers.

> **NOT** Peter told George that he was a terrible baseball player. He was very angry.
>
> **BUT** George was very angry because Peter called him a terrible baseball player.
>
> **OR** Because Peter was very angry, he called George a terrible baseball player.

2. Use pronouns to refer only to nouns or pronouns, not to possessive adjectives such as *his, her, their, Shakespeare's*.

> **NOT** James broke the girl's flute who was visiting his mother.
>
> **BUT** James broke the flute of the **girl who** was visiting his mother.

3. *This* and *which* should be used only to refer to a specific noun or pronoun immediately preceding them, not to the idea of the preceding sentence or clause. Rewrite the sentence or supply the missing noun or pronoun.

> **NOT** He didn't know whether to go or to stay. **This** made him very anxious.
>
> **BUT** He didn't know whether to go or to stay. **This uncertainty** made him very anxious.
>
> **OR** Because he didn't know whether to go or to stay, **he was** very anxious.

EXERCISES

A. Revise the following sentences to eliminate ambiguous pronoun references.

1. An important part of being a successful goalie is to build up his determination to defend the net. It must occupy his complete attention.

2. Many people who renovate to make their houses energy efficient are unaware of how it will increase their property values and are surprised when they assess their property for increased taxes.

3. Gradually the public grew to accept the theory of evolution, which forced the clergy into being less vocal in their opposition.

4. She left flowers in the teacher's office who had been such a help to her.

5. The two children hid their margarine sandwiches from their class-mates because they were ashamed to let them see how poor they were.

B. In the following paragraph circle inconsistent pronouns of address, pronoun-agreement errors, and ambiguous pronoun references. Then revise the paragraph to eliminate these problems, without omitting any ideas or changing sentences more than is necessary.

> In Shakespeare's *King Lear* he shows that lack of self-knowl-edge has disastrous consequences for a person, for without self-knowledge, they are unable to judge the motives and actions of others. Lear accepts the flattery of Goneril and Regan as sincere and appropriate to his dignity, which is obviously exaggerated. When Cordelia refuses to compete with her sisters, she wounds Lear's vanity. This is the reason he banishes her. When Kent tries to intervene, he banishes him because he refuses to admit that his judgment might have been in error. Lear's unwillingness to admit the truth about himself thus initiates the tragedy, for in his blindess he deprives himself of everyone most loyal to their king.

Section 6

PUNCTUATION

Punctuation marks have often been compared to traffic signals be-cause they give your reader directions. Commas, semicolons, and end punctuation marks do tell your reader when to slow down and when to stop. More important, however, punctuation is a guide to meaning. Punctuation marks indicate how your ideas are related, when you are quoting, and what kinds of sources you are referring to.

The following sections set out guidelines for using commas, semi-colons, colons, parentheses, dashes, quotation marks, and italics in formal writing.

COMMA

The comma is used in the following cases.

1. **Independent Clauses**: Use a comma to separate independent clauses

joined by a coordinate conjunction (**and, but, or, so, yet, for**).

> Inflation is under control, but unemployment is still a problem.

> No one has succeeded in proving the existence of UFOs, yet many have tried.

2. **Dependent Clauses**: Use a comma to set off a dependent clause at the beginning of a sentence.

> When economic conditions are poor, the incidence of family violence rises.

> Because the highways were icy, we postponed our trip.

3. **Introductory Phrases**: Use a comma to set off long or potentially confusing phrases at the beginning of a sentence.

> In his search for the meaning of life, he examined many religions. (long phrase)

> In winter, darkness comes early. (could be misread)

> In winter we go skiing. (would not be misread)

4. **Items in a Series**: Use a comma to separate more than two items (words or phrases) joined by *and* or *or*. In Canadian usage, the comma before the conjunction is optional. Some instructors prefer the comma before the conjunction to prevent the possibility of reading the last two items as a unit.

> We watched the children slide, swing, and climb.

> The horses galloped over the field, across the stream and down the road.

> He ordered toast, eggs, coffee, and milk for breakfast. (comma indicates four items were ordered)

5. **Non-restrictive Modifiers**: Use a comma to set off non-restrictive modifiers (words, phrases, or clauses that could be omitted from the sentence without changing its meaning).
a. Adjectives and verbal modifiers following nouns.

> The play, witty and well-acted, delighted the audience.

> The actors, after removing their greasepaint, celebrated their success.

b. Appositives (nouns or noun phrases that rename the preceding noun).

> The Beatles, the most popular rock group of the sixties, sold millions of records.

Note: Do not set off an appositive that is necessary to the meaning of the sentence (restrictive).

> The film *The Compleat Beatles* is a history of the group's rise and fall. (restrictive)

c. Non-restrictive clauses beginning with *which, who, whom,* or *whose*.

> The development of fibre optics, which revolutionized communications, also had a great impact on medicine.

> Orthopedic surgeons, who often treat athletic injuries, use fibre optic instruments to assess knee damage.

Note: Do not set off clauses that are **restrictive** (necessary to the meaning of the sentence). Clauses beginning with *that* are always restrictive.

> Tom Smith, whose knees were badly injured in a skiing accident, is slowly recovering. (clause is non-restrictive)

> Athletes who injure their knees often recover slowly. (clause is restrictive)

> The hand that rocks the cradle rules the world. (clause is restrictive)

6. **Parenthetical Expressions**: Use a comma to set off transitional words and phrases and other expressions that break the flow of the sentence.

> Third World countries, in contrast, may be resource-rich but capital-poor.

> This situation, I believe, leads to economic instability.

> Well, I'd better be going.

> Yes, there were thirty thousand people at the demonstration.

7. **Dates and Place Names**: Use a comma to set off dates and place names when more than one item of information is given.

> The centre of the Canadian automobile industry is Windsor, Ontario.

> Canada officially entered World War II on September 10, 1939.

8. **Quotations**: Use a comma to set off brief quotations from introductory material.

> One minister said, "This policy should never have been adopted."

> "This policy," said one minister, "should never have been adopted."

EXERCISES

A. Add commas where appropriate.

1. Because he could find no way to avoid the task he got to work.

2. In the morning light shone through the cracks in the roof.

3. An employee who suggests possible improvements in working conditions should be rewarded.

4. Torville and Dean elated after winning the gold medal for ice-dancing were surrounded by adoring fans.

5. Each of these companies which are now facing bankruptcy once employed more than a thousand workers.

6. Marvin on the other hand is steady hard-working and rather un-imaginative.

7. Indeed some of the arguments deserve more serious consideration.

8. The negotiators were tired and hungry and they made little progress.

9. The film *Fiddler on the Roof* has attracted large and enthusiastic audiences.

10. According to William Blake "Imagination has nothing to do with Memory."

11. Returning home after the conquest of Gaul Julius Caesar announced "I came I saw I conquered."

B. Insert commas as necessary in the following sentences. Together these sentences constitute a paragraph on the reasons for the expulsion of the Acadians in 1755. The information is taken from W.S. MacNutt, *The Atlantic Provinces: The Emergence of Colonial Society 1712-1857*, The Canadian Centenary Series (Toronto: McClelland and Stewart, 1965).

1. Between 1713 when their land was ceded to the British and 1755 when they were forcibly expelled the Acadians descendants of early French settlers were pawns in the struggle between the French and the British for control of North America.

2. According to MacNutt the Acadians who "abhorred war" (p. 42) signed a British oath of allegiance in 1730 only because a separate treaty granted them "the right not to bear arms on the King's behalf" (p. 32).

3. This treaty was the basis for their claims to neutrality in later wars.

4. The boundaries of Acadia were never defined however and as a consequence the Acadians became embroiled in disputes between the French and English.

5. The French who continued to claim the territory north of the Bay of Fundy attempted to confine the British to the Acadian peninsula by fomenting Indian attacks on the English settlements.

6. The British on the other hand tried to secure the area by bringing

in thousands of British colonists and by encouraging intermarriage among the Acadians the Indians and the British settlers.

7. If more drastic measures became necessary the British were prepared to expel the Acadians by force.

8. With these opposing forces to contend with the Acadians could not expect much protection from their claim to neutrality.

SEMICOLON

The semicolon indicates a stronger separation between sentence elements than the comma does. Use a semicolon in the following cases.

1. **Independent Clauses**: Use a semicolon to join independent clauses when there is no coordinate conjunction (*and, or, but, yet, so, for*) between them.

> Hegel was an idealist; Dewey was a pragmatist.

2. **Independent Clauses**: Use a semicolon to join independent clauses when the second clause begins with a conjunctive adverb (*accordingly, consequently, therefore, thus, then, hence; furthermore, moreover, besides, likewise; nevertheless, however, otherwise, still*). Put a comma after the conjunctive adverb if there is any chance of misreading.

> Byron's poetry soon eclipsed Scott's; therefore Scott turned to writing novels.
>
> Few members of the legislature thought an election was necessary; nevertheless, the premier called one.

If you have trouble distinguishing conjunctive adverbs from coordinate and subordinate conjunctions, remember this simple guide: coordinate and subordinate conjunctions must appear at the beginning of a clause, but conjunctive adverbs can be moved to other positions, as in this sentence:

> Few members of the legislature thought an election was necessary; the premier nevertheless called one.

3. **Independent Clauses**: Use a semicolon and a coordinate conjunction to join independent clauses when the clauses are long or contain commas.

> The hard-boiled detective, as we have seen in the works of Dashiell Hammett, Raymond Chandler, and Ross MacDonald, is a distinctively American creation; but the amateur sleuth, popularized by British writers such as Dorothy Sayers, Agatha Christie, and Michael Innes, also appears in American detective fiction.

4. **Items in a Series**: Use a semicolon to separate items within a series that contains commas.

> The defence attorney called three witnesses: her client's brother, who testified that his sister was with him the night of the crime; the brother's caretaker, who testified that he saw the defendant arrive at 10 p.m.; and the brother's neighbour, who glimpsed the sister as she left at 11:30 p.m.

COLON

In most cases, a colon indicates that what follows is an expansion of what has already been said. Use a colon for the following purposes.
1. **Enumeration**: Use a colon to introduce a list or a summary. The items following the colon should be grammatically parallel.

> Car manufacturers have introduced several improvements: better restraint systems, better pollution-control devices, and better rust-proofing.

2. **Expansion**: Use a colon to introduce a phrase or clause that explains a preceding statement.

> He wanted only one thing out of life: to make money.

3. **Quotation**: Use a colon to introduce a formal quotation. (The quotation must be a grammatically complete sentence.)

> Goldberg dismissed the arguments against changes in the Fisheries Act: "Contrary to the opinions expressed by packers and the fisheries unions, the proposed changes are not designed to increase federal control over the fishing industry."

4. **Salutation**: Use a colon after the salutation of a business letter.

> Dear Dr. Samuels:

PARENTHESES

Parentheses indicate explanatory material that is not essential to the meaning of the sentence. Use parentheses for the following purposes.
1. **Bibliographical Information**: Use parentheses to enclose bibliographical information in the body of your essay.

> Alice Harwood's *The Game Is Over* (Toronto: Dominion Press, 1984) is a study of the decline of amateur sports.

2. **Explanatory Material**: Use parentheses to enclose explanatory material that would interrupt the logical flow of the sentence.

> At a council meeting this morning, the mayor (who holds stock in several land development companies) disqualified himself from voting on the proposal to annex areas to the north and west of the city.

DASH

Dashes indicate interruptions in a train of thought or in the structure of the sentence. They lend an air of informality to a sentence and therefore should be used sparingly in formal writing. Use dashes for the following purposes.

1. To set off abrupt shifts in thought.

> My Aunt Sadie—you remember her, don't you?—lived to be a hundred.

2. To set off a list or summary when it comes in the middle of a sentence.

> She had established her goals in life—to travel, to have an interesting career, to develop close relationships—before she was sixteen.

Note: When the list or summary comes at the end of the sentence, use a colon instead of a dash unless you want to indicate special emphasis.

> Before she was sixteen, she had established her goals in life: to travel, to have an interesting career, to develop close relationships.

EXERCISES

A. Insert semicolons, colons, parentheses, and dashes where appropriate.

1. In many societies work is divided in the following way men do the jobs that the society as a whole considers important or dangerous the other jobs are left to women.
2. *Cabaret* directed by Bob Fosse and starring Liza Minelli and Michael York adds a new dimension to the concept of the musical.
3. Adolescence a necessary stage of physical and emotional development in most theories can also be studied as a cultural phenomenon.

4. Invulnerable children thrive on adversity their hardships stimulate in them a desire and a capacity to overcome obstacles.

5. Dickens vividly portrays the monotonous, mechanical lives of factory workers in his description of Coketown "It contained several large streets all very like one another . . ." p. 213.

6. The goal of modern correctional institutions should not be punishment or revenge it should be the rehabilitation of the whole person.

7. *The Stone Angel* Macmillan 1964 established Margaret Laurence as an important Canadian novelist.

8. The Pope needed only to show Galileo the instruments of torture Galileo's medical knowledge of what these instruments would do did the rest.

9. When I returned home most unexpectedly I might add I was astounded at the changes that had occurred during my absence.

10. Ancient Chinese and Hindu societies had much in common both were unified through changeless religious and cultural patterns both had little curiosity about foreign lands both were exploited by the West.

B. Insert semicolons, colons, parentheses, and dashes in the sentences below as necessary. Do not make any other changes. Together these sentences form a paragraph on certain types of criminal behaviour.

1. There are two types of crimes in which the criminal deliberately chooses evil over good crimes of desperation and crimes of defiance.

2. The motive for these crimes is different from the motive for other types of crime therefore the punishment should also be different.

3. The first type the crime of desperation is motivated by the need for survival.

4. A woman with a limited income perhaps a single parent might steal food, for example, in order to feed her family.

5. The woman is fully aware that in stealing she is doing wrong she is driven to it by her circumstances.

6. Society would make this judgment this woman has committed a crime and should be sent to jail.

7. But if she were placed in a job-training programme one that would lead to permanent employment, not a make-work scheme she would have a better chance of becoming a productive member of society.

8. The second type the crime of defiance is motivated by the need for rebellion.

9. Young teenagers, for example, may commit crimes pulling fire alarms, stealing hubcaps, shoplifting taking drugs just for the thrill of doing something wrong.

10. The proper punishment for them would be to arrange for them to get their "thrills" in constructive ways mountain-climbing, travelling, helping others.

QUOTATION MARKS

Use quotation marks to indicate dialogue, quotations from other writers, and the titles of short works. This section covers only the appropriate use of quotation marks as punctuation. For suggestions on integrating quotations into your writing, see Section 8: Quotations.

1. Put quotation marks around direct speech.

> Marie said, "I should get more exercise." (direct speech)
> Marie said that she should get more exercise. (indirect speech)

2. Put quotation marks around any three or more consecutive words that you have taken from a printed text when you have incorporated the quotation into your own sentence.

> In *The Last Spike: The Great Railway 1881-1885* Pierre Berton, describing the large number of casualties that occurred as the railroad was put through the Rockies, says that "the hopsital at Yale had to be enlarged to take care of the accident victims" (p. 193).

Do not put quotation marks around indented quotations unless the quotation marks appear in the original text (as indications of dialogue, for example).

3. Commas and periods are always placed inside quotation marks.

> "Many plant species," he said, "are in danger of extermination."

4. Other punctuation marks (question marks, exclamation marks, semicolons, colons, dashes) are placed inside quotation marks if they punctuate only the quoted words. They are placed outside quotation marks if they punctuate the sentence containing the quotation.

> The first lines of the poem are "O, what can ail thee, knight-at-arms,/ Alone and palely loitering?"

> Do you agree with Keats's statement that "Beauty is truth, truth beauty"?

5. Use single quotation marks for quotations within quotations.

> In her interpretation of *Macbeth*, Carlyle argues that "the audience's sense of the futility of Macbeth's actions is confirmed in the 'She should have died hereafter' speech."

6. Use quotation marks to enclose titles of brief works (essays, magazine and newspaper articles, poems, short stories, songs, single episodes of a television series). Notice that these are usually parts of larger works.

> In his article "The Influence of Popular Culture on the Poetry of John Doak," Martin Sommers points out that Doak's poem "Coming on Down" contains echoes of the Rolling Stones' song "Jumpin' Jack Flash."

ITALICS

In typed and handwritten work, italics are indicated by underlining. Use italics in the following cases.

1. Underline the titles of works published separately (books, magazines, newspapers, record albums, films, television series). Also underline the names of ships and airplanes, works of art, and long musical compositions.

> The book <u>False Economies</u> consists of a series of articles first published in <u>Journal of Economic Analysis</u>.

2. Underline words or letters referred to as words or letters.

> The word <u>truly</u> does not contain an <u>e</u>.

3. Underline foreign words or phrases that have not been incorporated into English.

> The setting epitomized what the Germans would call <u>Gemütlichkeit</u>.
>   BUT
> We had croissants for breakfast.

EXERCISE

Insert quotations marks or underline as necessary in the following sentences. Together these sentences form a paragraph on the theme of exile in V.S. Naipaul's collection *In a Free State* (Harmondsworth: Penguin, 1971).

1. The most interesting aspect of the treatment of exile in In a Free State is the complex relationship Naipaul creates between the concept of freedom and the movement from order to disorder.

2. For all of Naipaul's major characters, whether they are in the burning streets of Washington, the alien environment of England, or the war-torn deserts of Africa, the word freedom is highly ambiguous.

3. In the first story, One out of Many, Santosh reflects on the freedom

of the exile: I was a free man; I could do anything I wanted. . . . I could, if it were possible for me to become again what I once was, go to the police and say, I am an illegal immigrant here. Please deport me to Bombay. . . . It didn't matter what I did, because I was alone. And I didn't know what to do (pp. 54-55).

4. The only way for Santosh to become an American citizen, and thus to free himself from the threat of exportation, is to give up his freedom by marrying a hubshi, an American black.

5. The first-person narrator of the story Tell Me Who to Kill and the main character of the title story, In a Free State, have also left their homeland and its restricting order to enter a state of disorder where the freedom that surrounds them becomes the one aspect of life they cannot deal with.

6. Thus for the main characters of the book In a Free State, the absence of restrictions does not bring freedom but rather an aimless drifting into exile.

REVIEW EXERCISES

A. Insert or change punctuation in the paragraph below as necessary. Do not make any other changes. This paragraph is from an essay on the character of the Duke in Browning's poem "My Last Duchess."

> Once we know the dramatic situation in Browning's poem My Last Duchess we can see how calculating the Duke's treatment of the envoy is. Throughout his speech the Duke addresses his listener as Sir so that even though the other is not allowed to reply we are reminded of his presence. We are also reminded of the purpose of the Duke's revelations. The apparent candour with which he confesses his pride I choose/ Never to stoop 11. 42-43 is designed to disarm his guest just as his passing reminders of his wealth and power are designed to intimidate him. Yet the Duke stoops to treat the envoy as an equal by suggesting that they descend the stairs together. The aim of this gesture is to ensure the envoy's goodwill in the delicate negotiations over the dowry as the Duke's flattering comment about the Count's generosity The Count your master's known munificence 1. 19 makes clear. The silent presence of the envoy thus reveals the means the Duke is willing to employ to achieve his ends.

B. Insert or change punctuation in the two paragraphs below as necessary. Do not make any other changes. These paragraphs are from an essay on the film *Network*.

> The movie Network released in 1976 presents a complex analysis of the state of North American society in the 1970s. The

central characters in the film Howard Beale a middle-aged news broadcaster who has been told that he will be fired because his ratings have dropped Max Schumaker fired when he refuses to relinquish the autonomy of the news department and Diana Christenson head of programming who rises to power through a cold-blooded dedication to the god of higher ratings force us to ask some fundamental questions about the society we live in and the television programming that both creates and reflects it. The story of the decline and fall of Howard Beale suggests that we are no longer capable of controlling the technology we have created. The relationship between Max and Diana suggests that television has the power to change us so that we are no longer recognizably human.

When Howard Beale Peter Finch is allowed to continue in his new-found role as a messiah we see the exploitation of people on both sides of the television screen. For Beale's television show does exactly what Diana Christenson's market research suggests that television should do articulate the rage and frustration of the television viewer in order to defuse it. In keeping with the emphasis on self-expression in the '70s Beale's pronouncements give people the chance to substitute the release of emotion for the activities that bring about real change. Because viewers can no longer distinguish between the illusion of reality presented to them on television and the reality of their own lives the show's ratings climb even as Beale urges his viewers to turn off their television sets. The words I'm mad as hell and I'm not going to take it anymore! become a slogan mindlessly screamed by the studio audience at every newscast. When Beale collapses on stage after his prophetic outbursts the audience applauds it's just another part of the show.

Section 7

SPELLING AND CAPITALIZATION

Misspellings and related errors, such as faulty use of the apostrophe and faulty capitalization, are important for several reasons. Sometimes a misspelled word will mislead your readers. If you write "Class moral began to falter towards the end of term," for example, your readers may think that you are commenting on the decline of ethical standards in the class when you intended to comment on the decline in class spirit.

Other spelling errors, such as writing "occassionally" instead of "occasionally" or "existance" instead of "existence," will not interfere with your meaning, but they are likely to be irritating. If you make a large number of spelling errors, your readers may even doubt the validity of what you are saying. They may conclude, however unfairly, that a person who makes so many spelling errors can't possibly know what he or she is talking about. If you want your work to be considered seriously, then you have to take a professional attitude towards your finished product. And this means paying close attention to your spelling.

This section is divided into seven parts:

1. Careless errors
2. Commonly confused words
3. Commonly misspelled words
4. Preferred Canadian spellings
5. Three basic spelling rules
6. Apostrophes
7. Capitalization

It's a good idea to read through all seven parts before you proofread so that you will know what to look for in your own work.

This information is intended primarily to remind you of the importance of correct spelling and to give you some pointers on how to avoid the most common errors. If spelling is a real problem for you, there are a number of useful books devoted entirely to spelling. Here are two you might find useful:

Buck, Vernon, and Theodore Rappaport. *Basic Spelling Skills: A Program for Self-Instruction.* New York: McGraw-Hill, 1970.

Fergus, Patricia M. *Spelling Improvement: A Program for Self-Instruction*, 4th ed. New York: McGraw-Hill, 1983.

The number one rule about spelling is this: if you are in doubt, check a dictionary.

CARELESS ERRORS

These are among the most irritating of spelling errors because, like hairs in your soup, they suggest lack of attention or slipshod work. In this category belong misspellings of names, places, titles, and concepts you refer to in your essay. Check your sources to make sure you have correctly differentiated between Margaret Laurence and D.H. Lawrence; Saint John, New Brunswick, and St. John's, Newfoundland; *The Stone Angel* and *The Right Angle*; psychology and physiology.

COMMONLY CONFUSED WORDS

1. One-word and two-word forms that differ in meaning.

already   He is already half an hour late.

all ready   We are all ready to go.

altogether   The project is altogether (entirely) too costly.

all together   All together the costs of the project are enormous.

everyday   Playing video games is an everyday (ordinary) pastime for him.

every day   He takes the bus every day.

everyone   Everyone had a good time.

every one   Every one (emphasis) of the candy bars was gone.

maybe   Maybe (perhaps) I'll come.

may be   I may be late for dinner.

2. Words with similar spellings but different meanings. The most common uses are indicated; for other uses, consult your dictionary.

affect   v. to influence. The weather affects our moods.

effect   n. result. One effect of high interest rates is higher mortgage payments.

coarse   adj. rough. The shirt was made of coarse cloth.

course   n. subject; line of action. I dropped one course.

complement   v. to make complete. Her paintings complement the room's decor.

compliment   v. to praise. He complimented her on her performance.

conscience   n. sense of right and wrong. His conscience troubled him.

conscious   adj. aware; deliberate. She was conscious of being stared at.

foreword   n. preface. A well-known columnist wrote the foreword for the book.

forward   adv. ahead. The line slowly moved forward.

local   adj. pertaining to a certain place. We take the local newspaper.

locale   n. location. He was familiar with the locale.

loose   adj. not tight. Wear loose clothing.

lose   v. to misplace. Don't lose your shoes.

moral   adj. ethical. That was a moral decision.

morale   n. mental attitude; spirits. Morale was low.

principal   adj. main. Her principal goal was to win the election. n. chief person. The principal talked with the students.

principle   n. a fact, belief, or rule that governs ideas or actions. The principle of free speech must be upheld.

than   conj. indicating comparison. He is taller than I. She would rather talk than fight.

then   adj. at that time. Then the alarm went off.

their belonging to them. Their car is new.
there at that place. We went there after work.
they're contraction for *they are*. They're our friends.
to prep. toward. The car came to the intersection.
too adv. also; more than enough. The driver braked too quickly.
two adj. number more than one. He hit two cyclists.
your belonging to you. Don't forget your prize.
you're contraction for *you are*. You're late.

COMMONLY MISSPELLED WORDS

The following words are so frequently misspelled that they merit special attention. If you are a weak speller, this is a good list to memorize.

accidentally	dependent	prejudice
accommodate	despair	privilege
acquire	desperate	professor
a lot	embarrass	pronunciation
all right	existence	recommend
analyze	heroes	restaurant
argument	leisure	rhyme
basically	loneliness	rhythm
business	maintenance	separate
category	occasion/occasionally	tragedy
commitment	occurred/occurrence	truly
convenient	parallel	unnecessary
definite/definitely	possess/possession	villain

PREFERRED CANADIAN SPELLINGS

For the most part, Canadians tend to retain the *u* in words like *colour*, *flavour*, *labour*, *behaviour*, *armour*, and *vigour*, whereas in American spelling these words are spelled without the *u*. Canadians also prefer the *-re* to the *-er* ending in words like *centre*, *theatre*, and *fibre* and in metric measurements such as *metre* and *litre*. Other preferred Canadian spellings are *cheque* rather than *check* and *defence* rather than *defense*.

The issue here is consistency rather than correctness, since in most cases both Canadian and American spellings are acceptable. In other words, you want to avoid a mixture of Canadian and American spellings such as the following:

> The defense player coloured with rage as he watched the behavior of the fans throwing garbage in the center of the arena.

A consistent use of preferred Canadian spellings would give you this:

> The defence player coloured with rage as he watched the behaviour of the fans throwing garbage in the centre of the arena.

If you are not sure which is the preferred Canadian spelling of a word, check a Canadian dictionary, such as *Funk and Wagnalls Standard College Dictionary (Canadian Edition)*, *Gage Canadian Dictionary*, or *Houghton-Mifflin Canadian Dictionary of the English Language*.

THREE BASIC SPELLING RULES

i before *e* except . . .

When you are not sure whether the *i* or the *e* comes first, it's helpful to remember that the *i* usually comes before the *e* (as in *yield, diesel, believe*) except in the following cases:

> a. the long sound of *e* follows a *c*: *receive, perceive, ceiling* (but not *ancient*)
> b. the *e* and *i* are pronounced together and sound like a long *a*: *neighbour, weigh, freight*
> c. The *e* and *i* are pronounced together and sound like a long *i*: *height, sleight, Heidelberg*
> d. The *e* and *i* are pronounced together as a short *i* after an *f*: *counterfeit, forfeit*

Common exceptions to these rules: *weird, seize, either, neither, their*

Adding Suffixes

A. Adding suffixes to words ending with a single consonant preceded by a single vowel

1. Double the final consonant before adding a suffix beginning with a vowel in the following cases:

a. If the word is one syllable

> *Examples*   beg + ed = begged
> run + ing = running
> flat + en = flatten

b. If the accent is on the last syllable in words of more than one syllable

> *Examples*   confer + ed = conferred
> begin + er = beginner
> commit + ing = committing

2. Do not double the final consonant when adding a suffix in the following cases:

a. If the accent in words of more than one syllable shifts to the first syllable after you have added the suffix.

> *Examples* confer + ence = conference
> prefer + ence = preference
> refer + ence = reference

b. If you are adding a suffix that begins with a consonant.

> *Examples* commit + ment = commitment
> top + less = topless

B. Adding suffixes to words ending in *e, ie,* and *y*
1. Words ending with a silent *e* preceded by a consonant
a. Keep the *e* if you are adding a suffix beginning with a consonant.

> *Examples* definite + ly = definitely
> excite + ment = excitement
> lone + some = lonesome
> use + less = useless

b. Drop the final *e* if the suffix begins with a vowel.

> *Examples* excite + ing = exciting
> ice + y = icy
> lose + ing = losing
> use + able = usable

Exceptions: to keep the final *c* or *g* soft in words such as *advantage, outrage, change,* and *notice,* keep the finel *e* when you add a suffix beginning with *a, o,* or *u.*

> *Examples* advantage + ous = advantageous
> outrage + ous = outrageous
> change + able = changeable
> notice + able = noticeable

2. In words ending in *ie,* change the *ie* to *y* if you are adding *ing.*

> *Examples* lie + ing = lying
> die + ing = dying
> tie + ing = tying

3. Words ending in *y* preceded by a consonant
a. Change the *y* to *i* when you are adding any suffix except *ing.*

> *Examples* weary + ed = wearied
> busy + ly = busily
> tiny + est = tiniest
> cry + ed = cried

b. Retain the *y* if you are adding *ing*.

> *Examples*   Cry + ing = crying
> fly + ing = flying
> rely + ing = relying

Irregular Plurals

As you know, you can make most nouns plural by adding *s*, as in *dogs, tables, chairs*. The following guidelines will help you with nouns that do not form the plural by adding *s*.

A. Nouns ending in *s, ss, x, z, ch,* and *sh* are made plural by adding *es* because you need the extra syllable to pronounce the word.

Examples	SINGULAR	PLURAL
	Jones	Joneses
	waitress	waitresses
	tax	taxes
	buzz	buzzes
	match	matches
	brush	brushes

B. Nouns ending in *y*
1. Nouns ending in *y* preceded by a vowel are made plural by adding *s*.

Examples	SINGULAR	PLURAL
	monkey	monkeys
	attorney	attorneys
	valley	valleys

2. Nouns ending in *y* preceded by a consonant are made plural by changing the *y* to *i* and adding *es*.

Examples	SINGULAR	PLURAL
	baby	babies
	fly	flies
	company	companies

C. Nouns ending in *o*.
1. Nouns ending in *o* preceded by a vowel are made plural by adding *s*.

Examples	SINGULAR	PLURAL
	studio	studios
	video	videos
	duo	duos

2. Some nouns ending in *o* preceded by a consonant are made plural by adding *s*; others are made plural by adding *es*.

Examples	PLURAL = o + s	PLURAL = o + es
	pianos	heroes
	gigolos	vetoes
	solos	embargoes
	piccolos	potatoes

D. Foreign words
1. Some foreign words retain their original plural forms.

Examples	SINGULAR	PLURAL
	phenomenon	phenomena
	criterion	criteria
	analysis	analyses
	thesis	theses
	curriculum	curricula
	medium	media
	datum	data

2. Other foreign words more commonly taken English plurals.

Examples	SINGULAR	PLURAL
	formula	formulas (formulae)
	campus	campuses (campi)
	bureau	bureaus (bureaux)
	memorandum	memorandums (memoranda)

APOSTROPHES

1. Use an apostrophe to indicate the missing letters in a contraction. **Note**: Some instructors consider contractions inappropriate for formal writing.

> *Examples*
> I am—I'm
> you are—you're
> He could not go—He couldn't go.
> The pool is empty–The pool's empty.

2. Use an apostrophe (with or without an *s*) to make nouns possessive.
A. Singular nouns
(1) If the noun does not end in *s*, add *'s*.

> *Examples*   Hamlet's father is dead.
>   The teacher's books were stolen.

(2) If the noun has one syllable and ends in *s*, add *'s*.

> *Examples* James's car is red.
> The boss's enemy shot him.

(3) If the noun has more than one syllable and ends in *s*, add an apostrophe after the final *s* in the word.

> *Examples* Joan Williams' car is red.
> The waitress' customers left in disgust.

B. Plural nouns
(1) If the plural ends in *s*, the apostrophe goes after the final *s*.

> *Examples* Both boys' bathing suits were lost.
> All the students' marks were excellent.

(2) If the plural is irregular and does not end with *s*, treat it as a singular and add *'s*.

> *Examples* Children's toys, men's coats, and women's shoes are all on sale.

(3) Be careful not to make every plural a possessive. Use the apostrophe only when you want to indicate that something belongs to something else.

C. Compound nouns (nouns joined by a conjunction)
(1) To indicate joint possession—one thing shared by two or more people—put *'s* (or *'*) after the second noun.

> *Examples* Bill and Joe's cafe—indicates that Bill and Joe own the cafe together
>
> Kathy and Janis' friendship—indicates that the two women are friends

(2) To indicate separate possession, put *'s* (or *'*) after each noun.

> *Examples* Bill's and Joe's cafes—indicates that the two men own separate cafes
>
> Kathy's and Janis' friendships—indicates a reference to the separate friendships of the two women

D. Possessive pronouns do not take an apostrophe: *yours, his, hers, its, ours, theirs.* Watch especially for these troublesome forms:

> **who's** means *who is,* as in "Who's coming for dinner?"
> **whose** means *belonging to whom,* as in "Whose keys are on the table?"

it's means *it is*, as in "It's cold today."
its means *belonging to it*, as in "The dog opened its eyes."

CAPITALIZATION

Capitalization is used to distinguish proper nouns from common nouns. Proper nouns are capitalized because they name specific things.

Examples	COMMON NOUN	PROPER NOUN
	girl	Mary
	boy	Tom
	school	Riverside Elementary School
	building	Royal Plaza Hotel
	a king	King George VI

Here are guidelines to follow in cases where it is not so easy to distinguish common nouns from proper nouns.

1. Do not capitalize the names of family members unless you are using these words as names.

> *Examples*   Give this book to Uncle John.
> Give this book to your uncle.
> Father said that Mother would be working late tonight.
> Please ask your mother or father to call me later this afternoon.

2. Capitalize the days of the week and months, but not seasons: January, April, Tuesday, Saturday, summer, winter, spring, fall.
3. Capitalize the names of languages, nationalities, and religions: English, French, Chinese, Chilean, Jewish, Catholic, Hindu.
4. Do not capitalize colour words used to refer to races: black, white.
5. Do not capitalize *the* unless it is used as part of a name: the United States, The Hague.
6. Capitalize the first word of titles and every other word except articles (*a, an, the*), conjunctions (*and, or*, etc.), and short prepositions (*of, to, for, with, by*, etc.).

> *Examples*   *For Whom the Bell Tolls*
> *A Jest of God*
> "Time in the Middle Ages"
> "Politics and the English Language"
> "The Fastest Gun in the West"

7. Do not capitalize the names of directions unless they are used as the names of places.

> *Examples*   Turn north after you cross the bridge.
> The old priest had lived in the North for twenty years.

SECTION 7

EXERCISE

There are more than fifty errors in spelling (including apostrophes) and capitalization in the following essay. See how many you can find and correct.

WHY A GOOD WINTER IS BAD FOR ALBERTA

Weather they admit it or not, Albertans revel in the harshness of prairie winter. By mid-october they begin to assemble there winter wardrobes, hunting for last years gloves, boots, and hates, and wondering if last years coat will last another winter. The athletic plan ski holidays and skating partys, while the non-athletic lay in alot of firewood and brochures about sunny places. City dwellers buy new batteries and snow tires, and farmers order new machinery for spring delivery. If the weather has not turned bitterly cold by mid-November, Albertans begin too worry about the consequences.

All though farmers like to tell tall tails about twenty-foot snow drifts as much as city folks do, they're principle interest in the weather is financial. To them a mild Winter means a dry Spring, with to little moisture for their crops. Many of them are conscience of the drought year's of the Depression, when ungerminated seeds blew in the august dust. As indian summer stretches into December, they start canceling their orders for new tractors and combines.

Farmers are'nt alone in their plight. Eventhough tow truck operators may be releived to find their telephones jangling less insistently, other buisness people miss the clinking of the cash register. The clothing and sporting good's industries are both ef-fected. Women occassionally resist the temptation to buy a new fur coat untill the January sales and children manage alright with last years snow suits. Shops that specialize in skies and ski apparel go broke and tow bars stand idol. If ski resorts loose money, so do other parts of the tourist industry. During the coarse of a mild January, bookings' for flights to hawaii fall drastically. Basking in Waikiki seems less of a privaledge when the neighbors arent freezing in Edmonton.

Although Albertans insist that they enjoy a mild winter, there moral plummets when the temperature dosen't. Fall colds and flu persist until february. Distressing rumors of rats crossing the border to escape Saskatchewan's -30 temperatures plague the prov-ince. Definately convinced that a mild winter is immorale, every one takes comfort in the prospect of a rainy summer. Nostalgic memories of the wild exhilaration of spring break-up after a harsh Winter deepen the lonliness and gloom.

But the worst thing about a good winter is that it is basicly borring. Their maybe nothing to do accept sniffle at home and lis-ten to the complaints of farmers and the frantic sails pitches of travel agencys and clothing stores. The only escape from the woe's of a mild winter is the hope that the next one will be worse.

Section 8

USING QUOTATIONS

When you are analyzing texts or writing research papers, you will often need to use direct quotations. Used effectively, quotations are a good means of supporting and illustrating your points. Used awkwardly or excessively, quotations can detract from the orderly presentation of your ideas.

WHEN TO QUOTE

1. When the precise wording of a short passage of prose or poetry is the starting point for your analysis or evaluation of a concept, theory, proposal, or text, such as Freud's definition of narcissism; a statement by a public official; the last four lines of Keats's "Ode on a Grecian Urn."

2. When you can use a particularly well-expressed opinion by an authority on your topic to lend support to your position, such as a statement on the need for nuclear disarmament by a respected military leader; a literary critic's interpretation of the lines from Keats.

3. When you need to give an example to illustrate a point you are making about a text. If you were analyzing the character of the Duke in Browning's poem "My Last Duchess," for example, you might use a quotation to illustrate the point below.

> The Duke in Robert Browning's poem "My Last Duchess" suggests that his wife's courtesy to other men indicated her lack of respect for his name and position:
>
>> She thanked men,—good! but thanked
>> Somehow—I know not how—as if she ranked
>> My gift of a nine-hundred-years-old name
>> With anybody's gift.
>> (11. 31-34)

WHEN NOT TO QUOTE

1. When you can paraphrase someone's words or ideas without loss of meaning or impact.

Note: When you paraphrase, you must still acknowledge where the material came from by footnoting your source. For suggestions about

SECTION 8

how to summarize, see Chapters 11 and 12. For the format of footnotes and bibliographies, see Handbook Section 9.

2. When you are summarizing factual information.

3. When the quotation merely repeats your point.

4. When you have used the quotation elsewhere in your paper. Find another passage to illustrate your point.

INTRODUCING QUOTATIONS: GENERAL CONSIDERATIONS

1. When you are using a quotation to illustrate a point, make the point first, then give the quotation. In this way, you let your reader know what to look for in the quotation.

> **NOT** "My hair was naturally curly but today I wanted the protection of all possible female rituals" (p. 151). In these words the protagonist of Alice Munro's story "The Red Dress" acknowledges the importance society places on good looks.
>
> **BUT** In preparing for the high school dance, the protagonist of Alice Munro's story "The Red Dress" acknowledges the importance society places on good looks: "My hair was naturally curly but today I wanted the protection of all possible female rituals" (p. 151).

2. Whenever you quote, establish the context of the quotation by identifying its source or purpose.

> **NOT** Magazine advertising is aimed at those who can afford the products. "When you sell Cadillacs, one rich reader is worth a hundred times as much as a hundred men on welfare."
>
> **BUT** Magazine advertising is aimed at those who can afford the products. As one advertising executive has said, "When you sell Cadillacs, one rich reader is worth a hundred times as much as a hundred men on welfare."

3. Make your quotations as short as possible. You can often quote only part of a sentence or part of a line of poetry and paraphrase the rest, as in the following examples.

> PROSE
>
> The Acadians, who according to one historian "abhorred war and preferred to be left out of the military reckoning," signed a British

oath of allegiance in 1730 only because they were granted "the right not to bear arms on the King's behalf" by a separate treaty.[1]

POETRY

Apparently there are those who still believe that war will accomplish what the narrator of Tennyson's *Maud* thought it would do: unify a nation in a purpose higher than the material concerns of peacetime; wreak "God's just wrath . . . on a giant liar" (III, 45); and bring glory to those who would otherwise live in obscurity.

4. Do not string quotations together to make a series of points. Separate quotations by paraphrase or explanations.

> **NOT** In his essay "The Superiority of the Bilingual Brain," Wilder Penfield says, "There is good evidence that familiarity with additional languages, even though limited, in the first decade endows the normal child with a more efficient and useful brain." "When the uncommitted cortex is conditioned early, the individual becomes a better linguist; the child is better prepared for the long educational climb." "In the years that follow man or woman will more easily become the 'well-educated' adult for which the future calls so urgently" (*Second Thoughts* [Toronto: McClelland and Stewart, 1970], pp. 37-38).

> **BUT** In his essay "The Superiority of the Bilingual Brain," Wilder Penfield argues that the child who acquires some knowledge of a second language during the first ten years develops a "more efficient and useful brain" and thus will be more successful in school and "will more easily become the 'well-educated adult' for which the future calls so urgently" (*Second Thoughts* [Toronto: McClelland and Stewart, 1970], pp. 37-38).

5. Do not take quotations out of context and use them in a way that is misleading, as in the following example.

> The Bible says, "Cain rose up and slew his brother Abel." In another place it says, "Go thou and do likewise." Therefore we should kill our brothers.

---

[1] W.S. MacNutt, *The Atlantic Provinces: The Emergence of Colonial Society 1712-1857*, The Canadian Centenary Series (Toronto: McClelland and Stewart, 1965), pp. 42, 32.

SECTION 8

6. Make sure that the quotation fits grammatically with the sentence or phrase that introduces it.

> **NOT** Satan says that the fallen angels will look great when:
>> Our greatness will appear
>
>> Then most conspicuous, when great things
>>> of small,
>
>> Useful of hurtful, prosperous of adverse,
>>> We can create.
>
>> (*Paradise Lost*, II, 257-60)

> **BUT** Satan says that the greatness of the fallen angels will be "most conspicuous, when great things of small,/ Useful of hurtful, prosperous of adverse,/ We can create" (*Paradise Lost*, II, 258-60).

> **NOT** Stalin emphasized the idea that the constitution represented the reality of the present. It was not a programme for the future, as can be seen in "Thus, the draft of the new constitution is a summary of the path that has already been traversed, a summary of gains already achieved" (*Selected Writings*, p. 387).

> **BUT** Stalin insisted that the new constitution represented present reality, that it was not a programme for the future but "a summary of the path that has already been traversed, a summary of gains already achieved" (*Selected Writings*, p. 387).

HOW TO QUOTE: FORMAT

Prose

1. **Long Quotations**.

a. If you are quoting more than five lines of prose, the quotation should be set off from the body of your essay. Leave one blank line before and after the quotation if you are writing longhand; triple space if you are typing. Single space the quotation itself, indenting ten spaces from both the right- and left-hand margins. Do not put quotation marks around the quotation unless they appear in the passage. The footnote number, if one is necessary, comes at the end of the quotation. Remember to introduce the quotation.

> Mausner and Platt conclude their study of smoking among college students with this observation:
>> Our research supports the widely held concept that smoking is initiated by forces in the social environment of adolescents.

It also presents some evidence for the thesis that smoking throughout life is highly dependent on the social environment.[2]

b. If no footnote number is required, the page reference appears on a separate line after the quotation, in parentheses, near the right-hand margin.

on the social environment.

(p. 171)

2. **Short Quotations**. Prose quotations shorter than five lines may be indented for emphasis, but they are usually included within the body of your text, in quotation marks. Footnote numbers, if necessary, go after the final quotation mark. Page references included in your text should come after the final quotation mark, in parentheses followed by a period. Quotations within a quotation are indicated by single marks.

Example: Quotation with footnote number

Bynner discovered that boys who smoke "saw non-smokers as completely lacking in toughness, and thus the act of giving up smoking involved identification with a group which had a very unattractive characteristic."[3]

Example: Quotation with page reference

Bynner discovered that boys who smoke "saw non-smokers as completely lacking in toughness" (p. 93).

Example: Quotation within quotation

Bynner also found that "more smokers (48%) than non-smokers (13%) thought that 'too much fuss was being made about smoking' " (p. 34).

Poetry

1. **Long Quotations**. If you are quoting three or more lines of poetry, the quotation should be set off from your text. Skip a line before and after the quotation if you are writing longhand or triple space if you are typing. Centre the lines in the middle of the page, exactly as they appear in the original. Do not use quotation marks unless they appear

---

[2]Bernard Mausner and Ellen S. Platt, *Smoking: A Behavioral Analysis* (New York: Pergamon Press, 1971), p. 171.

[3]J.M. Bynner, *The Young Smoker* (London: Her Majesty's Stationery Office, 1969), p. 93.

in the lines you are quoting. Place footnote numbers, if necessary, after the last word in the quotation. Put line numbers, if appropriate, in parentheses on the line below the quotation, near the right-hand margin. Remember to introduce quotations.

Example: Poetry with footnote number

> The protagonist in Alden Nowlan's poem "Warren Pryor" represents all children who are molded to fill their parents' dreams:
>
> > When he went in the Bank their cups ran over.
> > They marvelled how he wore a milk-white shirt
> > work days and jeans on Sundays. He was saved
> > from their thistle-strewn farm and its red dirt.[4]

Example: Poetry with line reference

> In "El Greco: Espolio" Earle Birney suggests that the carpenter who made Christ's cross, like most of us, is unconcerned about the significance of his actions.
>
> > He doesn't sense perhaps that one of the hands
> > is held in a curious gesture over him—
> > giving or asking forgiveness?—
> > but he'd scarcely take time to be puzzled by poses.[5]
>
> (11. 14-17)

2. **Short Quotations**. If you are quoting fewer than three lines of poetry, include the quotation in the body of your essay. Use a slash to indicate divisions between lines. Footnote and line references are handled the same as for prose. Example:

> The carpenter in Earle Birney's poem "El Greco: Espolio" is willing to "build what's wanted/ temples or tables mangers or crosses" (11. 25-26).

3. Quotations of fewer than three lines of poetry are sometimes set off for special emphasis.

Plays

Depending on the play, you may be quoting either prose or poetry. Follow the guidelines above for prose or poetry as appropriate.

---

[4]From *Under the Ice* (Toronto: Ryerson, 1961), pp. 18-19; reprinted in *Fifteen Canadian Poets Plus Five*, ed. Gary Geddes and Phyllis Bruce (Toronto: Oxford University Press, 1978), p. 188. By permission of the author.

[5]From *Collected Poems by Earle Birney*, reprinted by permission of The Canadian Publishers, McClelland and Stewart, Toronto.

1. **Verse Plays**. For plays so divided, give the act, scene, and line numbers in parentheses, as in the following example, rather than the page number.

> Mark Antony begins his eulogy of the slain Caesar by suggesting that all men, even Caesar, are more likely to be remembered for their weaknesses than for their strengths:
>
> > I come to bury Caesar, not to praise him.
> > The evil that men do lives after them.
> > The good is oft interred with their bones;
> >
> > (III.ii.79-81)

2. **Prose Plays**. If the play is not divided into acts, scenes, and lines, give the page or pages on which the quotation appears.

> Near the end of *Who's Afraid of Virginia Woolf?* Martha reveals that her role in the cruelty and sadness of her relationship with George has been caused not by hatred of him, but by hatred of herself. Martha tells Nick that she cannot forgive George
>
> > for having come to rest; for having seen me and
> > having said: yes; this will do; who has made the
> > hideous, the hurting, the insulting mistake of
> > loving me and who must be punished for it.
> > George and Martha: sad, sad, sad.[6]

HOW TO INDICATE CHANGES IN QUOTATIONS

You know, of course, that it's important to quote accurately. Most of the time you will give quotations exactly as they appear in the text you are quoting from, with the same wording, spelling, and punctuation. Occasionally, however, you may need to add a word or phrase to clarify something in the quotation, to omit words, to make minor changes so that the quotation will fit into the grammatical structure of your sentence, or to indicate an error or possible error in the original. Here are guidelines for making these changes.

Passage from which you are quoting

> "The war had not only recalled the province to a sense of its being part of a larger world, but had also given it a new sense of being part of the Canadian nation" (W.L. Morton, *Manitoba: A History,* 2nd ed. [Toronto: University of Toronto Press, 1967], p. 359).

---

[6]Edward Albee, *Who's Afraid of Virginia Woolf?* (New York: Pocket Books, 1964), p. 191.

SECTION 8

Insertions. Put added words in square brackets.

> As W.L. Morton points out, "The war had not only recalled the province [Manitoba] to a sense of its being part of a larger world, but had also given it a new sense of being part of the Canadian nation" (p. 359).

Deletions. Use an ellipsis (three spaced dots) where words are omitted.

> As W.L. Morton points out, "The war . . . recalled the province to a sense of its being part of a larger world" (p. 359).

Changes. Put changed word or letter in square brackets.

> As W.L. Morton points out, the war "not only recalled the province to a sense of its being part of a larger world, but . . . also [gave] it a new sense of being part of the Canadian nation" (p. 359).

Error in text. Put [sic] after the error. This symbol is used to indicate typographical errors, deviant spellings, grammatical mistakes, or confused wording in the original quotation.

> According to one study, "Each of the provinces are [sic] contributing to the problem of acid rain."

EXERCISE

This exercise is designed to give you practice in integrating quotations and examples. In each case, introduce the quotation or example appropriately, quote only the most relevant material, and punctuate the quotations correctly. Bibliographical information for these quotations appears in Exercise A, Handbook Section 9.

1. "I have learned that neither kindness nor cruelty by themselves, independent of each other creates any effect beyond themselves; and I have learned that the two combined together, at the same time, are the teaching emotion."[1] This lesson Jerry has learned from his encounters with the dog in *The Zoo Story* applies equally well to the painful human relationships in Albee's other plays.

2. If he had not been so crafty, Mrs. Dempster would not have gone simple. "I felt myself tied to her by the certainty that I was responsible for her straying wits, the disorder of her marriage, and the frail body of the child who was her great delight in life. I had made her what she was."[2] This statement shows that Dunstan feels guilty.

3. Human life begins with a single fertilized cell, within which the basic laws of inheritance determine our individual features. "In the past 20 years, it has been shown that the inherited blueprint that determines the shape of our noses, colour of eyes and hair, etc., actually is a chemical substance or molecule commonly called DNA (deoxyribonucleic acid),"[3] as Suzuki says in his essay on genetics.

4. "Slightly lighter of heart, Brian left the store."[4] This is an example of how Brian found some relief in talking with his father.

5. To fulfill "his vast responsibilities as sovereign of France" was the main reason Louis XIV wanted glory, according to William Church.[5]

6. One can recognize Jake's belief that England would be much better than Canada by the following:[6] "Earlier in Montreal, Jake had earnestly assured his troubled relatives that their city was a cultural wasteland, a colonial pimple, and that he was off to nourish himself at the imperial fountainhead."

7. Gwendolyn MacEwen's poem "One Arab Flute" begins as follows: "I was innocent as a postcard/ among the dark robes and bazaars;/ my exiled smile shone under/ the stern judicial sun;" (11. 1-4).[7]*

8. In the eighteenth century, as Alfred Cobban points out, the middle and upper classes in France were becoming aware of the increasing numbers of poor people.

> "The pressure of the unpropertied populace on those with property and social position was something which respectable society was becoming acutely conscious of in the eighteenth century. Its basic cause, indeed the dominating fact in eighteenth-century France, was the great rise in population, perhaps from some 15 millions at the beginning of the century to 26 at the end. Admittedly all such figures before the nineteenth century are speculative, but there can be little actual doubt that there was substantial growth, both actual and proportional, in population, and along with this a great increase in the numbers of poor—the landless, craftless, statusless workers in both country and town" (p. 133).[8]

9. The idea that blindness is a mental rather than a physical condition is clear when Gloucester perceives that he

> I stumbled when I saw. Full oft 'tis seen,
> Our means secure us, and our mere defects
> Prove our commodities. O dear son Edgar,
> The food of thy abused father's wrath!
> Might I but live to see thee in my touch
> I'd say I had eyes again![9]   (11. 21-26)

---

*"One Arab Flute" from *Earthlight: Selected Poetry of Gwendolyn MacEwen.* Reprinted by permission of the author and General Publishing Co. Limited, Toronto, Canada.

SECTION 8

Section 9

FOOTNOTES AND BIBLIOGRAPHY

Footnotes and bibliographies serve two basic purposes: to acknowledge your sources of information and opinion and to enable your reader to locate those sources as easily as possible. To satisfy these requirements, citations must be both **accurate** and **complete**. Various disciplines have their own standard format for references, and advanced students are expected to learn the appropriate format for their discipline. In lower-level courses, instructors are generally satisfied if you use any accepted format.

The guidelines and examples below demonstrate how to set out the most common types of entries for footnotes and bibliographies. Our suggestions are based on the *MLA Handbook for Writers of Research Papers, Theses and Dissertations* (New York: Modern Language Association of America, 1977), a widely used guide for the humanities. If you need to cite material not covered by our examples, consult this work or similar guides.

FOOTNOTES

What to Footnote

1. Footnote every idea or piece of information which is not your own, as well as every sequence of three or more words. In addition to footnoting quotations and paraphrased or summarized material, be sure to acknowledge general sources of facts and ideas within the essay by using blanket footnotes (illustrated below).

2. It is normally not necessary to footnote information obtained through lectures or discussions in the class for which you are writing the paper. Remember that it is better to do your own thinking than to rely on notes from previous classes or on study aids such as *Coles Notes*; however, if you do use such sources, footnote them.

3. It is not necessary to footnote information considered "common knowledge." What constitutes "common knowledge" is not always clear, unfortunately. Readily available, undisputed factual information certainly falls under the category of "common knowledge." You would not need to footnote the fact that Earth is the third planet from the sun, for example, since you could consult ten different astronomy books and they would all agree. You should footnote the source of factual information that is not readily available or that may differ

according to the source you consult, however. For example, you would footnote the source of unemployment figures, since those figures not only change over time but also vary according to the criteria used to measure unemployment. Always footnote **interpretations** of data and of texts.

How to Footnote

1. General Format

(a) Footnotes (or endnotes, as they are called if they appear at the end of your essay) are numbered consecutively throughout the essay. Footnote numbers appear after the quotation or paraphrase, raised slightly above the line, after the punctuation, if any, and without any punctuation after or around them. In other words, like this.[1] **Note**: You may find it easier to put in footnote numbers by hand, especially if you are using a computer or word processor.

(b) Put your notes either at the bottom of the page on which the number appears (footnotes) or collect them on a separate sheet headed "Notes" (without the quotation marks) at the end of your essay.

(c) When notes appear at the bottom of the page, leave four spaces between the text of your essay and the footnote; single space within the footnote; and double space between footnotes. If you are listing notes on a separate sheet, double space within notes and triple space between them. Indent the first line of the note five spaces.

(d) In your footnotes, your bibliography, and your essay, underline the names of the following: titles of books, plays, long poems (especially if they have been published separately), magazines, scholarly journals, newspapers, radio and television programmes, films, ballets, operas, titles of songs and pieces of music (if they are not identified by form, number, and key), names of ships and aircraft, and works of classical literature (but not sacred writings such as the Bible or the Koran). These items appear in italics in printed texts.

Put quotation marks around titles of short poems, stories, articles, essays, chapters of books, individual episodes of radio and television programmes, lectures and speeches, and unpublished works (such as theses and dissertations).

2. First and Subsequent References

(a) The first time you quote, paraphrase, or summarize information from any source, put a footnote number after the material and give complete bibliographical information, as illustrated in the sample footnotes below.

(b) After the first complete citation of a work to which you will be referring frequently, such as a text you are analyzing, add a sentence saying that "All other references to this edition will appear in parentheses in the text." Thereafter, do not use footnotes for this work. Instead, put the page numbers (for prose), line numbers (for poetry), or act, scene, and line numbers (for plays so divided) in parentheses after the quotation. If you are quoting from more than one work by the same author, include a short form of the title in the parenthetical reference. For examples of parenthetical references, see Handbook Section 8: Using Quotations.

(c) After the first complete citation to works for which you are not using parenthetical references, give only the following information in subsequent footnotes: the author's name; a short form of the title if you are quoting from more than one work by the same author; and the page, line, or act, scene, line reference.

⁶Taylor, p. 206
⁹Berton, *Last Spike*, p. 104.

(d) Acknowledge general sources of facts and ideas within the essay by using blanket footnotes such as these:

¹Unless otherwise noted, the factual information in this essay comes from Albert Soboul's *The French Revolution, 1787-1799*, trans. Alan Forrest and Colin Jones (New York: Vintage Books, 1975).

²For my approach to this aspect of the French Revolution, I am indebted to Alfred Cobban's *The Social Interpretation of the French Revolution* (London: Cambridge University Press, 1964), pp. 53-78.

Sample Footnotes

ARTICLES
1. In a scholarly journal
Author's name in normal order, "Title in Full," Name of Periodical, volume number in Arabic numerals (year), number or numbers of pages from which you have taken material without "p." or "pp."

¹Evelyn J. Hinz, "The Paradoxical Fall: Eternal Recurrence in D.H. Lawrence's The Rainbow," English Studies in Canada, 3 (1977), 468.

2. In a mass circulation magazine
Author's name in normal order (if given), "Title in Full," *Name of Periodical*, complete date of issue, page number or numbers preceded by "p." (for one page) or "pp." (for more than one page).

¹Richard Ellis, "Dolphins: The Mammal Behind the Myths," Science Digest, January 1982, p. 67.
¹Shona McKay, "Out of Work," Maclean's, March 28, 1983, p. 30.

3. In an encyclopedia

If the article is signed, the author's name comes first; if not, the title of the article comes first. If the encyclopedia is well known, omit place of publication and publisher, but include edition (if given) and the year. If the work is arranged alphabetically, omit the volume number and the page number unless you are referring to one page of a multipage article.

[1]"Immortality," Encyclopaedia Britannica, 1972.

[1]"Home Bank," Encyclopaedia Canadiana, 1968.

[1]"Grasslands of Africa," The Random House Encyclopaedia (New York: Random House, 1977), 586.

BOOKS

Author's name in normal order, *Title* (Place of Publication: Publisher, date), p. or pp.

[1]George G.F. Stanley, The Birth of Western Canada (Toronto: Longmans, Green, 1936), pp. 323-24.
[1]R.D. Laing, The Politics of Experience and The Bird of Paradise (Harmondsworth, England: Penguin, 1967), p. 90.

PARTS OF BOOKS

1. In a book by a single author

Author's name in normal order, "Title of Essay, Short Story, or Poem," in *Title of the Work* (Place of Publication: Publisher, date), p. or pp.

[1]V.S. Naipaul, "One Out of Many," in In a Free State (Harmondsworth, England: Penguin Books, 1971), p. 31.

[1]John Harrington, "Point of View," in The Rhetoric of Film (New York: Holt, Rinehart and Winston, 1973), pp. 51-52.

2. In a collection or anthology with an editor

Author's name in normal order, "Title of the Essay, Short Story, or Poem," in *Title of the Work*, ed. John Doe, edition or volume (Place of Publication: Publisher, date), p. or pp. (1. or 11. for poetry; act, scene, line number(s) for plays so divided). If a volume number appears, give the location of the quotation or information without using p. or pp. (1. or 11.).

[1]Northrop Frye, "The Educated Imagination," in Modern Canadian Essays, ed. William H. New (Toronto: Macmillan, 1976), pp. 93-94

[1]Lewis Carroll, "The Walrus and the Carpenter," in The Norton Anthology of English Literature, ed. M.H. Abrams, 2 (New York: W.W. Norton, 1979), 16-17.

FILMS

A footnote for a film must include the title (underlined), the distributor, and the date. If you feel the information is useful to your reader, include the names of the principal actors, the director, and the producer. You can also give the print size (16mm., 35mm.) and the showing time in parentheses after the date.

> [1]Bob Fosse, dir., <u>Cabaret</u>, with Liza Minelli and Michael York, Allied Artists, 1972 (35 mm., 124 min.).

> [2]Robert Altman, dir., <u>McCabe and Mrs. Miller</u>, with Warren Beatty and Julie Christie, Warner Brothers, 1971 (35 mm., 120 min.).

BIBLIOGRAPHIES

What to Include

There are two common kinds of bibliographies: bibliographies of works consulted and bibliographies of works cited. The first includes all the reading you have done in preparation for writing an essay or a research paper. The second includes only those items cited within the essay. At the undergraduate level, you should normally restrict your bibliography to works you have referred to in your essay or research paper. .

General Format

On a separate sheet headed "Bibliography of Works Cited" (without the quotation marks), list bibliographical entries in alphabetical order by the last name of the author. If the work has more than one author, give the authors' names in the order in which they appear in your source, inverting only the first name. If no author is given, alphabetize the entry by the first word of its title (ignoring the articles *a, an, the*). Dictionaries and other reference works are commonly listed by title rather than by the name of the editor. Double space within entries and triple space between entries. Indent the second and succeeding lines five spaces. Include the subtitle of books, separating it from the main title with a colon. Do not number bibliographical entries.

Sample Bibliographical Entries

ARTICLES

Author's name, last name first. "Title of the Article." *Name of the Periodical*, volume number in Arabic numerals (year), inclusive page number(s). Do not use "p." or "pp." when there is a volume number.

> Suzuki, David. "Genetics: Will This Science Save Us or Kill Us?"
> Canada and the World, 27 (February 1972), 108-20.

BOOKS
Author's name, last name first. *Title*. Place of Publication: Publisher, date.

> Stanley, George G.F. The Birth of Western Canada: A History of
> the Riel Rebellions. Toronto: Longmans, Green, 1936.
> Shroyer, Frederick B. and Louis G. Gardemal. Types of Drama.
> Glenville, Illinois: Scott, Foresman, 1970.
> Dictionary of Greek and Roman Biography and Mythology. Ed.
> William Smith. 3 vols. New York: AMS Press, 1967.

PARTS OF BOOKS
Author's name, last name first. "Title." In *Title of Work*, ed. Name (if applicable). Place of Publication: Publisher, date, inclusive page numbers (if applicable).

> Frye, Northrop. "The Educated Imagination." In Modern Cana-
> dian Essays, ed. William H. New. Toronto: Macmillan, 1976,
> pp. 93-109. "Immortality," Encyclopaedia Britannica, 1972.

SUBSEQUENT WORKS BY THE SAME AUTHOR
Type ten hyphens in place of the author's name. Continue as for the appropriate entry.

> Naipaul, V.S. "One Out of Many." In In a Free State.
> Harmondsworth, England: Penguin, 1971.
> ———— "Tell Me Who to Kill." In In a Free State. Harmond-
> sworth, England: Penguin, 1971.

FILMS
A bibliographical entry for a film contains the same information as the footnote: title of the film (underlined), the distributor, the date. Like the footnote, the bibliographical entry can also include the names of the director and producer, the names of the principal actors, and the print size and showing time if you think this information will be useful to your reader.

> Altman, Robert, dir. McCabe and Mrs. Miller. With Warren Beatty
> and Julie Christie. Warner Brothers, 1971.
> Fosse, Bob, dir. Cabaret. With Liza Minelli and Michael York.
> Allied Artists, 1972.

SECTION 9

EXERCISES

A. This exercise is designed to give you practice in using a standard format for footnotes. All the necessary information for footnoting the quotations in the exercise for Handbook Section 8 is given below, but not in a standard form. Correct the footnote entries so that they follow the format for first references outlined above. =

> [1]Albee, Edward, The Zoo Story, pp. 35-36 (New York: Signet Books, 1959).

> [2]Davies, Robertson. Fifth Business (New York: Signet), 1971, pp. 28.

> [3]David Suzuki, "Genetics: Will This Science Save Us or Kill Us?" In William H. New, ed. Modern Canadian Essays. (Macmillan of Canada: Toronto, 1976), p. 172.

> [4]W.O. Mitchell. "Who Has Seen the Wind." Toronto: Macmillan of Canada, 1973, P. 75.

> [5]John C. Rule, ed., Louis XIV and the Craft of Kingship. "Louis XIV and Reason of State," by William Church (n.p.: Ohio State University Press, 1969), p. 381.

> [6]Richler, Mordecai, St. Urbain's Horseman, Toronto, 1972, Bantam of Canada, pp. 178.

> [7]Gwendolyn MacEwen, "One Arab Flute," in Gary Geddes and Phyllis Bruce, ed., "15 Canadian Poets Plus 5", 1. 1-4 (Oxford University Press: Toronto, 1978).

> [8]The Social Interpretation of the French Revolution, by Alfred Cobban. (Cambridge: 1964, Cambridge University Press, p. 133).

> [9]Neilson, William Allan, and Hill, Charles Jarvis, editors. The Complete Plays and Poems of William Shakespeare. King Lear (Cambridge, Mass.: Riverside Press, 1942), Act IV, scene i, 11. 21-26

B. This exercise is designed to give you practice in using a standard format for bibliographical entries. Following the format outlined above, make up a bibliography from the footnotes in Exercise A.

Section 10

ESSAY FORMAT

MANUSCRIPT CONVENTIONS

1. Use white, standard-sized paper (no note-sized paper or oversized computer sheets). Paper should be ruled if you write longhand, un-ruled if you type.

2. Use blue ink or black typewriter ribbon. Most instructors prefer typed essays, especially if your handwriting is difficult to read.

3. Write or type on only one side of the paper.

4. Double space typewritten essays; check with your instructor about single or double spacing handwritten essays.

5. Leave generous margins, both to improve appearance and to provide a place for comments. Margins should be about 3.5cm (1 1/2 in.) on the left and at the top, and about 2.5 cm (1 in.) on the right and at the bottom.

6. Number the pages, starting with page 2. Put your name before the page number in case sheets become separated.

7. Staple or clip pages together. Do not fold corners or use pins.

8. Do not fold the essay or put it in any kind of folder unless instructed to do so.

9. Keep a copy of your essay.

TITLE PAGE

1. Title your essay with a short form of your thesis.

2. Centre your title in the middle of your title page. Capitalize the first word and all other words except articles (*a, an, the*) and short prepositions (such as *on, at, to, in, of, for*).

3. Do not underline your title or put quotation marks around it. If your title includes the name of a book or other separate publication (play, film, newspaper, magazine, or long poem), underline the name. If your title includes the name of a short poem, short story, essay, or song, put the name in quotation marks. Examples:

> False Pride in Dickens' <u>Great Expectations</u>

> The Theme of Possession in D.H. Lawrence's
> "The Rocking-Horse Winner"

4. Put your name, course and number, section number, the name of your instructor, and the date on your title page.

PART 4

Reference
Section

GENERAL CATEGORIES FOR CONTENT ANALYSIS

GENERAL CATEGORIES	SAMPLE SUBCATEGORIES
FEATURES What are the main parts of this event, set of data, concept, or theory?	**Social:** What are the main aspects of this event, set of data, concept, or theory relating to the organization of a community or group? (e.g., What are the most important features of inner city decay?) **Psychological:** What are the main aspects of this event, etc., concerning the organization of needs, drives, etc., within the individual? (e.g., The Oedipus complex, unconscious associations, and childhood sexuality are all features of Freud's theory of psychological development.) **Economic:** What are the ways in which this event, etc., is related to the production, circulation, or distribution of wealth or goods, or to the conditions of labour? **Political:** What are the main ways in which this event, etc., is related to a system of government, authority, or power?
CAUSES What has brought about, or might have brought about, this event, set of data, concept, or theory?	**Social:** How has the particular way a group or community is organized influenced the form taken by this event, set of data, concept, or theory? **Psychological:** What motivations, drives, needs within the individual influenced the form taken by this event, etc.? **Economic:** How has a particular way of organizing the production, circulation and distribution of goods or the conditions of labour influenced the form of this event, etc.? (e.g., The need to maintain overseas markets forced the British to remain in India.)

CAUSES	**Political:** How has a particular structure of government, authority, or power influenced the form taken by this event, etc.? (e.g., How has the structure of authority within the school system contributed to these data indicating serious dissatisfaction among students, teachers, and parents?)
EFFECTS What has happened, or might happen, as a result of this event, set of data, concept, or theory?	**Social:** What effects has this event, set of data, concept, or theory had on an organized group or community? **Psychological:** What has happened to the individual's inner organization of needs, drives, motivations, etc., as a result of this event, data, concept, or theory? **Economic:** What has happened to the production, circulation, or distribution of goods, or to the conditions of labour, as a result of this event, etc.? **Political:** What has happened to the organization of government, authority, or power as a result of this event, etc.? (e.g., The concept of a master race allowed the reorganization of the power structure in Germany along less democratic lines.)

GENERAL AND SPECIAL CATEGORIES FOR TEXTUAL ANALYSIS: OUTLINE

GENERAL CATEGORIES	SPECIAL CATEGORIES	
	NON-FICTIONAL PROSE	**FICTION**
Subject What is the work about?	**Subject** What issue, idea, event, or person is the article, essay, review, biography, etc. about?	**Subject** What is the novel or short story about?
Structure How is the work put together?	**Structure** How is the argument and/or narrative and/or description selected and arranged?	**Narrative Structure** What is the principle behind the selection and arrangement of events ("plot")?
Development What are the particular details that give the work substance?	**Evidence and Detail** What kind of evidence does the author give to support the argument? What kind of detail to develop narrative or descriptive writing?	**A. Setting** What is the place, time, and social environment within which events take place? **B. Characterization** What are the characters like? What techniques are used to portray them?
Style How does the author/director use the "language" of the medium?	**A. Diction** What do usage level and word choice tell me? **B. Images and Symbols** Are these used to comment on the subject? How? **C. Sentence Structure** What do sentence patterns tell me?	**A. Diction** What do usage level and word choice tell me? **B. Images and Symbols** Do these create patterns of meaning? How? **C. Sentence Structure** What do sentence patterns tell me?
Tone What is the author's/director's attitude towards the subject and audience, as conveyed by the work?	**Tone** What is the author's attitude to subject and reader, as conveyed by the work?	**A. Point of View** Who is the narrator? How does this affect the way the story is told? **B. Tone** What attitude does the narrator (and/or author) adopt towards the story and the reader?
Theme or Thesis What is the central idea of the work?	**Thesis** What is the central point of the work?	**Theme** What is the central idea of the novel or short story?

POETRY	DRAMA	FILM and TV
Subject What is the poem or sequence of poems about?	**Subject** What is this play about?	**Subject** What is this film or programme about?
Poetic Structure What is the principle behind the selection and arrangement of details in the poem?	**Dramatic Structure** What is the principle behind the selection and arrangement of events ("action")?	**Structure** What is the principle behind the selection and arrangement of events ("action")?
A. Setting What is the place, time, and social environment within which the development of the poem takes place? **B. Characterization** What are the characters like? What techniques are used to portray them?	**A. Setting** What is the place, time, and social environment within which the action takes place? What do costuming, music, lighting, sets, etc., indicate about the setting? **B. Characterization** What are the characters like? How are various techniques, including dialogue and acting, used to portray them?	**A. Setting** What is the place, time, and social environment established by the locations, by music, etc.? **B. Characterization** What are the characters like? How are various techniques, including dialogue and acting, used to portray them?
A. Diction What do usage level and word choice tell me? **B. Images and Symbols** Do these create patterns of meaning? How? **C. Prosody** How are sound and rhythm used in the poem?	**A. Diction** What do usage level and word choice in individual characters and in the play as a whole tell me? **B. Images and Symbols** Do these create patterns of meaning? How? **C. Pacing** What is the rhythm of dialogue and action?	**A. Shooting Techniques** What do camera angles, shot length, etc., convey about setting or characters? **B. Images and Symbols** Do these create patterns of meaning? How? **C. Editing Techniques** What movement of action does the editing create?
A. Point of View Who is the speaker in the poem? How does this affect the way the poem is written? **A. Tone** What is the tone and how does it reflect the speaker's attitude?	**Tone** a) Playwright: What attitude to subject and audience is evident? b) Director: What attitude to subject and audience is evident?	**Tone** What is the director's attitude to the subject and audience, as conveyed by the film or programme?
Theme What is the central idea of the poem?	**Theme** What is the central idea of the play?	**Theme** What is the central idea of the film or programme?

SPECIAL CATEGORIES:
QUESTIONS TO ASK IN ANALYZING NON-FICTIONAL PROSE

A. Identifying Textual Features

Subject and Genre
1. What issue, idea, event, or person is this work about?
2. Does this work belong to a particular genre (kind) of non-fictional writing (e.g., autobiography, biography, historical writing, scientific article)? What are the main characteristics of this genre?

Structure   The selection and arrangement of points, narrative incidents, and/or descriptive detail.
1. Is the main purpose of the work to present an **evaluation** (another commonly used term is **argument**)? If so, what principle determines the order in which points are presented (e.g., pro-con structure)?
2. Is the main purpose of the work to present an **analysis** (another commonly used term is **exposition**)? If so, what principle determines the order in which points are presented (e.g., order of ascending interest)?
3. Is the main purpose of the work to present a narrative or a description? If so, what principle governs its order (e.g., past to present, near to far)?
4. If the work mixes evaluation and/or analysis with narration and/or description, what is the organizing principle?

Evidence and Detail   The material used to support evaluative or analytical points, or to give substance to narration or description.
1. What material does the author use to support evaluative or analytical points? Examples? Facts? Statistics? References to, or quotations from, authorities on the subject? Imaginary situations? Predictions?
2. Does the author give substance to narration by extended accounts of a small number of events or by brief accounts of many events? Is description **panoramic** (using selected details to summarize a wide range of experience), or **dramatic** (using lots of details to convey a particular experience)?

Diction   The author's general level of usage and particular word choices.
1. Is the general level of usage in the work that of formal, educated speech; informal, everyday speech; the colloquial speech associated with a particular dialect or subculture; or a mixture of these levels? Are there significant shifts between levels of usage?

2. Is a specialized vocabulary (e.g., the vocabulary of the biologist or the banker) important to this work?
3. Are there significant patterns of word choices (e.g., euphemisms designed to hide unpleasant facts)?

Images and Symbols   **Images** are figures of speech and, more generally, descriptions of sensations; **symbols** are objects, actions, gestures, or patterns of images used to express a more abstract idea.
1. Does the author use any significant figures of speech (metaphor, simile, personification) or descriptions of sensations (sight, hearing, touch, smell, taste, body movement) in discussing issues, ideas, events, or persons (e.g., Carl Sagan's comparison between the behaviour of caged chimpanzees and the behaviour of prison inmates in *The Dragons of Eden*)?
2. Are there any objects, actions, gestures, or images that have or take on a symbolic meaning (e.g., shooting an elephant in George Orwell's essay of that title; the motorcycle in Robert Pirsig's *Zen and the Art of Motorcycle Maintenance*)?

Sentence Structure   Sentence length and type.
1. What are the characteristic features of the author's sentences? Long or short? Simple or complex? Is there a distinctive use of parallelism or of other rhetorical devices?
2. Are there significant exceptions to, or changes in, the author's habitual sentence structure?

Tone   The author's attitude towards his or her subject and readers as conveyed in the work; the counterpart of "tone of voice" in speech.
1. Is there a narrator who is distinctly different from the author (e.g., the narrator of Jonathan Swift's "A Modest Proposal")? If so, how would you characterize the narrator's attitude towards the subject and/or the reader? Contemptuous? Confiding? "Reasonable," as Swift's narrator seems?
2. How would you characterize the author's attitude towards his or her subject (and narrator)? Serious? Humorous? Detached? Impassioned? etc.
3. How would you characterize the author's attitude towards his or her readers? Friendly? Pompous? Critical? Condescending? etc.
4. Are there significant shifts in tone? If so, where and to what purpose?
5. How apparent, and how important to the work, is the personality of the author?

Thesis
Does the author state a thesis directly? If so, what is it?

B. Connecting Textual Features

1. If the work belongs to a distinct genre (kind), in what ways does it conform to and depart from the conventions of the genre?
2. How does the title relate to the work as a whole?
3. What is the relationship between structure and evidence/detail? Is one part of the evaluation or analysis supplied with more evidence or detail than another, for example?
4. How do elements of style (diction, image and symbol, sentence structure) relate to structure and evidence/detail? Does the style seem appropriate to the purpose of the work?
5. What is your interpretation of the author's thesis, based on your analysis of the work and your sense of how its elements are related?
6. Is there a difference between your interpretation of the thesis and the thesis stated in the work? If so, what accounts for this difference?

SPECIAL CATEGORIES: QUESTIONS TO ASK IN ANALYZING FICTION

A. Identifying Textual Features

Subject and Genre
1. What is this novel or short story about?
2. Does this work belong to a particular genre (kind) of fiction or fictional tradition (e.g., romance, Gothic novel, science fiction)? What are the main characteristics of this genre?

Narrative Structure The selection and arrangement of events ("plot").
1. Are events presented in chronological order? If not, in what order are they presented? Are flashbacks used?
2. To what extent are events presented as a series of dramatic scenes? To what extent are events summarized (e.g., "Five years had passed, five hard years in which the cow had died, the barn had burned, and Jane had married Tom.")?
3. What is the principle by which events are linked? Cause-and-effect (e.g., the consequences of wife-selling in Thomas Hardy's *The Mayor of Casterbridge*)? The development of the main character (e.g., Mordecai Richler's *The Apprenticeship of Duddy Kravitz*)? A physical, mental, or spiritual quest (e.g., *Lord of the Rings*)? A seemingly random association?
4. Is the work divided into parts? Do these parts correspond to stages in the development of the action?
5. Does the action lead towards a climax or turning point? Is there a resolution of conflicts or a revelation? If there is no climax and resolution, how does the action develop?
6. Why does the work end as it does?

Setting   The place, time, and social environment within which the action takes place.
1. What are the most important locations in the work? Are they interior locations (inside houses, prisons, caves) or exterior ones? How extensively are they described?
2. During what historical period is the work set? What period of time does it encompass?
3. Does the work create a particular social environment through the portrayal of manners, customs, and moral values?

Characterization   The techniques used in portraying the characters.
1. Is the main character a hero(ine), a villain, or an anti-hero (a character presented as decidedly **unheroic**)? Are the characters round (with complex or contradictory aspects) or flat (type characters, stereotypes). Is there a broad or narrow range of characters?
2. What physical, psychological, and moral traits are associated with particular characters, and how are these traits revealed? Through dialogue? Through description of physical appearance or mental process? Through distinctive behaviour? Through the perceptions or comments of other characters? In some other way?
3. Do these traits change in the course of the novel or short story? If so, how and to what purpose?
4. What do the characters think about each other? Are there significant differences in characters' conceptions of each other?

Diction   The general level of usage (formal, informal, colloquial) within the narrative, as well as the speech styles and word choices of particular characters.
1. Is the general level of usage in the narrative that of formal, educated speech; informal, everyday speech; the colloquial speech associated with a particular dialect or subculture; or a mixture of these levels?
2. What is the general level of usage of specific characters? Are there characters who shift among these levels of usage? If so, in what situations? Why?
3. Do any characters use a distinctive vocabulary (e.g., the Jungian psychoanalyst in Robertson Davies' *The Manticore*)?

Images and Symbols   **Images** are figures of speech and, more generally, descriptions of sensations; **symbols** are objects, actions, gestures, or patterns of images used to express a more abstract idea.
1. Are there figures of speech (metaphors, similes, personification) employed in the narrative or by the characters that seem significant because of repetition or placement (e.g., Hagar's statement that she "turned to stone" the night her son John died in Margaret Laurence's *The Stone Angel*)?

2. Are there descriptions of sensations (e.g., heat, cold, light, dark, colours, smells, sounds) that seem significant because of repetition or placement (e.g., engulfing vegetation in Ken Kesey's *Sometimes a Great Notion*).

3. Are there any objects, actions, gestures, or images that have or take on a symbolic meaning? Are there any **conventional** symbols (as a bishop's mitre symbolizes religious power)? Are there any **universal** symbols (as still water symbolizes the unknown in Janet Frame's story "The Reservoir")? Are there any **contextual** symbols (as the rocking horse symbolizes relentless ambition in D.H. Lawrence's story "The Rocking Horse Winner")?

4. Do images and symbols combine to form significant patterns of meaning in the novel or story (e.g., food and eating in Margaret Atwood's novel *The Edible Woman*)?

Sentence Structure   Sentence length and type.
1. What are the characteristic features of the sentences of the narrator and/or main characters? Are the sentences long or short, simple or complex? Is there a pronounced use of parallelism or of other rhetorical devices?
2. Are there significant exceptions to or changes in characteristic sentence structure? If so, where? What is their purpose?

Point of View   Vantage point from which the action is presented.
1. What is the point of view from which the story is told? First person ("I"); third-person limited (restricted to one character's thoughts and feelings) or omniscient (moving in and out of characters' minds at will); "camera eye" (objective narration)?
2. How does the title relate to the work as a whole?
3. Is the narrator also a major or minor character in the action? Is his or her part in the action likely to affect his or her reliability as narrator?
4. Does the novel or short story draw your attention to the process of narration by addressing the reader directly, by discussing the difficulty of telling the story, or by other means?

Tone   Attitude to subject and audience.
1. How would you describe the tone of the novel or short story? Serious? Playful? Ironic? Detached?
2. Is there a difference in tone between the narrator's attitude towards the story and the narrator's attitude towards the reader (e.g., Jane Austen presents the dilemmas of her main characters seriously and sympathetically, but the narrative voice also invites readers to maintain some degree of ironic detachment)?
3. Does the tone of the novel or story change at any point? If so, where and to what purpose?

B. Connecting Textual Features to Discover Theme

1. If the novel or story belongs to a particular genre (kind) of fiction, in what ways does it conform to and depart from the conventions of the genre?

2. How does the narrative structure of the novel or story help to reveal character?

3. How does setting contribute to characterization and narrative structure? Are particular events or particular characters associated with particular places (e.g., in Emily Bronte's *Wuthering Heights*, Wuthering Heights is associated with Heathcliff and the Earnshaws, while Thrushcross Grange is associated with the Lintons)?

4. How do the elements of style (diction, image and symbol, and sentence structure) help to portray action, setting, and character?

5. How do action, setting, characterization, style, point of view, and tone combine to convey the theme of the novel or story?

6. What is this theme?

SPECIAL CATEGORIES: QUESTIONS TO ASK IN ANALYZING POETRY

A. Identifying Textual Features

Subject and Genre

1. What is this poem about?

2. Does this poem belong to a distinct genre (kind) of poetry or poetic tradition (e.g., lyric, elegy, ballad, dramatic monologue)? What are the main characteristics of this genre?

Poetic Structure The selection and arrangement of events, ideas, sensations and feelings, as well as the arrangement of lines.

1. What is the organizing principle of the poem? A sequence of events? A train of thought? The movement of sensations or feelings? A mixture of these?

2. Why does the poem begin and end as it does? What are the main stages in its development? Is there a turning point?

3. Is the work divided into regular poetic units (e.g., stanzas)? Do these units correspond to stages in the development of the poem?

4. Is there a particular arrangement of lines (e.g., sonnet form)? How is the development of the poem related to this arrangement?

Setting The place, time, and social environment within which the development of the poem takes place.

1. What are the most important locations in the poem?

2. Is the poem set during a specific historical period? What period of time does the poem itself encompass?

3. Is a particular social environment portrayed or suggested?

Characterization   The techniques used in portraying characters.

1. Does the poem present various characters, or only a speaker? Is the speaker distinctly different from the poet (as in dramatic monologues)? Or does the speaker appear to speak for the poet (i.e., to be a **persona** of the poet)?

2. What physical, psychological, and moral traits are associated with the character(s) of the poem? How are they portrayed? Do these traits change in the course of the poem?

3. Do we, as readers, see characters differently from the way they are perceived by the speaker or by other characters?

Diction   The general level of usage, as well as particular word choices, in the poem.

1. Is the general level of usage in the poem that of formal, educated speech; informal, everyday speech; the colloquial speech associated with a particular dialect or subculture; or a mixture of these levels?

2. Can you identify any distinctive word choices in the poem (e.g., use of archaisms, deliberate alteration of expressions normal in prose)?

Images and Symbols   **Images** are figures of speech and, more generally, descriptions of sensations; **symbols** are objects, actions, gestures, or patterns of images used to express a more abstract idea.

1. Are there any figures of speech (e.g., metaphors, similes, personification) that seem significant because of repetition or placement (e.g., Burns' "My Luv's like a red, red rose")?

2. Are there descriptions of sensations (sight, hearing, touch, smell, taste, body movement) that seem significant because of repetition or placement (e.g., references to sleep in Frost's "Stopping by Woods on a Snowy Evening")?

3. Do images in the poem group into significant patterns (e.g., controlling metaphor or metaphysical conceit, as, for example, the compasses in John Donne's "A Valediction: Forbidding Mourning")?

4. Are there any objects, actions, gestures, or images that have or take on a symbolic meaning? Are there any **conventional** symbols (as the church in Philip Larkin's "Church Going" stands for traditional religious beliefs)? Are there any **universal** symbols (as spring represents a time of rebirth in Shelley's "Ode to the West Wind")? Are there any **contextual** symbols (as the skunk is a symbol of persistent, ignorant life in Robert Lowell's "Skunk Hour")?

5. Are the symbols in the poem part of a larger symbolic pattern in the poet's work as a whole (e.g., roses in Blake's poems, gyres in Yeats's poems)?

Prosody   The use of sound and rhythm in poetry.
1. What is the rhythm of individual lines in the poem? Do they have a regular **metre** (e.g., iambic, trochaic)? Or no regular metre (e.g., free verse, prose poems)?
2. Is the line length regular (e.g., tetrameter, pentameter) or irregular (free verse)? Does the poem combine metre and line length in a special form (e.g., blank verse—unrhymed iambic pentameter)?
3. Do lines correspond to units of meaning? How are pauses used (e.g., end-stopping, caesura)?
4. Does the poem use rhyme? If so, is it regular end rhyme or a special form of rhyme (e.g., internal rhyme, slant rhyme, eye rhyme)?
5. Does the poem use sound in other ways (e.g., alliteration, assonance, consonance, onomatopoeia)?

Point of View   The vantage point from which the development of the poem is presented.
1. From which point of view is the poem presented? First person? Third-person limited? Omniscient? Camera eye?
2. Is the speaker of the poem closely involved in the events, ideas, sensations, or feelings developed in the poem? Is the speaker's account to be trusted?

Tone   Attitude to subject and/or audience.
1. How would you describe the tone of the poem? Melancholy? Playful? Sarcastic? Conversational?
2. Does the tone change at any point in the poem? If so, where, how, and to what purpose?
3. Is the tone of the poem determined by the attitudes to subject and audience of a **persona** speaking for the poet, or by those of a speaker distinct from the poet? If the attitudes are those of a distinct speaker, are there indications of the poet's attitudes as well?

B. Connecting Textual Features to Discover Theme

1. If the poem belongs to a particular genre (kind), in what ways does it conform to and depart from the conventions of the genre?
2. How does the title relate to the work as a whole?
3. How is the structure of the poem linked to characterization and setting?
4. How do elements of style (diction, images and symbols, and prosody) contribute to structure, characterization, and setting?
5. How do poetic structure, setting, characterization, diction, images and symbols, prosody, and tone combine to convey the theme of the poem?
6. What is the theme?

SPECIAL CATEGORIES:
QUESTIONS TO ASK IN ANALYZING DRAMA

A. Identifying Textual Features

Subject and Genre
1. What is this play about?
2. Does this play belong to a particular genre (kind) of drama (e.g., comedy, tragedy)? What are the main characteristics of this genre?

Dramatic Structure   The selection and arrangement of events ("action").
1. Does the action begin with the gradual unfolding of the plot (as *King Lear* begins with Lear's testing of his daughters), or does it begin after the occurrence of some significant event revealed early in the play (as *Hamlet* begins after the murder of Hamlet's father)?
2. Does the action lead towards a climax (rising action) and a resolution of conflicts (falling action)? If not, how does the action develop?
3. If the play is divided into acts (and scenes), what is the principle that governs these divisions?
4. Why does the play end as it does?

Setting   The place, time, and social environment within which the action takes place.
1. In what particular location(s) is the play set (e.g., park, city apartment, classroom)? Is a larger geographical location indicated (e.g., a particular city, region, country)?
2. Is the play set during a specific historical period? What period of time does the play itself encompass?
3. Is a particular social environment conveyed through the portrayal of manners, customs, and moral values?
4. How is the setting created? Through characters' comments (e.g., "Here we are in Rome.")? Through stage directions? Through costumes, lighting, make-up, music, props?
5. Does the kind of stage on which the play is presented (Renaissance, proscenium arch, thrust, theatre-in-the-round) contribute to the setting?

Characterization   Techniques for portraying characters.
1. Which are the major and which are the minor characters? Is there a distinct **protagonist** (hero or heroine) and **antagonist** (villain)? Are there one or more characters who serve as **foils** for another character by exaggerating his/her qualities? Are there any **type** characters (confidante, revenger)? Are there any **stock** (stereotyped) characters (nosy neighbour, faithful servant, tyrannical boss)?

2. What physical, psychological, and moral traits are associated with particular characters, and how are these traits revealed? Through what the character says, or what is said about the character, in dialogue, monologue, soliloquy, or asides? Through the character's (or actor's) actions or gestures? Through physical appearance (including costuming and make-up)?

3. Do these traits change in the course of the play? If so, where, how, and to what purpose?

4. What do the characters think about each other? Are there significant differences in characters' conceptions of each other? Are there significant differences between the characters' conceptions and the audience's (e.g., to Othello, Iago is "honest Iago"; to the audience, Iago is a villain)?

Diction   The general level of usage (formal, informal, colloquial) within the play as a whole, as well as the speech styles and word choices of particular characters.

1. Is the general level of usage of a particular character that of formal, educated speech; informal, everyday speech; the colloquial speech of a particular dialect or subculture; or a mixture of these levels? What is the general level of the play as a whole?

2. Are there characters who shift among these levels of usage? If so, in what situations? Why?

3. Do any characters use a distinctive vocabulary (e.g., the vocabulary of salesmanship in *Death of a Salesman*)?

Images and Symbols   **Images** are figures of speech and, more generally, descriptions of sensations; **symbols** are objects, actions, gestures, or patterns of images used to express a more abstract idea.

1. Are there any figures of speech (metaphors, similes, personification) that seem significant because of repetition or placement (e.g., repetition of metaphors of disease in *Hamlet*)?

2. Are there descriptions of sensations (sight, hearing, touch, smell, taste, body movement) that seem significant because of repetition or placement (e.g., repetition of images of sight and blindness in *King Lear*)?

3. Are there any objects, actions, gestures, or images that have or take on a symbolic meaning? Are there any **conventional** symbols (as a flag symbolizes patriotism, or a certain posture symbolizes despair)? Are there any **universal** symbols (light, dark, water, fire, etc.)? Are there any **contextual** symbols (as Laura's glass animals symbolize life's fragility in Tennessee Williams' *The Glass Menagerie*)?

4. Do images and symbols combine to form significant patterns of meaning in the play?

5. Do costumes, lighting, make-up, sets, music, or props have any symbolic value?

Pacing   The rhythm of dialogue and action.
1. Does the rhythm of language in the play have a specific form (e.g., blank verse), or can it be described more impressionistically (e.g., deliberate, philosophical, light, staccato, fast-paced, etc.)?
2. Are there distinctive features of sentence structure in characters' speech? Does a particular character speak in monosyllables or in long, complex sentences? Is there a pronounced use of parallelism or other rhetorical devices?
3. What is the pace of the action? Is it fast-paced or slow-paced? Does it proceed with deliberation or with unexpected turns and twists?

Tone   Attitude to subject and/or audience.
1. How would you describe the tone of the play as a whole? of particular acts? of particular scenes? Serious? Romantic? Nostalgic? Ironic?
2. Are there significant shifts in tone? If so, where and why?
3. For performances: How do elements under the director's control (acting, sets, make-up, lighting) contribute to the tone?

B. Connecting Textual Features to Discover Theme

1. If the play belongs to a distinct genre (kind), in what ways does it conform to and depart from the conventions of the genre?
2. How does the title relate to the work as a whole?
3. How does the dramatic action reveal character?
4. How does setting affect plot and characterization?
5. Are particular images or symbols associated with particular events, places, characters? If so, what is the purpose of this association?
6. How do diction and pacing help to create tone?
7. How do structure, setting, characterization, style, and tone help to convey the theme?
8. What is the theme?

SPECIAL CATEGORIES: QUESTIONS TO ASK IN ANALYZING FILMS AND TV*

A. Identifying Textual Features

Subject and Genre
1. What is this film or programme about?
2. Does it belong to a particular genre (kind) of film or television production (e.g., disaster movie or soap opera)? What are the main characteristics of this genre?

---

*To analyze documentaries, newscasts, and similar programmes, use the Special Categories for Analyzing Non-fictional Prose in conjunction with the questions on shooting and editing techniques given here.

Structure   The selection and arrangement of events ("action").
1. How does the action begin? What is conveyed by the opening titles, the opening scene?
2. Are there distinct stages in the development of the action? If so, what are they?
3. Do events lead to a climax (turning point) and resolution of conflicts? If so, where does the climax occur and how are conflicts resolved? If not, what happens?
4. Why does the film or television programme end as it does? What is conveyed by the closing scene, closing shots, closing titles?

Setting   The place, time, and social environment within which the action takes place.
1. What are the important locations in this film or programme? Are they interior, exterior, or both?
2. During what historical period is the film or programme set?
3. What picture do you get of the society in which the action takes place? What features of the setting convey the society's manners, customs, and moral values (e.g., expensive houses, cars, and clothes might suggest a society that values material possessions)?
4. What special techniques (lighting, music, shot length, angle, etc.) are used to portray setting? What do these techniques convey?

Characterization   Techniques for portraying characters.
1. What physical, psychological, or moral traits are associated with particular characters, and how are these traits revealed? Through what the character says, or what is said about the character? Through the character's (and actor's) actions and gestures? Through physical appearance (including costuming and make-up)?
2. Do these traits change in the development of the action? If so, where, how, and to what purpose?
3. Are there significant differences in characters' conceptions of each other? Are there significant differences between the characters' conceptions and the audience's?

Shooting Techniques   Ways of photographing with a motion picture or television camera.
1. Is there a distinctive use of camera placement (close-up, medium shot, long shot) or camera movement (panning, tracking, craning, zoom) in the film or programme? If so, what is its purpose (e.g., close-up = intensity; long shot = detachment)?
2. Is there a distinctive use of camera angle (e.g., high angle, low angle, oblique angle, tilt shots) in the film or programme? If so, what is its purpose?
3. Is there a distinctive use of composition (e.g., symmetry, asymmetry) in the shots? If so, what is its purpose?

4. Is there a distinctive use of camera speeds (e.g., slow motion, time lapse, speed-up) or lenses (wide angle, telephoto)? If so, what is its purpose?
5. Is there a distinctive use of colour, texture (e.g., graining), or lighting (high key, low key)? If so, what is the purpose?

Images and Symbols   **Images** are figures of speech and, more generally, descriptions of sensations; **symbols** are objects, actions, gestures, or patterns of images used to express a more abstract idea.
1. Are there images that seem important because of repetition or placement (e.g., the hovering helicopter that conveys menace in *Missing*)?
2. Are there objects, actions, gestures, or images in the film or programme that have or take on a symbolic meaning (e.g., the tossing of the football at the end of *Tender Mercies* symbolizes the continual movement between opposites in life)?
3. Do images and symbols combine to form significant patterns of meaning in the film or programme (e.g., *Apocalypse Now* uses images and symbols to establish parallels with Conrad's "Heart of Darkness" and thus to suggest the evil in American involvement in the Vietnam War)?

Editing Techniques   Methods governing the sequence and combination of individual shots.
1. Does the film or programme make any distinctive use of cuts (cross cuts, jump cuts, flash cuts) and fades (fade-out, fade-in, dissolves) within scenes? If so, to what purpose?
2. How are episodes put together to convey the passage of time (cuts, fades, dissolves)? Are there flashbacks or other special techniques used in between-scenes editing?
3. How are sound effects, including music, used?

Tone   The director's attitude to subject and/or audience, as conveyed by the film or programme.
1. How would you describe the tone of the film or programme as a whole? Menacing? Comic? Romantic? Nostalgic? Are there shifts in tone? If so, where and why?
2. What techniques (e.g., shooting, editing, music, lighting) are used to help establish the tone of the film or programme?

B. Connecting Textual Features to Discover Theme
1. If the film or programme belongs to a distinct genre, in what ways does it conform to and depart from the conventions of the genre?
2. How does the title relate to the work as a whole?

3. How does the structure of the film or programme contribute to characterization?

4. How does setting affect plot and characterization? For example, are particular places associated with certain characters or significant events?

5. Are particular images or symbols associated with particular events, places, characters? If so, what does this association convey?

6. How are shooting or editing techniques used to convey action, setting, character?

7. How are action, setting, and characterization linked to the tone?

8. How do the elements of the film or programme combine to convey the theme?

9. What is the theme?

STEPS IN PREPARING, WRITING, AND REVISING ANALYSIS ESSAYS

Preparing to Write

STEP 1. Clarifying the Topic
Do I understand the terms used in the topic?
Does this topic require content analysis or textual analysis?
Do I know what kind of material to use in my essay?
Do I need to limit the topic?
Have I chosen a topic that fits my interest, knowledge, time, and writing skills?

STEP 2. Gathering Material
What source or sources of material can I draw on if I am analyzing content?
What source or sources of material can I draw on if I am analyzing a text?

STEP 3. Categorizing Material
What general or special categories of analysis should I divide my material into?

STEP 4. Finding a Thesis
For content analysis:
What generalization can I make about the nature of the thing I am analyzing?
Why does the thing I am analyzing have this particular nature?

For textual analysis:
What generalization can I make about the theme or thesis of the work I am analyzing?
A. What pattern of conflict does the work establish between sets of values?
B. How is this conflict resolved?
C. What is the work's theme or thesis?
Why does the work I am analyzing have this particular nature?
A. What features of the work led me to my interpretation?
B. Why does the author or director present this particular point of view?

Writing the Draft

STEP 5. Selecting Material
Which categories of analysis best support my thesis and thus will work best as paragraph topics for my first draft?

STEP 6. Ordering Material
Should I arrange points in my draft in a chronological, spatial, or logical order?
Is the order I have chosen an order of ascending interest?

STEP 7. Writing the Draft
In writing the draft, have I concentrated on getting my ideas on paper rather than getting every sentence perfect?

Revising the Draft

STEP 8. Revising the Thesis
Does the thesis state an opinion and support it, without merely restating the topic, summarizing information, stating a general opinion, or sounding confused or pretentious?
Do I need to work out a better thesis from my first draft?

STEP 9. Revising Essay Structure
Do my paragraphs correspond to the analytical categories I selected for writing the first draft? If not, is there a good reason?
Have I arranged points in an appropriate order?

STEP 10. Revising Middle Paragraphs
Does each middle paragraph have a topic sentence that serves as a mini-thesis for the paragraph?
If a single aspect of my material occupies more than one paragraph, have I used an "umbrella" topic sentence?

Does each middle paragraph provide enough explanation and detail to support the point made in its topic sentence?

STEP 11. *Revising Introductions and Conclusions*
Does the introduction establish an appropriate context for the essay, outline in order the points to be covered, and end with the thesis? Does the conclusion restate the thesis in different words, summarize the main points, and suggest the wider implications of the subject, if any?

STEP 12. *Final Editing*
Have I used the Checklist for Final Editing to identify and correct problems in tone, sentence structure, grammar, spelling, punctuation, and format?

STEPS IN PREPARING, WRITING, AND REVISING COMPARISON ESSAYS

Preparing to Write

STEP 1. *Clarifying the Topic*
Do I understand the terms used in the topic?
Does this topic require comparison of content or comparison of texts?
Is the basis of comparison given?
Do I know what kind of material to use in my essay?
Do I need to limit the topic?
Have I chosen a topic that fits my interest, knowledge, time, and writing skills?

STEP 2. *Gathering Material*
What source or sources of material can I draw on if I am comparing content?
What source or sources of material can I draw on if I am comparing texts?

STEP 3. *Categorizing Material*
What matching categories should I divide my material into?

STEP 4. *Finding a Thesis*
What generalization can I make about the nature of the things I am comparing?
A. What is my basis of comparison?
B. What patterns do I perceive in my material?
C. What is the central likeness or difference between these patterns? Why are the things I'm comparing similar or different?

Writing the Draft

STEP 5. Selecting Material
Which matching categories best support my thesis and thus will work best as paragraph topics for my first draft?

STEP 6. Ordering Material
Should I arrange points in my draft in a chronological, spatial, or logical order, as well as an order of ascending interest?
Should I use the block method or the alternating method of organizing comparisons?

STEP 7. Writing the Draft
In writing the draft, have I concentrated on getting my ideas on paper rather than getting every sentence perfect?

Revising the Draft

STEP 8. Revising the Thesis
Does the thesis state an opinion and support it, without merely restating the topic, summarizing information, stating a general opinion, or sounding confused or pretentious?
Does the thesis explain the central likeness and/or difference between the things I'm comparing?
Do I need to work out a better thesis from my first draft?

STEP 9. Revising Essay Structure
Do my paragraphs correspond to the matching categories I selected for writing the first draft? If not, is there a good reason?
Have I arranged points in an appropriate order?
Have I consistently used either the block or the alternating method of organizing comparisons?

STEP 10. Revising Middle Paragraphs
Does each middle paragraph have a topic sentence that serves as a mini-thesis for the paragraph?
If I am using the alternating method, does each topic sentence compare a single aspect of the things being compared?
If a single aspect of my material occupies more than one paragraph, have I used an "umbrella" topic sentence?
Does each middle paragraph provide enough explanation and detail to support the point made in its topic sentence?
If I am using the alternating method, does each paragraph provide all the explanation about one of the things being compared before shifting to the other?

STEP 11. Revising Introductions and Conclusions
Does the introduction give equivalent background information for each thing being compared, outline in order the points to be covered, indicate the basis of comparison, and end with the thesis?
Does the conclusion restate the thesis in different words, summarize the main points, and suggest the wider implications of the comparison, if any?

STEP 12. Final Editing
Have I used the Checklist for Final Editing to identify and correct problems in tone, sentence structure, grammar, spelling, punctuation, and format?

STEPS IN PREPARING, WRITING, AND REVISING EVALUATION ESSAYS

Preparing to Write

STEP 1. Clarifying the Topic
Do I understand the terms used in the topic?
Does this topic require content evaluation or textual evaluation?
Is the standard of evaluation given or implied?
Do I know what kind of material to use in my essay?
Do I need to limit the topic?
Have I chosen a topic that fits my interest, knowledge, time, and writing skills?

STEP 2. Gathering Material
What source or sources of material can I draw on if I am evaluating content?
What source or sources of material can I draw on if I am evaluating texts?

STEP 3. Categorizing Material
What analytical and evaluative categories should I divide my material into?

STEP 4. Finding a Thesis
What generalization can I make about the nature of the things I am evaluating?
A. What standard(s) of evaluation am I using?
B. What patterns of strengths and weaknesses do I perceive in my material?

C. What is my evaluation of the relationship between overall strength and overall weakness?
Why have I come to this evaluation?

Writing the Draft

STEP 5. Selecting Material
Which categories of strengths and weaknesses best support my thesis and thus will work best as paragraph topics for my first draft?

STEP 6. Ordering Material
Should I arrange points in my draft in a chronological, spatial, or logical order, as well as an order of ascending interest?
Should I use a pro-con structure for presenting my points?

STEP 7. Writing the Draft
In writing the draft, have I concentrated on getting my ideas on paper rather than getting every sentence perfect?

Revising the Draft

STEP 8. Revising the Thesis
Does the thesis state an opinion and support it, without merely re-stating the topic, summarizing information, stating a general opinion, or sounding confused or pretentious?
Does the thesis explain the relation between strengths and weaknesses in the thing(s) I'm evaluating?
Do I need to work out a better thesis from my first draft?

STEP 9. Revising Essay Structure
Do my paragraphs correspond to the categories of strengths and weaknesses I selected for writing the first draft? If not, is there a good reason?
Have I arranged points in an appropriate order?
If I have used a pro-con structure, have I consistently moved from con to pro arguments?

STEP 10. Revising Middle Paragraphs
Does each middle paragraph have a topic sentence that serves as a mini-thesis for the paragraph?
If I am using pro-con structure, does each topic sentence show the relationship between strengths and weaknesses of a single aspect of my material?
If I am not using pro-con structure, does the topic sentence evaluate one aspect of the thing I'm evaluating?

If a single aspect of my material occupies more than one paragraph, have I used an "umbrella" topic sentence?

Does each middle paragraph provide enough explanation and detail to support the evaluation made in its topic sentence?

If I am using pro-con structure, do I finish the discussion of the con side before shifting to the pro side?

STEP 11. *Revising Introductions and Conclusions*

Does the introduction give enough background information to establish the purpose of the evaluation, outline in order the points to be covered, indicate the standard of evaluation, and end with the thesis?

Does the conclusion restate the thesis in different words, summarize the main points, and suggest the wider implications of the evaluation, if any?

STEP 12. *Final Editing*

Have I used the Checklist for Final Editing to identify and correct problems in tone, sentence structure, grammar, spelling, punctuation, and format?

STEPS IN PREPARING, WRITING, AND REVISING RESEARCH ESSAYS

Preparing to Write

STEP 1. *Clarifying the Topic*

Do I understand the terms used in the topic?

Does this topic require analysis, comparison, or evaluation of content, or of one or more texts?

Do I know what kind of material to use in my essay?

Do I need to limit my topic?

Have I chosen a topic that fits my interest, knowledge, time, and writing skills?

STEP 2. *Gathering Material*

What preliminary sources of material can I draw on?

What categories can I use for gathering research material?

What sources of reference material can I draw on to compile my working bibliography?

A. Is there a bound bibliography available?

B. Is there a relevant periodical index or annual bibliography available?

C. Can I find references through my library's card or microfiche catalogue?

How do I choose, record, and track down references for my working bibliography?

How do I evaluate and take notes on the references I have found?

What should I do if I have to change my original research direction?

STEP 3. *Categorizing Material*
What categories should I use for my combined preliminary material (if any) and research material?

STEP 4. *Finding a Thesis*
What is the nature of the thing I am researching?

Why does the thing I am researching have this particular nature?

Writing the Draft

STEP 5. *Selecting Material*
Which categories of material best support my thesis and thus will work best as paragraph topics for my first draft?

STEP 6. *Ordering Material*
Should I arrange points in my draft in a chronological, spatial, or logical order, as well as an order of ascending interest?

If I am comparing or evaluating, should I use alternating or pro-con structure?

STEP 7. *Writing the Draft*
In writing the draft, have I concentrated on getting my ideas on paper rather than getting every sentence perfect?

STEP 8. *Revising the Thesis*
Does the thesis state an opinion appropriate to this kind of research essay and support that opinion?

Does the thesis reflect my own opinion, rather than merely summarizing the opinions of writers I have consulted?

Do I need to work out a better thesis from my first draft?

STEP 9. *Revising Essay Structure*
Do my middle paragraphs correspond to the composite categories I selected for writing the first draft? If not, is there a good reason?

Have I arranged points in an appropriate order?

Is my research material fully incorporated into the order I have chosen?

STEP 10. *Revising Middle Paragraphs*
Does each middle paragraph have a topic sentence that serves as a mini-thesis for the paragraph?

Does each topic sentence for paragraphs using research material clearly indicate how this material relates to a single aspect of my thesis? Does each paragraph provide enough explanation and detail to support the point made in its topic sentence? In the case of research material, is there an appropriate mixture of summary and quotation?

STEP 11. Revising Introductions and Conclusions
Does the introduction establish an appropriate context for the essay, indicate the relation between my research material and my own line of thinking, outline in order the points to be covered, and end with the thesis?
Does the conclusion restate the thesis in different words, summarize the main points (and, if appropriate, the relation between primary and secondary material), and suggest the wider implications of the subject, if any?

STEP 12. Final Editing
Have I used the Checklist for Final Editing to identify and correct problems in tone, sentence structure, grammar, spelling, punctuation, and format (including footnotes and bibliography)?

STRATEGY FOR LIBRARY RESEARCH

What sources of reference material can I draw on for my working bibliography?

A) Bound Bibliography?

Find through
(1) bibliography or bibliographies
(2) subject index in library catalogue

Choose by annotations, date, comprehensiveness

B) Periodical Index or Annual Bibliography?

Find through
(1) bound bibliography
(2) serials list under title
(3) card catalogue under subject or title

Choose by recency, scope, annotations

C) The Library Card or Microfiche Catalogue?

STRATEGY FOR LIBRARY RESEARCH *(continued)*

How do I find references in these sources?	**A) Check** relevant sections for references
	B) Check relevant sections in each yearly volume, working backward from present
	C) Check under relevant subject headings, using *Library of Congress Subject Headings* volumes if necessary
What bibliographical information do I need?	**Books:** Author, title, place of publication, publisher, date of publication
	Articles: Author, title of article, title of periodical, volume number (for scholarly journals), date, page numbers
How do I locate these books and articles?	**Books:** (1) Check card catalogue under author or title (2) Record call number (3) Search shelves by call number, or request from closed stacks librarian
	Articles: (1) Check card catalogue or serials list under title of periodical (2) Check holdings for volume wanted; record call number (3) Search shelves or request from librarian

CHECKLIST FOR FINAL EDITING

Each question in the checklist represents a summary of matters discussed in the designated section and pages of the handbook. Common marking symbols are indicated in parentheses; page references are given in square brackets.

HANDBOOK SECTION **1**

TONE

Is my tone appropriate for the subject and reader of my essay? [p. 292]

(*P add*)   Have I used appropriate pronouns of address for referring to myself, my subject, and my reader? [p. 292]

(*Dic*)   Is my diction appropriate in level, clear in connotation, and correct in meaning? [p. 295]

HANDBOOK SECTION **2**

SENTENCE PROBLEMS

Are my sentences grammatically complete and structurally unambiguous? [p. 300]

(*Frag*)   Are there any sentence fragments? [p. 301]
(*CS*)   Are there any comma splices? [p. 304]
(*R-O*)   Are there any run-on sentences? [p. 306]
(*MM,DM*)   Are there any misplaced or dangling modifiers? [p. 308]
(*Mix*)   Are there any mixed constructions? [p. 310]
(*//ism*)   Is there any faulty parallelism? [p. 311]

HANDBOOK SECTION **3**

SENTENCE EFFECTIVENESS

Are my sentences concise, varied, and effectively linked? [p. 313]

(*Rep*)   Have I eliminated wordy constructions and unnecessary repetition from my sentences and paragraphs? [p. 313]

(*Emph*) Have I altered sentence patterns to distinguish among main points, explanations, and details? [p. 318]

(*Trans*) Do I use words, phrases, or clauses to provide transitions and to maintain continuity? [p. 319]

HANDBOOK SECTION **4**

VERBS

Are my verbs correct in regard to agreement, tense, and voice? [p. 324]

(*Agr*)   Does each verb agree with its subject? [p. 324]

(*Tense*)   Are there any unnecessary shifts in tense? [p. 326]

(*Pass*)   Have I used the passive voice unnecessarily? [p. 328]

HANDBOOK SECTION **5**

PRONOUNS

Is my use of pronouns consistent, correct, and clear? [p. 330]

(*P Shift*) Are there unnecessary shifts in pronouns of address? [p. 330]

(*P Agr*) Are there errors in pronoun agreement? [p. 332]

(*P Ref*) Are there problems with ambiguous pronoun reference? [p. 333]

HANDBOOK SECTION **6**

PUNCTUATION

Is my punctuation a correct and reliable guide to my meaning? [p. 335]

 Have I used **commas** to separate independent clauses and items in a series (list)? Have I used **commas** to set off from a sentence's main clause all the clauses, phrases, modifiers, and other expressions not essential to its meaning? [p. 335]

(↷ ⟍) Have I used **semicolons** to separate independent clauses not joined by a conjunction? [p. 339]

(↷ ⟍) Have I used **colons** to introduce an expansion of what has already been said? [p. 340]

(⟨↑⟩ ⟨↗⟩) Have I used **parentheses** to enclose non-essential explanatory material? [p.340]

(⌒ ⟍) Have I used **dashes** to set off interruptions in thought or sentence structure? [p. 341]

(↷ ⟍) Have I used **quotation marks** for direct speech, quotations from a text if not indented, and titles of works contained within larger works? [p. 343]

(⌒ ⟍) Have I used **italics** or underlining for titles of separately published works and for foreign words or phrases? [p. 344]

HANDBOOK SECTION **7**

SPELLING AND CAPITALIZATION

Is my spelling, use of apostrophes, and capitalization correct? [p. 346]

(*Sp*) Have I checked my **spelling** to eliminate careless errors, common misspellings, and non-Canadian spellings? [p. 347]

(*apos*) Have I used **apostrophes** to indicate contractions and possessives? [p. 353]

(*Cap*) Have I used **capitalization** to distinguish proper nouns from common nouns? [p. 355]

HANDBOOK SECTION **8**

QUOTATIONS

Have I used quotations effectively to support and illustrate my points? [p. 357]

(*Quot*) Am I right to quote rather than to explain or to paraphrase? [p. 357]

(*Quot*) Are my quotations introduced effectively? [p. 358]

(*Quot*) Are my quotations precise, accurate, and set out in the appropriate format for long or short quotations from prose, poetry, or drama? [p. 360]

HANDBOOK SECTION **9**

FOOTNOTES AND BIBLIOGRAPHY

Have I used footnote and bibliographical references accurately to indicate references to ideas, information, and words from other sources? [p. 366]

(*Source?*) Have I used a footnote or endnote to identify the source of every idea, piece of information, or sequence of words that is neither my own nor common knowledge? [p. 366]

(*Foot*) Have I set out my footnotes or endnotes according to an accepted format? [p. 367]

(*Bib*) Have I set out my bibliography according to an accepted format? [p. 370]

HANDBOOK SECTION **10**

ESSAY FORMAT

Is my essay set out in the appropriate general format? [p. 373]

(*EF*) Have I followed conventions as to paper, ink, spacing, margins, page numbering, and presentation? [p. 373]

(*EF*) Does my title page contain the required information, presented in an appropriate format? [p. 373]

SAMPLE RESEARCH PAPER: COMPARISON OF CONTENT

In Chapter 11 we demonstrated the process of preparing to write a research paper on a content topic by showing how you would find material and reach a thesis comparing the founding of the Red River Settlement and Fort Victoria. The final draft of the essay, including the title page, notes, and bibliography, is reprinted here to serve as a model for your research papers.

The Effects of the Hudson's Bay Company

on the Development of the

Red River Settlement and Fort Victoria

Marlyn Lyall

History 205 (Section 07)

Dr. E.S. Smith

March 30, 1985

1

The Red River Settlement was begun in 1812 in what is now southern Manitoba; Fort Victoria was begun in 1843 on Vancouver Island. Although both were originally established as fur trading posts by the Hudson's Bay Company, Fort Victoria developed into a successful agricultural colony, but the Red River Settlement did not. Two factors that contributed to the failure of the Red River Settlement and the success of Fort Victoria were the quality of the land and the quality of the administrators. The most important factor, however, was the attitude of the Hudson's Bay Company. Because the activities of the farmers in the Red River Settlement were perceived as incompatible with the more immediately profitable fur trade, the Company's attitude towards settlers there was indifferent, if not openly hostile. But because the activities of the farmers in Fort Victoria were almost immediately profitable, the Hudson's Bay Company supported their efforts fully.

From the beginning, the Hudson's Bay traders were opposed to an agricultural settlement on the Red River and did nothing to promote its establishment or to encourage its survival. The settlement was established as a result of the efforts of Thomas Douglas, the fifth Earl of Selkirk, who bought a controlling interest in the Hudson's Bay Company and through it attempted to build a colony.[1] Although Selkirk believed that agricultural settlements were essential in North America, the fur trading companies, both the Hudson's Bay Company and its competitor, the North-West Company, disagreed. The fur traders felt that the presence of settlers would likely cause the animal population to decrease. They found the settlement on the Red River especially threatening because it was located in some of the best fur country in North America.

2

From the beginning, then, the Red River farmers were in a precarious position. Although the settlement was established with the official support of the Hudson's Bay Company, the Company traders resented its existence and refused to get involved except to criticize the policies of settlement administrators. The North-West Company, on the other hand, worked openly to sabotage the settlement and tried to convince its Métis employees that the settlers would oust them from their lands.[2] Because the British government was antagonistic at this time to all monopolies, and to the Hudson's Bay Company in particular, the British did nothing to help Selkirk establish his tiny agricultural settlement.[3] Thus the survival of the Red River settlement was undermined from the beginning by the powers most necessary to ensure its success.

The attitude of both the British government and the Hudson's Bay Company towards the establishment of an agricultural settlement at Fort Victoria, in contrast, was much more enthusiastic. Britain had begun to recognize the importance of colonization in retaining possession of its land, especially on the Pacific coast where the Americans were pressing for the annexation of all the territory to the Alaskan boundary.[4] Instead of regarding farming as an unwelcome interference with the fur trade, the Hudson's Bay Company traders in Fort Victoria quickly perceived the advantages of producing agricultural goods for export in a location that was superb for trade with America, Russia, and Asia.[5] With the support and encouragement of the Hudson's Bay Company, the settlement at Fort Victoria was soon securely established, with farming as an important enterprise.

The difficulties of the settlers on the Red River, who struggled along from one disaster to another as they attempted to farm in an

3

"unbroken, undrained, uncontrolled" wilderness, were made worse by the ineptitude of the administrators.[6] Miles Macdonell, whom Selkirk had appointed governor of the settlement, exacerbated the already bad relations between the settlers and the fur traders with the Pemmican Proclamation of January 8, 1814, which prohibited the export of pemmican from the district for one year.[7] This policy, designed to prevent food shortages in the settlement as the War of 1812 dragged on, angered the traders of both companies. Since the North-West Company depended on provisions from the colony for its fur brigades, which travelled far beyond the immediate district, this proclamation convinced the North-Westers that the Hudson's Bay Company had deliberately established the settlement in order to destroy its competitor's trade routes. The embargo also angered the Hudson's Bay traders because they too were prohibited from exporting pemmican. Hostilities came to a head on June 19, 1816, when twenty men from the colony, including its new governor, Robert Semple, were killed in the battle of Seven Oaks by a band led by an employee of the North-West Company. As a result, the colonists were forced to abandon the settlement temporarily.[8] Thus a combination of poor management from its officials and antagonism from the fur traders nearly succeeded in destroying the settlement.

Fort Victoria's early years, in contrast, were peaceful apart from a few minor difficulties. These minor problems show, however, that if the Hudson's Bay Company had not fully supported the colony and if the problems had been handled less skilfully, much trouble could have developed. A year after the post was founded, Chief Factor James Douglas turned over the running of the post to his assistant, Roderick Finlayson. Unlike Macdonell and his successor, Finlayson was

4

extremely skilful in maintaining good relations between the colonists
and the original inhabitants of the area. Some of the neighbouring
Indians, for example, became part of the settlement, aiding in the
farming and being paid the same as other employees of the Company.[9]
Finlayson was able to maintain these good relations and thus preserve
the stability of the settlement even when trouble did arise between the
settlers and the Indians. When a group of local Indians killed and ate
some of the livestock and then declared war on the fort, Finlayson,
instead of declaring war in return, fired a cannon ball at a deserted
cedar lodge on the edge of the Indian village. When a group of Indians
came to the fort, Finlayson explained that he had enough arms to
destroy them but that he wished only to do good. The Indians paid for
the cattle, the peace pipe was smoked and vows of friendship were
exchanged.[10]

By 1847, four years after Fort Victoria was founded, the settlement
was well established. Three hundred acres of land were cultivated,
dairy cattle were producing abundant quantities of milk and butter,
and food was being exported to Russia.[11] But ironically, success itself
was becoming a problem for the settlement. To maintain control, the
Hudson's Bay Company instituted policies designed to curtail the
growth of the settlement by making it nearly impossible for any
settler who was not an employee of the Company to buy land and by
keeping land prices high.[12] Most important, the Company refused to
cooperate with the British government when it attempted to declare
Fort Victoria a British colony in 1849 and sent over Richard Blanshard
as governor.[13]

Although some of the settlers wanted more independence from the
Hudson's Bay Company,[14] the Company was determined to maintain

Fort Victoria as a Hudson's Bay operation and the Company's employees, who comprised the majority of the settlement, refused to accept Blanshard's authority. There was no open opposition, but Blanshard soon found himself so completely isolated that, in the words of one Company employee, "he could scarcely realize he was governor except by taking out his commission and reading it to himself occasionally."[15] Blanshard gave up and returned to England in 1851, and James Douglas, the man the Company had wanted all along, became governor.[16] The British government thus accepted the Hudson's Bay Company's power over Fort Victoria. Ultimately this power became a stranglehold that nearly suffocated the colony, but initially the good management and support of Company officers helped the settlement to become secure and profitable.

The failure of the settlement on the Red River, in contrast to the success of the settlement at Fort Victoria, clearly demonstrates the enormous influence of the attitude of the Hudson's Bay Company. Because the agricultural pursuits at Fort Victoria were the source of immediate profits, the Company promoted the prosperity of the settlement and encouraged its growth until it showed signs of a desire for independence. In the Red River Settlement, on the other hand, the prolonged difficulties in establishing an agricultural base, along with continuous hostility from both the surrounding native peoples and from the fur traders, hostility made worse by inept colony officials, meant that the colony limped along from hardship to hardship until Manitoba joined confederation and the hold of the Hudson's Bay Company was finally loosened.

6

Notes

[1]Chester Martin, Lord Selkirk's Work in Canada (Toronto: Oxford University Press, 1916), p. 15.

[2]Martin, p. 36.

[3]Martin, p. 47.

[4]Margaret A. Ormsby, British Columbia: A History (Vancouver: Macmillan of Canada, 1958), pp. 84-88.

[5]Ormsby, pp. 84-88.

[6]W.L. Morton, Manitoba: A History, 2nd ed. (Toronto: University of Toronto Press, 1967), pp. 56-57.

[7]Morton, pp. 50-51.

[8]Morton, p. 54.

[9]Alexander Begg, History of British Columbia from Its Earliest Discovery to the Present Time (Victoria: Ryerson Press, 1894 [reissued 1972]), p. 174.

[10]Begg, pp. 162-64.

[11]Begg, p. 174.

[12]Begg, p. 196.

[13]Begg, p. 190.

[14]Begg, p. 196.

[15]Begg, p. 191.

[16]Begg, p. 195.

Bibliography of Works Cited

Begg, Alexander. History of British Columbia from Its Earliest Discovery to the Present Time. Victoria: Ryerson Press, 1894 (resissued 1972).

Martin, Chester. Lord Selkirk's Work in Canada. Toronto: Oxford University Press, 1916.

Morton, W.L. Manitoba: A History. 2nd ed. Toronto: University of Toronto Press, 1967.

Ormsby, Margaret A. British Columbia: A History. Vancouver: Macmillan of Canada, 1958.

Glossary of Rhetorical Terms

Asterisks indicate terms defined elsewhere in the glossary.

ANALYZE   To divide something into parts in order to understand both the parts and the whole. The main purpose of analysis is to explain something, such as a concept, a text, an event, or a set of data, by examining its parts in detail.
See Also: Content Analysis; Content Analysis, General Categories For; Content Analysis, Special Categories For; Textual Analysis; Textual Analysis, General Categories For; Textual Analysis, Special Categories For.

COMPARE   To show the similarities and differences between two things or among more than two things in order to reveal the qualities of each more clearly.

COMPARISON, BASIS OF   The common element in terms of which two or more things are compared. Topics that can be put in the form "Compare X and Y in terms of Z" specify the basis of comparison, Z. The basis of comparison tells you which features of the things you are comparing are relevant and thus gives you a focus for gathering information and writing your essay.

COMPARISON, METHODS OF ORGANIZING   The **block method** consists of organizing your middle paragraphs* so that you finish everything you have to say about one of the things you are comparing before taking up another.
The **alternating method** consists of organizing your middle paragraphs so that in each paragraph or series of paragraphs you discuss only one aspect of each of the things you are comparing.

CONCLUSION   The concluding paragraph in your essay provides the chance for both you and your reader to step back from the essay and survey the development of your thesis.* The conclusion should restate the thesis, tie together the points developed in the middle paragraphs* and mention the wider implications of the discussion, if any.

CONTENT ANALYSIS   The analysis of behaviour, data, written works, and other sources of information without regard to the form in which the information is communicated.

CONTENT ANALYSIS, GENERAL CATEGORIES FOR   The categories of causes, effects, and features that you can divide your material into when your topic does not state or imply a more specific set of categories.

CONTENT ANALYSIS, SPECIAL CATEGORIES FOR   The categories used by a particular discipline to analyze a body of material without regard to the form in which the material is communicated.

DEVELOPMENT   The use of evidence or detail to give substance to a point.

DICTION   A writer's level of word usage (formal, informal, colloquial) and particular word choices. An aspect of style* that also contributes to tone.*

DISCUSS   An ambiguous term frequently used in essay topics. It does not mean "summarize the relevant information." Check the essay topic carefully to determine whether you are expected to analyze,* compare,* or evaluate* a body of information. "Discuss the significance of X in Y" means to analyze the relationship between X and Y; "discuss X and Y" means to compare X and Y; "discuss the validity of X" means to evaluate X.

EVALUATE   To determine the strengths or weaknesses of something—a plan, a performance, a work of art, or a theory, for example. Content evaluation usually asks you to evaluate an idea, position, argument, or viewpoint. Textual evaluation usually asks you to determine how effective the presentation of a theme* or thesis* is.

EVALUATION, STANDARD OF   A set of criteria based on accumulated judgments of things of the same kind that you can use as a standard against which to measure the material you are evaluating. The most common standards of evaluation are aesthetic (how effective is the relationship between form and content in the work?), logical (how convincing is the reasoning?), practical (will it work and is it useful?), and ethical (is it morally right or wrong?).

EVIDENCE   The factual information, examples, and references to and quotations from authorities that you use to support your thesis.

GENRE   A distinct kind of literary work. The term is used to refer both to the general form (e.g., novel, play) and to more specific types within the form (e.g., Gothic novel, Greek tragedy).

INTRODUCTION   The introductory paragraph prepares your reader both intellectually and emotionally for the essay to follow. It establishes the context by defining necessary terms, giving historical background, etc., and indicates the structure of the essay by mentioning, in order, the main points you plan to cover. The introduction usually ends with your thesis.*

MIDDLE PARAGRAPHS   Paragraphs between the introduction and conclusion that explain and illustrate subpoints of the thesis.* The purpose of each paragraph is defined by a topic sentence* that links the paragraph to the thesis. Middle paragraphs usually contain both **explanations** of the point made in the topic sentence and specific **details** illustrating that point. **Transitional words and phrases** show how points, explanations, and details are related.

MIDDLE, PARAGRAPHS, ORDER OF   There are four common ways of organizing a sequence of middle paragraphs.
1. Chronological order: The arrangement of material according to units of time. The simplest chronological order starts with events furthest away in time and ends with events closest in time.
2. Spatial order: The arrangement of material according to locations in space. Spatial order may move from near to far, top to bottom, right to left, etc.
3. Logical order: The arrangement of material according to a chain of reasoning. The order in which material is presented is determined by the need to establish one point so that it will serve as the basis for the next.
4. Order of ascending interest: The arrangement of material to lead up to the most important or most interesting point. An order of ascending interest may also accommodate a chronological, spatial, or logical order.
See also: Comparison, Methods of Organizing; Pro-Con Structure

PRIMARY SOURCE   Any first-hand source of information, such as the literary work you are analyzing, a performance you have seen, your own observations and experience, the raw data from a scientific experiment, or the historical documents on which historians base their interpretations of events.
See also: Secondary Source

PRO-CON STRUCTURE   The method of arranging points in an argument so that you consider the points against (con) your position as well as the points for (pro) your position. A pro-con structure is a way of refining the principle of arranging material in an order of ascending interest to fit the special demands of the evaluation essay.
See also: Middle Paragraphs, Order Of

RESEARCH PAPER   An extended analysis, comparison, or evaluation essay that includes information from secondary sources* as well as from primary sources.* A research paper is not merely a summary of other writers' ideas; it is an essay in which you develop your own opinion on your subject and use your research material as part of your evidence to support that opinion.

SECONDARY SOURCE   Material that provides information about, or criticism and analysis of, a primary source. A historian, for example, may write a book (secondary source) interpreting the meaning of historical documents (primary sources). An anthropologist may collect data (primary sources) about various cultures and write an article comparing those cultures (secondary source). A literary critic may write a review (secondary source) of a new novel (primary source). In secondary sources, material is selected and presented to support a particular point of view.

STRUCTURE   The selection and arrangement of parts in a written work or performance.

STYLE   The distinctive way of writing that belongs to a particular writer. For analytical purposes, it is helpful to see style as consisting of a writer's use of diction,* image and symbol, and sentence structure.

SUBJECT   The text, issue, theory, proposal, etc., that a writer writes about. If your essay topic is "Assess the role of the peasants in the French Revolution," the **subject** of your essay is the role of the peasants in the French Revolution.

TEXTUAL ANALYSIS   The analysis of written works or performances (such as plays, television programmes, and films) with attention both to what is being said and to how the work or performance is presented. Your purpose in analyzing a text is to determine the relation between the work's form (its manner of presentation) and its content.

TEXTUAL ANALYSIS, GENERAL CATEGORIES FOR   The parts into which you can divide the text you are analyzing if you are not familiar with the special categories appropriate to that particular kind of text (e.g., play, film, poem). The general categories of textual analysis are subject,* structure,* development,* style,* tone,* and theme* or thesis.*

TEXTUAL ANALYSIS, SPECIAL CATEGORIES FOR   The categories commonly used in literary criticism and related fields to analyze written works and performances.

THEME   The main statement made about a subject in fiction, drama, poetry, film, and imaginative literature generally. A theme is usually implied, whereas a thesis* is usually stated directly.

THESIS   The main statement made about a subject in non-fictional prose. In your essay, the thesis will consist of an opinion with one or more reasons to support it. The purpose of the essay is to develop and confirm the thesis. Like the hypothesis in a scientific experiment, the thesis is the thing you are proving.

TONE   The attitude a writer takes to a subject and to a reader, the equivalent of "tone of voice" in conversation. The tone of a work can be described as serious or light, witty or ponderous, condescending or apologetic, and in many other similar ways. In your own essays, tone can be thought of as a product of diction* and pronouns of address.

TOPIC SENTENCE   The sentence in a middle paragraph,* usually at the beginning, that states the main idea of the paragraph and shows how the material in the paragraph supports the thesis* of the whole essay. Topic sentences are thus the bridge between the generalization you make in your thesis and the specific details you give in your middle paragraphs. An "umbrella" topic sentence covers points made in more than one paragraph.

Subject Index

(*denotes Canadian materials)

Index

CORRECTION SYMBOLS

The following list contains the correction symbols we have used in the Checklist for Final Editing and in the Handbook, as well as a few other common symbols. Page numbers in parentheses indicate the pages of the text in which we discuss the subject. Since correction symbols vary somewhat from instructor to instructor, you may want to add others that your instructors use.

adj	error in adjective form
adv	error in adverb form
agr	error in subject-verb agreement (p. 324)
apos	error in the use of the apostrophe (p. 353)
awk	awkward expression
Bib	error in bibliographical format (p. 370)
Cap	error in capitalization (p. 355)
CS	comma splice (p. 304)
Dic	error in diction (p. 295)
DM	dangling modifier (p. 309)
EF	error in the conventions of essay format (p. 373)
Emph	emphasis—failure to alter sentence patterns to fit meaning or to distinguish explanation and detail (p. 264)
foot	error in footnote format (p. 366)
Frag	sentence fragment (p. 302)
Mix	mixed construction (p. 310)
MM	misplaced modifier (p. 308)
New ¶	start new paragraph here (p. 319)
No ¶	combine this paragraph with the previous one (p. 320)
¶ det	paragraph lacks adequate detail (p. 264)
¶ exp	paragraph lacks adequate explanation (p. 265)
P add	inappropriate pronouns of address (p. 292)
P agr	error in pronoun agreement (p. 332)
P Ref	error in pronoun reference (p. 333)
P Shift	unnecessary shifts in pronouns of address (p. 330)
//ism	faulty parallelism (p. 311)
Pass	unnecessary use of the passive voice (p. 328)
Pn	punctuation [caret indicates punctuation to be inserted; slash indicates punctuation to be deleted]

︿ , /	misuse of comma (p. 335)
︿; ;/	misuse of semicolon (p. 339)
︿: :/	misuse of colon (p. 340)
( ) (/)	misuse of parentheses (p. 340)
⌒ —/	misuse of dash (p. 341)
❝❞ ″/	misuse of quotation marks (p. 343)
⌒ _/_	misuse of italics (p. 344)

Quot	error in use, introduction, content, or format of quotations (p. 357)
Rep	wordy constructions or unnecessary repetition (p. 313)
R-O	run-on sentence (p. 306)
Source?	absence of adequate footnotes to indicate source of material (p. 366)
Sp	spelling error (p. 349)
Tense	unnecessary shift in verb tense (p. 326)
Tone	inappropriate attitude towards subject and/or reader (p. 292)
Trans	transition needed (p. 319)
TS	topic sentence inadequate or missing (p. 84)